The Cambridge Companion to Postcolon

The Cambridge Companion to Postcolonial Literary Studies offers an introduction and overview of one of the most important strands in recent literary theory and cultural studies. The volume aims to introduce readers to key concepts, methods, theories, thematic concerns, and contemporary debates in the field. Drawing on a wide range of disciplines, contributors explain the impact of history, sociology, and philosophy on the study of postcolonial literatures and cultures. Topics examined include everything from anticolonial nationalism and decolonization to globalization, migration flows, and the "brain drain" which constitute the past and present of "the postcolonial condition." The volume also pays attention to the sociological and ideological conditions surrounding the emergence of postcolonial literary studies as an academic field in the late 1970s and early 1980s. The Companion turns an authoritative, engaged, and discriminating lens on postcolonial literary studies.

THE CAMBRIDGE
COMPANION TO

POSTCOLONIAL
LITERARY STUDIES

EDITED BY
NEIL LAZARUS

CAMBRIDGE
UNIVERSITY PRESS

PUBLISHED BY THE PRESS SYNDICATE OF THE UNIVERSITY OF CAMBRIDGE
The Pitt Building, Trumpington Street, Cambridge, United Kingdom

CAMBRIDGE UNIVERSITY PRESS
The Edinburgh Building, Cambridge, CB2 2RU, UK
40 West 20th Street, New York, NY 10011–4211, USA
477 Williamstown Road, Port Melbourne, VIC 3207, Australia
Ruiz de Alarcón 13, 28014 Madrid, Spain
Dock House, The Waterfront, Cape Town 8001, South Africa

http://www.cambridge.org

First published 2004
Reprinted 2006

Printed in the United Kingdom at the University Press, Cambridge

Typeface Sabon 10/13 pt.   *System* LATEX 2$_\varepsilon$ [TB]

A catalogue record for this book is available from the British Library

Library of Congress Cataloguing in Publication data
The Cambridge companion to postcolonial literary studies / [edited by] Neil Lazarus.
p.   cm. – (Cambridge companions to literature)
Includes bibliographical references and index.
ISBN 0 521 82694 2 (hardback) – ISBN 0 521 53418 6 (paperback)
1. Postcolonialism in literature.   2. Decolonization in literature.   3. Postcolonialism.
4. Criticism – History – 20th century.   I. Lazarus, Neil, 1953–   II. Series.
PN56.C63C36   2004
809′.93358 – dc22   2004040754

ISBN 0 521 82694 2 hardback
ISBN 0 521 53418 6 paperback

For Edward Said (1935–2003), who taught all of us

CONTENTS

CONTENTS

CONTRIBUTORS

DEEPIKA BAHRI is Associate Professor of English at Emory University. She has published *Native Intelligence: Aesthetics, Politics, and Postcolonial Literature* (2003), numerous essays in journals and collections, and co-edited *Realms of Rhetoric* (2003) and *Between the Lines: South Asians and Postcoloniality* (1996).

TIMOTHY BRENNAN is Professor of Cultural Studies and Comparative Literature, and English, at the University of Minnesota, and the Director of the Humanities Institute there. He has published widely on postcolonial studies, social and cultural theory, comparative literature, and the problem of intellectuals. He is the author of *At Home in the World: Cosmopolitanism Now* (1997), *Salman Rushdie and the Third World: Myths of the Nation* (1989), and has edited and introduced Alejo Carpentier's *Music in Cuba* (2001). He has just completed a book titled *Cultures of Belief*.

LAURA CHRISMAN has published in the fields of postcolonial cultural theory, black Atlantic cultural studies, South African literature, and British imperial literature and ideology. She is the author of *Postcolonial Contraventions: Cultural Readings of Race, Empire and Transnationalism* (2003) and *Rereading the Imperial Romance: British Imperialism and South African Resistance in Haggard, Schreiner and Plaatje* (2000).

FERNANDO CORONIL teaches in the Departments of History and Anthropology, and directs the Latin American and Caribbean Studies Program, at the University of Michigan. He is the author of *The Magical State: Nation, Money, and Modernity in Venezuela* (1997), and has published widely in such journals as *Public Culture* and *Cultural Anthropology*. His research interests include historical anthropology, capitalism, state formation, gender, and popular culture in Latin America.

KEYA GANGULY is Associate Professor in the Department of Cultural Studies and Comparative Literature at the University of Minnesota. She is the author of *States of Exception: Everyday Life and Postcolonial Identity* (2001) and a senior editor of *Cultural Critique*. Her interests are in the social philosophy of the Frankfurt School, postcolonial studies, film theory, cultural studies, and the intellectual history of modernism/modernity. She has published essays on critical theory, Indian cinema, popular culture, and the politics of ethnography, and is currently writing a book on the films of Satyajit Ray.

SIMON GIKANDI is Robert Hayden Professor of English Language and Literature at the University of Michigan, Ann Arbor. He is author and editor of numerous works on postcolonial theory and the postcolonial literatures of Africa, the Caribbean, and the black Atlantic, including *Writing in Limbo: Modernism and Caribbean Literature* (1992); *Maps of Englishness: Writing Identity in the Culture of Colonialism* (1997); and *Ngugi wa Thiong'o* (2001). He is the editor of the Routledge *Encyclopedia of African Literature* (2002), and co-editor (with Abiola Irele) of the *Cambridge History of African and Caribbean Literature* (2004).

PRIYAMVADA GOPAL is a University Lecturer at the Faculty of English, Cambridge University, and a Fellow of Churchill College. Her book on the Indian Progressive Writers' Association, *Literary Radicalism in India: Gender, Nation and the Transition to Independence*, will be published in 2004.

NEIL LAZARUS is Professor of English and Comparative Literary Studies at the University of Warwick. He has published widely on postcolonial studies, social and cultural theory, and is the author of *Resistance in Postcolonial African Fiction* (1990) and *Nationalism and Cultural Practice in the Postcolonial World* (1999), and co-editor, with Crystal Bartolovich, of *Marxism, Modernity and Postcolonial Studies* (2001).

JOHN MARX is completing a book manuscript entitled "Modernist English" and beginning another called "Skepticism and the Arts of Global Administration." His work has appeared in *Modernism/Modernity, Diaspora,* and *Novel*. He teaches modernist and contemporary literature and culture at the University of Richmond.

BENITA PARRY is currently Honorary Professor in the Department of English and Comparative Literary Studies at the University of Warwick. She is the author of *Delusions and Discoveries: Studies on India in the*

British Imagination, 1880–1930 (1972, republished 1998) and *Conrad and Imperialism: Ideological Boundaries and Visionary Frontiers* (1983). A collection of essays, *Postcolonial Studies: A Materialist Critique*, will be published in 2004.

TAMARA SIVANANDAN is Principal Lecturer in the Sociology and Criminology group, School of Health and Social Sciences, at Middlesex University. Her research interests are in race and representation, education, black British and Third-World politics and culture. She has written on postcolonial literatures and on issues of race in education.

ANDREW SMITH is currently the *Sociological Review* Fellow at the University of Keele, and was previously an honorary research fellow of the Department of Sociology, University of Glasgow. His doctoral research focused on migration and the Nigerian expatriate community in Scotland, and he has published articles dealing with postcolonial theory and with popular culture in West Africa.

INDICATIVE CHRONOLOGY

Compiling a chronology for a volume such as this is a fraught undertaking. The more inclusive and comprehensive one tries to be, the greater becomes the risk that the whole exercise will end up a baggy monster, shapeless and undiscriminating. Criteria for inclusion and exclusion are always relatively difficult to justify and must, obviously, remain open to challenge. In drawing up the list that follows, I did not want merely to re-present in tabular form the material presented in the various chapters that make up this volume. Rather, my intention was to construct a list that gestures towards the multiplicity and huge diversity, both of the literary works actually or potentially implicated by the term "postcolonial literary studies," and of the social and political events that provide the overarching contexts for these works. As a field of academic specialization, postcolonial studies has tended (as several of the chapters in this volume suggest) to be overly schematic, restricted – not to say attenuated – in its coverage, range of reference, and field of vision. What follows is intended, therefore, in a rather utopian sense, as the outline of what scholars in the field might – or ought to – consider within their purview.

This chronology takes 1898 as its cut-off date. It would have been possible to begin earlier, of course – in 1870, say, or 1776, depending on what one chose to emphasize; perhaps even *much* earlier, in 1492. To have done so would have enabled one to reference some of the key historical events relating to colonial conquest and resistance to it, to slavery, maroonage, and emancipation, and to the emergence of creole republicanism, anticolonial revolution, and decolonization in the "New World" of the Americas. However, while an expanded chronology of this kind would obviously have been more encyclopedic in its scope, and perhaps more fully representative of the work done in the field of postcolonial studies, it would also have been much bulkier, more unwieldy, and, arguably, less reader-friendly than the one that follows. Moreover, 1898 does at least make a *plausible* cut-off date, inasmuch as it is often taken to mark the emergence of the United States as an imperialist power onto the world stage, and therefore to look forward to the developments of the second half of the twentieth century – developments that would leave the United States, by the end of that century, as the world's only hegemon and superpower.

With respect to the historical events itemized, I have obviously referenced those that might be said to be world-historical in their significance, as well as those whose significance has resonated far beyond their specific location in time and place. Uncontroversial examples of the first category would include the American destruction of the Spanish fleet in Manila Bay in 1898, the Japanese sacking of Nanking (1937), the nuclear strikes on Hiroshima and Nagasaki (1945), the partition of India (1947), the Chinese and Cuban revolutions, the Vietnamese victory over the French at Dien Bien Phu in 1954, the ethno-genocide in Rwanda in the mid-1990s, and the events of 11 September 2001. Similarly uncontroversial examples of the second category would include the massacre at Jallianwallagh Bagh in Amritsar (1919), Abd al-Krim's armed resistance to colonial domination in Morocco (1921–26), the massacre of Palestinian villagers by Zionist extremists at Dair Yasin (1948), the events at Sharpeville and Soweto in South Africa (1960 and 1976, respectively), the American-assisted ouster and assassination of elected President Salvador Allende in Chile (1973), the Indonesian invasion and occupation of East Timor (1975), and the military crackdown on student demonstrators at Tiananmen Square in Beijing (1989).

In addition to events of these kinds, however, I have also chosen to include references to events that might not themselves be world-historical, but that are nevertheless epochal or otherwise decisive for those involved in them. It seems particularly important to register events of this kind inasmuch as critiques of Eurocentrism and of elitist or top-down historiography have been among the foundational gestures of postcolonial studies from the outset. So while it might be conceded that such events as the uprising against the French in Madagascar (1898–1904), the 1926 riots in Java and Sumatra, and the 1964 overthrow of Cheddi Jagan's government in Guyana did not in themselves change the map of the world, they were nevertheless deeply consequential for those impacted by them, and they remain deeply consequential for contemporary researchers in postcolonial studies. Indeed, even if such events are deemed relatively inconsequential when considered on their own, their accumulative significance, as individual events in a sequence of events of a similar kind, is salutary. Thus if, between Madagascar in 1898 and the East Indies in 1926, one inserts such events as the Ashanti Rebellion of 1900 in the Gold Coast, the 1904 uprisings by the Nama and Herero peoples in South West Africa and the Acehnese in Sumatra, the Maji Maji revolt of 1905–7 in Tanganyika, the Bambatha Rebellion of 1906 in South Africa, insurrections in Cuba (1906) and Nicaragua (1909), the onset of the Mexican revolution in 1910, and the overthrow of the empire and the establishment of a republic in China (1911), one comes very quickly to an understanding of how ubiquitous and how continuous has been the resistance to colonial rule and imperialist domination.

By the same token, let us think of the ouster of Cheddi Jagan in 1964 not on its own but alongside such other more or less contemporaneous events as the following: the military coup in Thailand (1959) that served to usher in Sarit Thanarat's dictatorship; the crisis in the Congo (1960) occasioned by the overthrow and then subsequently the murder of Patrice Lumumba; the toppling of the US-sponsored dictatorship of Syngman Rhee in the April 19 revolution of 1960, followed, all too soon, by General Park Chung-hee's military coup and the restoration of dictatorship in South Korea; the US-sponsored Bay of Pigs episode (1961); the massive clamp-down on leftists in Peru (1963); the escalation of the US military campaign against Vietnam throughout the mid-1960s; the US-backed military coup against a left-wing government in Brazil (1964); the Western-assisted military coups of Bokassa in the Central African Republic, Mobutu in the Congo, Suharto in Indonesia, and Boumedienne in Algeria (all 1965); the intervention of US troops in the Dominican Republic and the installation there of a puppet regime (1965); the assassination of Mozambican liberation struggle leader Eduardo Mondlane (1965); and the ousting of Kwame Nkrumah of Ghana in a military coup (1966). To consider these events together is to understand that if it has, self-evidently, been hideously difficult to construct democracy in the postcolonial world, one of the primary reasons for this has been the continuous and active subversion of democracy and the "will of the people" by imperialist intrigue and military might, deriving invariably (in the post-1945 world) from the United States.

The Chronology includes dates for the acquisition of political independence in numerous former colonial territories, from Syria and Lebanon in 1945, the Philippines in 1946, and India in 1947 to Namibia in 1990 and Eritrea in 1993. It does not, however, detail the formation of the myriad parties, organizations, fronts, and alliances that fought for independence in all these territories. The one exception to this is the Indonesian Communist Party (PKI), formed in 1920, which warrants special mention both because it grew to become the largest such party outside the Soviet Union, and because it was so brutally crushed, with the physical liquidation of hundreds of thousands of its members, by the police and military of Suharto's "New Order" regime in 1965–66.

Also not included in the Chronology are details relating to the "white" Anglophone settler colonies of Canada, New Zealand, and Australia. There has been some debate in postcolonial studies over the status of these societies as erstwhile colonies and therefore contemporary "post-colonies." Without going into this debate, however, it seems to me that little would be gained by treating twentieth-century developments in Canada, New Zealand, Australia, and, for that matter, the United States in analogy with developments in such societies as Cuba, East Timor, Mali, Malaysia, and Mexico.

The left-hand column in the Chronology is devoted to "Political/Historical Events," in terms of the criteria specified above. The right-hand column is then devoted to writings of various kinds. These writings can be categorized under the following rubrics:

a) instances of colonial discourse (fictional or non-fictional) – examples include Joseph Conrad's *Heart of Darkness* and Albert Sarraut's *The Economic Development of the French Colonies*;

b) writings by Western authors that have proved valuable to the general cause of anticolonialism or anti-imperialism – examples include E. D. Morel's *The Congo Slave State* and Lenin's *Imperialism: The Highest Stage of Capitalism*;

c) important political writings by representatives of "colonial" peoples – examples include M. N. Roy's *India in Transition* and Sun Yat-sen's *The Three Principles of the People*;

d) works of literature by colonial and postcolonial writers – examples include Rabindranath Tagore's *Home and the World* and Nizar Qabbani's *On Entering the Sea*;

e) important critical and/or scholarly writings by colonial and postcolonial authors: examples include José Enrique Rodó's *Ariel* and Eric Williams's *Capitalism and Slavery*;

f) key texts in the academic field of postcolonial studies: examples include Edward W. Said's *Culture and Imperialism* and Declan Kiberd's *Inventing Ireland: The Literature of the Modern Nation*.

I have used the following abbreviations to signal the status of the writings cited:

A   autobiography
CD   colonial discourse
D   drama
F   fiction
NF   non-fiction
P   poetry
KT   key text in postcolonial studies

In most cases, writers are cited only once – to signal their entry into prominence or else their most significant work. Thus the Ghanaian writer Ayi Kwei Armah is listed under 1968, the date of publication of his first, and still his best-known, novel, *The Beautyful Ones Are Not Yet Born*. In some limited cases, however, writers are cited more than once, to signal their writing of a second (or even third) especially significant work. Thus Gabriel García Márquez is listed under 1967 (the date of publication of *One Hundred Years of Solitude*) but also 1985 (the date of publication of *Love in the Time of Cholera*, which many consider to be an even greater work); and the same is true of Nadine Gordimer, Ngugi wa Thiong'o, and Salman Rushdie, among others. Still other writers receive double (or multiple) citations because their work has been important in different contexts: thus Wole Soyinka appears as the author of the drama *The Road* in 1965, the volume of poetry, *Idanre* in 1967, the critical volume *Myth, Literature and the African World* in 1976, and of course as the recipient of the Nobel Prize for Literature in 1986.

In almost every case, I have listed the work cited under an English title, even where (as in the case of Yi Kwang-su's 1917 novel, *Heartlessness*, or Hafiz Ibrahim's 1937 *Diwan*, for example) no translation exists as yet. Where translations into English exist, I have used the available title, but indexed to the date of original publication of the work in question: Edouard Glissant's *La lézarde* was translated into English under the title of *The Ripening* only in 1985, for instance, but it appears in the Chronology as *The Ripening* (1958) – the date of original publication of *La lézarde*.

Finally, it needs to be said that the list of works of creative literature provided here is not intended to serve as a "postcolonial canon" in any sense. Rather it is meant to testify to the vast range and sheer diversity of the literary works that might be said to fall within the compass of "postcolonial studies" as a field of academic specialization.

Neil Lazarus

Chronology

Date	Political/historical events	Literary and other writings
1898	Spanish–American War: destruction of Spanish fleet in Manila Bay announces emergence of US as imperialist power; in victory, US acquires Philippines, Cuba, Puerto Rico, and Guam from Spain; US immediately moves to put down insurrection (1896–1902) in the Philippines Sudan: Battle of Omdurman, Mahdist forces defeated by British Madagascar: revolt against French colonial power (–1904)	
1899	South Africa: outbreak of Anglo-Boer War (–1902)	Joseph Conrad, *Heart of Darkness* (F; CD) Rudyard Kipling, *The White Man's Burden* (NF; CD)
1900	China: Boxer Rebellion, anti-Western uprising; forcibly put down Foraker Act renders Puerto Rico a colony of the US Gold Coast: Ashanti rebellion First Pan-African Conference, London	Solomon T. Plaatje (South Africa), *Boer War Diary* (NF) José Enrique Rodó, *Ariel* (NF)
1901		Rudyard Kipling, *Kim* (F; CD)
1902	Cuba: Platt Amendment; US appropriates part of Guantánamo Bay; imposes quasi-protectorate status on Cuba	J. A. Hobson, *Imperialism* (NF)
1903	US occupies Panama, forcing its separation from Colombia	E. D. Morel, *The Congo Slave State* (NF)
1904	Russo-Japanese War, ends (1905) with defeat of Russians Namibia: uprising of Herero and Nama against German rule East Indies: revolt by Acehnese in Sumatra; forcibly put down	Joseph Conrad, *Nostromo* (F; CD)
1905	India: launch of *swadeshi* ("of our own country") movement (–1908), in protest at British decision to partition Bengal Tanganyika: Maji Maji revolt (–1907)	

(*cont.*)

Date	Political/historical events	Literary and other writings
1906	South Africa: Bambatha Rebellion (Zulu uprising), begins as protest against poll tax US troops occupy Cuba (–1909).	
1907	Britain grants dominion status to its self-governing (white) colonies	
1908		Ch'oe Nam-son (Korea), "From the Sea to a Youth" (P) Rabindranath Tagore (India), *Home and the World* (F)
1909	India: Morley–Minto reforms US troops occupy Nicaragua (–1925)	Mohandas K. Gandhi (India), *Hind Swaraj* (NF)
1910	Korea: annexation by Japan; colonial rule to 1945 Mexico: revolution begins with constitutional and guerrilla challenges to the dictatorship of Porfirio Díaz	
1911	China: Revolution ends imperial regime, establishes provisional republic Mexico: Díaz regime falls; liberal reformer Francisco Madero assumes presidency	Iliya Abu Madi (Lebanon), *The Memorial of the Past* (P) J. E. Casely-Hayford (Gold Coast), *Ethiopia Unbound* (F) Muhammad Iqbal (India), "Complaint" (P)
1912	Cuba: uprising led by Independent Movement of People of Color, forcibly put down with assistance of US	
1913	South Africa: Native Land Act Mexico: Madero deposed, then murdered; Pancho Villa resumes guerrilla campaign	Rabindranath Tagore wins Nobel Prize for Literature
1914	Outbreak of First World War	Gabriela Mistral (Chile), *Sonnets of Death* (P)

1915
- Ceylon: Sinhala anti-Muslim riots; colonial government declares martial law
- US troops occupy Haiti to prevent acession to presidency of Rosalvo Bobo; occupation lasts until 1934

Nikolai Bukharin, *Imperialism and World Economy* (NF)
Mariano Azuela (Mexico), *The Underdogs* (F)

1916
- Ireland: Easter Rising

1917
- Bolshevik Revolution, first erupts in St. Petersburg
- Balfour Declaration, promises a "national home" for Jews in Palestine and protection of civil and religious rights of non-Jews in the territory

V. I. Lenin, *Imperialism: The Highest Stage of Capitalism* (NF)
Rabindranath Tagore (India), *Nationalism* (NF)
Yi Kwang-su (Korea), *Heartlessness* (F)

1918
- Armistice treaty signed, brings First World War to an end
- Declaration of the Irish Republic

Lu Hsun (China), "A Madman's Diary" (F)

1919
- League of Nations created at Peace Conference, Versailles
- German colonies in Africa transferred to Britain, France, and Belgium as Mandates
- China: May Fourth Movement – demands radical modernization, opposes imperialism
- India: Montagu–Chelmsford reforms (permitting limited self-government); Rowlatt Act (gives colonial police widespread powers to investigate and crush opposition); Gandhi calls for all-India mass protest movement; massacre of civilians at Jallianwallah Bagh in Amritsar
- Establishment of the Third International (Comintern)
- Outbreak of Anglo-Irish War (–1921)
- Mexico: rebel leader Emiliano Zapata killed by government troops
- Korea: uprising against Japanese colonialism
- Third British–Afghan War
- First Palestinian National Congress rejects Balfour Declaration, calls for Arab independence

Li Ta-chao (China), "A New Era" (NF)
Chu Yo-han (Korea), *Fireworks* (P)

(cont.)

Date	Political/historical events	Literary and other writings
1920	Britain gains mandate control over Iraq, Trans-Jordan, Palestine; anti-British revolt in Iraq Government of Ireland Act India: Gandhi launches Non-Cooperation movement Mozambique: colonial rule in Mozambique systematized: population subjected to forced labor Indonesia: Communist Party (PKI) is formed; becomes largest such party in the world outside of socialist state bloc before it is obliterated by Suharto in brutal campaign (1965–66)	
1921	Ireland: outbreak of civil war (–1923) Morocco: armed resistance to French and Spanish domination, led by Abd al-Krim (–1926) China: Sun Yat-sen elected president; civil war breaks out between his regime and warlords in the north	
1922	Declaration of the Irish Free State	Frederick Lugard, *The Dual Mandate in British Tropical Africa* (NF; CD) M. N. Roy (India), *India in Transition* (NF) René Maran (Martinique), *Batouala* (F)
1923	Ceylon: general strike, militant fusion of nationalist and class-based demands Mexico: Pancho Villa murdered	Albert Sarraut, *The Economic Development of the French Colonies* (NF; CD) Zhu Ziqing (China), "Destruction" (P)
1924	China: Sun Yat-sen dies; leadership of Kuomintang (National People's Party) assumed by the anti-communist Chiang Kai-shek India: communalist violence between Hindus and Muslims; Gandhi begins hunger strike as "a penance and a prayer"	E. M. Forster, *A Passage to India* (F; CD) Pablo Neruda (Chile), *Twenty Love Poems and a Song of Despair* (P) José Eustasio Rivera (Colombia), *The Vortex* (F)
1925	China / Hong Kong: massive strike, boycott of foreign goods (–1926) Syria: Druze revolt (–1927)	Sun Yat-sen (China), *The Three Principles of the People* (NF) Kim So-wol (Korea), *Azaleas* (P)

1926	Indonesia: riots in Java and Sumatra, forcibly put down by Dutch China: Chiang moves to establish hegemony over parts of the country still under control of warlords; captures Wuhan (1926) and Shanghai (1927); in Shanghai, orchestrates massacre of labor organizers, communists, and other activists; subsequent communist-led uprisings in Nanch'ang and Hunan are crushed Nicaragua: rebellion against authoritarian regime of Adolfo Díaz; US intervention, successfully resisted by forces under Augustino César Sandino	Ho Chi Minh (Vietnam), *Colonization on Trial* (NF) Ricardo Güiraldes (Argentina), *Don Segundo Sombra* (F) Martín Luis Guzmán (Mexico), *The Eagle and the Serpent* (F) Thomas Mofolo (South Africa), *Chaka* (F)
1927	International Conference Against Imperialism and Colonial Oppression, Brussels Bolivia: massive revolt of indigenous people against government	André Gide, *Voyage to the Congo* (NF; CD) Cho Myong-hui (Korea), *The Naktonggang River* (F) Taha Husain (Egypt), *The Days* (vol. II, 1939) (A) José Vasconcelos, *The Cosmic Race* (NF)
1928	China: capture of Beijing by Chiang's forces; he becomes national president	Mário de Andrade (Brazil), *Macunaíma* (F) José Carlos Mariátegui, *Seven Essays towards an Interpretation of Peruvian Reality* (NF)
1929	Nigeria: Aba "women's riots" India: Meerut Conspiracy Case against 31 labor leaders Palestine: riots sparked by founding of the Jewish Agency; several hundred killed, many by British soldiers Geneva Convention signed, regulating treatment of prisoners of war	Rómulo Gallegos (Venezuela), *Doña Bárbara* (F) Wen I-to (China), *Dead Water* (P)
1930	India: Gandhi launches Civil Disobedience Movement Vietnam: peasant uprising, coincides with formation of Communist Party Brazil: military coup	Mao Tse-tung (China), "A Single Spark Can Start a Prairie Fire" (NF) Launch of Négritude movement in Paris by Francophone intellectuals including Léopold Sédar Senghor, Aimé Césaire, and Leon Damas Nicolás Guillén (Cuba), *Son Motifs* (P) Solomon T. Plaatje (South Africa), *Mhudi* (F)

(cont.)

Date	Political/historical events	Literary and other writings
1931	British Commonwealth of Nations created Japanese invade Manchuria	Evelyn Waugh, *Black Mischief* (F; CD) Gregorio López y Fuentes (Mexico), *The Land* (F) Ahmad Shauqi (Egypt), *Diwan*
1932	Thailand: absolute monarchy overthrown in bloodless civilian–military coup El Salvador: insurrection led by Farabundo Martí crushed; supported by US, dictator Maximiliano Hernández oversees pogrom in which 30,000 are killed	Mulk Raj Anand (India), *Untouchable* (F) Tewfiq al-Hakim (Egypt), *The People of the Cave* (D) Claude McKay (Jamaica), *Banana Bottom* (F) Mao Tun (China), *Midnight* (F) Gilberto Freyre, *The Master and the Slaves* (NF)
1933	Nicaragua: take-over of power by Anastasio Somoza García, supported by US; Sandino murdered	George Orwell, *Burmese Days* (F; CD) Hsiao Hung (China), *The Field of Life and Death* (F) Jorge Icaza (Ecuador), *Huasipungo* (F) Alfred Mendes (Trinidad), *Pitch Lake* (F) Shen Ts'ung-wen (China), *Border Town* (F) Hu Shih, *The Chinese Renaissance* (NF)
1934	China: "Long March" begins, as Mao Tse-tung and his supporters trek to remote Yenan to escape liquidation by KMT forces	Jorge Luis Borges (Argentina), *A Universal History of Infamy* (F)
1935	Mussolini's forces invade and occupy Ethiopia Passage of Government of India Act Wave of strikes in Central African copper-belt China: Japanese forces seize Beijing, set up puppet regime in north	Meo Tse-tung (China), *Problems of Strategy in China's Revolutionary War* (NF) Jayaprakash Narayan (India), *Why Socialism?* (NF) Jawarharlal Nehru (India), *An Autobiography* Manik Bandopadhyay (India), *The History of Puppets* (F) C. L. R. James (Trinidad), *Minty Alley* (F) Lao She (China), *Camel Hsiang-tzu* (F) Premchand (India), *The Gift of a Cow* (F)
1936	Spanish Civil War erupts Paraguay: military coup; fascist regime installed Palestine: Arab revolt (–1939), protesting British rule and dispossessions caused by Zionist settlement; brutally crushed by British, with more than 1,000 Palestinian deaths	

1937	China: Shanghai falls to Japanese; Nanking sacked, more than 100,000 killed; Mao issues "National Salvation Program" calling for united front against Japanese; forms temporary military alliance with Chiang's KMT Jamaica: riots against British rule (–1938) Trinidad: nationalist riots	Karen Blixen (Denmark), *Out of Africa* (NF; CD) Hafiz Ibrahim (Egypt), *Diwan* R. K. Narayan (India), *The Bachelor of Arts* (F) Siburapha (Thailand), *Behind the Painting* (F)
1938		Jomo Kenyatta (Kenya), *Facing Mount Kenya* (NF) Ciro Alegría (Peru), *The Hungry Dogs* (F) María Luisa Bombal (Chile), *The House of Mist* (F) D. O. Fagunwa (Nigeria), *The Forest of a Thousand Daemons* (F) Sadeq Hedayat (Iran), *The Blind Owl* (F) Graciliano Ramos (Brazil), *Barren Lives* (F) Raja Rao (India), *Kanthapura* (F) George Antonius, *The Arab Awakening* (NF) C. L. R. James, *The Black Jacobins* (NF)
1939	German invasion of Poland; outbreak of Second World War	Joyce Cary, *Mister Johnson* (F; CD) Aimé Césaire (Martinique), "Notebook of a Return to the Native Land" (P, revised 1947, 1956) Juan Carlos Onetti (Uruguay), *The Pit* (F) Tuan-mu Hung-liang (China), *The Steppe of the Khorchin Banner* (F)
1940	Fall of France to Nazi forces Vietnam: revolts in southern Mekong Delta	Tarashankar Bandyopadhyay (India), "The Witch" (F) Ts'ao Yü (China), *Peking Man* (D) César Vallejo (Peru), *Spain, Take This Cup from Me* (P) Fernando Ortiz, *Cuban Counterpoint: Tobacco and Sugar* (NF)

(cont.)

Date	Political/historical events	Literary and other writings
1941	Ethiopia: Allies capture Addis Ababa from Italians, enabling Haile Selassie to return after five-year absence Japanese troops capture Cambodia, Vietnam, Thailand; in response, Ho Chi Minh launches Viet Minh independence movement Japan bombs US fleet in Pearl Harbor, precipitating US into War; Japanese invade and occupy Hong Kong, Malaya	H. I. E. Dhlomo (South Africa), *Valley of a Thousand Hills* (P) Edgar Mittelholzer (Guyana), *Corentyne Thunder* (F) Ibrahim Tuqan (Palestine), *Diwan*
1942	India: Gandhi launches Quit India Movement Japanese forces capture Singapore, Java, Burma, and the Philippines; attack Solomon Islands and New Guinea	Albert Camus, *The Outsider* (F; CD) Jorge Amado (Brazil), *The Violent Land* (F)
1943	India: armed struggle under leadership of Subhas Chandra Bose launched against British forces in north-east; devastating famine in Bengal (−1944) kills almost 4 million people	Ishaq Musa al-Husaini (Palestine), *A Chicken's Memoirs* (F)
1944	Vietnam: major famine kills 2 million people US: Bretton Woods conference; foundation of International Monetary Fund (IMF) and World Bank Guatemala: regime of General Castañeda overthrown in "October Revolution" Palestine: Zionist forces begin guerrilla warfare against British; tactics include terror and assassinations	José María Arguedas (Peru), *Everyone's Blood* (F) Ismat Chughtai (India), *The Quilt and Other Stories* Jacques Roumain (Haiti), *Masters of the Dew* (F) Eric Williams, *Capitalism and Slavery* (NF)
1945	War ends in Europe US drops nuclear bombs on Hiroshima and Nagasaki in Japan, leading to Japanese surrender Algeria: French repression of nationalists; major uprising follows; thousands killed Revolution in Vietnam brings Ho Chi Minh's Viet Minh to power; French forces attempt to recapture colonial power; war ensues (−1954)	Gabriela Mistral wins Nobel Prize for Literature Gopinath Mohanty (India), *Paraja* (F)

	Indonesia: "Revolution of 1945" in which Republic is declared; fierce fighting as Dutch attempt to reinstall colonial power (–1949); civil war in Java (–1948) in which many leftists are murdered Philippines liberated from Japanese occupation Syria, Lebanon gain independence Fifth Pan-African Congress held in Manchester, England, proclaims "right of all colonial peoples to control their own destiny"	Truong Chinh (Vietnam), *The August Revolution* (NF) Jawaharlal Nehru (India), *The Discovery of India* (NF) Peter Abrahams (South Africa), *Mine Boy* (F) Miguel Angel Asturias (Guatemala), *Mr. President* (F)
1946	United Nations convenes for the first time Thailand: military overthrows nationalist leader Pridi Phanomyong Indochina: fierce resistance to French attempt to reinstall colonial rule after Second World War (–1954) Argentina: General Juan Perón assumes presidency Philippines gains independence Palestine: militant right-wing Zionist guerrillas blow up British Army headquarters in Jerusalem; Arab anti-Zionist protests continue	
1947	India gains independence; birth of Pakistan following partition of sub-continent; hundreds of thousands die in inter-communal violence; 8.5 million refugees cross border in both directions Burma: U Aung San, hero of independence movement, assassinated Palestine: UN announces plan for partition, granting bulk of land to minority Jewish population Korea: US establishes Syngman Rhee as leader of government in South; pursues authoritarian policies, targets the mass revolutionary movement that had developed after liberation from Japanese occupation in 1945	Jawaharlal Nehru delivers "Tryst with Destiny" speech Babani Bhattacharya (India), *So Many Hungers!* (F) Ch'ien Chung-shu (China), *Fortress Besieged* (F) Birago Diop (Senegal), *Tales of Amadou Koumba* (F) Suryakant Tripathi "Nirala" (India), *The Earthly Knowledge* (P) Pa Chin (China), *Cold Nights* (F) Badr Shakir al-Sayyab (Iraq), *Withered Fingers* (P)
1948	Burma, Sri Lanka (Ceylon) gain independence; insurrectionary challenge to fledgling Burmese state from left parties South Africa: Afrikaner Nationalist Party comes to power, implements policy of *apartheid*	Graham Greene, *The Heart of the Matter* (F; CD) Alan Paton (South Africa), *Cry, the Beloved Country* (F; CD) G. V. Desani (India), *All About H. Hatterr* (F)

(cont.)

Date	Political/historical events	Literary and other writings
	Indo-Pakistan war over disputed state of Kashmir India: Gandhi assassinated Palestine: fighting between Palestinians and Zionists escalates into civil war; massacre of Palestinian villagers at Dair Yasin by Zionist ultras; Palestinians driven out of their homes and off their land; independent Jewish state declared; declaration immediately recognized by US; by year's end, number of Palestinian refugees estimated at 1 million Malaya: massive, communist-inspired insurgency, guerrilla war against British colonial rule (–1953); eventually defeated Philippines: Huk rebellion – peasant struggle against landed oligarchy – begins; eventually crushed (1954) Cambodia gains independence UN adopts Declaration of Human Rights	Saadat Hasan Manto (Pakistan), "Toba Tek Singh" (F) Ernesto Sábato (Argentina), *The Tunnel* (F) Léopold Sédar Senghor, ed. *Anthologie de la nouvelle poésie nègre et malgache de langue française* (P) Jean-Paul Sartre, "Black Orpheus" (NF)
1949	China: victory of communist forces under Mao Tse-tung; People's Republic proclaimed; Chiang Kai-shek's nationalists take refuge in Taiwan Indonesia gains independence under Sukarno Laos gains independence	Miguel Angel Asturias (Guatemala), *Men of Maize* (F) Alejo Carpentier (Cuba), *The Kingdom of This World* (F) Khalil Mutran (Lebanon), *Diwan* V. S. Reid (Jamaica), *New Day* (F) Ma'ruf al-Rusafi (Iraq), *Diwan* Ting Ling (China), *The Sangkan River* (F)
1950	Outbreak of US–Korean war (–1953); casualties will top 1 million Tibet: China invades, assumes control Jordan annexes West Bank, absorbing 600,000 Palestinians	Doris Lessing, *The Grass is Singing* (F; CD) Pablo Neruda (Chile), *Canto general* (P) Octavio Paz, *Labyrinth of Solitude* (NF)
1951	Egypt: guerrilla war against British forces in Suez Canal Zone Libya gains independence Iran nationalizes its oil industry	Nirad C. Chaudhuri (India), *The Autobiography of an Unknown Indian*

Year	Events	Literary works
1952	South Africa: African National Congress launches Defiance Campaign Kenya: State of Emergency declared as anti-colonial insurrection ("Mau Mau") intensifies Vietnam: France launches massive offensive against Viet Minh forces	Ralph de Boissiere (Trinidad), *Crown Jewel* (F) Andrée Chedid (Egypt), *From Sleep Unbound* (F) Mochtar Lubis (Indonesia), *A Road with No End* (F) Amos Tutuola (Nigeria), *The Palm-Wine Drinkard* (F) Frantz Fanon, *Black Skin, White Masks* (NF)
1953	Cuba: Fidel Castro leads abortive assault on Moncada Barracks in Santiago de Cuba; many of the militants are killed; others, including Castro, are captured Iran: CIA-backed coup deposes nationalist leader, Mossadegh British Guiana: uprising, led by People's Progressive Party, against colonialism; put down by military force; constitution suspended	Fidel Castro (Cuba), "History will absolve me" (NF) Alejo Carpentier (Cuba), *The Lost Steps* (F) George Lamming (Barbados), *In the Castle of My Skin* (F) Camara Laye (Guinea), *The African Child* (F) Roger Mais (Jamaica), *The Hills Were All Joyful Together* (F)
1954	Vietnamese army led by Ho Chi Minh defeats French colonial forces at Dien Bien Phu; France sues for peace; the Viet Minh take Hanoi Egypt: Gamal Abdel Nasser takes power Algeria: war of independence begins (–1962) Guatemala: US orchestrates overthrow of nationalist government of Jacobo Arbenz	Samira 'Azzam (Palestine), *Little Things* (F) Martin Carter (Guyana), *Poems of Resistance* Driss Chraïbi (Morocco), *The Simple Past* (F) Kamala Markandaya (India), *Nectar in a Sieve* (F) Nicanor Parra (Chile), *Poems and Antipoems* Abd al-Rahman Sharqawi (Egypt), *The Earth* (F)
1955	Bandung Conference of independent Asian and African states; declaration upholds principles of national sovereignty, human rights, and equality among nations and states South Africa: Freedom Charter adopted at Congress of the People Vietnam: outbreak of civil war in South; Ngo Dinh Diem declares South Vietnam a republic	Aimé Césaire (Martinique), *Discourse on Colonialism* (NF) U Nu (Burma), *An Asian Speaks* (NF) Amrita Pritam (India), *Messages* (P) Juan Rulfo (Mexico), *Pedro Páramo* (F) Saadi Youssef (Iraq), *Songs Not for Others* (P) Wang Meng (China), *The Young Newcomer* (F)

(cont.)

Date	Political/historical events	Literary and other writings
1956	Egypt: Nasser nationalizes Suez Canal; Egypt invaded by Israel, with British and French support; withdrawal of these forces negotiated Sudan gains independence; armed resistance continues in the south (–1972) Morocco, Tunisia gain independence Cuba: Castro initiates revolution when he returns to Cuba with small armed force Yemen: anti-British strikes in Aden; clashes between British and Yemeni troops (–1957) Soviet Union: at 20th Congress of the Communist Party of the Soviet Union, Nikita Khruschev denounces Stalin's crimes; initiates de-Stalinization Hungary: anti-Stalinist uprising crushed by Soviet troops China: Mao introduces "Hundred Flowers" campaign ("Let a hundred flowers bloom, let a hundred schools of thought contend")	First international conference of black writers and artists (Paris) George Padmore (Trinidad), *Pan Africanism or Communism?* (NF) Carlos Bulosan (Philippines), *America is in the Heart* (A) Mongo Beti (Cameroon), *The Poor Christ of Bomba* (F) Chang Ai-ling (China), *Naked Earth* (F) David Diop (Senegal), *Hammer Blows* (P) Faiz Ahmed Faiz (Pakistan), *Prison Thoughts* (P) João Guimarães Rosa (Brazil), *The Devil to Pay in the Backlands* (F) Naguib Mahfouz (Egypt), *Cairo Trilogy* (–1957) (F) Ferdinand Oyono (Cameroon), *Houseboy* (F) Samuel Selvon (Trinidad), *The Lonely Londoners* (F) Kushwant Singh (India), *Train to Pakistan* (F)
1957	Ghana gains independence; also peninsular Malaya (becomes Malaysia in 1963 with incorporation of Sarawak, Sabah and Singapore) Indonesia: Sukarno declares martial law; revoked 1963 Algeria: Battle of Algiers	Kwame Nkrumah (Ghana), *Ghana: Autobiography* (NF) Octavio Paz (Mexico), *Sunstone* (P) Albert Memmi, *The Colonizer and the Colonized* (NF)
1958	Pakistan: military coup brings Mohammed Ayub Khan to power Guinea gains independence Cameroun: Reuben Um Nyobé, UPC leader, killed All-African People's Conference, Accra	Chinua Achebe (Nigeria), *Things Fall Apart* (F) Edouard Glissant (Martinique), *The Ripening* (F) N. V. M. Gonzalez (Philippines), *Bread of Salt* (F) Ludu U Hla (Burma), *The Caged Ones* (F)

Year	Events	Literature
	Sri Lanka: riots erupt, as Sinhala chauvinists attack Tamils; hundreds killed; state of emergency eventually declared Venezuela: dictator Marcos Pérez Jiménez ousted in coup China: Mao launches "Great Leap Forward", programme of rapid industrialization and collectivization, marked also by denigration of intellectuals	Qurratulain Hyder (India), *River of Fire* (F) Es'kia Mphahlele (South Africa), *Down Second Avenue* (A)
1959	Cuba: overthrow of Batista regime; Fidel Castro assumes power China: devastating famine (–1961), kills as many as 40 million Zambia: Kenneth Kaunda imprisoned, United Independence Party banned; leads civil disobedience campaign when released Thailand: Sarit Thanarat seizes power through coup; installs dictatorship, continued by his successors (–1973) Tibet: rebellion crushed by Chinese forces; Dalai Lama flees into exile Laos: Pathet Lao communist rebels launch major offensive against state	
1960	Harold Macmillan's "winds of change" speech South Africa: Sharpeville massacre, as police open fire on unarmed gathering – 67 killed; ANC and Pan-African Congress banned Benin, Burkina Faso, Central African Republic, Chad, Congo, Gabon, Ivory Coast, Madagascar, Mali, Mauritania, Niger, Nigeria, Senegal, Somalia, Togo gain independence Congo: attempted secession of Katanga province; martial law declared by new president Patrice Lumumba; military seizes power, supported by US and Belgium; Lumumba arrested South Korea: April 19 student revolution topples regime of Syngman Rhee; democracy short-lived, as General Park Chung-hee takes power in military coup	Wilson Harris (Guyana), *Palace of the Peacock* (F) Hwang Sun-won (South Korea), *Trees on a Cliff* (F) Ousmane Sembene (Senegal), *God's Bits of Wood* (F) George Lamming, *The Pleasures of Exile* (NF)

(cont.)

Date	Political/historical events	Literary and other writings
1961	US-sponsored Bay of Pigs invasion of Cuba thwarted Cameroon, Sierra Leone, Tanzania gain independence Congo: Lumumba murdered while in custody Angola: armed struggle begins South Africa: Albert Luthuli, President of ANC, awarded Nobel Peace Prize First Conference of Non-Aligned Countries, Belgrade	Nnamdi Azikiwe (Nigeria), *Zik: Selected Speeches* (NF) Frantz Fanon (Martinique), *The Wretched of the Earth* (NF) Vo Nguyen Giap (Vietnam), *People's War People's Army* (NF) Ernesto "Che" Guevara (Argentina/Cuba), *Guerrilla Warfare* (NF) Adonis (Syria), *Songs of Mihyar the Damascene* (P) Cyprian Ekwensi (Nigeria), *Jagua Nana* (F) Attia Hosain (India), *Sunlight on a Broken Column* (F) Cheikh Hamidou Kane (Senegal), *Ambiguous Adventure* (F) V. S. Naipaul (Trinidad), *A House for Mr. Biswas* (F)
1962	Algeria, Burundi, Jamaica, Rwanda, Trinidad and Tobago, Uganda gain independence Border war between India and China Cuban missile crisis: US President Kennedy authorizes blockade of Cuba in bid to prevent deployment of Soviet nuclear weapons	Mehdi Ben Barka (Algeria), "Resolving the Ambiguities of National Sovereignty" (NF) Kenneth Kaunda (Zambia), *Zambia Shall Be Free* (A) Patrice Lumumba (Congo), *Congo My Country* (NF) Albert Luthuli (South Africa), *Let My People Go* (NF) Carlos Fuentes (Mexico), *The Death of Artemio Cruz* (F) F. Sionil José (Philippines), *The Pretenders* (F) Alex La Guma (South Africa), *A Walk in the Night* (F) Carlos Martínez Moreno (Uruguay), *The Wall* (F) Mario Vargas Llosa (Peru), *The Time of the Hero* (F)

1963	Formation of Organization of African Unity (OAU)	Julio Cortázar (Argentina), *Hopscotch* (F)
	Kenya gains independence	Ghassan Kanafani (Palestine), *Men in the Sun* (F)
	Peru: massive clamp down on left-wing activists	Severo Sarduy (Cuba), *Gestures* (F)
	Guinea-Bissau: PAIGC launches armed resistance	C. L. R. James, *Beyond a Boundary* (NF)
1964	Malawi, Zambia, Malaya gain independence	Govan Mbeki (South Africa), *South Africa: The*
	Vietnam: "Gulf of Tonkin Resolution" enables US administration to escalate its military campaign; air war against North Vietnam begins; also huge increases in number of US combat troops	*Peasants' Revolt* (NF)
	Mozambique: FRELIMO launches armed struggle	Forugh Farrokhzad (Iran), *Another Birth* (P)
	Guyana: Cheddi Jagan's government is overthrown	
	Brazil: left-wing government overthrown in US-backed military coup	
	South Africa: ANC leaders Nelson Mandela and Walter Sisulu sentenced to life imprisonment for treason – incarcerated on Robben Island	
	China: long-term deterioration in relations between China and Soviet Union (1956–) leads to breach between two communist powers	
1965	White Rhodesian government declares unilateral independence from Britain	Nelson Mandela (South Africa), *No Easy Walk to Freedom* (NF)
	Central African Republic: Jean Bedel Bokassa takes power in coup; has himself crowned "Emperor"; dictatorship until 1979	Kwame Nkrumah (Ghana), *Neo-Colonialism: The Last Stage of Imperialism* (NF)
	Congo (Zaire): Mobutu takes power in coup; dictatorship until 1997	Michael Anthony (Trinidad), *The Year in San Fernando* (F)
	Indonesia: Suharto takes power in coup; initiates pogrom (–1966) against the left: half a million people are murdered; hundreds of thousands more imprisoned in brutal conditions	Guillermo Cabrera Infante (Cuba), *Three Trapped Tigers* (F)
	Thailand: rural insurgency, led by Communist Party (–1978)	Kamala Das (India), *Summer in Calcutta* (P)
		Shahnon Ahmad (Malaysia), *Rope of Ash* (F)
		Wole Soyinka (Nigeria), *The Road* (D)

(cont.)

Date	Political/historical events	Literary and other writings
	Singapore breaks from Malaysia and becomes separate state under authoritarian rule of Lee Kwan-yew	Paul Scott, *The Jewel in the Crown* (F; CD)
	Dominican Republic: intervention of US forces to overthrow constitutional revolution headed by Colonel Francisco Caamaño Deño; puppet regime installed	U. R. Ananthamurthy (India), *Funeral Rites* (P)
	Mozambique: FRELIMO leader, Eduardo Mondlane, assassinated	Louise Bennett (Jamaica), *Jamaica Labrish* (P)
	Algeria: Colonel Houari Boumedienne seizes power from President Ben Bella	José Lezama Lima (Cuba), *Paradiso* (F)
		Flora Nwapa (Nigeria), *Efuru* (F)
		Jean Rhys (Dominica), *Wide Sargasso Sea* (F)
		Marta Traba (Argentina/Colombia), *Rites of Summer* (F)
		Mario Vargas Llosa (Peru), *The Green House* (F)
1966	Barbados, Botswana, Guyana, Lesotho gain independence	Oginga Odinga (Kenya), *Not Yet Uhuru* (A)
	Zimbabwe: armed struggle launched	José Maria Sison (Philippines), *Struggle for National Democracy* (NF)
	Namibia: armed struggle launched	Miguel Angel Asturias wins Nobel Prize for Literature
	Ghana: Kwame Nkrumah ousted in coup	Gabriel García Márquez (Colombia), *One Hundred Years of Solitude* (F)
	First Tricontinental Conference, Havana	V. S. Naipaul (Trinidad), *The Mimic Men* (F)
	China: Mao inaugurates "Cultural Revolution" (–1976), emphasizing permanent revolution and class struggle; vilification and widespread persecution of intellectuals one consequence of the movement's radical anti-urban and anti-bourgeois ideology	Ngugi wa Thiong'o (Kenya), *A Grain of Wheat* (F)
		Wole Soyinka (Nigeria), *Idanre, and Other Poems*
1967	Nigeria: civil war erupts as federal government moves to combat secession of Biafra (–1970)	
	Six-day Arab–Israeli war; crushing victory for Israel, which seizes Sinai and Gaza from Egypt, West Bank from Jordan; Israeli annexation of Old City of Jerusalem	
	India: peasant unrest in Naxalbari, West Bengal; Maoist "Naxalite" agitation spreads across several states (–1975)	
	Bolivia: capture and execution of Ernesto "Che" Guevara by Bolivian Rangers in collaboration with CIA operatives	

		Andre Gunder Frank, *Capitalism and Underdevelopment in Latin America* (NF)
		Wilson Harris, *Tradition, the Writer and Society* (NF)
1968	US: Martin Luther King assassinated	Julius K. Nyerere (Tanzania), *Ujamaa: Essays on Socialism* (NF)
	Student-led uprisings world-wide, especially France, Mexico, US	Ayi Kwei Armah (Ghana), *The Beautyful Ones Are Not Yet Born* (F)
	Czechoslovakia: "Prague Spring" crushed by Soviet troops	Dennis Brutus (South Africa), *Letters to Martha* (P)
	Vietnam: "Tet Offensive"; Vietcong capture Hue, drastically weaken American military and civilian confidence	Ahmadou Kourouma (Ivory Coast), *The Suns of Independence* (F)
		Yambo Ouologuem (Mali), *Bound to Violence* (F)
		Nizar Qabbani (Iraq), "Comments on the Notebook of Decadence" (P)
		Andrew Salkey (Jamaica), *The Late Emancipation of Jerry Stoker* (F)
		Wong Phui Nam (Malaysia), *How the Hills Are Distant* (P)
1969	Britain sends troops to Northern Ireland to quell rioting	Eduardo Mondlane (Mozambique), *The Struggle for Mozambique* (NF)
	Cambodia: US begins massive secret bombing campaign	Elena Poniatowska (Mexico), *Until We Meet Again* (F)
	Argentina: urban uprisings in various cities (Cordoba, Rosario, others), popular radicalization (–1973)	Tayeb Salih (Sudan), *Season of Migration from the North* (F)
		Fadwa Tuqan (Palestine), *Horsemen and the Night* (P)

(cont.)

Date	Political/historical events	Literary and other writings
1970	Fiji, Tonga gain independence Laos: intensive US bombing of Vietcong supply line Cambodia: Prince Sihanouk overthrown in right-wing coup Chile: socialist Salvador Allende elected to presidency Jordan: "Black September"; fighting between Jordanian army and Palestinian guerrillas; Palestinians expelled from Jordan	Salah Abd al-Sabur (Egypt), *Journey at Night* (P) Ama Ata Aidoo (Ghana), *No Sweetness Here* (F) Merle Hodge (Trinidad), *Crick Crack Monkey* (F) Hwang Sok-yong (South Korea), *The Strange Land* (F) Jabra Ibrahim Jabra (Palestine), *The Ship* (F)
1971	Civil war breaks out in East Pakistan, following declaration of independent state of Bangladesh; subsequent war between India and Pakistan ends with defeat of the latter; Zulfikar Ali Bhutto elected Prime Minister, ending 13 years of military rule Uganda: Idi Amin comes to power in coup; dictatorship to 1979 Bahrain gains independence	Pablo Neruda wins Nobel Prize for Literature Mahmoud Darwish (Palestine), *Lover from Palestine* (P) Christopher Okigbo (Nigeria), *Labyrinths* (P) Yu Kwang-Chung (Taiwan), *Acres of Barbed Wire* (P) Roberto Fernández Retamar, "Caliban" (NF)
1972	Philippines: Ferdinand Marcos declares martial law; rebellion by Filipino Muslims in south; met with extreme violence Northern Ireland: "Bloody Sunday," British paratroops kill 13 marchers in Derry; IRA retaliates; direct rule imposed	Steve Biko (South Africa), *I Write What I Like* (NF) Dhoomil (India), *From the Parliament to the Street* (P) Athol Fugard (South Africa), *Sizwe Banzi is Dead* (D) Nick Joaquin (Philippines), *Tropical Gothic* (F) Manohar Malgonkar (India), *The Devil's Wind* (F) Simone Schwarz-Bart (Guadeloupe), *The Bridge of Beyond* (F) Paulo Freire, *Pedagogy of the Oppressed* (NF) Walter Rodney, *How Europe Underdeveloped Africa* (NF)

1973	"Oil crisis" as Organization of Petroleum Exporting Countries raises prices and curtails production	Amilcar Cabral (Guinea-Bissau), *Return to the Source* (NF)
	Collapse of Bretton Woods political-economic system; US comes off gold standard; paves way for globalization of capital and neo-liberal economic policies	Le Duan (Vietnam), *The Vietnamese Revolution* (NF)
	Thailand: dictatorship is brought down; but subsequent years are marked by instability and increased violence against left-wing activists, until coup (1976) re-establishes military rule	Mahasweta Devi (India), *Mother of 1084* (F)
	Chile: Salvador Allende, elected president, assassinated in coup led by General Augusto Pinochet, with active assistance of the CIA; Pinochet initiates violent campaign of repression of leftists; dictatorship lasts until 1990	Eduardo Galeano, *The Open Veins of Latin America* (NF)
	Bahamas gains independence	
	Egypt and Syria launch joint attack on Israel; Israel victorious after fierce exchange	
	Guinea-Bissau: Amilcar Cabral, leader of PAIGC, assassinated by Portuguese agents	
1974	Guinea-Bissau gains independence after armed struggle	M. Gopalakrishna Adiga (India), *Song of the Earth and Other Poems*
	Grenada gains independence	Nadine Gordimer (South Africa), *The Conservationist* (F)
	Ethiopia: Haile Selassie deposed after general strike	Emile Habiby (Palestine), *The Secret Life of Saeed, the Ill-Fated Pessoptimist* (F)
		Bessie Head (South Africa / Botswana), *A Question of Power* (F)
		Daniel Moyano (Argentina), *The Devil's Trill* (F)
		Agostinho Neto (Angola), *Sacred Hope* (P)
		Augusto Roa Bastos (Paraguay), *I the Supreme* (F)
		José Luandino Vieira (Angola), *The Real Life of Domingos Xavier* (F)
		Adonis, *The Fixed and the Changing: A Study of Conformity and Originality in Arab Culture* (NF)

(cont.)

Date	Political/historical events	Literary and other writings
1975	Vietnam war ends with defeat of US and capture of Saigon by People's Army of Vietnam Cambodia: seizure of power by Khmer Rouge under Pol Pot; people living in Phnom Penh forced into countryside; intellectuals murdered; state seals itself off from outside world Angola, Mozambique, Cape Verde gain independence after armed struggles Civil wars continue in Angola and Mozambique after independence Indonesia invades and occupies East Timor India: High Court in Allahabad finds Indira Gandhi guilty of electoral malpractice; sets aside her election; in response Indira declares State of Emergency in India (–1977); under Emergency, tens of thousands of activists and opponents of the regime are arrested Bangladesh: Sheikh Mujibur Rahman, first Prime Minister of the new state (1972–75) murdered in military coup; strong evidence of American CIA involvement; event issues in two decades of military dictatorship Papua New Guinea gains independence Lebanon: outbreak of civil war	Ruth Prawer Jhabvala (India), *Heat and Dust* (F) Bharati Mukherjee (India/US), *Wife* (F) Nawal el Saadawi (Egypt), *Woman at Point Zero* (F) Indira Sant (India), *The Snake-skin and Other Poems* Antonio Skármeta (Chile), *I Dreamt the Snow Was Burning* (F)
1976	South Africa: student uprising; begins in Soweto township, spreads to other parts of the country; hundreds killed Argentina: Isabel Péron ousted in military coup; General Roberto Videla takes power, inaugurates "dirty war" against leftists, unionists, community organizers, intellectuals (–1983) Seychelles gains independence Peru: general strikes (–1977), popular radicalization, contribute to growing challenge to military rule	Jayanta Mahapatra (India), *A Pain of Rites* (P) Manuel Puig (Argentina), *The Kiss of the Spider Woman* (F) Antônio Torres (Brazil), *The Land* (F) Wole Soyinka, *Myth, Literature and the African World* (NF)

Year	Events	Literary works
1977	South Africa: Steve Biko dies in police custody India: Janata Party elected; Congress Party defeated for first time since independence Pakistan: Bhutto ousted in military coup led by General Zia-ul-Haq; Zia pledges to establish Islamic social order Djibouti gains independence	Bessie Head (South Africa / Botswana), *The Collector of Treasures* (F) Elias Khoury (Lebanon), *Little Mountain* (F) Clarice Lispector (Brazil), *The Hour of the Star* (F) Ngugi wa Thiong'o (Kenya), *Petals of Blood* (F) Sergio Ramirez (Nicaragua), *To Bury Our Fathers* (F) Manuel Rui (Angola), *Yes, Comrade!* (F) Edwin Thumboo (Singapore), *Gods Can Die* (P) Samir Amin, *Imperialism and Unequal Development* (NF)
1978	Vietnamese forces invade Cambodia in attempt to oust Pol Pot's Khmer Rouge regime; regime is toppled (1979), but guerrilla activity continues until 1989; National Salvation Front under leadership of Heng Samrin installed in Phnom Penh Iran: mass demonstrations against Shah; imposition of martial law Afghanistan: Soviet-backed military coup Egypt/Israel: Camp David accords; Israel agrees to withdraw from Sinai; "self-rule" pledged for Palestinians in occupied territories	Dambudzo Marechera (Zimbabwe), *The House of Hunger* (F) O. V. Vijayan (India), *Short Stories* Edward W. Said, *Orientalism* (KT)
1979	Soviet invasion of Afghanistan Pakistan: Bhutto hanged on orders from Zia-ul-Haq; Islamic Law introduced War between China and Vietnam: heavy casualties on Chinese side force withdrawal Nicaragua: popular uprising overthrows Somoza dictatorship, brings Sandinista National Liberation Front (FSLN) to power; Washington immediately moves to destabilize the Sandinista regime; 30,000 will be killed in ensuing violence	Mariama Bâ (Senegal), *So Long a Letter* (F) Buchi Emecheta (Nigeria), *The Joys of Motherhood* (F) Nuruddin Farah (Somalia), *Sweet and Sour Milk* (F) Nadine Gordimer (South Africa), *Burger's Daughter* (F) Roy Heath (Guyana), *The Armstrong Trilogy* (−1981) (F)

(cont.)

Date	Political/historical events	Literary and other writings
	Iran: Revolution; the Shah flees to US; Ayatollah Khomeini returns to country and assumes power; American Embassy occupied and personnel taken hostage; eventually released (1981) St. Lucia, St. Vincent gain independence Uganda: Idi Amin toppled with assistance of troops from Tanzania Grenada: New Jewel Movement comes to power under Maurice Bishop	Earl Lovelace (Trinidad), *The Dragon Can't Dance* (F) Lu Wenfu (China), *The Gourmet* (F) Pak Mogwol (South Korea), *Unordered* (P) Pramoedya Ananta Toer (Indonesia), *Buru Quartet* (–1988) (F)
1980	Zimbabwe gains independence; Robert Mugabe elected to power India: Congress Party under Indira Gandhi returns to power El Salvador: Archbishop Oscar Romero assassinated by rightist paramilitaries at San Salvador Cathedral Antigua, Barbuda gain independence Outbreak of Iran–Iraq war (–1988) Peru: demise of military rule; election of right-wing civilian government	Yu Luojin (China), *A Chinese Winter's Tale* (A) J. M. Coetzee (South Africa), *Waiting for the Barbarians* (F) Anita Desai (India), *Clear Light of Day* (F) Pepetela (Angola), *Mayombe* (F) Ricardo Piglia (Argentina), *Artificial Respiration* (F) Salman Rushdie (India), *Midnight's Children* (F) Osvaldo Soriano (Argentina), *A Funny Dirty Little War* (F) Michael Thelwell (Jamaica), *The Harder They Come* (F) Albert Wendt (Samoa), *Leaves of the Banyan Tree* (F)
1981	Belize gains independence Iran: 149 "leftist militants" executed by Khomeini regime Egypt: President Sadat assassinated by soldiers	Ariel Dorfman (Chile), *Widows* (F) Mongane Wally Serote (South Africa), *To Every Birth Its Blood* (F) Aminata Sow Fall (Senegal), *The Beggars' Strike* (F) Malek Alloula, *The Colonial Harem* (NF)

1982

Falklands/Malvinas war between UK and Argentina; loss of the war weakens hold of military regime in Argentina

Lebanon: Israeli invasion; Israeli commander Ariel Sharon facilitates Lebanese Christian militia's massacre of Palestinian refugees in camps of Sabra and Shatila

Nicaragua: counter-revolutionary attack on Sandanista forces, armed and sponsored by US; war continues until 1990, when Sandinista government is defeated in election by coalition supported by US

Guatemala: military regimes of Rios Montt (–1983) and Humberto Mejía (1983–85); brutal pogroms unleashed against leftists, activists, Indian communities; over 100,000 murdered

Mexico: moratorium on loan repayment sparks international debt crisis

Benedict Anderson, *Imagined Communities: Reflections on the Origins and Spread of Nationalism* (KT)

Edouard Glissant, *Caribbean Discourse* (KT)

Gabriel García Márquez wins Nobel Prize for Literature

Inaugural issue of the series *Subaltern Studies*, edited by Ranajit Guha

Isabel Allende (Chile), *The House of the Spirits* (F)

Reinaldo Arenas (Cuba), *Farewell to the Sea* (F)

Edward Kamau Brathwaite (Barbados), *The Arrivants* (P)

Lloyd Fernando (Malaysia), *Scorpion Orchid* (F)

1983

Philippines: assassination of opposition leader, Benigno Aquino, as he returns to country to fight election against Marcos

Sri Lanka: communalist violence against Tamils; armed resistance and ruthlessness of LTTE ("Tamil Tigers") escalates in response

Grenada: following murder of Prime Minister Maurice Bishop, US forces intervene to topple New Jewel Movement

Argentina: Raúl Alfonsín's election brings to an end 8 years of military dictatorship, during which at least 30,000 were killed

Jamaica Kincaid (Antigua), *Annie John* (F)

Njabulo Ndebele (South Africa), *Fools and Other Stories*

Grace Nichols (Guyana), *i is a long-memoried woman* (P)

Sony Labou Tansi (Zaire), *The Antipeople* (F)

Luisa Valenzuela (Argentina), *The Lizard's Tail* (F)

Nirmal Verma (India), *The Crows of Deliverance* (F)

Johannes Fabian, *Time and the Other* (NF)

Abdelkebir Khatibi, *Magbreb pluriel* (NF)

Date	Political/historical events	Literary and other writings
1984	India: pitched battle between Indian army and Akali Dal extremists in Golden Temple, Amritsar; Indira Gandhi assassinated in October, in retaliation; riots against Sikh community, especially in New Delhi Brunei gains independence Uruguay: massive protests and general strike topple military dictatorship after 11 years Ethiopia: devastating famine kills 500,000	Rigoberta Menchú (Guatemala), *I, Rigoberta Menchú: An Indian Woman in Guatemala* (A) Bai Xian Yong (Taiwan), *Vile Spawn* (F) Miguel Bonasso (Argentina), *Memory of Death* (F) Maryse Condé (Guadeloupe), *Segu* (F) Abdelrahman Munif (Saudi Arabia), *City of Salt* (F) Cristina Peri Rossi (Uruguay), *The Ship of Fools* (F) Edward Kamau Brathwaite, *History of the Voice* (NF)
1985	Brazil: return to civilian government after 20 years of military dictatorship Peru: Alan García, social democratic candidate, voted into power; proves unable to combat runaway inflation and rising insurrection of Sendero Luminoso guerrillas; voted out of office in 1990	Pipit Rochijat Kartawidjaja (Indonesia), "Am I PKI or Non-PKI?" (NF) Tahar Ben Jelloun (Morocco), *The Sand Child* (F) Assia Djebar (Algeria), *Fantasia, An Algerian Cavalcade* (F) Gabriel García Márquez (Colombia), *Love in the Time of Cholera* (F) Nayantara Sahgal (India), *Rich Like Us* (F) Ken Saro-Wiwa (Nigeria), *Sozaboy* (F)
1986	Philippines: "People Power Revolution" topples Marcos dictatorship Haiti: dictatorship of Jean-Claude Duvalier overthrown	Wole Soyinka wins Nobel Prize for Literature Nuruddin Farah (Somalia), *Maps* (F) Sahar Khalifeh (Palestine), *Memoirs of an Unrealistic Woman* (F) Waleed Khazindar (Palestine), *Present Verbs* (P) Hanif Kureishi (UK), *My Beautiful Laundrette* (F) Alvaro Mutis (Colombia), *The Snow of the Admiral* (F)

Year	Events	Cultural developments
1987	Fiji: right-wing coup; new leader, Colonel Sitiveni Rabuka, proposes racialist new constitution Burkino Faso: President Thomas Sankara assassinated in counter-revolutionary military coup Israel: insurrection (*intifada*) breaks out as Palestinians protest continuing Israeli oppression (–1990); several hundred killed South Korea: massive popular protests, strikes, calling for democratization, social and economic security	Caryl Phillips (St. Kitts), *A State of Independence* (F) Anton Shammas (Israel), *Arabesques* (F) Linda Ty-Casper (Philippines), *Wings of Stone* (F) Derek Walcott (St. Lucia), *Collected Poems* Wang Anyi (China), *Love in a Small Town* (F) Partha Chatterjee, *Nationalist Thought and the Colonial World: A Derivative Discourse* (KT) Peter Hulme, *Colonial Encounters: Europe and the Native Caribbean 1492–1797* (KT) Ngugi wa Thiong'o, *Decolonising the Mind: The Politics of Language in African Literature* (KT) Fredric Jameson, "Third-World Literature in the Era of Multinational Capitalism" (KT) Agha Shahid Ali (India), *The Half-Inch Himalayas* (P) Jesús Díaz (Cuba), *The Initials of the Land* (F) Daniel Maximin (Guadeloupe), *Soufrières* (F) Horacio Vázquez Rial (Argentina), *Triste's History* (F) Shrikant Verma (India), *Magadh* (P) Benita Parry, "Problems in Current Theories of Colonial Discourse" (KT)
1988	Pakistan: Benazir Bhutto, daughter of Zulfikar Ali Bhutto, elected Prime Minister as country again returns to civilian rule Brazil: labor and human rights activist, Chico Mendes, murdered at instigation of big landowners Burundi: inter-communal violence kills thousands Afghanistan: uncompromising resistance from guerrillas forces withdrawal of Soviet troops; civil war ensues as rival factions bid for power	Naguib Mahfouz wins Nobel Prize for Literature Upamanyu Chatterjee (India), *English, August* (F) Amit Chaudhuri (India), *Afternoon Raag* (F) Michelle Cliff (Jamaica/US), *No Telephone to Heaven* (F) J. M. Coetzee (South Africa), *Foe* (F) Tsitsi Dangarembga (Zimbabwe), *Nervous Conditions* (F)

(cont.)

Date	Political/historical events	Literary and other writings
	Chile: Chilean electorate repudiates Pinochet dictatorship in plebiscite; votes against his plan to extend rule for a further 8 years	Amitav Ghosh (India), *The Shadow Lines* (F) Duong Thu Huong (Vietnam), *Paradise of the Blind* (F) Chenjerai Hove (Zimbabwe), *Bones* (F) Tomás Eloy Martínez (Argentina), *The Perón Novel* (F) Ninotchka Rosca (Philippines), *State of War* (F) Salman Rushdie (India), *The Satanic Verses* (F) Bapsi Sidhwa (Pakistan), *Cracking India* (F) Héctor Tizon (Argentina), *The Man Who Came to a Village* (F) Chandra Talpade Mohanty, "Under Western Eyes: Feminist Scholarship and Colonial Discourses" (KT) V. Y. Mudimbe, *The Invention of Africa: Gnosis, Philosophy, and the Order of Knowledge* (KT) Gayatri Chakravorty Spivak, "Can the Subaltern Speak?" (KT)
1989	Fall of Berlin Wall; collapse of Soviet Union and communist states of Eastern Europe US invasion and occupation of Panama; deposition of their erstwhile ally, President Noriega China: military crackdown on student demonstrators at Tiananmen Square; thousands of intellectuals and activists arrested in aftermath	Ayatollah Khomeini issues *fatwa* on Salman Rushdie, citing the alleged blasphemy of *The Satanic Verses* Nissim Ezekiel (India), *Collected Poems* Kazuo Ishiguro (UK), *The Remains of the Day* (F) Ngugi wa Thiong'o (Kenya), *Matigari* (F) M. K. Vassanji (Kenya/Canada), *The Gunny Sack* (F) Yun Heung-gil (South Korea), *The House of Twilight* (F) Bill Ashcroft, Gareth Griffiths, and Helen Tiffin, *The Empire Writes Back: Theory and Practice in Post-Colonial Literatures* (KT) Jean Bernabé, Patrick Chamoiseau, and Raphaël Confiant, *In Praise of Creoleness* (KT)

1990	South Africa: release of Nelson Mandela after 28 years in prison Namibia gains independence India: president's rule declared in Jammu and Kashmir; repeated confrontations between Indian security forces and armed militants; thousands are killed (~present day) Haiti: Jean Bertrand Aristide overthrown in bloody coup Burma: National League for Democracy wins electoral victory; military annuls election, arrests Aung San Suu Kyi	Octavio Paz wins Nobel Prize for Literature Bei Dao (China), *The August Sleepwalker* (P) Mia Couto (Mozambique), *Every Man is a Race* (F) Jessica Hagedorn (Philippines), *Dogeaters* (F) Abd al-Wahhab Bayati (Iraq), *Love, Death and Exile* (P) Terry Eagleton, Fredric Jameson, Edward W. Said, *Nationalism, Colonialism, and Literature* (KT)
1991	First Gulf War, US-led coalition forces bomb Iraq following invasion of Kuwait (1990) India: Rajiv Gandhi assassinated by Tamil Tiger militants from Sri Lanka East Timor: massacre of unarmed Timorese by Indonesian military in Santa Cruz church; 250 killed Somalia: President Siad Barre overthrown; but country collapses into civil war	Nadine Gordimer wins Nobel Prize for Literature Bao Ninh (Vietnam), *The Sorrow of War* (F) Khalil Hawi (Lebanon), *From the Vineyards of Lebanon* (P) Timothy Mo (UK), *The Redundancy of Courage* (F) Ben Okri (Nigeria), *The Famished Road* (F) Derek Walcott (St. Lucia), *Omeros* (P) Salman Rushdie, *Imaginary Homelands: Essays and Criticism 1981–1991* (KT)
1992	India: destruction of Babri Mosque in Ayodhya by Hindutva militants from Bharatiya Janata Party (BJP) Algeria: with Islamic party (FIS) poised to win national elections, huge anti-Islamic demonstrations; election cancelled; State of Emergency declared when President Boudiaf assassinated; FIS dissolved; the years following (to present) plagued by widespread violence and terrorism attributed to Islamist groups El Salvador: peace accord between government and FMLN guerrillas brings an end to 12 years of fighting in which 75,000 have died Somalia: UN-sanctioned intervention, to restore order and save victims of famine; 40,000-strong force, 30,000 of them from US	Derek Walcott wins Nobel Prize for Literature Ambai (C. S. Lakshmi) (India), *The Purple Sea* (F) Patrick Chamoiseau (Martinique), *Texaco* (F) Cheng Naishan (China), *The Banker* (F) Michael Ondaatje (Sri Lanka / Canada), *The English Patient* (F) Aijaz Ahmad, *In Theory: Classes, Nations, Literatures* (KT) Mary Louise Pratt, *Imperial Eyes: Travel Writing and Transculturation* (KT)

(cont.)

Date	Political/historical events	Literary and other writings
	Peru: President Fujimoro suspends constitution; capture of Abimael Guzman, leader of Sendero Luminoso guerrillas Mozambique: peace treaty signed between President Chissano and South African-backed Renamo forces; casualties in war exceed 1 million	Arturo Uslar Pietri, *The Creation of the New World* (NF) Roberto Schwarz, *Misplaced Ideas: Essays on Brazilian Culture* (NF)
1993	India: communalist violence; many Muslims killed in Bombay and Gujarat Eritrea gains independence, after long armed struggle against Ethiopia	Toni Morrison wins Nobel Prize for Literature Amin Maalouf (Lebanon), *The Rock of Tanios* (F) Vikram Seth (India), *A Suitable Boy* (F) Ivan Vladislavic (South Africa), *The Folly* (F) Edward W. Said, *Culture and Imperialism* (KT)
1994	South Africa: non-racial, democratic elections; Nelson Mandela elected president Mexico: uprising in Chiapas state, led by Zapatista Army of National Liberation Haiti: US pressurizes military to allow President Aristide to return	Muhammad al-Maghut (Syria), *Joy Is Not My Profession* (P) Shyam Selvadurai (Sri Lanka / Canada), *Funny Boy* (F) Shu Ting (China), *Selected Poems* Homi K. Bhabha, *The Location of Culture* (KT)
1995	Rwanda: long-simmering civil war degenerates into vast inter-ethnic massacres; death-toll reaches 1 million Nigeria: military regime executes Ogoni leader and writer Ken Saro-Wiwa	Subcommandante Marcos (Mexico), *Shadows of Tender Fury* (NF) Keki Daruwalla (India), *A Summer of Tigers* (P) A. K. Ramanujan (India), *Collected Poems* Declan Kiberd, *Inventing Ireland: The Literature of the Modern Nation* (KT)
1996	Afghanistan: extreme Islamist faction, the Taliban, take power Guatemala: peace pact signed	Rohinton Mistry (India/Canada), *A Fine Balance* (F) Nizar Qabbani (Syria), *On Entering the Sea* (P)

1997	Hong Kong returned by Britain to China Zaire: Moburu's dictatorship ousted in coup; but civil war ensues Brazil: massive mobilization of landless people demanding reform	Vikram Chandra (India), *Love and Longing in Bombay* (F) Arundhati Roy (India), *The God of Small Things* (F) A. Sivanandan (Sri Lanka), *When Memory Dies* (F)
1998	General Pinochet, former Chilean dictator, arrested in London on human rights charges filed in Spain; British government intervenes to transfer Pinochet back to Chile; precedent is set for indicting those charged with human rights crimes Indonesia: Suharto dictatorship overturned after 32 years	Yvonne Vera (Zimbabwe), *Butterfly Burning* (F)
1999	East Timor: Indonesia withdraws its troops	Gao Xingjian (China), *One Man's Bible* (F)
2000	Israel: second *intifada* breaks out	Gao Xingjian wins Nobel Prize for Literature Naiyer Masud (India), *Essence of Camphor* (F) Zadie Smith (UK), *White Teeth* (F)
2001	Islamist suicide bombers hijack planes, fly them into World Trade Center towers and Pentagon building in US; casualties exceed 3,000; in response, US declares "War on Terrorism," invades Afghanistan in pursuit of Osama Bin Laden, alleged mastermind of hijackings, and overthrows ruling Taliban	V. S. Naipaul wins Nobel Prize for Literature
2002	Brazil: Luiz Inácio Lula de Silva ("Lula") elected to presidency as Workers' Party (PT) wins general election	
2003	Invasion and occupation of Iraq by coalition dominated by US forces	J. M. Coetzee wins Nobel Prize for Literature

I

NEIL LAZARUS

Introducing postcolonial studies

I

Before the late 1970s, there was no field of academic specialization that
went by the name of "postcolonial studies." Today, by contrast, postcolonial studies occupies a position of legitimacy and even relative prestige, not
only within the Euro-American academy but also in universities in many
countries of the formerly colonized world. Postcolonial studies centers have
been set up in many institutions – mostly linked to departments of literature
but inviting significant input also from scholars based in cultural studies, history, anthropology, art, and other disciplines – and innumerable conferences
and colloquia have been convened. Advertisements for academic positions in
postcolonial studies have become fairly routine. Several dedicated academic
journals have begun publication, and any number of other journals have
devoted special issues to "postcolonial literature," "postcolonial theory," or
"the postcolonial condition." Literary anthologies and critical readers, as
well as compilations of essays in the field, have been published, and many
of these have sold very well.[1] And in addition to the hundreds of scholarly
books and thousands of critical articles that might be said to be *in* the field or
indeed to make it up – from the works of Edward W. Said, Homi K. Bhabha,
Benedict Anderson, V. Y. Mudimbe, Peter Hulme, and Gayatri Chakravorty
Spivak to the mass of less influential work on particular authors, periods,
situations, events, and concepts – there has recently emerged a burgeoning production of scholarly texts that take the *critical field itself* as their
object.[2]

To say that postcolonial studies as an institutionalized field of academic
specialization did not exist before the late 1970s is not to say that there was
no work being done then on issues relating to postcolonial cultures and societies. On the contrary, there was a large amount of such work, much of it
deeply consequential and of abiding significance. There were political studies
of state-formation in the newly decolonized countries of Africa, Asia, and

the Caribbean; economic and sociological studies of development and under-development (typically centered on Latin America); historical accounts of anticolonial nationalism and of the various and diverse nationalist leader-ships which had fought or campaigned against colonial rule in territory after territory – Jamaica, Ghana, Algeria, India, Indonesia – and which had then themselves come to power when independence had finally been won; literary studies of the new writing that was being produced by writers from these territories; and so on. In every discipline, there were presses specializing in the publication of academic material relating to postcolonial issues. More-over, in most disciplines, dedicated journals had latterly come into existence to carry the emerging debates and to sponsor wider scholarship. (In the context of African literature, to give just one example, the first issue of the influential periodical, *African Literature Today*, was published in 1968, and the first issue of what is still the field's flagship journal, *Research in African Literatures*, appeared in 1970.)

The word "postcolonial" occasionally appeared in this scholarship, but it did not mean then what it has come to mean in "postcolonial studies." Thus when Hamza Alavi and John S. Saul wrote about the state in "post-colonial" societies in 1972 and 1974, respectively, they were using the term in a strict historically and politically delimited sense, to identify the period immedi-ately following decolonization, when the various leaderships, parties, and governments which had gained access to the colonial state apparatuses at independence undertook to transform these apparatuses, to make them over so that instead of serving as instruments of colonial dictatorship they would serve these new leaders' own social and political interests, whether social-ist or bourgeois, progressive or reactionary, popular or authoritarian (Alavi 1972; Saul 1974). "Post-colonial" (or "postcolonial" – the American vari-ant), in these usages from the early 1970s, was a periodizing term, a historical and not an ideological concept. It bespoke no political desire or aspiration, looked forward to no particular social or political order. Erstwhile colonial territories that had been decolonized were "postcolonial" states. It was as simple as that. Politically charged and ideologically fraught terms were all around, and were fiercely contested – capitalism and socialism; imperialism and anti-imperialism; first-world and third-world; self-determination and neo-colonialism; center and periphery; modernization, development, depen-dency, under-development, mal-development, "dependent development" – but the notion of "postcoloniality" did not participate, on any side, in these debates. To describe a literary work or a writer as "postcolonial" was to name a period, a discrete historical moment, not a project or a politics.[3] It was far more usual to see writers and works characterized in terms of their communities of origin, identity, or identification. Thus Chinua Achebe was described variously as an Igbo writer, a Nigerian writer, an African writer, a Commonwealth writer, a third-world writer, but seldom if ever as a "postcolonial" one. To have called Achebe a "postcolonial" writer would have been, in a sense, merely to set the scene, historically speaking, for the analysis to come.

To begin to appreciate how much things have changed in this respect, consider the following passage from Homi K. Bhabha's essay, "The Postcolonial and the Postmodern: The Question of Agency," in *The Location of Culture*. I quote from Bhabha's essay at length, both because of its relevance to my commentary and because Bhabha's work has been so influential in framing the parameters of postcolonial studies:

> Postcolonial criticism bears witness to the unequal and uneven forces of cultural representation involved in the contest for political and social authority within the modern world order. Postcolonial perspectives emerge from the colonial testimony of Third World countries and the discourses of "minorities" within the geopolitical divisions of East and West, North and South. They intervene in those ideological discourses of modernity that attempt to give a hegemonic "normality" to the uneven development and the differential, often disadvantaged, histories of nations, races, communities, peoples. They formulate their critical revisions around issues of cultural difference, social authority, and political discrimination in order to reveal the antagonistic and ambivalent moments within the "rationalizations" of modernity. To bend Jürgen Habermas to our purposes, we could also argue that the postcolonial project, at the most general theoretical level, seeks to explore those social pathologies – "loss of meaning, conditions of anomie" – that no longer simply "cluster around class antagonism, [but] break up into widely scattered historical contingencies" . . . The postcolonial perspective . . . departs from the traditions of the sociology of underdevelopment or "dependency" theory. As a mode of analysis, it attempts to revise those nationalist or "nativist" pedagogies that set up the relation of Third World and First World in a binary structure of opposition. The postcolonial perspective resists the attempt at holistic forms of social explanation. It forces a recognition of the more complex cultural and political boundaries that exist on the cusp of these often opposed political spheres.
>
> (1994: 171, 173)

We can see straight away that in Bhabha's thinking, "postcolonial" has ceased to be a historical category. The term does not designate what it sounds like it designates, that is, the moment, or more generally the time, *after* colonialism. There *are* temporal words and phrases in Bhabha's formulation – "no longer," for instance – but these do not appear to relate in any discernible way to *decolonization* as a historical event, that is to decolonization as a "cut" or break in time, such that one could speak of a colonial "before" and a postcolonial "after." Bhabha writes that "postcolonial criticism" concerns itself with "social pathologies" that can "no longer" be referred to the explanatory factor of class division: "postcolonial criticism" is thus opposed to (and for Bhabha evidently comes after or supersedes) class analysis. No explanation is given, however, as to why the term "colonial" is felt to be implicated in the putative obsolescence of class analysis. Indeed, on the basis of what Bhabha says, "postcolonial criticism" could as easily be called "post-Marxist criticism."

Or even "post-modern criticism," since Bhabha is at pains to emphasize that the "post-" in "postcolonial criticism" is directed against the assumptions of the "ideological discourses of modernity," which are said to flatten out complexity, to simplify the sheer heterogeneity and unevenness of real conditions, to reduce these to "a binary structure of opposition."[4] For Bhabha, "postcolonial" is a fighting term, a theoretical weapon, which "intervene[s]" in existing debates and "resists" certain political and philosophical constructions. "Postcolonial criticism," as he understands and champions it, is constitutively anti-Marxist – departing not only from more orthodox Marxist scholarship but even from "the traditions of the sociology of underdevelopment or 'dependency' theory"; it evinces an undifferentiating disavowal of all forms of nationalism and a corresponding exaltation of migrancy, liminality, hybridity, and multiculturality (see Smith, in this volume); it is hostile towards "holistic forms of social explanation" (towards totality and systematic analysis) and demonstrates an aversion to dialectics (see Ganguly, in this volume); and it refuses an antagonistic or struggle-based model of politics in favor of one that emphasises "cultural difference," "ambivalen[ce]" and "the more complex cultural and political boundaries that exist on the cusp" of what "modern" philosophy had imagined as the determinate categories of social reality.

Between Alavi's and Saul's "post-colonialism" and Bhabha's, a sea-change has occurred. It is within the context of this sea change that postcolonial studies has emerged to prominence as a field of academic specialization. The task then becomes to account for this sea-change, to explore its causes and consequences. This is by no means an easy task, because it requires us to operate on many levels simultaneously. At the level of political economy, thus, we can speak (and indeed must, since it is an important part of the whole story) of the reassertion of imperial dominance beginning in the 1970s, that is, of the global re-imposition and re-consolidation both – economically – of what Samir Amin has called "the logic of unilateral capital" (1997: 95) and – politically – of an actively interventionist "New World Order," headquartered in Washington, DC. One of the fundamental preconditions of this re-imposition and re-consolidation (Walden Bello [1999] calls it "rollback") was the containment and recuperation of the historic challenge from the third world that had been expressed in the struggle for decolonization in the post-1945 period. (Chapter 2 in this volume, by Lazarus, deals centrally with this issue, which is also taken up, to some degree, in the chapters by Sivanandan, Parry, Brennan, and Chrisman.) Postcolonial studies not only emerged in close chronological proximity to the end of the era of decolonization.[5] It also has characteristically offered something approximating a monumentalization of this moment – a rationalization of and pragmatic adjustment to, if not quite a celebration of, the downturn in the fortunes and influence of insurgent national liberation movements and revolutionary socialist ideologies in the early 1970s. In this context it is also necessary to mention the collapse of historical communism in 1989. For "[t]he fall of the Berlin Wall and the crisis of the Soviet world," as Robert Gwynne and Cristóbal Kay have written, served to "reassert . . . the dominance of the world capitalist system . . . The demise of the bipolar world, which had been based around Cold War political ideologies, shifted the emphasis to the variations of political economy within the world system" (1999: 9). After 1975, as many commentators have observed, political sentiment in the West tended to turn against nationalist insurgency and revolutionary anti-capitalism; after 1989, socialism itself was pronounced dead and buried (see Parry, in this volume).

This goes quite a long way towards explaining the strong anti-nationalist and anti-Marxist dispositions of most of the scholars working within postcolonial studies – an academic field that has scarcely been immune to the *Zeitgeist* or spirit of the age. Yet too much of the commentary on postcolonial studies (including the critical or dissenting scholarship) has been reductive. There has been a tendency to read postcolonial studies as *mere* ideology, as though in fact the class position of its leading practitioners relative to the class position of most members of postcolonial societies were in itself a mark, or brand, of inauthenticity. Kwame Anthony Appiah's fiercely oppositional definition has been much admired, for instance – "Postcoloniality is the condition of what we might ungenerously call a comprador intelligentsia: of a relatively small, Western-style, Western-trained, group of writers and thinkers who mediate the trade in cultural commodities of world capitalism at the periphery" (1992: 149) – as has Arif Dirlik's reformulation of it – "I think [Appiah] . . . is missing the point because the world situation that justified the term comprador no longer exists. I would suggest instead that postcoloniality is the condition of the intelligentsia of global capitalism" (1994: 356). However, both of these definitions are guilty of a certain unwarranted determinism, as they move surreptitiously and in the absence of any analysis from one kind of "standpoint" to another, from an identification of the social location of the postcolonialist to an identification of the political and philosophical position that the postcolonialist will (necessarily? probably?) assume or take up.

It is not, of course, that the class position of the postcolonial theorist relative to that of the people whom he or she is theorizing ought not to be a matter of concern. Of course it should: and in fact, precisely this "gap" *has* been a major matter of concern in the scholarly literature. Yet what really needs to be addressed in this respect – and it has to be said that it has not thus far been addressed with the requisite degree of subtlety and precision in the scholarly literature – is how postcolonial studies, as a particular field of academic specialization, has been shaped by this gap, or how scholars, using the particular resources generated by their work in the field of postcolonial studies, have sought to bridge or shrink or destroy this gap. Dirlik comes close to identifying this theoretical task when he states that "[t]he question . . . is not whether this global intelligentsia can (or should) return to national loyalties but whether, in recognition of its own class-position in global capitalism, it can generate a thoroughgoing criticism of its own ideology and formulate practices of resistance against the system of which it is a product" (1994: 356). It is clear, however, that for Dirlik himself, this is a rhetorical question. As he has defined it, "this global intelligentsia" – the community of postcolonial scholars – cannot be imagined formulating "a thoroughgoing criticism of its own ideology."

Consider in this context the following formulation by Anthony D. King, intended to give a sense of what postcolonial studies is about, a sense of what it does and why, and of what theoretical and methodological investments govern its practice:

> What might be called the modern history of postcolonial (literary) criticism, informed by poststructuralism, began seriously in the early 1980s. Its early exponents (Homi Bhabha, Edward Said, Gayatri Spivak) focused on a critique of literary and historical writing and . . . were located in the humanities of the western academy. The critique was directed especially at Eurocentricism and the cultural racism of the West. Subsequently, the objects of the deconstructive postcolonial critique expanded to include film, video, television, photography, all examples of cultural praxis that are mobile, portable, and circulating in the West. Yet given that such literature, photography, or museum displays have existed for decades, why did this postcolonial critique only get established in the 1980s? . . . The answer is apparently simple. Postcolonial criticism in the West had to wait until a sufficient number of postcolonial intellectuals, an audience for them, was established in the Western academy.

(1995: 543–44)

Large sections of this passage are unexceptionable, indeed, admirably clear. King identifies (without specifying) the close connection between poststructuralism and postcolonial criticism (see Gikandi, in this volume); he identifies the critique of Eurocentrism as a foundational aspiration within postcolonial studies, and the fact that the field emerged initially in departments of literature and then, having achieved critical mass there, was taken up in culture studies generally, and in anthropology and history (see Parry, Marx, in this volume). Still, King's final sentence is deeply problematical, for two reasons. First, it makes the strange suggestion that the emergence of "postcolonial studies" was merely a matter of the demographic density of "postcolonial intellectuals" in "the Western academy" – a suggestion that crudely quantifies and renders one-dimensional a phenomenon that was clearly qualitative and multi-dimensional. The result is to strip postcolonial studies of any particular *content*. Second, it seems to suppose that "postcolonial studies" was, as it were, *there* in the Western academy all along, merely waiting for its audience of "postcolonial intellectuals" – a supposition that neutralizes the particular *history* (global and political-economic as well as more concretely institutional and academic-theoretical) of the field. In opposition to King, we could argue that "postcolonial criticism" could not possibly have existed before the 1980s, not because it would have lacked an adequate audience then, but because it would have made no sense at all in the historico-ideological context of the 1970s.

2

Colonial rule, as V. Y. Mudimbe notes in *The Invention of Africa*, was established and consolidated on the basis of "the domination of physical space, the reformation of *natives'* minds, and the integration of local economic histories into the Western perspective. These complementary projects constitute what might be called the colonizing structure, which completely embraces the physical, human, and spiritual aspects of the colonizing experience" (1988: 2). To the extent that the ideological legitimation of colonialism took the forms of a denigration of "native" cultures and a silencing of "native" voices, the responses of the colonized to colonialism included, centrally, an ideological dimension, in which colonial representations were contested and the validity and integrity of "native" cultures reclaimed (Said 1993: 191–281). Among the best-known instances of such resistance are those offered by Chinua Achebe in his "auto-ethnographic" novel, *Things Fall Apart* (1976 [1958]) and by Aimé Césaire, in his searing *Discourse on Colonialism*. In a key passage in *Discourse*, Césaire self-consciously assumes the agency and sovereignty of the speaking subject in order to throw the various apologies for colonialism back in the faces of the colonizers. "They talk to me about progress, about 'achievements,' diseases cured, improved standards of living," he says. But

> I am talking about societies drained of their essence, cultures trampled under-foot, institutions undermined, lands confiscated, religions smashed, magnifi-cent artistic creations destroyed, extraordinary *possibilities* wiped out.
>
> They throw facts at my head, statistics, mileages of roads, canals, and rail-road tracks.
>
> I am talking about thousands of men sacrificed to the Congo-Océan. I am talking about those who, as I write this, are digging the harbor of Abidjan by hand. I am talking about millions of men torn from their gods, their land, their habits, their life – from life, from the dance, from wisdom.   (1972: 21–22)

This kind of rhetorical–political gesture has come to be known, in the scholarly literature, under the playful rubric of "the empire writing [or striking] back" (Ashcroft, Griffiths, and Tiffin 1989). Nevertheless, what marks a specifically *post*-colonial inflection of it is the awareness that the subalternizing and silencing propensities of the colonialist representations are often – and symptomatically – evident, too, in *élite* representations issu-ing from within the colonized – and then, after decolonisation, the post-colonized (nominally independent) – society: in the language and thought of members of the political classes, national and local leaders and spokes-people, men and women of substance, the rich, the landed, the propertied, the educated. Confronted with this relatively late-breaking awareness, the progressive intellectual response, since the 1980s, has been to raise again the question of "the people," to re-direct attention to the disenfranchised sectors of the society – actually a majority and typically an *overwhelming* majority of the population – to insist that both the reclamation of tradition and the (re-)construction of national culture *after* colonialism require a recovery of popular consciousness across the full range of its social articulations. In the domain of scholarship, this new – or perhaps renewed – emphasis has seen the rise of a veritable battery of projects – in Europe and North America as well as in the "Third World" – aimed at the recovery and adequate theoriza-tion of popular consciousness and popular practice: a variety of "histories from below," insurgent sociologies, new approaches in political economy, mould-breaking developments in anthropology, feminist and environmen-talist work in all sectors of the social sciences, and so on.

In *The Invention of Africa*, Mudimbe follows Jean Copans in propos-ing that this "intellectual evolution" was powered in the early 1960s by "the advent of sociology and Marxism as major events" (1988: 176).

"Sociology," Copans had written in 1976, with particular reference to the African context

> was not just a new specialization, it constituted a complete break on several counts; empirically, as it was taking into consideration the real history of African peoples; in scale, as it moved on from the village to national social group (from "mini" to "maxi"); theoretically, as a materialistic and historical explanation took the place of Griaulian idealism which ignored the realities of colonialism. (qtd. Mudimbe 1988: 176)

Such is the *culturalist* emphasis in postcolonial studies, however, that little of this pioneering work in sociology or political economy or development studies is known; and even less is it taken on board (see Brennan, in this volume). From the standpoint of postcolonial studies, the turn from élite (understood as axiomatically élitist) forms of representation to popular ones seems to have derived not from sociology or political economy but from the more culturally inflected disciplines of history and anthropology: the work of James Clifford and Néstor García Canclini, Arjun Appadurai and Partha Chatterjee, Jean and John Comaroff is routinely cited, not that of, for example, Peter Gutkind, Walter Rodney, John Saul, Catherine Coquery-Vidrovitch, or Anouar Abdel-Malek.

It is, indeed, Subaltern Studies that has come to provide the methodological template for the approach to the question of popular consciousness in postcolonial studies (see Gopal, Coronil, in this volume). Importantly, however, what is considered exemplary is not the work that initially appeared under that imprimatur in the early 1980s, and that was still committed to the enterprise of recovering or uncovering the contents and forms of consciousness of "the people," those spoken of and for in élite representations, but never afforded the public, sanctioned space to speak of and for themselves: "the wretched of the earth," in Fanon's famous formula (1968); the "people without history," in Eric Wolf's (1982). Instead, the version of subalternity that has proved most influential in postcolonial studies is that proposed by Gayatri Chakravorty Spivak.[6]

Spivak defines subalternity very strenuously in terms of a structured inarticulacy at the élite levels of state and civil society – such that to be positioned as subaltern in any discursive context is to be incapable of representing oneself within that context (see Bahri, in this volume). The subaltern is the object of discourse, never the subject. Subaltern practice, on Spivak's construction, cannot signify "as itself" across the divide that separates social élites from whose who are not élite. Within the élite spheres, "[t]he subaltern cannot speak" (1988b: 308); or, as Spivak puts it in a more recent essay, "[t]he gendered subaltern woman . . . can yield 'real' information as agent with the greatest difficulty, not the least because methods of describing her sympathetically are already in place. There is a gulf fixed between the anthropologist's object of investigation and the activist's interlocutor" (1994: 143). On Spivak's reading, the actual contents of the social practice of "the people" are always, indeed definitionally, unrepresentable, including by intellectuals. Whatever is read (that is, represented) as "subaltern" within élite discourse has for her always-already been made over, appropriated, translated, traduced. It is precisely the irreducible gap between popular practice and its (misrecognizing) construal in élite discourse that the term "subalternity" designates on her usage of it. This conceptualization seems to me to come close to fetishizing difference under the rubric of incommensurability. The central problem with Spivak's theorization of subalternity is that in its relentless and one-sided focus on the "gap" of representation, representation as political ventriloquization, it contrives to displace or endlessly defer other questions – among them an *epistemological* question, concerning not the conditions of possibility of representation, but its *adequacy*, and a *methodological* question, concerning the relation between theory and practice.[7]

3

I have already mentioned that contestation of colonialist representations of the colonial enterprise and of "native" cultures was from the outset central to the response of the colonized to colonial rule. Certainly since the publication of Edward Said's *Orientalism* in 1978 – and significantly prior to this date in such disciplinary fields as anthropology – the attempt to "unthink Eurocentrism" has been lodged as a foundational aspiration of most scholarship, including that deriving from the West, on the subject of colonial discourse.[8]

It is, however, worth drawing attention to two distinctive features of the critique of Eurocentrism in postcolonialist scholarship, both deriving – directly or indirectly, warrantedly or unwarrantedly – from Said's example in *Orientalism*. First, there is the emphasis placed upon the socially constitutive role of Orientalist (or Eurocentric) discourse: such discourse is said literally to have *produced* the fantasmatic worlds which it designates, such that they thereby cease to be fantasmatic and become real. "The Orient" emerges as an effect of Orientalist discourse: representation precedes and produces the reality which it can then claim merely to re-present, having obscured if not obliterated the earlier reality which, as a colonizing discourse, it had begun by misrepresenting. Hence Said's reference to "the enormously systematic discipline by which European culture was able to manage – and even produce – the Orient politically, sociologically, militarily, ideologically, scientifically, and imaginatively during the post-Enlightenment period" (1978: 3). Hence also the proliferation of scholarly monographs with titles like *Inventing India* (Crane 1992), *Imagining India* (Inden 1990), *Inventing Ireland* (Kiberd 1995), *Writing Ireland* (Cairns and Richards 1988), and Mudimbe's *The Invention of Africa* (1988), already mentioned. Such works take very seriously the idea that language (in the broad sense) is not only world-disclosing but also world-constituting. Beyond Said, they may be said to derive their framing assumptions from Michel Foucault, who had similarly insisted upon both the materiality and the social productivity of discourse.

The interpretation of Said's own epistemology has not been particularly well handled by postcolonial scholars, who have consistently misread him, assuming that his commitment to an anti-essentialist critical practice derives from a conventionalist epistemology. "[T]here seems to be, in [Said's] . . . concern with the material conditions of writing, a constant tendency to impute a real world behind the structures of signification that represent the world," Ashcroft and Ahluwalia write, in irritation, in their study of Said and his work (1999: 4); "Yet this is something Said continually denies. He says time and again that there is, for instance, no 'real' Orient, obscured by the misrepresentations of Orientalism." In fact, this is not at all what Said says. What he *actually* writes in *Orientalism* is more or less just the reverse: "In the first place, it would be wrong to conclude that the Orient was *essentially* an idea, or a creation with no corresponding reality . . . There were – and are – cultures and nations whose location is in the East, and their lives, histories, and customs have a brute reality obviously greater than anything that could be said about them in the West" (1978: 5). *Pace* Ashcroft and Ahluwalia and many other scholars in postcolonial studies, Said is in fact an epistemological *realist*. For him – as for such thinkers as Samir Amin, who writes in his book *Eurocentrism* that Orientalist discourse "merits reproach for the simple reason that it produced false judgements" (1989: 101) – it is quite obvious that there is an "East" and that it is systematically misrepresented in Orientalist discourse. However, what Said then goes on to say is that his book, *Orientalism*, will be concerned less with this question of misrepresentation – with "the correspondence between Orientalism and Orient" – than with "the internal consistency of Orientalism and its ideas about the Orient" (1978: 5).[9]

The second feature of the new scholarship consists in the fact that it has tended to situate Eurocentrism less as an *ideological formation* than as an *episteme*. The difference between these two modes of conceptualization has been usefully glossed by Mudimbe, with reference to anthropology – although his own estimate of their respective analytical powers as modes of conceptualization is the opposite of my own. Mudimbe distinguishes

> two kinds of "ethnocentrism": an epistemological filiation and an ideological connection. In fact they are often complementary and inseparable. The first is a link to an episteme, that is, an intellectual atmosphere which gives to anthropology its status as discourse, its significance as a discipline, and its credibility as a science in the field of human experience. The second is an intellectual and behavioral attitude which varies among individuals. Basically this attitude is both a consequence and an expression of a complex connection between the scholar's projection of consciousness, the scientific models of his time, and the cultural and social norms of his society.   (1988: 19)

If we understand Eurocentrism as an ideology (as I myself do), then it can become subject to critique. Our methodological assumption would be that it is always in principle (and indeed in practice) possible to stand outside any given problematic in order to subject its claims to scrutiny. This, of course, is the classical notion of critique as encountered in Immanuel Kant and exemplified most significantly for radical scholarship in Karl Marx's various critiques of bourgeois political economy, German idealist philosophy, anarchism, and so on. It is ideology critique on this model that had been activated in anticolonialist scholarship prior to the advent of postcolonial studies: in the many critiques of anthropology (usually by anthropologists themselves), for instance, or of modernization theory, or of development studies.

However, scholars in postcolonial studies have tended to address Eurocentrism along the first of the axes specified in the quotation above, that is, as an episteme or intellectual atmosphere. Said himself defined Orientalism as "the corporate institution for dealing with the Orient – dealing with it by making statements about it, authorizing views of it, describing it, by teaching it, settling it, ruling over it: in short, Orientalism as a Western style for dominating, restructuring, and having authority over the Orient"; and he added that

> so authoritative a position did Orientalism have that I believe no one writing, thinking, or acting on the Orient could do so without taking account of the limitations on thought and action imposed by Orientalism . . . This is not to say that Orientalism unilaterally determines what can be said about the Orient, but that it is the whole network of interests inevitably brought to bear on (and therefore always involved in) any occasion when that peculiar entity "the Orient" is in question.   (1978: 3)

Building on this formulation – or, better, working from sets of similar assumptions – postcolonialist scholars have tended to situate Eurocentrism as an intellectual atmosphere or hegemonic mode of conceptualization, whose structuring propensities are so deeply and insidiously layered that they cannot but be determinative of all scholarly production on questions relating to "Europe and its Others." On this reading, Eurocentrism is not susceptible to critique, since it is entailed in the very fabric of modern thought, scholarship, knowledge production, disciplinarity.

This essentially Foucauldian understanding of Eurocentrism as an intellectual atmosphere then gives way almost inevitably in much contemporary postcolonial theory to a further proposition, as to the constitutive Eurocentrism of all "Western" thought. In the work of such very different critics as Dipesh Chakrabarty (2000a, 2000b), Jan Nederveen Pieterse (1995, 2001), Tsenay Serequeberhan (1994, 1997), and the Robert Young of *White Mythologies* (1990), for instance, we encounter the argument, not that the *dominant* modes of thinking in the modern West have been rationalist, modernist, and Eurocentric, but that this is the *only* kind of thinking to have been elaborated in modernity, or in the West – the only kind of thinking, indeed, that is *conceivable* in those orders. On the basis of this (to my mind, false) inference, these critics then move – as, in terms of their convictions, it must seem only right for them to do – to disavow modernity, Europe, and rationality themselves, as all inherently imperialistic and totalitarian. From their standpoint, as Jürgen Habermas has written in a powerful critique, not just rationalist thought but reason itself – and, *mutatis mutandis*, not just Eurocentric thought but Europe itself, and not just modernist thought but modernity itself – "becomes unmasked as the subordinating and at the same time itself subjugated subjectivity, as the will to instrumental mastery." The attempt for these critics then becomes to "pull . . . away the veil of reason [or of modernity or "the West"] from before the sheer will to power" (Habermas 1987: 4).

4

The last quarter of the twentieth century has borne witness to a profound decentring of the dominant traditions of the literary world. This transformation has been registered at all levels – reading, writing, publishing, and criticism – including at the highest levels of institutional consecration. Thus while no African writer had won the Nobel Prize for Literature before the mid-1980s, four have done so since then – Wole Soyinka (1986), Naguib Mahfouz (1988), Nadine Gordimer (1991), and J. M. Coetzee (2003). The Caribbean writers, Derek Walcott and V. S. Naipaul won the Nobel Prize in 1992 and 2001, respectively; and the African American novelist, Toni Morrison, did so in 1993. In Britain, the Booker Prize has since the early

1980s been dominated by writers either living in, raised in, or with close connections to the former colonial world: Salman Rushdie, J. M. Coetzee (twice), Keri Hulme, Ben Okri, Michael Ondaatje, and Arundhati Roy, among others.[10] Much the same is true of the Prix Goncourt in France. Everywhere in Anglophone and Francophone literatures, much of the most vibrant, audacious, and inspiriting contemporary writing is being produced by such writers, whose work derives from and reflects upon the experiences of colonialism and post-coloniality, even if the intellectual and ideological formation of these writers cannot be separated from the metropolitan *studium*, the various "great traditions." In the Hispanophone and Lusophone worlds, this process has an even longer history, as witness the legacies bequeathed by such writers as Jorge Amado, Miguel Angel Asturias, Alejo Carpentier, and Cesar Vallejo. (Several Latin American writers have won the Nobel Prize, starting with Gabriela Mistral in 1945: Asturias, 1967; Pablo Neruda, 1971; Gabriel García Márquez, 1982; and Octavio Paz, 1990.)

To read, teach, or write about contemporary literature today is inevitably to feel the impact of this decentring (see Marx, in this volume). Where previously "English" literature, for instance, meant, more or less unproblematically, writing produced by white Britons – or, at most, by them and Anglo-Americans – today not only is it the case that English is demonstrably a world language, spoken by millions more people outside of Britain and North America than within the borders of the United Kingdom and the United States; it is also obvious that the cultivation, preservation, and enrichment of English (as a literary language) are today tasks undertaken as much by "non-Anglo" as by "Anglo" writers (to use terms which, though problematical, have a certain currency in the US). The point has been made well by Salman Rushdie in his 1983 essay, "'Commonwealth Literature' Does Not Exist," from *Imaginary Homelands*: "What seems . . . to be happening is that those peoples who were once colonised by the language are now rapidly remaking it, domesticating it, becoming more and more relaxed about the way they use it – assisted by the English language's enormous flexibility and size, they are carving out large territories for themselves within its frontiers" (1991: 64). Today courses in post-1945 "English" literature that ignore "minority" or "postcolonial" writers and the issues of decolonization, migration, and diaspora are simply anachronistic. The same is true of courses in modern French literature that ignore such writers as Assia Djebar, Sony Labou Tansi, and Patrick Chamoiseau, and that have nothing to say about *Beur* culture. Nor is it a case of "adding" these writers (and issues) to courses that stand in other respects unreconstructed. On the contrary, the advent of "colonial discourse theory" and "postcolonial literary studies" (one can, for convenience, link their simultaneous emergence to 1978, the date of publication of Said's *Orientalism*) has transformed the way in which metropolitan writing is read too – even that metropolitan writing (canonical or non-canonical) that has no ostensible reference to empire, race, nation, colonialism, and anticolonialism (see Parry, Marx, Smith, in this volume).

5

In its widest reaches, the study of "postcolonialism" might be said to implicate most of the humanities and social sciences – from anthropology and political science to philosophy, musicology, economics, and geography. No single volume could plausibly attempt to survey the vast range of this material. The present volume, therefore, is of necessity restricted in its focus. It takes as its object of examination both the academic sub-field of postcolonial literary studies and the domains implicated by that sub-field: "postcolonial theory," "postcolonial" literatures and cultures, globalization, and what some have called "the postcolonial condition." The volume's aims are threefold:

1. to introduce readers to key concepts, methods, theories, thematic concerns, and contemporary debates in the academic field of postcolonial literary studies;
2. to situate these concepts, theories, and debates institutionally, by thinking about them in relation to developments in academic work in fields and disciplines (e.g., history, sociology, philosophy) that abut and influence postcolonial literary studies;
3. to contextualize the emergence and defining trajectories of postcolonial literary studies in broad socio-historical terms, that is, relative to wider social and political developments at the level of the world-system – everything from anticolonial nationalism and decolonization to globalization, migration flows, and the "brain drain."

The volume is structured as follows: after this Introduction, the three chapters in Part 1, "Social and Historical Context" (by Lazarus, Sivanandan, and Parry), explore the great historical experiences (imperialism, anticolonialism, decolonization, globalization) that constitute the past and present of "the postcolonial condition," as well as the sociological and ideological conditions surrounding the emergence of postcolonial literary studies as an academic field in the late 1970s and early 1980s. The five chapters of Part 2, "The Shape of the Field" (by Marx, Gikandi, Brennan, Gopal, and Ganguly), offer an overview of the theoretical and substantive range of the field, discuss its intellectual provenance, trajectory, and effects, and evaluate some of the key concepts and methods developed and deployed by postcolonialist scholars. Part 3, "Sites of Engagement" (Chrisman, Bahri, Coronil, Smith), comprises four chapters analyzing central debates and points of disagreement in the field, and drawing out their implications for politics and theory. This structure is designed to afford an authoritative, but at the same time engaged and discriminating, perspective on postcolonial literary studies – a field currently alive with activity and invention.

NOTES

1 For literary anthologies, see for example Biddle 1995; Ross 1999; Thieme 1996. The best-known Readers are probably Ashcroft, Griffiths, and Tiffin 1995; Castle 2001; Mongia 1996; Schwarz and Ray 2000; and P. Williams and Chrisman 1993. Influential compilations of critical essays include Ansell-Pearson, Parry, and Squires 1997; Barker, Hulme, and Iversen 1994; Bartolovich and Lazarus 2002; and Bhabha 1990a.

2 Examples include Afzal-Khan and Seshadri-Crooks 2000; Childs and Williams 1997; Gandhi 1998; Huggan 2001; Loomba 1998a; McLeod 2000; Moore-Gilbert 1997; Quayson 2000; San Juan 1998.

3 For a late example of such usage, see Lazarus 1990.

4 A quite different reading of the relation between the "posts" of postcolonialism and postmodernism is to be found in Appiah 1991.

5 A compelling date to cite as a reference here is 1975, since it marked the acquisition of independence, finally, after many years of armed struggle and revolutionary warfare, not only in Vietnam, but also in Angola, Mozambique, and Guinea-Bissau / Cape Verde.

6 The commentary on Spivak that follows is derived substantially from my book, *Nationalism and Cultural Practice in the Postcolonial World* (Lazarus 1999a: 109–15).

7 For other pertinent critiques of Spivak's theory of subalternity, see Larsen 2002; Parry 1987, 1994.

8 The slogan, "unthinking Eurocentrism," is drawn from the title of Ella Shohat and Robert Stam's book, *Unthinking Eurocentrism: Multiculturalism and the Media* (1994).

9 For other studies of Said and his work, see Sprinker 1992; Kennedy 2000; Hussein 2002.

10 For discussions of the significance of this, see Huggan 2001; Amireh and Majaj 2000; Strongman 2002.

I

SOCIAL AND HISTORICAL CONTEXT

2

NEIL LAZARUS

The global dispensation since 1945

I

The purpose of this chapter is to provide an overview of political and economic developments in the world system since the end of the Second World
War in 1945. There are several reasons why it seems important to begin
a volume devoted to postcolonial studies with an account of this kind –
not only to "set the scene," as it were, to discuss the conditions prevailing in the post-war years, as the great movements for independence and
national liberation in Africa, Asia, and the Caribbean gathered momentum
in the drive towards decolonization; but also to sketch the contours of the
global dispensation into which the new countries were subsequently precip-
itated at independence (joining the Latin American states, most of which
had achieved political independence in the nineteenth century), and in the
context of which they had to take their place, for the most part as relatively
poor and relatively poorly resourced nation-states (both undeveloped and
under-developed) in an inegalitarian, unevenly integrated, and highly polarized world system of nation-states. It is impossible to understand the fraught
trajectories of developments in these new nation-states in the decades since
their decolonization – hard-won victories as well as an abundance of what
the historian of Africa, Basil Davidson, has called "setbacks and defeats"
(1983: 95) – without a consideration of the global picture, both of the shifting balance of geopolitical forces and of transformations and restructurings
in capitalism and capitalist class relations world-wide. The dispositions of
power in the world system have not only set certain untranscendable limits
to what it has been possible, and what impossible, for the newly decolonized
states to achieve; they have also been such as to determine – or at the very
least powerfully influence – policies and practices in these new states (as also
in their older Latin American counterparts) even in situations where their
leaders have imagined and sought to put forward and implement credible
alternatives.

The point here is not, of course, to suggest that the setbacks and defeats of the postcolonial era ought automatically to be referred beyond the "post-colonies" themselves, to the world system. This would be to exculpate the clearly culpable leaderships of any number of postcolonial states, whose record, in human rights terms as well as in terms of the provision of standards of living, welfare, and social empowerment, has been dismal. It is obvious that we ought not to let the murderousness, brutality, and corruption – not to mention the ineptitude, cowardice, and greed – of so many postcolonial leaders disappear from view in our reckoning of developments in the decades since decolonization. "The trouble with Nigeria is simply and squarely a failure of leadership," as Chinua Achebe once succinctly put it in the opening sentence of a broadside of his on the venality and abuse of power of the Nigerian political class (1984: 1) – and we ought never to allow ourselves to forget or ignore the general truth contained in Achebe's statement.

Yet there is no contradiction between identifying the criminality and ineptitude of postcolonial rulers and recognizing that they were and are at the same time the creatures of larger powers and forces in the world system. Economically speaking, the poverty and, indeed, ever-deepening immiseration and indebtedness of so many postcolonial nations is a structural feature of the terms of their insertion into the global economy, from which it has been simply impossible for them to "de-link" or disconnect themselves. To lay the blame for the destruction of the environment, the impoverishment of communities, and the exploitation of workers in Nigeria, Malaysia, Venezuela, and Trinidad on corrupt and autocratic national rulers, without also taking into account the central roles played by the massive and hugely powerful Western-based oil conglomerates, for instance, would clearly be to invert reality (see Galeano 1973: 289–91). The same truth holds in the political realm. Thus it takes nothing away from the revulsion that we rightly feel for Pinochet, Suharto, Mobutu, and Saddam Hussein – brutal dictators who used all of the resources of the police states which they commanded to maintain themselves in power and to crush opposition – to observe that it is likely that none of them would have been able to come to power, and that it is certain that none of them would have been able to *stay* in power for as long as they did, without the direct, active, and sustained support of the United States, self-proclaimed "keeper of the peace" in the post-1945 period.

2

Commentators of all political persuasions tend to agree that the sixty years between 1945 and the present can be divided more or less neatly into two distinct eras. First, a quarter-century or so of explosive growth, marked by significant gains and the unprecedentedly wide dispersal of social, political, and economic benefits to populations at large. This boom-period came to an end sometime around the end of the 1960s or the beginning of the 1970s (the steep hike in oil prices in 1973 is often cited as a key moment in the transition), as the world system stumbled into economic recession and attendant political crisis; and it has been followed by a period marked by the global assertion and consolidation of US political hegemony and what Samir Amin has called "the logic of unilateral capital" (1997: 95). Thus Immanuel Wallerstein, in a fairly representative summary, suggests that the economics of the period since 1945

> are in broad outline easy to expound. There was a major expansion of the capitalist world-economy following the end of the Second World War. It came to an end perhaps in 1967, perhaps in 1973. It was the greatest single expansion in the history of this world-system going back to 1500 (measured by any of the usual criteria, except that of expansion of land area included within the world-economy) . . . For all the standard economic reasons, this expansion came to an end and has been followed by an economic stagnation.
>
> (1991: 123–24)

If we focus exclusively on the advanced capitalist world – the "West" – to begin with, we can note that the Second World War ended with the definitive eclipse of European political hegemony by US political hegemony. The strength of European economies had been shattered by the war, and needed to be rebuilt. The US-sponsored Marshall Plan "paved the way for a rapid rebuilding of Europe, where the United States encouraged reconciliation and a commitment to economic integration" (Amin 1994: 26). The rebuilding was secured on the basis of a selective internationalization of capital: on the one hand, there was the development and promotion of markets that were both open and globally integrated; on the other hand, policies were instituted which protected *national* capitals and allowed and encouraged them to grow free from "open" competition in the world market. Boom-era capitalism was global in its overall posture, but growth unfolded everywhere "within the framework of autocentric national economies" (Samir Amin 1997: 93; see also Arrighi 1994; Brett 1985; Hobsbawm 1994; Szentes 1988; Therborn 1996).

The stabilization of capitalism in the core societies of Western Europe and the United States in the immediate post-war period was secured on the basis of what some political economists have characterized as a *Fordist* regime of accumulation. (The name "Fordism" is derived from the American

automobile manufacturer, Henry Ford, and refers to the way in which labor
was organized in his factories and labor-power reproduced around them.)
Post-war Fordism, as Simon Clarke has explained, was based

> on the mass production of homogeneous products, using the rigid technology
> of the assembly line with dedicated machines and standardized . . . work rou-
> tines. Increased productivity [was] attained through economies of scale as well
> as the deskilling, intensification and homogenization of labor. This [gave] rise
> to the mass worker, organized in bureaucratic trade-unions which negotiate[d]
> uniform wages that [grew] proportionately with productivity increases. Homo-
> geneous consumption patterns reflect[ed] the homogenization of production
> and provide[d] a market for standardized commodities, while rising wages
> provide[d] growing demand to match the growing supply. The overall bal-
> ance between supply and demand [was] achieved through Keynesian macro-
> economic policies, while the overall balance between wages and profits [was]
> achieved through a collective bargaining supervised by the state. The educa-
> tion, training, socialization, etc. of the mass worker [was] organized through
> the mass institutions of a bureaucratic welfare state.   (1990: 73)

The *social* dimensions of post-war Fordism need to be emphasized here,
both in terms of what they entailed and in terms of what they achieved.
Centrally, as Clarke's account intimates, Fordism as a generalized social
regime entailed a historic compromise between capital and labor, a compromise that has frequently gone under the name of "the welfare state." For
a combination of reasons – the relative strength of organized labor and the
relative weakness of "organized capital" in the immediate post-war years,
and an exhausted disenchantment on all sides with the politics of confrontation – post-war reconstruction in the core capitalist societies took the form
of social democracy. Growth on the one hand was complemented by the
dispersal of social and economic benefits on the other. During this period of
thirty years or so, as Colin Leys has written,

> the industrialized countries experienced steady economic growth, distributed
> the benefits with a degree of equity (however modest) between capital and
> labour and between town and country, invested in their infrastructure, increas-
> ingly recognized and assisted disadvantaged groups and pursued all sorts of
> other social and cultural objectives, from gender equality to care for the envi-
> ronment, even if such goals were only very imperfectly attained. (1996: 193)

Much the same point is made also by Jürgen Habermas, in a rather magis-
terial summary that warrants quoting at length:

> In the affluent and peaceful Western European democracies, and to a lesser
> degree in the United States, Japan, and some other countries, mixed economies
> made possible the establishment and effective realization of basic social rights.

Of course, the explosive growth of the global economy, the quadrupling of industrial production, and an exponential increase in the world trade between the early 1950s and the early 1970s also generated disparities between the rich and the poor regions of the world. But the governments of the OECD [Organization of Economic Cooperation and Development] nations, who were responsible for three-quarters of global production and four-fifths of global trade in industrial goods during these two decades, had learned enough from the catastrophic experiences of the period between the two world wars to pursue intelligent domestic economic policies, focussing on stability with a relatively high rate of economic growth, and on the construction and enhancement of comprehensive social security systems. In welfare-state mass democracies, highly productive capitalist economies were socially domesticated for the first time, and were thus brought more or less in line with the normative self-understanding of democratic constitutional states.

(2001: 48; see also Larrain 2000: 114)

It is worth picking up on Habermas's term "domesticated" here and emphasizing that the welfare state was a political *settlement*, reflecting no magnanimous or "natural" aspiration on capital's part to harmonize its interests with those of labor but, on the contrary, the bitterly hard-won ability of organized labor to constrain capital. Even so, the period of sustained economic growth that the welfare state or "social Keynesianism" made possible could not be sustained indefinitely. Beginning in the late 1960s, a series of related developments combined to put an end to what Eric Hobsbawm (1994) has called the "golden age" and to bring the post-war boom to a shuddering halt. The immanent instability of the Keynesian welfare state – the final incompatibility between capitalist class relations and social democracy – caused the rate of growth to slow and then to stagnate. The various socioeconomic contradictions that had been both masked and exacerbated by the social democratic class compromise of Fordism began (once again) in the late 1960s and early 1970s to stage themselves as the sites of open confrontation. Having developed as far as it was possible to develop within the framework of Keynesianism, capital began to chafe under the bit of the restrictions it had been obliged by the power of organized labor to accept. (As Samir Amin has written, social democracy was never capable of "challeng[ing] the hegemony of capital, but only [of] temper[ing] it with the power of the workers in the political arena" [1992: 20].) It was in this context, as Nicholas Costello, Jonathan Michie, and Seumas Milne, among many other commentators, have noted, that

a consensus started to emerge among the ruling classes of the major western states that without the discipline of redundancy and mass unemployment on the workforce there was no possibility of overcoming the stagflationary crisis of the period and carrying out the economic restructuring necessary to meet the challenge from Japan and the Far East. In Britain, this ideology emerged in the form of monetarism which in due course turned into the free-market crusade of Thatcherism. In the US it started life as Reaganomics. In France it arrived in a dramatic form in 1983 when the socialist government conducted a U-turn strongly reminiscent of the British Labour government's capitulation to the IMF seven years earlier. (1989: 62)

From the standpoint of the ruling classes in the core capitalist nation-states, the required "economic restructuring" could not be achieved through any re-consolidation of the welfarist order of Fordism and Keynesian class compromise. Instead, as Michael Rustin has written,

> new strategies [began to be] developed by capital, both intellectually and in political practice. These included the internationalization of its operations, transferring "Fordist" forms of production to less developed countries, while maintaining crucial command and research functions in the metropolises; the imposition of more stringent market disciplines on capital and labour, through the international "de-regulation" of trade, movements of capital, and labour; the internal "marketization" of operations within large firms, through the institution of management by local profit-centres; the development of new technologies and forms of production and marketing . . . and a dispersal and reduction of the scale of production in order to elude the countervailing cultures and institutions of organized labour. (1989: 55)

It is in this general context that the subjects of "post-Fordism" and "globalization" have tended to enter the scholarly literature. The suggestion is that these "new strategies" developed by capital starting in the late 1960s and early 1970s – and intended both to restructure the social relations of production and to install new technologies and forms of production – might have been sufficiently consequential in their scope and tendency to oblige us to think of them as inaugurating a new regime of accumulation. According to David Harvey, so striking is the new flexibility on capital's part "with respect to labour processes, labour markets, products, and pattern of production," and so pointedly at odds is it with "the rigidities of Fordism," that the contemporary commentator is more or less compelled to entertain the "hypothesis of a shift from Fordism to what might be called a 'flexible' regime of accumulation." At the very least, Harvey suggests, this hypothesis might stand as "a telling way to characterize modern history" (1989: 124, 147; see also Burbach and Robinson 1999; Castells 1998; J. Harris 1999; Harvey 1995; Howells and Wood 1993; J. Kolko 1988; Lash and Urry 1987; Lipietz 1987; Robinson 1996a, 1996b).

As with the welfare state, so too with "globalization," it is necessary to specify its social implications as well as its causes and conditions of emergence. The general result of the capitalist-sponsored restructuring of class relations since 1970 has been devastating for the broad majority of people affected by it. Confining our analysis still to the core capitalist societies, the record is one of

> declining real wages for the least skilled, dramatic increases in inequality of incomes and wealth, higher unemployment and declining levels of collective provision across a whole range of goals that only yesterday had defined the kind of societies people wanted to live in (such as support for gender and other kinds of equality, and the steady improvement of social services and social security) with corresponding increases in social distress, marginalization, racism, crime, violence, and political alienation. (Leys 1996: 194)

The practical effects of globalization in the contemporary period in Western Europe and the United States have been to privatize social provision, thereby dismantling the welfare state and stripping vast sectors of metropolitan populations of security across wide aspects of their lives (health, welfare, education, etc.); to drive millions of people out of work, forcing them not only into unemployment but into *structural* unemployment; and to enact legislation which makes it increasingly difficult for people to represent themselves collectively, to campaign and fight for their interests and the rights formally accorded them (Bauman 1998; Bourdieu 1998; Brecher and Costello 1994; Cockburn 1997; Martin and Schumann 1997; Moody 1997; Tabb 2001).

The politics of globalization are inseparable from the unfolding hegemony of neoliberal ideology. The social thought and practice of the "transnational capitalist class" (Sklair 2001) – the social fraction whose members Tim Brennan has suggestively dubbed the "new cosmopolitans" (1997) – proceed upon the assumption that the world market is the overriding motive force of contemporary economic development and that nation-statist policy has therefore become irrelevant to economic practice. To these new cosmopolitans – a cohort made up pre-eminently of politicians at the helm of neoliberal states, executives and senior operatives of transnational corporations, and professional and managerial élites in the financial and information sectors of the contemporary world system – globalization appears in the guise of "a tide sweeping over borders in which technology and irresistible market forces transform the global system in ways beyond the power of anyone to do much to change" (Tabb 1997: 20).

One could, of course – and should – immediately object that what is stereotypically projected in neoliberal ideology as a behemoth or a brakeless train is in fact the direct outcome of social and economic *policy* and is hence subject to direction or alteration. Thus Alan Scott, who helpfully points out that

> Globalization must be seen in part at least as the outcome of an idea, and specifically the idea of a free market . . . [G]lobalization on such a view is the realization or side-effect of economic deregulation and the lowering of social costs within national communities . . . Deregulation . . . is not a *response* to competition, but a means of extending it into areas which were previously protected, or partially protected, from commodification. It is deregulation that undermines the ability of nation states to protect themselves from the social destructiveness of markets, but it is also the nation state that is the key actor in bringing deregulation about internally . . . and externally . . . [C]ontemporary neoliberalism has been successful because it has persuaded many politicians, and perhaps voters also, that the direction of causality runs from economic development to political response and thus presents itself merely as an objective or at least neutral diagnosis rather than as a contributor to the emergence of the very conditions it purports to analyse. (1997: 9–10)

Scott's reminder is salutary, since so much of the contemporary debate about globalization is premised upon the false assumption that, good or bad, it is a development that cannot be withstood, cannot be managed or regulated. "There is no alternative": this invidious mantra is cited everywhere in the scholarly literature, as also in the wider political and public spheres, such that even those who deplore the effects that neoliberal policies have had upon social life are disposed to believe that there is nothing that can be done about it. Thus John Gray, for instance. Gray was a fierce champion of Mrs. Thatcher's "free market" policies during the first years of her Prime Ministership in Britain, beginning in 1979. By the 1990s he had come to recognize that neoliberal policies of the kind espoused by Thatcher had "harmonized" the social relations of production downwards, disembedding people from their local or regional networks and submitting them to the tender mercies of a labor market driven by technologically determined developments in the forces of production and utterly indifferent to their interests. Yet, enemy of neoliberalism though he has become, Gray is still only capable of painting a picture of an unstable, unsteerable, rampaging juggernaut, which it is quite beyond the capacity of any human agency to temper or domesticate. Today, he writes, all social actors – even corporate ones – are obliged to operate in

> an environment so transformed by market forces that no institution – not even the largest transnational corporation or sovereign state – can master it. In this environment the most unmanageable forces spring from a torrent of technological innovations. It is the combination of this unceasing stream of

new technologies, unfettered market competition and weak or fractured social institutions that produces the global economy of our times . . . In the late twentieth century there is no shelter – for corporations or for governments – from the global gale of creative destruction. (1998: 76)

The main reason to reject this way of thinking – widespread right across the political spectrum – is that, for all its criticism of neoliberalism, it *depoliticizes* the recent developments in the world system. In its fatalism and technological determinism, it fails to register that globalization directly serves the interests of some people, and that there is an intimate structural connection between the obscenely burgeoning prosperity of this minority and the steady immiseration of the large majority of the world's population. Gray laments this immiseration, but he presents it as the outcome of an agentless and irreversible process, of which there are only victims. In these terms, Barry Gills's critique of the politics of what he calls the "New Hellenism" might cogently be directed against Gray and those whose analyses are similar to his:

[N]o argument that depoliticises the processes of globalization should be politically or intellectually acceptable. On the contrary, globalization should actually serve to focus our attention precisely on the type of political responses it sets in motion, rather than feed the idea that politics is becoming the predictable epiphenomena [*sic*] of technological processes. In reality, the politics of globalization is all around us, and like all politics, it is a fairly fluid and open situation, the outcomes of which will be determined by "struggle" or contest, and by the balance of forces on each question . . . Above all, no account of globalization should "write out" the response to these processes by popular forces and social movements, including traditional labour movements and "opposition" political parties. (1997: 66)

3

The schematic narrative of the political economy of capitalism in the post-1945 era outlined above is sound as far as it goes. However, it is essentially partial and incomplete. To bring it into line with reality, it is necessary to supplement the narrative in two respects, the first comparative-historical, the second (and more important) geo-political. First, a caveat needs to be entered concerning the impression of *discontinuity* that is likely to be conveyed by the analytical starkness of the narrative's juxtaposition of the epochs of expansion (1945 to 1968 or 1973, say) and of crisis (1968/1973 to the present). The suggestion in the political economic literature, as we have already seen, is that in its attempts to resolve the crisis of profitability that set in towards the end of the 1960s, capital launched a new offensive against labor world-wide, dissolving the welfarist class compromise that had marked its dealings with the Western working class in the post-1945 period and accelerating or intensifying its rate of exploitation of workers in the peripheries and semi-peripheries. Yet the strategies aggressively deployed by capital during this period – among them the transnationalization of production, the development of new productive forces and technologies, the installation of newly rationalized productive regimes and new modes of marketing, the prioritization of speculative or financial over productive capital – were not new. On the contrary, every one of these strategies, generally conceived, has had a long and chequered career in the development of capitalism over the course of the past several hundred years (Hirst and Thompson 1996; Mandel 1993; E. M. Wood 1997, 1998, 2002). Salutary here is Wallerstein's characteristically macro-historical reading of the recurring drama of overproduction: "[w]hat seems to have happened every fifty years or so" in the history of capitalist development, he writes,

> is that in the efforts of more and more entrepreneurs to gain for themselves the more profitable nexuses of commodity chains, disproportions of investment occurred such that we speak, somewhat misleadingly, of overproduction. The only solution to these disproportions has been a shakedown of the productive system, resulting in a more even distribution. This sounds logical and simple, but its fall-out has always been massive. It has meant each time further concentration of operations in those links in the commodity chains which have been most clogged. This has involved the elimination of both some entrepreneurs and some workers . . . Such a shift also enabled entrepreneurs to "demote" operations in the hierarchy of the commodity chains, thereby enabling them to devote investment funds and effort to innovative links in the commodity chains which, because initially offering "scarcer" inputs, were more profitable. "Demotion" of particular processes on the hierarchical scale also often led to geographical relocation in part. Such geographical relocation found a major attraction in the move to a lower labour-cost area. (1996: 34–35)

It scarcely remains after this for Wallerstein to add, as the clincher, that "[w]e are living through precisely such a massive world-wide relocation right now of the world's automobile, steel, and electronics industries. This phenomenon of relocation has been part and parcel of historical capitalism from the outset" (35).

The second respect in which it is necessary to supplement the narrative of the political economy of post-1945 capitalism offered hitherto derives from its focus on the core capitalist nation-states of Western Europe and the United States. Left without further elaboration, the narrative might leave the impression that inasmuch as the world system is headquartered in these states, the only developments that are worth recording in detail are those that take place in them – that what happens on the peripheries of the world system doesn't really matter or make any difference to it. The truth is quite otherwise, however. It is clear that the prosperity of the period from 1945 until the late 1960s was indeed substantially predicated upon the welfarist class compromise in the core capitalist nations of Western Europe and the United States. Yet the achievement of the welfare state – measured not only in terms of economic growth but also in terms of social democracy – needs to be properly situated. It is in fact complementary with, and indeed partially dependent on, two other world-historical social projects, which, following Samir Amin, we might identify as the Soviet system – "called an attempt to build socialism, although it really was an attempt to build 'capitalism without capitalists,' which nevertheless set itself up as a challenge to capitalism and so stimulated it" – on the one hand, and "the attempts of national-capitalist development in the peripheral countries, which were made possible by the victories of national liberation movements," on the other (Amin 1998: 21–22). These three social projects operated in tandem and – notwithstanding their structural and ultimately definitive limitations – initially met with considerable success in the post-1945 era. Amin writes that they

> either unfolded within the framework of autocentric national economies or, in the case of the countries of the East and the South, aspired to construct such autocentric economies. They differed in their relationship ("interdependence") with the world economy: Atlanticism, the construction of Europe, in the case of the developed countries of the West; a "negotiated" opening to the world economy in the case of the countries of the South; quasi-autarky for the countries of the East. (1997: 93)

Amin insists that the growth with democratization that we have seen to have been a feature of the boom-era in the West was complemented by substantial gains in the East and South. Thus he maintains that "[t]he victory of the Soviet Union and the Chinese revolution created internal and international conditions favouring the development of the countries of the East" – and that to the extent that these developments "contributed [also] to pressures exerted on capital to engage in the historic social-democratic compromise" in the context of the Cold War, they contributed to further advances in the West too. Moreover, "[t]he simultaneous rise of national liberation movements in the third world and the ability of postcolonial regimes to harness the benefits of East–West competition favoured economic growth in the south in a number of ways" (94–95). The net result of all these developments, Amin writes, was a period, or interregnum, in which "capital was constrained to operate within structures relatively favourable to the peoples of the world" (95).

4

Limitations of space prevent us from exploring post-1945 developments in the Soviet Union and the Soviet satellite regimes in Eastern Europe.[1] However, developments in what Amin calls "the Third World" during this period are central to this volume and require some elaboration here. For purposes of analysis, we can separate out a political and an economic strand, although in practice the two are manifestly and even inextricably interwoven. Politically, we need to start by registering as decisively as possible the sheer, irreversible gain represented by the attainment of political independence itself, that is, by the achievement of decolonization.[2] The articulation and elaboration of national consciousness; the mobilization of popular will or support; the tempering of this will in the fire of the anticolonial campaigns, of struggles for national liberation, when the least response of the colonial states was intransigence and the arrogant refusal even to contemplate reform, and the more typical response was to call out the police and very often the army to silence dissent and quell resistance – these developments, concerted in their nevertheless uncoordinated appearance across the globe in the immediate post-war period, were (and remain) of world-historical significance (see Sivanandan, in this volume). In no instance was independence merely bestowed upon a colonial population as a gift. (The colonial discourse of "tutelage," of "preparing" native populations for self-rule, was from the outset an ideological ruse in the strict sense.) In every case, it was necessary to mobilize against the colonial state – which we would do best to think of as a kind of dictatorship – to campaign against it at every level, from the courts and the press and the schools to labor militancy, from strikes and non-violent mass action, civil disobedience, and passive resistance to direct action and the taking up of arms. Resistance to colonial rule had of course begun even before it had been imposed on the basis of conquest. Yet, as Colin Legum writes,

> it was not until the Second World War that the modern anticolonial struggle spread from Indonesia and Indochina in the East across Southeast Asia, the Middle East, and Africa to the Caribbean. Two principal factors account for the decline of western imperialism. World War II had depleted the military and economic resources of the metropolitan powers; the propaganda of a war "fought for democracy" infected public opinion and governments in Europe,

as well as anti-imperialism movements in the colonies led by modernizing élites. The other factor was that colonial possessions had begun to lose their economic value for Britain and France, though not yet for Portugal, Spain, and Belgium.   (1999: 5–6)

Even where what historians have termed the "transfer of power" was finally settled through negotiation – in the Indian subcontinent, Egypt, Ghana, Senegal, and Jamaica, say – the decolonizing process was never without violence, and required steady courage, discipline, resilience, and resourceful intelligence of those, at all levels, engaged in the campaign against colonial rule. In other regions – Cuba, Algeria, Kenya, and Vietnam, for instance – the demand for sovereignty was met by blank refusal and further repression and violence, and the independence movements had to resort to armed struggle to achieve their ends. In such cases, the national liberation struggle is properly regarded as revolutionary.

It is important to emphasize the achievement of decolonization, to remind ourselves of the heroism commonly displayed by ordinary people in the struggle for independence, and of the solidarities built in the process. The era of decolonization was marked by heady expectancy, dynamism, a sense of uplift and vibrant hopefulness. "The world became a larger and happier place," as Basil Davidson writes of these years (1992: 196) – not "*seemed* to become a larger and happier place," note, but actively *became* such. What Davidson writes of Africa is generalizable to the postcolonial world at large in this respect:

> there were many reasons for optimism. The old empires were falling fast and would not be restored. The social freedoms that had provided the real magnet behind nationalism were making themselves increasingly felt; and the grim silence of the colonial years was already shattered by a hubbub of plans and schemes for a more favorable future. People even talked of a "new Africa," and yet it did not sound absurd. A whole continent seemed to have come alive again, vividly real, bursting with creative energies, claiming its heritage in the human family, and unfolding ever more varied or surprising aspects of itself.
> (195–96)

Politically speaking, this new sense of uplift and regeneration proved to be of relatively short duration. In *The Black Man's Burden: Africa and the Curse of the Nation-State*, the book from which I have just quoted, Davidson attempts to analyze the processes through which, in the postcolonial era, the gap between People and State has widened rather than (as might have been anticipated, and was certainly hoped for) narrowed. Increasingly, he argues, "social" imperatives – those concerning the distribution of capital, resources, and services – have been subordinated to the "national" requirements of élite entrenchment – that is, where they have not been cynically jettisoned altogether. Not only has "the extraction of wealth from an already impoverished Africa . . . in no way [been] halted by the [ending of colonial rule]"; in addition, "the 'national conflict,' embodied in the rivalries for executive power between contending groups or individuals among the 'élites' . . . [has] take[n] priority over a 'social conflict' concerned with the interests of most of the inhabitants of these new nation-states" (219, 114). Although this commentary is focused on sub-Saharan Africa, what Davidson says is readily applicable elsewhere in the postcolonial world as well. For in South, Southeast, and East Asia, the Maghreb and the Mashriq, Latin America and the Caribbean, as in Africa, leaders and ruling élites have come to identify their own maintenance in power as being of greater importance than the broader "social" goods of democratization, opportunity, and equality, and they have increasingly used the repressive apparatuses and technologies of the state (often inherited from the colonial order) to enforce order and to silence or eliminate opposition: Banzer, Somoza, and the Duvaliers, Abacha, Mengistu, and Mugabe, Indira Gandhi and Zia ul-Haq, Suharto and Marcos – the list is a dispiritingly long one. As Arundhati Roy puts it, in a recent commentary on developments in postcolonial India:

> Fascism has come to India after the dreams that fueled the freedom struggle have been frittered away like so much loose change. Independence itself came to us as what Gandhi famously called a "wooden loaf" – a notional freedom tainted by the blood of the hundreds of thousands who died during Partition. For more than half a century now, that heritage of hatred and mutual distrust has been exacerbated, toyed with and never allowed to heal by politicians. Over the past fifty years ordinary citizens' modest hopes for lives of dignity, security and relief from abject poverty have been systematically snuffed out. Every "democratic" institution in this country has shown itself to be unaccountable, inaccessible to the ordinary citizen, and either unwilling or incapable of acting in the interests of genuine social justice. And now corporate globalization is being relentlessly and arbitrarily imposed on India, ripping it apart culturally and economically. (2002: 18)

This is a remarkable formulation, but I want to signal up one problem with it. It is interesting to compare Roy's words here with those of her great predecessor, Rabindranath Tagore, who, writing just before independence in India, observed that "[i]t does not need a defeatist to feel deeply anxious about the future of millions when all their innate cultures and peaceful traditions are being simultaneously subjected to hunger, disease, exploitation (foreign and indigenous), and the seething contents of communalism" (qtd. Legum 1999: 49).

It might seem to Roy herself, perhaps, that there is a straight line to be drawn between Tagore's fears on the eve of independence and her own eloquent indictment of modern Indian politics. For Roy, too, speaks of "exploitation (foreign and indigenous)"; she too speaks of the furies of communalism[3] and laments the destruction of democratic institutions (whether "traditional" or of colonial provenance). Only with respect to the predations of "corporate globalization" does she refer to the present conjuncture as in any sense *different* from that which has obtained since decolonization in 1947 – and she phrases globalization as merely the last (or at least the most recent) in a long list of calamities to have befallen India over the course of the half-century since that date.

The problem with this way of thinking is that it is "presentist" – that is, it tends to construe the past as the history of the present,[4] a construction that leads Roy, I think, to the surprisingly unhistorical inference that what has happened in India is the only thing that *could have happened*, that this thing that has happened has, in a sense, *always been happening* or has always been *about to happen*. Philosophically, of course, something that happens had to have *been able* to happen: it had to have been a *possibility*, or else it could not have become a reality. Yet, in Roy's formulation, the destruction of democracy in India, the fomenting of communalist hatred and violence, the immiseration of "ordinary citizens," have been continuous, unbroken features of the postcolonial era. This, I take it, is why she categorizes the hopes and expectations that attended independence, and that had increasingly inspired collective action towards that political end in the years leading up to 1947, as mere *dreams*. When she refers to the "dreams that fueled the freedom struggle," she allows her readership to imagine that they were never more than this, that they always lacked substance, plausibility, realism. Her readership might then be led to wonder whether the winning of independence was so great an achievement after all.

Many scholars active in postcolonial studies are, indeed, positively cynical about decolonization and national liberation. As Aijaz Ahmad – who dislikes this cynicism – has rightly complained, the tendency in contemporary scholarship is to focus not on the "revolutionary heroism" that was everywhere in evidence in the anticolonial struggle, but on the setbacks and defeats that have followed in the years since independence, "the failures, the distortions, the bureaucratization; that there [were] also . . . other kinds of solidarities no longer [seems to] matter" (Ahmad 1992: 28, 33).

It is important to recollect the energy, dynamism, and optimism of the decolonizing and immediate post-independence era both for the sake of the historical record, and also to enable us to register the *successes* of this period, however slender, partial, provisional, or unsustainable they proved to be in the long term. The Vietnamese army's defeat of the French at Dien Bien Phu in 1954; the staging of the Bandung Conference in 1955; the resolution of the Suez crisis in 1956; the acquisition of independence in Ghana in 1957 – these were all events which fired the minds and imaginations of millions of people world-wide, placing on to the world stage, perhaps for the first time, the principled and resolute figure of "Third-World" self-determination. Nor were such successes related only to "internationalism" in its various guises (see P. Anderson 2002). For domestically, too, the newly inaugurated postcolonial regimes undertook all manner of ambitious projects intended to improve the livelihood and welfare of their citizenry, from literacy and adult education campaigns to the construction and provision of hospitals, from the building of roads and sewage facilities to vast irrigation schemes (as most notably in the Sudan, for instance), and from the redistribution of land to the outlawing of feudal rights over the labor of others. Here, women were granted the right to vote, and to own property. There, workers were granted the right to organize and strike. Still elsewhere, compulsory education of children was introduced. Constitutions were framed; new laws were passed; many tyrannical and bitterly resented colonial laws and edicts were struck down.

Such social gains bear comparison with those secured in the core capitalist states under the rubric of the welfare state. It is in this context that the new states of Africa, Asia, and the Caribbean, which were decolonized only during the post-1945 period, were brought into alignment with the Latin American states, most of which had been decolonized during the nineteenth century. From the 1930s, under the rubric of "modernization," economic policy in the Latin American states had been national-developmental. In response to the global depression of 1929, the Latin American states had abandoned laissez-faire economics and embarked on policies characterized, as Robert Gwynne and Cristóbal Kay have explained, "by greater state involvement in the management of the economy, an attempt to reduce the linkages with the wider world economy and promote industrialization" (1999: 3). These policies were sustained in Latin America throughout the "golden age" of post-war capitalism; and they also became the policies overwhelmingly favored by the leaders of the newly decolonized states elsewhere. What such policies entailed in general, as Samir Amin has observed, "was a bourgeois-nationalist modernization scheme designed to lead to the construction of relatively endocentric and industrialized national economies within an international framework of controlled interdependence on the world scale, as opposed to the Soviet framework of disengagement"

(1997: 147). Most of the Latin American states "developed interventionist and protectionist policies which controlled most of economic life, but they also introduced some aspects of a welfare state in health, social security and housing. In spite of all this, the benefits of modernity continued to be highly concentrated and the masses of the people continued to be excluded" (Larrain 2000: 116). The most successful of the developmental states were of course the so-called "Asian Tigers" – Hong Kong, Taiwan, South Korea, and Singapore – whose rapid economic growth was secured during the boom era on the basis of "the central role played by a national developmentalist state with a forceful industrial policy (imposed after sweeping land reform) in the pursuit of international competitiveness and growth . . . Contrary to initial claims by neoliberals . . . , the success of the NICs [Newly Industrializing Countries] of East Asia was state-induced rather than market driven" (Gwynne and Kay 1999: 6). Throughout the Third World in the quarter-century following the Second World War, developmentalism (or modernization) produced relatively impressive economic results, even if these cannot be correlated with any necessary democratization, either political or economic. As Walden Bello has observed "The 1960s and 1970s . . . saw significant gains for the Third World, or South . . . [S]timulated by development strategies in which the state played a central role, Southern economies grew. Latin America's gross domestic product (GDP) rose by an average of 5 per cent per annum between 1960 and 1982, while Africa's climbed by an average of 4 per cent" (Bello 1999: 7).

5

It is this order that Samir Amin sees as having collapsed in the years of crisis that set in during the late 1960s. Sometime between 1968 and 1971, he writes, "the world system entered a phase of structural crisis, which continues to this day. The crisis manifests itself in the return of a high and persistent unemployment accompanied by a slowing down of growth in the West, the collapse of Sovietism, and serious regression in some regions of the Third World, accompanied by unsustainable levels of external indebtedness" (1997: 94). The situation receives a fuller elaboration in Jorge Larrain's *Identity and Modernity in Latin America*:

> By 1973, a new phase had set in which was characterized by a slowing down of economic growth and a falling rate of profit in industrial nations. Everywhere in the capitalist world profits fell, trade contracted, and unemployment became very pronounced. This was compounded by the sharp rise in oil prices in October 1973. By 1974–5 a generalized recession was hitting the world capitalist

system for the first time since the Second World War. What was new about this recession and the period that followed it was that the anti-depression policies followed by most governments produced inflation without adequately stimulating the economy, thus provoking high levels of unemployment. Throughout the developing world the recession had damaging effects: it aggravated the chronic deficits of its balance of payments by bringing down the prices of raw materials and raising the prices of oil and other essential imports, thus producing inflation, unemployment and stagnation. This marked the beginning of the huge expansion of the Third World's international debt, which soon became an impossibly heavy burden for its very weak economies, with the result that several countries defaulted on their obligations.   (2000: 133)

It is worth spelling out the political and the economic dimensions of this ongoing crisis as it affects the postcolonial world in a little more detail. "[I]n the first flush of independence," Legum writes, with specific reference to Africa, the new leaders

> had been easily tempted by lavish offers of foreign aid, which they saw as a means of stimulating development and financing education and health infrastructure programs. While aid on reasonable terms can contribute to development, the necessary condition is that the loans should produce more than the interest and redemption costs. This did not happen, with the result that by the end of the 1980s, most sub-Saharan countries were forced to devote anything between 40 percent and 82 percent of their foreign exchange earnings to redeeming their foreign debt . . . The debt service to export goods and services was around 200 percent. Debt thus became one of the major obstacles to Africa's development.   (1999: 45)

The sheer size of the debts owed to foreign lending institutions was one problem, and a big one. Still, throughout the boom era, it had been possible to incur debt to repay debt, and African leaders had done so, risking everything on the naïve and, with hindsight, deluded assumption that the terms of world trade would not always disadvantage them, that their investments (political and economic) would one day produce redeemable dividends. Once the global downturn commenced at the end of the 1960s, however, any chance of their "catching up" and keeping a clean balance sheet disappeared definitively, and probably forever. The story is taken up by John Saul:

> Fatefully for Africa [the] . . . debt came due, in the 1980s, just as the premises of the dominant players in the development game were changing. The western Keynesian consensus that had sanctioned the agricultural levies, the industrialization dream, the social services sensibility, and the activist state of the immediate post-independence decades – and lent money to support all this – was replaced by "neoliberalism." For Africa this meant the winding down of

any remnant of the developmental state, the new driving premise was to be a withdrawal of the state from the economy and the removal of all barriers, including exchange controls, protective tariffs and public ownership (and with such moves to be linked as well to massive social service cutbacks), to the operation of global market forces. (2001: 23)

What has happened with respect to Africa has happened, too, to differing degrees, with respect to other regions of the postcolonial world. In Latin America, for instance, the crippling burden of debt repayment has led such major states as Mexico, Argentina, and Brazil to the brink. Growing indebtedness has contrived to render Latin American states ever more dependent on foreign capital at the very moment when foreign capitalists, themselves concerned with profitability, have become unwilling to extend credit and eager to get the highest possible short-term returns on their loans and investments. "In the aftermath of the debt crisis" of the early 1980s, as Gwynne and Kay write,

> the international financial institutions were by and large able to dictate economic and social policies to the indebted countries, especially the weaker and smaller economies, through structural adjustment programs (SAPs). While Brazil and Mexico were able to negotiate better terms with the World Bank and foreign creditors, Bolivia and other countries were unable to do so. Peru, during the government of Alan García, tried to defy the international financial institutions but was severely punished for it and, after a change of government, the country had to accept the harsh reality of the new power of global capital and implement a SAP. SAPs were used as vehicles for introducing neoliberal policies . . . ; they had particularly negative consequences for the poor of Latin American economies as unemployment soared and wages and social welfare expenditures were drastically reduced. (1999: 6)

Throughout the postcolonial world since the early 1980s, Structural Adjustment Programs have been imposed as conditions for the distribution of loans, which the recipient nations are not in any position to refuse. They typically mandate huge cuts in government spending and social provision; the slashing of wages; the opening up of local markets to imported goods and the removal of all restrictions on foreign investment; the privatization of state enterprises and social services; and deregulation in all sectors to ensure that all developments are driven by the logic of the market rather than by social need or government policy (Bello 1999: 27). SAPs have become a favored means of disciplining postcolonial states, domesticating them, and rendering them subservient to the needs of the global market. They have also become a means of ensuring that postcolonial states retain their peripheral status, neither attempting to delink themselves from the world system nor ever imagining themselves capable of participating in it from any position of parity, let alone power.

Peter Wilkin has written that, among other things, "globalization" involves the attempt on the part of the "dominant social forces in the Northern or core nation-states . . . in conjunction with major corporate institutions, . . . to overturn the limited gains made by working people throughout the world-system in the post-war period" (1997: 24). Saul suggests similarly that, with respect to Africa, at least, the term "recolonization" would not be too strong (2001: 25). Bello, for his part, speaks of "rollback," arguing that the United States is seeking today

> to reinforce a set of global economic practices whose observance would favor the continued dominance of the status quo powers, in particular the United States. The drive to institutionalize these practices, which come under the rubric of "free markets" and "free trade," is designed to make other models of capitalist development illegitimate. It is directed, in particular, at those development strategies in which the state – through planning, industrial targetting, protecting markets, favoring local investors, or engaging in production itself – spearheads the process of development and makes "catching up with the North" a real possibility. It aims, in fact, to make it very difficult for new Japans, new South Koreas, and new Taiwans to emerge from the South.
>
> (1999: 86)

Such formulations enable us to conceptualize globalization in terms of the political renewal and refurbishment of imperial power in what, since the collapse of the Soviet Union in 1989, is today, unprecedentedly, a unipolar world. We need to bear in mind that the stage upon which the immediate post-1945 developments unfolded was that of a *pax Americana*. It is not only that the East–West conflict, the Cold War, continually buffeted postcolonial states about, obliging them to present themselves in certain lights, to implement certain policies and to shut down or abort others, in order to secure favor or forestall disfavor; it is also that decolonization – the emergence of new autocentric or would-be autocentric regimes in the postcolonial world – was from the outset viewed by the United States, the post-war hegemon, as an insurgent and potentially dangerous development, to be monitored closely and crushed whenever it seemed too threatening.

There is a remarkable moment in Norman Mailer's great novel of the Second World War, *The Naked and the Dead* (first published in 1949), in which the demented and rabidly right-wing American general, Cummings, lectures his liberal junior officer, Hearn, about the historical significance of the war for the United States:

Historically the purpose of this war is to translate America's potential into kinetic energy . . . When you've created power, materials, armies, they don't wither of their own accord. Our vacuum as a nation is filled with released power, and I can tell you that we're out of the backwaters of history now . . . For the past century the entire historical process has been working toward greater and greater consolidation of power . . . Your men of power in America, I can tell you, are becoming conscious of their real aims for the first time in our history. Watch. After the war our foreign policy is going to be far more naked, far less hypocritical than it has ever been. We're no longer going to cover our eyes with our left hand while our right is extending an imperialist paw.

(Mailer 1993: 327)

As though performing to Cummings's script, the United States in the post-1945 period has made it its business to export counter-revolution, working ceaselessly, sometimes directly, sometimes covertly, to undermine, subvert, and overthrow regimes and movements which it deems to have stood in opposition to its interests and political philosophy (see Blum 2003; Chomsky 1987: 203–405; 1992). Brennan refers, in this context, to the "orchestrated mass killing of leftists in Indonesia, Chile, Mozambique, Nicaragua, Colombia, Vietnam, Afghanistan, and elsewhere" (1997: 33); and any casual listing of the states and regimes which the United States has actively sought to destabilize must give one pause: such a listing must start, of course, with Cuba; but it might then move outwards, to such "middle American" and Caribbean nations as Guatemala, Nicaragua, Guyana, Grenada, and Jamaica; then on to such properly continental Latin American states as Venezuela, Bolivia, Peru, and Chile; then on to Africa (Angola, Zaire, Libya, Ghana, for instance); the "Middle East" (a wide arc from Somalia to Afghanistan, and including Israel/Palestine, Iran, Iraq, Syria, and Saudi Arabia); and Southeast Asia (most notably Vietnam, the Philippines, and Korea, but also Indonesia, Cambodia, and Laos). It is in this context that the developments that have occurred since 11 September 2001, and especially the illegal invasion and occupation of Iraq, must be situated. The historical significance of these developments has been well conceptualized by Jonathan Schell, as follows:

In the past 200 years, all of the earth's great territorial empires, whether dynastic or colonial, or both, have been destroyed. The list includes the Russian empire of the czars; the Austro-Hungarian Empire of the Habsburgs; the German empire of the Hohenzollerns, the Ottoman Empire, the Napoleonic Empire, the overseas empires of Holland, England, France, Belgium, Italy and Japan, Hitler's "thousand-year Reich" and the Soviet empire. They were brought down by a force that, to the indignation and astonishment of the imperialists, turned out to be irresistible: the resolve of peoples, no matter how few they were or how poor, to govern themselves.

With its takeover of Iraq, the United States is attempting to reverse this universal historical verdict. It is seeking to reinvent the imperial tradition and reintroduce imperial rule – and on a global scale – for the twenty-first century. Some elements, like the danger of weapons of mass destruction, are new. Yet any student of imperialism will be struck by the similarities between the old style of imperialism and the new: the gigantic disparity between the technical and military might of the conquerors and the conquered; the inextricable combination of rapacious commercial interest and geopolitical ambition and design; the distortion and erosion of domestic constitutions by the immense military establishments, overt and covert, required for foreign domination; the use of one colony as a stepping stone to seize others or pressure them into compliance with the imperial agenda; the appeal to jingoism on the home front.

(2003: 8)

This is the encircling political context implicated today by the term "postcolonial studies." The chapters that follow will attempt to explore how, and to what degree, postcolonial studies has moved to register and position itself relative to this political context.

NOTES

1 The subject is treated in Hobsbawm 1994; Kagarlitsky 2000. The failures – ranging from the Great Terror and collectivization to bureaucratization and the depoliticization of the population at large – are in any event taken more or less for granted in the West. Amin makes the interesting point that these should not blind us to the successes: the construction of "modern autocentric economies such as no country of peripheral capitalism has succeeded in doing"; and "a society in which the workers . . . won social rights (the right to work and social welfare) that have no match even in developed central capitalism (where some of the rights were belatedly won by great struggle, usually after the world wars, in part because of the fear of Communism), and even more so in crude peripheral capitalism" (1994: 179).

2 The literature on decolonization is too vast to be cited here. Wide-ranging discussions include Betts 1998; Cain and Hopkins 1993; and Young 2001.

3 I derive this phrase from the title of Achin Vanaik's book, *The Furies of Indian Communalism: Religion, Modernity and Secularization* (1997).

4 The phrase is Foucault's, of course, though I am using it in a sense not intended by Foucault in his own discussions of history and genealogy.

3

TAMARA SIVANANDAN

Anticolonialism, national liberation, and postcolonial nation formation

No, we do not want to catch up with anyone. What we want to do
is to go forward all the time, night and day, in the company of Man,
in the company of all men . . . It is a question of the Third World
starting a new history of Man, a history which will have regard to
the sometimes prodigious theses which Europe has put forward, but
which will also not forget Europe's crimes.

(Fanon 1968: 314–15)

Though rarely acknowledged as such in European history texts, or even
in the critical conceptions of much of the recent work undertaken in the
humanities subjects in the West, decolonization must surely signify as one
of the key global processes of the second half of the twentieth century. In
the two decades after the Second World War, around a hundred new states
emerged (some fifty in Africa alone), having won independence from colonial rule. The largest number of these decolonizations occurred in what had
been the British Empire, which, at its zenith in 1914, extended to some
12,700,000 square miles of the earth's surface, ranging from the Caribbean,
to the Indian sub-continent, Australia, and large sections of Africa and Southeast Asia. The decolonizations, most of which occurred within a matter of
years after the Second World War, involved an enormous loss for Britain, not
just economically and politically, but culturally too, for as Edward W. Said,
among others, has demonstrated so powerfully in his work, "most cultural
formations presumed the permanent primacy of the imperial power" (1993:
199).

Most of the territories under European colonial domination achieved independence only after prolonged struggle. Such struggles ranged from the
epic campaigns for liberation in India (which spanned Home Rule Leagues,
Gandhi's *satyagraha* or non-violent mass action, his Civil Disobedience campaigns, and the Quit India movement), to armed struggle, guerrilla warfare,
and revolution, as was the case with the Land and Freedom Armies ("Mau

Mau") in Kenya, or the campaigns in Algeria, Indonesia, Malaysia, Vietnam, Angola, and Zimbabwe. As a result, most of the new nation-states achieved independence in a spirit of heady expectancy, a spirit captured by one of the principal characters in Ayi Kwei Armah's novel, *The Beautyful Ones Are Not Yet Born*, who reflects about the moment of independence in Ghana: "We were ready here for big and beautiful things . . . The promise was so beautiful. Even those who were too young to understand it all knew that at last something good was being born. It was there. We were not deceived about that" (1981: 81, 85).

It is distressing, therefore, to consider the situation of many of these post-colonial societies some fifty years later, and to reflect on how little of that apparent promise has materialised. The rhetoric of anticolonial nationalism and the dreams of what independence would bring seem misguided in retrospect, for what is common to many – if not most – of these societies is their failure to attain the hoped-for social and economic freedoms for their peoples. What is to be found rather, is increasing division and oppression on the basis of class, ethnicity, religion, and gender; the failure of the economy to provide even basic necessities, never mind prosperity, for the mass of the people; a lack of democratic participation by the masses in the political sphere; and the continued – often increasing – structural dependence, economically, politically, and ideologically, on Western imperial powers. This is a failure which has allowed commentators in the West to regard the politics of the decolonized world after the departure of European rulers with contempt, to caricature it, as Said puts it, as amounting to little more than "a nasty mix of tribal chieftains, despotic barbarians and mindless fundamentalists" (1993: 276). Internally, it is clear that successive generations of leaders of postcolonial states have indeed tended, as Colin Legum has written, "to embark on policies that [have] created non-democratic, non-accountable, and non-transparent institutions at the heart of the economy" (1999: 44–45). And externally, by the same token, many postcolonial states are today so far from self-sufficiency, so indebted to and dependent on Western-based capital, that it is as though decolonization had never taken place. As John Saul writes, with particular reference to Africa, although his point can be generalized:

The term "recolonization" may remain more evocative metaphor than scientific concept. Nonetheless, it does capture much of the reality of contemporary Africa . . . The situation in which Africa finds itself, shaped both by its long established weaknesses and by the terms of its current subordination, makes it a mere taker of global capitalist signals, forced at least for the moment merely to slot into the role . . . that has been defined for it by capital and its functionaries beyond the continent's borders. (2001: 25)

It has become increasingly evident that while the ideology of anticolonial nationalism may well have been a necessary condition for the forging of the unity necessary to spearhead the resistance to colonial domination, it has proved an insufficient one to lead these societies successfully into a post-independence state of liberation – either from continuing Western imperialism, or from their own internal contradictions. This chapter will begin by providing a brief overview of the long history of resistance to colonial rule, move on to a consideration of the role of anticolonial nationalism in the independence movements, and look in detail at a couple of key examples of liberation struggle. It will then seek to explore and provide some explanation for the failures of so many postcolonial nations to achieve meaningful transformation of their societies after attaining political independence.

Resistance to colonial rule

They grabbed what they could get for the sake of what was to be got. It was just robbery with violence, aggravated murder on a great scale . . . The conquest of the earth, which mostly means the taking it away from those who have a different complexion or slightly flatter noses than ourselves, is not a pretty thing when you look at it too much.   (Conrad 1982: 10)

The sentiments above, expressed by the character Marlow in Conrad's *Heart of Darkness*, were describing Belgian colonial rule in Africa, but are evocative of the entire colonial enterprise, which caused enormous suffering at a global level. The imposition of colonial rule, however, did not go unchallenged. There were rebellions and resistance of various kinds to European colonial rule and domination from the time it began, whether in the Americas, the "Middle East," the South Pacific, South and Southeast Asia, or Africa. By the dawn of the twentieth century, such struggles were not only ubiquitous, but were becoming increasingly concerted and beginning to take the form of campaigns for national independence.

The forms that this resistance took varied hugely, in response to the wide range of forms and practices that comprised colonialism itself. In their *Third World Atlas*, Alan Thomas and Ben Crow usefully map the major risings against European rule in Africa, Asia, and the Americas between 1790 and 1890 (1997: 44–45). The struggles that they represent range from the resistance to initial European conquest (as in the wars between the British and the Zulu in the 1870s and the Dutch and the people of Aceh in Sumatra in 1873–74), to the numerous rebellions against European rule (such as the Morant Bay rebellion of 1865 in Jamaica and the "Indian Mutiny" of 1857–58), to movements of religious revivalism (such as the Dipo Negara rebellion of

1825–30 in what is now Indonesia and the Maori Pai Maire movement of 1864–67 in New Zealand), and outbreaks of guerrilla radicalism (such as the innumerable Maroon wars throughout the Caribbean). Thomas and Crow's maps bear testimony to the variety and impressive number of struggles that took place, and this despite the fact that, as they acknowledge, they have had to be very selective. There were many more struggles than they have been able to document.

Following James C. Scott's lead, we should also mention here the myriad "everyday" forms of resistance to colonialism, particularly among the colonized peasantry – forms of resistance whose intensity was too low for them to be considered "rebellious" or "insurrectionary," and which were therefore seldom documented in the colonial archives, but which nevertheless tell a story of continuous low-level resistance to domination. Scott's *Weapons of the Weak* is concerned with peasant resistance as class struggle rather than as anticolonial struggle. What he says, however, is directly relevant to the everyday forms of resistance to colonial domination:

> The fact is that, for all their importance when they do occur, peasant rebellions, let alone peasant "revolutions," are few and far between. Not only are the circumstances that favor large-scale peasant uprisings comparatively rare, but when they do appear the revolts that develop are nearly always crushed unceremoniously . . . For all these reasons it occurred to me that the emphasis on peasant rebellion was misplaced. Instead, it seemed far more important to understand what we might call *everyday* forms of peasant resistance – the prosaic but constant struggle between the peasantry and those who seek to extract labor, food, taxes, rents, and interest from them. Most of the forms this struggle takes stop well short of collective outright defiance. Here I have in mind the ordinary weapons of relatively powerless groups: foot dragging, dissimulation, false compliance, pilfering, feigned ignorance, slander, arson, sabotage, and so forth. (Scott 1985: 29)

Anticolonial nationalism in twentieth-century liberation struggles

Seek ye first the political kingdom, and all things shall be added unto you.
(Nkrumah 1971 (1957): 164)

It wasn't for the most part until the end of the First World War in 1918 that the numerous kinds of resistance to colonial rule began to coalesce into organized, militant, and self-conscious independence movements in the Anglophone and Francophone worlds.[1] The Second World War (1939–45) then gave new impetus to this stirring nationalism in the colonies, helping to mature it, not least because of the wartime experience of soldiers drawn in to fight for the "mother country" (often unwillingly, as, for example, in India where the British Viceroy declared war on Germany on behalf of the Indian Congress without even securing the agreement of its leaders). Not only did returning servicemen look for freedom for their own countries, having fought a *vita vya uhuru* (in Swahili, a "war for freedom") elsewhere, but inasmuch as colonized men had for the first time legitimately fought against and even killed Europeans, the strictures against such action were seen to be undermined. As the narrator in Ngugi wa Thiong'o's *Weep Not, Child* reflects, "[i]n spite of the fact that they were all white, they killed one another with poison, fire and big bombs that destroyed the land. They had even called the [African] people to help them in killing one another" (Ngugi 1988: 6).[2] Europe was thus subjected to a huge and disorienting change in perspective in the West/non-West relationship which it had not before experienced, confronted not just by activists and intellectuals from within the colonized world such as Frantz Fanon – who turned colonial thinking on its head by arguing that "Europe is literally the creation of the Third World. The wealth which smothers her is that which was stolen from the underdeveloped peoples" (Fanon 1968: 102; see Macey 2000) – but, as Said has argued, by Europeans such as Jean-Paul Sartre, who echoed Fanon – instead of the other way round – in declaring in his introduction to Fanon's *Wretched of the Earth* that, "there is nothing more consistent than a racist humanism since the European has only been able to become a man through creating slaves and monsters . . . in the past we made history and now it is being made of us" (Sartre 1968: 26, 27).

Progress towards decolonization was not uniform across the different colonies; in all cases, however, anticolonial nationalism played a tremendous part, and it remained a vital component of colonial and postcolonial politics until about the mid 1970s. Said writes, "It is a historical fact that nationalism – restoration of community, assertion of identity, emergence of new cultural practices – as a mobilized political force instigated and then advanced the struggle against Western domination everywhere in the non-European world. It is no more useful to oppose that than to oppose Newton's discovery of gravity" (1993: 218). It is important to note, however, that the term "nationalism" signifies all sorts of undifferentiated beliefs and practices, and while it is a useful term with which to identify the mobilizing force that united resistance against empire, it is important to try and establish more precisely what it entailed.

The problem is compounded by the fact that, as Timothy Brennan (1989) has pointed out, the question of the "nation" fell out of favor in metropolitan circles in the post-1945 period. Nationalism came to be regarded with impatience if not outright hostility: it was pronounced passé as an ideology by critics of both the right and the left. These negative judgments were provoked partly by the developments which had led to the Second World War, and which were taken to demonstrate that in the case of the relative latecomers to national consciousness among the industrialized nations – those, such as Italy, Germany, and Japan, in which nationalism had only emerged powerfully in the latter half of the nineteenth century, unlike in Britain, France, and Holland, where it had arisen much earlier – nationalism had tended to take a socially virulent form. Confronted with the spectre of "national socialism" (fascism), so recently defeated and at such heavy cost, European and American commentators in the post-war period tended to conceptualize nationalism not in terms of identity and identification, sovereignty and self-consciousness, as they might have done in the nineteenth-century, but in terms of imperialism and genocidal aggressivity: the implication of nationalism for them was not liberty and freedom from tyranny, but rather the embodiment of tyranny. Hence Eric Hobsbawm writes, with reference to Europe in the inter-war period (1918–39), that "[t]he logical implication of trying to create a continent neatly divided into coherent territorial states each inhabited by a separate ethnically and linguistically homogeneous population, was the mass expulsion or extermination of minorities. Such was and is the murderous *reductio ad absurdum* of nationalism in its territorial version, although this was not fully demonstrated until the 1940s" (1993: 133). Tom Nairn, too, denounces nationalism's "Janus-face," its capacity to be both communal and authoritarian (socialist and national-socialist), friendly and bellicose, and sees it as a reactionary throwback impeding the solidarities of "internationalism" (Nairn 1977; see Brennan 1989: 3).

Some historians and political scientists (Hobsbawm among them) have conceived of nationalism as an essentially European movement and philosophy, and inappropriate for Third-World countries which were either not ready for it or undeserving of it. These commentators have by and large been quite insensitive to the particular use made of nationalism by anticolonial forces, to its use, in other words, as a *defensive* ideology which served to unite resistance movements against empire – what Said has dubbed an "antinomian nationalism" in so far as it expressed antagonism rather than co-operation (Said 1993; see also Said 2000: 474–83; Chrisman, in this volume). It could be, too, that the Euro-American recoil from nationalism has in part been *due* to its successful use by nationalist movements in the developing world *against* Europe. For it is striking that whereas during the period of "high" colonialism Western spokespeople were perfectly happy to license its ideologies as the legitimate ones for consumption by colonized societies, these ideologies are suddenly deemed unsuitable for export in the *anti* colonial moment.

In the field of postcolonial studies, too, scholars have spent a considerable amount of time debating the question of the relation between the forms of anticolonial nationalism in the twentieth century and the forms of European nationalism in the eighteenth and nineteenth centuries (Anderson 1991; Chatterjee 1986, 1993; Loomba 1998a; Parry 1994, 2002; Spivak 1999). The debate has centered on the "modularity" – or otherwise – of the distinct European forms, which Benedict Anderson suggests became available for "pirating" by anticolonial nationalists in the course of their own particular campaigns. It is clear that the forms assumed by the anticolonial nationalisms were not the same as those of nineteenth-century Europe – of France or Germany or even the Italy of the *Risorgimento*[3] – even if they were sometimes modeled on them. In the work of some postcolonial theorists, however – Lisa Lowe and David Lloyd (1997), Christopher Miller (1990), and Gyan Prakash (2000), for example – anticolonial nationalist discourse is disparaged not only as derivatively Eurocentric, but also as élitist: it is the ideology of the colonially educated, European-oriented middle-class. Anticolonial nationalist discourse may indeed have been derivative and middle-class; but such a view not only fails, as Ranajit Guha argues, "to acknowledge, far less interpret, the contribution made by the people *on their own*, that is, *independently of the élite*, to the making and development of this nationalism" (Guha 1982b: 3), it also fails to take on board that anticolonial nationalists were able to adapt the received or imposed nationalist ideology for their own needs (just as in so many other historical moments, when forms of resistance have been forged out of subverting the very concepts or ideologies that have been used to oppress or constrain people). Said has commented on this as being "the partial tragedy of resistance, that it must to a certain degree work to recover forms already established or at least influenced or infiltrated by the culture of empire" (1993: 210). In any event this whole notion of derivation is clearly quite flawed, for the history of *all* cultures is, as Said among others has demonstrated, the history of cultural borrowings: "Cultures are not impermeable; just as Western science borrowed from Arabs, they had borrowed from India and Greece. Culture is never just a matter of ownership, of borrowing and lending with absolute debtors and creditors, but rather of appropriations, common experiences, and interdependencies of all kinds among different cultures. This is a universal norm" (1993: 217; see also Said 2000).

It is rather fascinating, nevertheless, in the context of these debates about the derivativeness of anticolonial nationalism, to take account of arguments made by Brennan and Basil Davidson in the course of their considerations about the postcolonial nation-state. Brennan notes that it would be inaccurate to assign the *origins* of the nation-state to Europe in the first place:

The nation-state is not only the by-product of the conditions created by European exploration; it was, more or less from the start, begun in acts of separation from the European centres of Madrid, Paris and London. If one discounts the civil wars of England and France, the first nationalists are not Frenchmen, Spaniards or Englishmen, but the creole middle classes of the New World – people like Simon Bolívar, Toussaint L'Ouverture and Ben Franklin. Thus Europe was not able to formulate its own national aspirations until after the markets made possible by imperial penetration had motivated them. In short, European nationalism was possible only because of what Europe was doing in its far-flung dominions.   (1989: 21)

Davidson's argument is elaborated in response partly to the colonialist discourse that characterized precolonial Africa as having no real history or political cultures, and partly to more recent Eurocentric attributions of the failures of postcolonial African nation-states to atavistic "tribalism." Most interestingly, given that in much recent thought on nationhood its origins are associated with the development of capitalism, Davidson holds not only that the history of precolonial tribalism (which he distinguishes quite sharply from more recent forms of tribalism) is "in every objective sense a history of nationalism" (1992: 75), but that some precolonial African social formations, at least, had all the attributes of modern nation-states and cannot be viewed in terms other than this. The Asante people, for example, had "a given territory, known territorial limits, a central government with police and army, a national language and law, and, beyond these, a constitutional embodiment in the form of a council called the Asanteman" (1992: 59). "Besides this" Davidson adds mischievously, in a stab at the lack of reflexivity (not to mention humility) of presumed Eurocentric interlocutors, "the Asante polity proceeded to behave in the best accredited manner of the European nation-state. Having achieved its own unity and independence, it went to war with neighbors and subdued them" (59)!

The question remains then: why adopt nationalism, an ideology seen to have been forged in the countries of the dominating imperial powers? In beginning to answer this question, let us recall the simple truth that colonialism was viciously oppressive – not only economically and politically, but also at the level of culture. The colonizing power gave nothing out of good will. To fight against it, there had to be the largest possible alliances, involving mass support or, as Davidson has pointed out, "the ideological basis for a wider unity than any known before" (1978: 156). The boundaries of colonized lands had been defined by European powers in a way which had denied and repressed existing communities. Colonial borders had been drawn up without any knowledge of the peoples or cultures whose lives they affected. Not only did this sometimes result in peoples with little historical connection being thrown together; it also often resulted in communities being torn apart, internally divided on the basis of administrative fiat. Obviously, too, the construction of frontiers and borders wreaked havoc with the cultures and self-sufficiencies of nomadic peoples, who did not farm the land but subsisted by moving great distances across it, typically living in co-operation with more settled pastoralists and agriculturalists. Popular or insurgent nationalism served to reclaim or imagine forms of community again, to forge collective political identities within these imposed boundaries sufficient to challenge colonial rule. It also served as an instrument of cultural resistance against a racist colonial discourse which had long denied all cultural value to its subject peoples, claiming them culturally incapable, therefore, of ruling themselves in the modern world. Neil Lazarus has argued that nationalism is indispensable in the Third World because "it is only on the terrain of the nation that an articulation between cosmopolitan intellectualism and popular consciousness can be forged; and *this* is important, in turn, because in the era of multinational capitalism it is only on the basis of such a universalistic articulation . . . that imperialism can be destabilised" (Lazarus 1994: 216). It is not that wider or different affiliations couldn't be or indeed weren't imagined – one has only to think, for example, of regional or political alliances such as Pan-Arabism, the Pan-African Congress, or the Non-Aligned Movement – but that the geo-political legacies of the previous 200 years provided a concrete basis on which the imperial powers – eager to retain influence even after independence – might be made to concede sovereignty.

National liberation struggles

Sooner or later they will leave our country, just as many people throughout history left many countries. The railways, ships, hospitals, factories, and schools will be ours and we'll speak their language without either a sense of guilt or a sense of gratitude. Once again we shall be as we were – ordinary people – and if we are lies we shall be lies of our own making.   (Salih 1969: 49–50)

Though India was not the first nation to win independence, the dissolution of the British Indian Empire which gave India and the newly created Muslim state of Pakistan their independence at midnight on 15 August 1947 was a key moment in the dynamic of the decolonizations of the twentieth century. This dynamic would reach a particular intensity in Africa a decade later, beginning with the independence of Ghana in 1957; and it would continue as a rising tide until the mid 1970s. In general, colonies which had been settled by Europeans took longer to decolonize. In these territories, the colonized population often needed to resort to armed struggle against entrenched settler regimes to get self-government, whereas territories governed from the metropolis tended to be susceptible to constitutional pressure and other forms of anticolonial action.

It would be impossible here to go into details of all the different independence movements, but a closer look at the struggles that took place against the British in India, where the nationalist movement for the main part did not have to engage in armed struggle to gain freedom, and in Algeria, where the struggle against French colonial rule was a bitter and violent one, will serve to illustrate the two categories – colonies governed from the metropolis and those with European settlers – mentioned above.

Nationalism and liberation in the Indian sub-continent

Historians have suggested that there were three key reasons for the granting of independence to India and Pakistan in 1947: the strength of Indian nationalism; the changing nature of British interests in India by the 1930s and 1940s; and the effects on both India and Britain of the Second World War. The late nineteenth century is often identified as the moment of the birth of modern nationalism in India, as it was in this period that the growing numbers of Western-educated Indians in the country – imbued with Western notions of liberalism and nationalism – began to press for reforms which would enable them to play a greater role in governing their own country. Their developing awareness of an "Indian" identity, reinforced by the overt racism of Europeans and Anglo-Indians, began to take a decisively political direction. (It is important to bear in mind, nevertheless, the point made by Bose and Jalal, among others, that subaltern anticolonialism predated any attempts by the urban élites to engage in the politics of mass mobilization against British rule [2002: 115; see also Shahid Amin 1995; Hardiman 1992]).

In December 1885, the Indian National Congress – the first all-India political organization – was founded. Initially a middle-class movement dominated by professionals and landlords whose aims and methods were moderate and reformist, its failure to make much headway led to the development of a more radical wing that began to question British rule. The radicals' call for a boycott of British goods went hand in hand with the *swadeshi* ("of our own country") movement which encouraged self-help through the production of home-made goods. Some groups went further and resorted to revolutionary violence and terror to attain their ends. In 1905 the first mass agitation – in the form of Non-cooperation – and the program of *swaraj* (self-rule) were launched to resist the British Viceroy's decision to partition Bengal. The Indian nationalists gained encouragement from Japan's defeat of Tsarist Russia in the war of 1904–5: the first time in modern history that an Asian country had defeated a European power.

Political expectations and awareness were raised further as a result of the First World War to which India contributed large numbers of troops, as well as huge amounts of raw materials and money. Although in 1906 the Muslim constituency had left the Indian National Congress, which was Hindu-dominated, to form the Muslim League, the Congress and League came to agreement at Lucknow in 1916 to forge a united front in working for home rule. The British state was prompted to respond by offering at least enough for the moderate nationalists. It introduced a Reforms Act in 1919 (the Montagu–Chelmsford reforms) which gave Indian politicians responsibility for certain aspects of provincial government, but conflicting with this was repressive legislation passed by the Government of India in the form of the 1919 Rowlatt Act which gave the police wide powers to investigate conspiracy against the Government, authorized detention without trial, and so on. The Rowlatt Act aroused widespread opposition throughout India. Against it, Gandhi – then an up-and-coming Congress leader – launched his first major campaign of civil disobedience and deployed his weapon of *satyagraha*, or non-violent mass action (first developed in his fight against racist laws during his time in South Africa). The official response to *satyagraha* included the massacre, early in 1919, of civilians at Jallianwallah Bagh in Amritsar, where General Dyer's troops opened fire on a large but unarmed and non-violent political gathering.

Over the next twenty or so years Gandhi emerged as the key figure in the Indian National Congress, leading it in three major campaigns against the British. The first was the Non-Cooperation movement of 1920–22 aimed at winning *swaraj*, in which Gandhi joined forces with the Khilafat movement organized by India's Muslim leaders who were incensed by the Allies' treatment of the Turkish sultan, their Khalifa or spiritual head. This was the first all-India mass movement uniting Hindus and Muslims, and involving sections of the peasantry as well. Communal problems, however, undermined national unity in the mid 1920s. Gandhi's next campaign was the Civil Disobedience movement which began in 1930 with the famous "salt march" and was finally brought to an end in 1934. His last major campaign was the Quit India movement of 1942, which was launched at a time when Britain was at war with Germany and Japan, and was considered an act of treachery.

Although the defeats suffered by the European powers in the Second World War at the hands of the Japanese were later reversed, British power in India was severely undermined as a consequence. (During the war, while some sections of the Indian population supported Britain in war, others formed an Indian National Army. Led by Subhas Chandra Bose, it actually fought against the British in Southeast Asia.) After 1945, negotiations between the nationalists and the British entered a new phase and it was only a matter of time until full independence was granted. The partition of India and the creation of the separate Muslim state of Pakistan in 1947, however, defeated Gandhi's political ambition for a united India at independence, and portended the communalist violence that haunts the sub-continent to the present.[4]

The liberation struggle in Algeria

Whereas Indian nationalism relied mainly on non-violent methods of protest which the British responded to with a mixture of reforms and repression, nationalism in Algeria ended up taking a very different course.

The French conquest of Algeria – positioned in the center of the Maghreb area of North Africa and populated mostly by Arab-Berber tribes – began in 1830 with their defeat of the ruling Ottoman Turks. Over the next hundred years or so, despite strong resistance at various stages, the French gradually colonized the country through settlement and a fierce policy of assimilation. In practice this meant that, at various stages, the *colons* (French and European settlers) managed to wipe out the distinctive features of native society and put Muslim institutions and culture, as well as the native population's land, under attack.[5]

Over the years, the French government repeatedly gave in to the demands of the French *colons* in Algeria, thus losing the ear of the more moderate Algerian nationalists. A more radical Governor-General, Violette, for example, was recalled to France in 1927 due to pressure from the representatives of the *colons* because of his view that the educated Muslim élite in Algeria should be given the vote. His book *L'Algérie vivra-t-elle?* ("Will Algeria Survive?"), published in 1931, warned that: "In fifteen or twenty years, there will be more than 10 million natives in Algeria, of whom about one million men and women will be steeped in French culture . . . If the Metropole does not intervene to insist on a more just and more humane point of view, Algeria is doomed" (qtd. Ageron 1991: 81).

Violette's book proved to be prescient. The anticolonial war fought in Algeria was among the longest and most bitterly fought in Africa and was in large part due to the obdurate refusal of the French to make reasonable concessions to the Algerian nationalists over a long period. In the 1930s the French again failed to meet even some of the demands of the nationalists because of opposition from the settlers, but this only served to enable the different nationalist parties to achieve relative unity in their demands and plans for action.

The defeat of France in the Second World War in 1940 seriously undermined its colonial position but, nevertheless, post-war French governments attempted to tighten control of their colonies. This policy led to a disastrous war for them in French Indochina (subsequently Vietnam), forcing a complete withdrawal from their Southeast Asian colonial empire after their critical defeat at Dien Bien Phu in 1954 at the hands of Ho Chi Minh and the Vietminh. This defeat was followed immediately by armed insurrection in Algeria, where, despite the Algerian people's surprising support for the French in the war effort, French repression had worsened. In Tunisia and Morocco, the French response to nationalist demands was more accommodating. In Algeria, however, this proved to be out of the question, since Algeria was regarded as an indissoluble part of France – the dogma of *Algérie française* being based on France's extensive economic investments in Algeria (reinforced by the discovery of oil and natural gas in the Sahara in the 1950s), and the presence of over a million *colons* (the so-called *Pied Noirs* or Black Legs) whose lobby continued to have a huge influence on French politics. Hence François Mitterand, then Minister of the Interior in France, was able to declare in 1954 that: "Algeria is France . . . Who among you would hesitate to use all means in order to save France?" (qtd. Hrbek 1999: 133).

The beginning of the armed struggle finally put an end to the French illusion that Algeria could be maintained as part of the French nation. Increasing numbers of Algerians – urban dwellers as well as peasants – joined the Armée de Libération Nationale (ALN) during the course of the struggle as French reprisals and terror fell on all Muslim Algerians indiscriminately. In 1956 the Front de Libération Nationale (FLN) became the main political organization of the Algerian people and at its congress in August reiterated the aim of its struggle as being a single, democratic, and socialist Algerian Republic which would be Arab and Muslim in character. The issue of Algerian independence now began to take on an international dimension as it became supported by Arab, Asian, and socialist countries: 1955 was, after all, the moment of the celebrated Bandung Conference of newly independent nations.

Muslim direct action was met by French reprisals, persecutions, and torture. The terror reached a peak in 1957 when the eight-month Battle of Algiers ended with the destruction of the ALN organization in that city, a pyrrhic victory for the French however, as it led to a wave of hatred for them in the whole of Muslim Algeria, and alienated public opinion in France which was shocked by the vicious methods of the French paratroopers. General de Gaulle, who took over the reins of power in France in 1958, made a last attempt, in response to the FLN's formation in September of a government in exile – the GPRA (Gouvernement Provisoire de la République Algérienne) – at winning back Algeria with his Constantine plan. When this too failed, and with the UN about to pass a resolution, in 1959, recognizing the right of the Algerian people to independence, the de Gaulle government announced that Algerians were to be given the right to self-determination, and began negotiations. These were difficult and protracted, and marred by the terrorist activity of the right-wing European OAS (Organisation Armée Secrète) during the autumn and winter of 1961–62. The ceasefire of March 1962, however, was followed by a referendum which resulted in a vote of 99.7 percent of the population in favor of independence. This period was marked again by a final outburst of vicious terrorism by the OAS fascists, which ultimately compromised the position of the Europeans in Algeria, thus occasioning their mass exodus. The July 1962 referendum, which led to an independent, Arab state of Algeria, brought to an end the 132 years of French colonial rule there. However, "the cost of liberation was heavy: it is estimated that nearly one million Algerians lost their lives; another two million were uprooted; ten thousand houses and buildings were destroyed during the war, and subsequently by OAS terrorism. No other African nation paid such a high and tragic price for its independence" (Hrbek 1999: 139). The heroism of the Algerian people, however, was a testimony to their determination never to give in, and symbolic of the determination of all the remaining colonized nations to achieve independence from European colonial rule.[6]

Decolonization and the forging of postcolonial nation-states

In a kind of collective failure of imagination, we learned that we simply could not think our way out of our pasts.　　　　　　　　(Rushdie 1995: 118)

Aijaz Ahmad offers a suggestive periodization for the emergence of large numbers of sovereign states through anticolonial movements in the twentieth century: a first phase, occupying the twenty years just after the Second World War, when states acquired independence under the leadership of their respective national bourgeoisies (some radical, others conservative) within the broad context of "modernization" and integration within the capitalist world system; and a second phase, occupying the period from 1965 to

1975, dominated by wars of national liberation that had a distinctly socialist bearing, despite the possibilities for successful socialist construction being limited due to the "level of prior economic development and the scale of imperialist devastations" (Ahmad 1992: 30). Examples from the first phase might include India, Morocco, Nigeria, Senegal, Jamaica, and Malaysia, with Algeria obviously presenting itself as an exception or special case; examples from the second phase might include Vietnam and Laos in Indochina, and the Lusophone African colonies of Mozambique, Angola, Cape Verde, and Guinea-Bissau. If one extended Ahmad's second phase beyond 1975 somewhat, one could also include Zimbabwe (which gained its independence in 1980).

The years immediately following independence, whether in Asia, Africa, or elsewhere, were full of optimism as the barriers of colonial racism were thrown aside and the possibilities for independent social, economic, and political development seemed within reach. In most cases, however, this optimism turned out to be ill-founded and as the hoped-for social and economic freedoms failed to materialize, disillusionment set in. Several commentators have pointed out that the rhetoric of anticolonialism was reductive: it implied that there was only one struggle to be waged, that being the defensive one against colonialism which would bring independence. It was assumed that independence by itself would deliver the looked-for freedoms; the ideal of freedom was rarely given a content. Julius Nyerere, Tanzania's first Prime Minister, reflected some fifteen years after his country's independence that:

> Most of Africa is now free from colonial rule . . . I know that we were right in our united demand for freedom from colonial rule. I know that we are right to support the demand for political freedom which is still being made by the peoples of southern Africa, without being deflected by considerations of what might come after. Our mistake was not in our demand for freedom; it was in the assumption that freedom – real freedom – would necessarily and with little trouble follow liberation from alien rule. (Nyerere 1979: 248–49)

In thinking about anticolonial nationalism today, half a century after decolonization, we need to bear in mind that there were – and remain – lots of different nationalisms in the Third World, some liberatory, some retrograde. As Ahmad has so firmly asserted,

> nationalism itself is not some unitary thing with some predetermined essence and value. There are hundreds of nationalisms in Asia and Africa today; some are progressive, others are not. Whether or not a nationalism will produce a progressive cultural practice depends, to put it in Gramscian terms, upon the political character of the power bloc which takes hold of it and utilizes it, as a material force, in the process of constituting its own hegemony. (1992: 102)

We need also to register the salient point that Davidson makes with respect to Africa, but which holds true for all decolonized societies, no matter what has happened in the years since independence, namely that "not even the worst news has been able to cancel out the tremendous central gain of anticolonial independence, perhaps the only gain at the end of the day . . . the reaffirmation of Africa's humanity" (1992: 196).

In recent years, there has been an increase in literature on the nationalism of the Third World, much of it given over to excoriation of the failures of the nation-states that independence delivered, and decrying nationalism in its cultural dimension as being illusion, myth, a false totalizing narrative. The criticism and disappointment have not been restricted to European writers alone. Partha Chatterjee, a leading member of the Subaltern Studies group, shows in his work on nationalism in the Indian context that anti-imperial nationalism can, in fact, become a panacea for *not* dealing with economic disparities, the need for social transformation, or the capture of the state by the national élite. He argues that the political success of nationalism in ending colonial rule has not signified a true resolution of the contradictions inherent in this discourse (a contradiction he conceptualizes as being ultimately that between "capital and the people-nation") and the evidence of this appears in the cases of separatist movements based on ethnic identities (proof of the incomplete resolution of the "national question") and more significantly in the "anti-modern, anti-Western strands of politics . . . preaching either a fundamentalist cultural revival or a utopian millennialism" (1986: 169; see also Chatterjee 1997a, 1997b; Hansen 1999; Vanaik 1997).

Much of the analysis of postcolonial societies has placed the onus of responsibility for their current problems on to the shoulders of the indigenous élites who assumed power after independence. For in most cases, decolonization gave power "not to revolutionary vanguards but to the national bourgeoisie poised for reintegration into subordinate positions within the imperialist structure" (Ahmad 1992: 28). In nation after nation, the native élites moved, as they took over the state structures (structures which, significantly, predated nationalist sentiment and activity, having been established by the colonizers), to consolidate their power and wealth – to don, in Ariel Dorfman's coinage, the "Empire's Old Clothes" – and failed either to take their countries out of dependency or to transform social structures in the interests of the mass of the people. Even where they tried, they usually failed. Having won the war, we might say, they proceeded to lose the peace.[7] "There is no doubt that the great tide of national liberation (1945–1975) was marked by real gains for Africa, Asia, and Latin America," Samir Amin writes. "But the advances were inadequate since they fell short of their goal.

By the end of the postwar cycle, third world states were turned back into a comprador role" (1994: 30).

In many cases, it cannot even be said that the new leaders really tried. Having, many of them, received an education under colonialism (finished off very often in its élite institutions, military or academic – Sandhurst, Oxbridge, the Sorbonne) which paradoxically made them conscious of, and unhappy with, the colonial racism that held them down, they donned native garb to unite their peoples in the independence struggle. Their culture and mentality, however, remained deeply dependent and derivative, and their rule, far from being a search for the autonomous development of their societies, in effect continued the domination and exploitation of the people begun by imperialism, but this time in indigenous form. Peter Worsley has described the nationalist ambition of this cohort as aiming to overthrow "not capitalism, but *foreign* capitalism . . . All that was needed, it seemed, was control of one's own political institutions. The support of the masses for that project was won by telling them that independence was the precondition for economic expansion which would benefit everyone" (1984: 2). These rulers weren't necessarily conscious agents of capitalism from the beginning; they constituted rather a political élite which used state power in order to acquire vast wealth at the expense of the mass of the population, and to turn themselves into a propertied class. They were a *comprador* bourgeoisie – or a "lumpen" one to use Andre Gunder Frank's description (1972) from the Latin American context – rather than a "proper" bourgeoisie, as they were unable themselves to carry out the historic bourgeois project – that of creating capitalist societies. Most merely gave in to pressure from the capitalist world and contented themselves with self-enrichment while the economic bases of the states over which they presided remained unreconstructed. Nyerere has commented:

> Some of our people identify their own personal interests with the existing neo-colonial situation . . . the local agents of foreign capitalists, and . . . the local capitalists who have developed in the shadow of large foreign enterprises. Such people may feel that their wealth and status depend upon the continued dominance of the external economic power . . . They point to the statistics of their Gross National Product as an example of what can be gained from it – rather in the manner of a high-class prostitute glorying in her furs and jewels! (1979: 253–54)

Such rulers failed in particular to establish vital links with the poor or dispossessed of their nations, or to extend democratic participation to them. By the late 1960s, aided by Western or Eastern bloc powers whose own interests coincided with strong rulers, many of these societies were under some kind of authoritarian regime (often military) or one-party state, the elimination of opposition usually being justified on the grounds that national unity – essential for economic growth – was threatened by tribalism or separatism. Such regimes were often overthrown only to be replaced in turn by some new form of dictatorship. Raymond Betts points out that "some 75 *coups d'etat*, mostly military in nature, occurred in the former colonial world in the first three decades of independence" (1998: 67). The examples that he cites – Ghana, Nigeria, Indonesia, the Philippines, Algeria – demonstrate the ubiquitous nature of the phenomenon. One example in particular is telling: Betts writes of Mobutu Sese Seko, who seized power in Zaire (formerly Congo) in 1965 and was himself deposed only in 1997, that he "oppressed his people, imprisoned his opposition, and drained the nation of its wealth, with his personal financial wealth estimated in billions of dollars. Zaire . . . was the richest African nation in terms of natural resources. At the end of Mobutu's reign, its population was one of the poorest" (68). Even in a country like India, still parading itself as one of the world's biggest democracies, there have been numerous instances of the abuse of power, starting, most notably, with Indira Gandhi's assumption of Emergency powers for a two-year period in the mid 1970s.

Although the national élites must bear responsibility for their part in the failure to realize liberationist ideals, one must not underestimate the pressures of the institutions they inherited, and the continuing and constitutive presence of imperialism as a world system. To quote Nyerere again, "If deliberate countervailing action is not taken, external economic forces determine the nature of the economy a country shall have, what investment shall be undertaken and where, and what kind of development – if any – will take place within our national borders. Neo-colonialism is a very real, and very severe, limitation on national sovereignty" (1979: 251–52). Decolonization, in fact, occurred precisely in a period which witnessed historically unprecedented expansion of trade internationally, and a consequent unification and binding together (subject to the principle of uneven and combined development) of the world system as a whole (see Lazarus, chapter 2 in this volume). This expansion gave capital increased access to markets in the newly decolonized zones too. As Ahmad has explained,

> this consolidation and post-war expansion in all the homelands of advanced capital, reflected as much in the imperialist military machines as in the globalized corporate economy, meant that throughout this period capital was to command enormous power to condemn every country which even attempted to introduce socialism to a perpetual war economy under conditions of acute scarcity and low levels of social development, with no prior experience of even a bourgeois democracy, let alone a socialist one. (1992: 22)

Since the onset of the world capitalist slump in the early 1970s – and the rise to global hegemony of neoliberal ideology, which has followed in its wake, and has itself led to the imposition of austerity packages and Structural Adjustment Programs on Third-World states, all under the sign of "globalization" – the possibilities for escaping deepening poverty and indebtedness, let alone for achieving growth, in the Third World seem further away than ever. Today, more than half the export earnings of many countries are absorbed by the servicing of foreign debt. Everywhere, economic and political dependency on rich countries is increasing; the possibilities for radical renewal diminishing. "Although the developing world as a whole made economic progress in the last quarter of the twentieth century," Legum has written:

> the number of people living in "absolute poverty" – a description coined by Robert McNamara when he was president of the World Bank – increased to more than one billion . . . McNamara's definition of the "absolute poor" are those living, literally, on the margin of life. Their lives are so characterized by malnutrition, illiteracy, and disease as to be beneath any reasonable definition of human beings. Those who have seen "the absolute poor" swarming in homeless family groups in India will instantly recognize this condition; up to the mid-twentieth century these conditions were comparatively rare in most of Africa, but this is no longer true . . . The urban explosion and the flight from an impoverished countryside has begun to produce conditions of absolute misery in squatters' camps and slums across the continent. (1999: 84)

Much the same point has also been made by Walden Bello, though in his case with a sharper critical focus, directed against those responsible (in the North and the South) for the imposition of neoliberal policies upon the huge masses of the world's population. Bello argues that what he calls "rollback" in the post-1975 period – the imperialist "structural resubordination [of the South] to the North via the dismantling of the economic role of the state" – has had more or less identical effects "under leaders as politically diverse as the Peronist Carlos Menem in Argentina, the social democrat Michael Manley in Jamaica, the socialist Jerry Rawlings in Ghana, the Nasserite Hosni Mubarak in Egypt and the technocrat Carlos Salinas de Gortari in Mexico" (Bello 1999: 70). Despite the widespread conversion of postcolonial leaders to the neoliberal faith (one could add Thabo Mbeki of South Africa, Mahathir Mohamad of Malaysia, and Atal Behari Vajpayee of India to the list provided by Bello), the sweeping imposition of neoliberal policies upon postcolonial societies (often termed "shock treatment") has generally had disastrous consequences. While there have been some positive results – plausible rates of economic growth, for instance – these have tended to be concentrated among the better-off sectors of society; and they

have come at the cost of much greater social inequality, the increasing dis-
enfranchisement and exclusion of the poor from the political process, and
huge reductions in states' already slender social provision (Gwynne and Kay
1999).

Surveying the failures of nation-forming in Africa, Lazarus has criticized
radical anticolonial intellectuals and political leaders for having been too
much predisposed to what he terms a "messianic" and middle-class conception of decolonization as a revolutionary process, and for having so roman-
ticized the resistance movements that they underestimated the dissensions
within them. This is his charge against Fanon, for example (Lazarus 1990,
1994, 1999a). Nevertheless, it is important to remember that, at their best,
the arguments for national resistance *were* critical and self-reflective, demonstrating an awareness of the pitfalls of the kinds of triumphalism needed to
spearhead resistance, but necessarily carrying too the imaginative recon-
ceptions of society and culture which would be needed in order to avoid
old oppressions and injustices. Indeed, even the bourgeois inheritors of the
new political kingdoms often showed an awareness of what they were up
against. Kwame Nkrumah, for example, when offered the political leadership of what would become the state of Ghana after independence, told his
voters that "there is a great risk in accepting office under this new constitution which still makes us half-slaves and half-free." He warned of the need
for "vigilance and moral courage" in withstanding the temptations of "temporary personal advantage," given that "bribery and corruption, both moral
and factual, have eaten into the whole fabric of our society and these must
be stamped out if we are to achieve any progress" (qtd. Davidson 1992:
163).

The writings of Frantz Fanon and Amilcar Cabral are prescient in their
understanding of the potential perils of inheriting the postcolonial nation-
state together with its institutions (see Chrisman, in this volume). Fanon's
celebrated essay, "The Pitfalls of National Consciousness," in *The Wretched
of the Earth*, is compellingly and disturbingly accurate in its anticipation
of the weaknesses and potential dangers of nationalist ideology. He argues
that the national bourgeoisie that takes over from colonial rule is a parasitic
social fraction – he terms it a "privileged caste" – which lacks the dynamism
necessary to enable it to develop the economic base of the country so that
it ends up delivering the economy, for the sake of its own betterment, to
the ex-colonial power and neo-colonialism. He anticipates that the sort of
nationalism that this class invokes can crumble into regionalism, tribalism,
and religious splits. He warns that if the leadership in postcolonial Africa
remains with the national bourgeoisie, the whole momentum of the liberation
struggle will be lost. This is not for him an inevitable process, however. He

distinguishes between the bourgeois nationalism which represents the interests of the indigenous élites, and a liberationist, anti-imperial, internationalist nationalism (which Lazarus, borrowing the term from Anouar Abdel-Malek, terms "nationalitarianism" [Lazarus 1994; Abdel-Malek 1981]) which views the attainment of nationhood as a necessary but first step towards the wholesale reconstruction of society in the postcolonial era (Fanon 1968).

Cabral, theorist and activist in the struggle against Portuguese colonialism in the West African colony of Guiné and Cape Verde, a founder member of the anticolonial African Independence Party there (PAIGC), produced copious speeches and essays to explain himself at every stage in the struggle – to both internal and external audiences. Two key texts, "The Weapon of Theory," the transcript of a speech given in Havana in January 1966, and "National Liberation and Culture," the Eduardo Mondlane Memorial Lecture delivered at Syracuse University in the United States in 1970, are seminal works in the theory and practice of national liberation struggle, absolutely realistic in their anticipation of the pitfalls of national independence. Cabral argued that as Guiné had no "national bourgeoisie" or working class conscious of its nature or potential (this was a similar situation to other colonized societies), the only possible agent for initiating change was the embryonic petty bourgeoisie because through its urban, literate, and semi-privileged position in colonial society, it had learned to manipulate state institutions, and it was the social group soonest able to become aware of the nature of colonial domination and to come to resent it:

> events have shown that the only social stratum capable both of having consciousness in the first place of the reality of imperialist domination and of handling the State apparatuses inherited from that domination is the native petty bourgeoisie . . . By nature of its objective and subjective position (higher standard of living than that of the masses, more frequent humiliation, higher grade of education and political culture, etc.) it is the stratum that soonest becomes aware of the need to rid itself of foreign domination.   (1969: 108)

Cabral argued that, whilst in this situation the development of a fully fledged struggle for national liberation had to be led by a vanguard party drawn from a sector of the petty bourgeoisie, nevertheless, no worthwhile success could be gained without the growing and effective support and involvement of the mass of the people, here the rural peasantry. He fully realized that for the native petty bourgeoisie to inherit the state after colonialist rule, "this specific inevitability in our situation," was a potential "weakness for the liberation movement" (108). This was the occasion for his developing one of his best-known arguments: on the necessity for this stratum, after independence, to commit suicide in its class consciousness and class interests if it were to lead the country *beyond* merely reformist (neo-colonialist or collaborationist) nationalism. He stated:

> In order not to betray these objectives [of national liberation], the petty bour-
> geoisie has only one choice: to strengthen its revolutionary consciousness, to
> reject the temptations of becoming more bourgeois and the natural concerns
> of its class mentality . . . the revolutionary petty bourgeoisie must be capable of
> committing suicide as a class in order to be reborn as revolutionary workers,
> completely identified with the deepest aspirations of the people to which they
> belong.   (110)

Nevertheless, his optimism about liberation struggle was of no utopian kind. As Davidson, who knew him personally, has commented: Cabral, while he would have condemned it, would not have been greatly surprised by the resort to a *coup d'état* in November 1980 in the independent Guinea-Bissau, for "the dialectics of process were what, among many other things, he thoroughly understood" (Davidson 1986: 38; see also Davidson 1989).

Cabral was clear then that the aim of resistance struggles was not merely independence, but a national liberation which involved a struggle against *neo-colonialism* too, and this struggle, for him, was a revolutionary one: "the *liberation struggle is a revolution* and . . . it does not finish at the moment when the national flag is raised and the national anthem played" (1969: 107; emphasis in original). He argued in his essay on "National Liberation and Culture" that this involved initiating (and maintaining) a culture-changing process. This initiative could be gained only through the vanguard's steady and continued converting of rural support into participation, for it was participation that held culture-changing value. (This was particularly important in a society like Guiné where the people were deeply provincial.) The armed struggle, he argued, implies "a veritable forced march along the road to cultural progress" (1973: 55) which on the part of the leaders of the movement meant getting to know the rural population better, enriching their culture by knowledge of the peasant ones; and, on the part of the mass of the workers, meant, for example, that they must "lose the complexes which constrained them in their relationships with other ethnic and social groups . . . break the bonds of the village universe to integrate progressively into the country and the world" (54). His list of some of the profound changes necessary in the life of the population if the liberation struggle is to succeed in its "march along the road to cultural progress" must surely offer a blueprint for any society seeking liberation:

> the armed liberation struggle requires the mobilization and organization of
> a significant majority of the population, the political and moral unity of the
> various social classes, the efficient use of modern arms and of other means of

war, the progressive liquidation of the remnants of tribal mentality, and the rejection of social and religious rules and taboos which inhibit development of the struggle (gerontocracies, nepotism, social inferiority of women, rites and practices which are incompatible with the rational and national character of the struggle, etc.) . . . Consider these features inherent in an armed liberation struggle: the practice of democracy, of criticism and self-criticism, the increasing responsibility of populations for the direction of their lives, literacy work, creation of schools and health services, training of cadres from peasant and worker backgrounds – and many other achievements.   (54–55)

To maintain this progress after independence required a liberation movement which would be capable of continuing to act as the determinant of an independent and progressive culture, a culture which would draw critically on the best of diverse local cultures, but also on what was of value in other cultures.

This latter is a crucial point given the regression by several post-independence states into various forms of nativism, ethnicism or fundamentalism based on some distorted "return to the source" of their precolonial history. For as part of the resistance against colonialism's racist cultural discourse which had repressed the original history and cultures of colonized peoples through assertion of their inferiority or non-existence, some intellectuals and leaders valorized and sought to re-inscribe notions of "pure" precolonial cultures at the center of liberation struggles. (The discourse of *Hindutva* – "Hindu-ness" – provides a socially malign example; Léopold Sédar Senghor's particular articulation of *négritude* a more innocuous one.) Said has argued most passionately against such nativisms, for, "[t]o leave the historical world for the metaphysics of essences like *négritude*, Irishness, Islam or Catholicism is to abandon history for essentializations, that have the power to turn human beings against each other" (1993: 228–29). It is clear from the writings of both Cabral and Fanon that, while they saw the necessity of rediscovering and reasserting the universal value of native cultures, they were not arguing for a reductive vision of culture which would trap it in some utopian and mummified version of a traditional past. They were aware that if their societies were to survive, they needed to continue to develop. Fanon, critical of the elevation of custom into culture since this locked culture into a past detached from the positive effects of contemporary events argued that, "A national culture is not a folklore nor an abstract populism that believes it can discover the people's true nature . . . [It] is the whole body of efforts made by a people in the sphere of thought" (1968: 233). Cabral looked for development that assumed entirely new dimensions of independent self-realization and that translated into a "significant leap forward of the culture." He argued, "Our cultural resistance [to colonialism] consists in the following: *while we scrap colonial culture and the negative aspects of our own culture*, whether in our character or in our environment, *we have to create a new culture*, also based on our traditions but respecting everything that the world today has conquered for the service of mankind" (qtd. Davidson 1986: 36; my emphasis). For his part, Aimé Césaire – a co-founder of *négritude* with Senghor, though distinctly more materialist in his thinking – wrote, "the problem is not to make a utopian and sterile attempt to repeat the past, but to go beyond. It is not a dead society that we want to revive. We leave that to those who go in for exoticism . . . It is a new society . . . with all the productive power of modern times, warm with all the fraternity of olden days" (1972: 31).

Conclusion

Democracy is a habit, and habits take a long time to develop.

(Legum 1999: 59)

Although the problems of liberation have not yet by any means been resolved, the ideals that informed the theories of those such as Fanon and Cabral remain valid and need to be reasserted and made relevant to modern problems. Moreover, these cannot be dismissed as merely utopian. As Guha has pointed out, there always has been – as there still is – a "politics of the people," which remains autonomous from the domain of élite politics and which, while being equally modern, is "distinguished by its relatively greater depth in time as well as structure" (1982b: 4). The early work of the Subaltern Studies group demonstrated this with regard to peasant resistance in India, for example, and various writers such as Kumari Jayawardena (1986) have documented the struggles for the emancipation of women which were organically related to the fight for national liberation (see also Mallon 1995; Moghadam 1994; Urdang 1989). This "subaltern" activity is still everywhere chipping away at injustices. Davidson has shown in his work on Africa, for example, that whereas the ruling élite has maintained as sacred the frontiers maintained by colonialism, for "what else after all, could guarantee [their] privilege and power . . . ?", the common people subvert this "foreign and unwanted imposition" by their "incessant emigration and immigration across these lines on the map, as well as by their smuggling enterprises" (1986: 44; 1992). This is not, of course, to suggest that migration and smuggling constitute the route to future development, but that oppressed peoples everywhere continue to find myriad ways of resisting exploitation. Because, as Worsley has written, Third World nations have a common referent in the world – "the unequal institutionalized distribution of wealth and illth on a world scale" (in other words, neo-colonialism is a world system) – the need is thus to develop communities and cultures of resistance which, while not denying the rights and needs of autonomous national or cultural identities, move beyond narrow identitarian categories to reach for new levels of unity; which connect popular struggles with the consciousness of a new universality – the "universal culture, aiming at perfect integration in the contemporary world" that Cabral argued for; the international consciousness that was also part of Fanon's vision, evident in *The Wretched of the Earth* throughout which, as Said notes, "Fanon wants somehow to bind the European as well as the native together in a new non-adversarial community of awareness and anti-imperialism" (1993: 274). As Aimé Césaire so famously put it in his poem, "Notebook of a Return to the Native Land": "no race has a monopoly on beauty, on intelligence, on strength / and there is room for everyone at the convocation of conquest" (1983: 77).

NOTES

1 The qualification, "Anglophone and Francophone worlds" is important here, since, in the Hispanophone and Lusophone worlds of Latin America, the struggles for national liberation had typically taken place, and political independence been won, a century earlier, mostly in the single generation from 1808 to 1825. For a discussion of the significance of this fact, and of the neglect of Latin America in postcolonial studies, see Coronil, in this volume.

2 Among the most sustained and telling aesthetic representations of this theme is *Camp de Thiaroye*, a 1989 film by the Senegalese writer and filmmaker, Ousmane Sembene, which deals with the demobilization of French West African soldiers after the Second World War.

3 On the *Risorgimento*, Gramsci's "Notes on Italian History" (in Gramsci 1971) is still unsurpassed. For a discussion of Gramsci's reading of the *Risorgimento* and its relevance to postcolonial studies, see Brennan 2001. On France see Weber 1976; on Germany, Craig 1981 and Stern 1974. The standard general studies include Gellner 1983; Hobsbawm 1987, 1993; Hroch 1985; and Tilly 1975.

4 The scholarly literature on decolonization in India is, of course, vast. Useful general studies include Alam 1999; Aloysius 1997; Bayly 1998; Bose and Jalal 2002; Cain and Hopkins 1993; Chandavarkar 1998; Chandra 1979; Chandra *et al.* 1989; Datta Gupta 1980; Sarkar 1989a; Vanaik 1990; Wolpert 1982.

5 Assia Djebar's novel, *Fantasia: An Algerian Cavalcade* (1993), offers an extraordinarily evocative meditation on the 130-odd years of the French colonization of Algeria.

6 On Algeria, and the war of national liberation there from 1954 to 1962, see, in addition to Ageron 1991 and Hrbek 1999, Samir Amin 1970; Caute 1970; Clayton 1994; Macey 2000; Ruedy 1992; Talbott 1981; Tlemcani 1986; Young 2001.

7 This formulation is suggested by Gabriel Kolko's two-part study of Vietnam: the optimistic *Anatomy of a War* (1986), followed in 1997 by the fiercely critical *Anatomy of a Peace*.

4

BENITA PARRY

The institutionalization of postcolonial studies

Beginnings: colonial discourse analysis

Those wanting to understand the beginnings and development of postcolonial studies will readily find numerous Introductions, Readers, Companions, monographs, and journal articles offering a variety of definitions and genealogies, advising further reading, and proposing new objects of study.[1] If the scale of publications testifies to the rapid assimilation of a disparate interdisciplinary undertaking within academic curricula, then the range of analytic strategies suggests a volatile and contested discussion. Yet despite a project in which poststructuralists vie with Marxists, culturalists with materialists, textualists with realists, postcolonial criticism has come to be identified as postmodernist in its orientation – an alignment promoted more or less actively by prominent critics in the field. One consequence of this is that there has been a fluid, polysemic, and ambiguous usage of the term "postcolonial" within and beyond specialist circles. The plenitude of signification is such that "postcolonial" can indicate a historical transition, an achieved epoch, a cultural location, a theoretical stance – indeed, in the spirit of mastery favored by Humpty Dumpty in his dealings with language, whatever an author chooses it to mean.[2] As a result it is not uncommon to find the term used in connection with any discursive contest against oppression or marginalization – such as feminist or queer or disability studies.

Aijaz Ahmad has recalled that "the first major debate on the idea of the postcolonial took place . . . not in cultural studies but in political theory where the object of inquiry was 'the postcolonial state,'" and he notes that because these discussions were conducted in Marxist terms, the categories of colonialism and postcolonialism initially designated "identifiable structural shifts in state and society" (1995a: 5). Such connotations are distinct from the manifestly unsustainable contemporary use of the word "postcolonial" as a temporal category where the "colonial" is understood to have been superseded or left behind and the "postcolonial" establishment of

66

formally independent regimes is perceived as signalling the end of North/ South inequalities. Indeed, some dissenting critics argue that the very term, "postcolonial," mystifies the contemporary situation, which is marked by the *persistence* of an international stratification of labor and resources and would therefore more appropriately be classified as late imperialism (Miyoshi 1993; Dirlik 1997). Still other critics have made a case for defining "the post-colonial domain" in terms of the extent to which peripheral societies continue to be subjected to or are disengaged from metropolitan forces (Coronil 1992: 101) – a provocative usage, but one limited in its application by the constraints on recently constituted and legally sovereign states to detach themselves from a global system in which they are not the major players.

Historicizing colonialism's aftermath has not however been foremost on the agenda of most of the high-profile theorists, who have been preoccupied instead with authoring a suitable "postcolonial positionality." According to one such theorist, postcoloniality involves the assumption of a decon-structive philosophical position towards the logocentrism and identitarian metaphysics underpinning Western knowledge (Spivak 1988b, 1990). Hence the postcolonial critic, who occupies "the heritage of imperialism intimately but deconstructively," is enjoined to intervene in the structure of which s/he is a part and "to change something that . . . [s/he] is obliged to inhabit" by tampering with "the authority of Europe's story-lines . . . reversing, dis-placing and seizing the apparatus of value-coding" (Spivak 1990: 56). Here the purpose of postcolonial critique is understood as being to dismantle and displace the truth-claims of Eurocentric discourses;[3] while in the words of another eminent critic, the burden of the postcolonial undertaking is "to intervene in and interrupt the Western discourses on modernity" (Bhabha 1994: 241). The location occupied by such criticism has been glossed as "neither inside nor outside the history of western domination but in a tan-gential relation to it" (Prakash 1993: 16–17) – this double or semi-detached consciousness, it is maintained, facilitating an understanding of colonialism and its legacies different from the narratives handed down either by colo-nialism or by anticolonialist movements, and thus throwing the claims of both official and dissident historiographies into disarray.

Such intense self-reflection, focused on the critic's obligation to under-mine the text of colonial authority as well as to install a distance from the concepts of anticolonialist theory, marked the beginnings of postcolonial studies in the late 1970s and early 1980s in what was then called "colo-nial discourse analysis." To understand both the achievements and prob-lems of the postcolonial studies project it is helpful to revisit this inaugural moment and to trace its subsequent trajectory. Colonial discourse analysis coincided with the institutionalization in the early 1980s of an extensive platform of research initiatives, including gender, feminist, African American, "ethnic," and gay studies. Together these undertakings examined how dominant systems of knowledge had effected the discursive relegation and institutional oppression of subordinated communities and marginalized cultural traditions (JanMohamed and Lloyd 1990). What emerged from these enquiries took on the form of innovative cross-disciplinary exercises that either were belatedly accommodated within existing university departments (English, Anthropology, Music, Art History, for instance) or else generated new ones (Women's Studies, African American Studies, Asian American Studies, Cultural Studies, etc.). The early exponents of colonial discourse analysis were often confronted by considerable resistance from scholars and critics wedded to long-established disciplinary paradigms. Whereas the aversion of mainstream scholars to the disturbance of existing critical norms was typically ideological, it often manifested itself as hostility to the admittedly exorbitant claims of "theory" as the meta-discourse of the emergent scholarship.

At its inception, colonial discourse analysis concentrated on exposing the making, operation, and effects of colonialist ideology; and although contestation of colonialism's authorized version had begun decades previously within the political and intellectual cultures of anticolonial movements, the endeavor presented itself as new-born – and, in the sense that it had recourse to a set of recently devised critical paradigms, it was indeed distinct from the earlier critiques. Thus Spivak proposed that postcolonial criticism could seize the opportunity afforded by Derrida's deconstruction of the discursive apparatus to occidental reason, since his "sustained and developing work on the *mechanics* of the constitution of the Other" could be put to "much greater analytic and interventionist advantage than invocations of the *authenticity* of the other" (1988b: 294). For Bhabha (1994) it was the language model that offered the means to explain colonialism's past and the postcolonial present by opening up the enunciative act to the insights of psychoanalytic theory. Of special significance to the new scholarship was the disposal of poststructuralist methodology – even though the political purchase and even the epistemological tenability of this methodology were fiercely questioned from the outset. (For instance, one disbelieving critic wrote that poststructuralism contrived to block the "appeal to any kind of real-world knowledge and experience" and failed "to acknowledge any difference . . . between historical fact and literary or fictive representation" [Norris 1994: 112; 1993: 182]). However, so influential did the poststructuralist modes prove that, although the theoretical practices and trajectories of the pioneering critics (these are invariably cited as Spivak, Bhabha, and Edward W. Said) were very different from one another, their work was appropriated by participants to license the privileging of "discourse" as the model of social practice, and consequently to promote an incuriosity about enabling socio-economic and political institutions.

Yet if we consider how Said himself appropriated Foucault's notion of knowledge as implicated in relations of power, we see that for him the material and social determinants of discourse are always in place. For Said, the study of colonial discourse was enabled by Foucault's "understanding of how the will to exercise dominant control in society and history, has also discovered a way to clothe, disguise, rarefy, and wrap itself systematically in the language of truth, discipline, rationality, utilitarian value, and knowledge" (Said 1984: 216). According to Peter Hulme, the disciplinary formation known as colonial discourse analysis came into being as a *critique* of the continental theoretical work it enlisted, and it was Said's singular achievement to have brought "the rhetorical power of the textual readings offered by discourse analysis [together . . .] with a 'real' world of domination and exploitation, usually analysed by a Marxism hostile to poststructuralism's epistemological scepticism" (Hulme 1989: 3). Thus although Said recognized "the scrupulously ethnocentric nature" of Foucault's undertaking, Hulme argues that he chose to emphasize the inherent *possibilities* of this work in the interests of extending to a global terrain the concept of discourse with the constant implication of textuality within networks of history, power, knowledge, and society.

In acknowledging a debt simultaneously to poststructuralist theory, Western Marxism, and Anglo-American cultural criticism, Said not only interrogated the privileged inclusions and absences of these modes, observing their massive indifference to colonialism as *constitutive* of metropolitan society and culture; he also called attention to the failure of their authors to recognize that anticolonialist critics such as Aimé Césaire, Frantz Fanon, C. L. R. James, and George Antonius had confronted the contradictions and hierarchies in the institutionalized thought of the metropoles long before prominent theorists in Europe and North America got around to doing so. Said's own writings, then, can be seen to negotiate an alliance between metropolitan theory and the analyses developed by liberation movements, in the process producing elaborations which were not in either source, while always retaining a usage of colonial discourse as necessarily implying its source and effects in real-world situations (Said 1984, 1993; Brennan 1992; Parry 1992).

This opens up a consideration of the often unacknowledged contribution which Marxism made to colonial discourse analysis in providing a model of the reciprocal action between base and superstructure, between material conditions and ideas, thereby recuperating the Marxist formulation of a socio-economic *formation* within which a nexus of heterogeneous and contradictory determinations interact. The writings of the Italian Marxist, Antonio Gramsci, which made connections between culture and both state and civil institutions, proposed that the inventions of cultural activity kept the ideological world in movement; following his lead, British "cultural materialism" defined culture not in terms of the metaphor of a superstructure "reflecting" an underlying base, but as itself a set of social practices – as a specifically coded process of struggle and negotiation within which subjectivity, cognition, and consciousness are made and remade under determinate historical and political conditions. Particularly significant was Raymond Williams's redeployment of the favored Gramscian concept of hegemony to signify the expedients deployed in order to win the spontaneous consent of the great mass of the population to the intellectual and moral direction imposed on social life by dominant groups. Williams also expanded on the volatility and open structure of social interactions (class or other): theorizing these, he insisted, must accommodate complicity and hegemonically engineered consent, but also – and crucially – resistance, since the maintenance of domination depends on "continuous processes of adjustment, reinterpretation, incorporation, dilution," processes moreover which are conducted in relation to "alternative," "oppositional," "residual," and "emergent" social, cultural, and ideological formations (Williams 1977, 1980).

If some theoretical registers of a Marxist *cultural* criticism were absorbed into colonial discourse analysis, however, the historical materialist analysis of colonialism as inseparable from an expansionist capitalism, to which racial oppression was integral, was typically set aside. For postcolonial critics, as already stated, tended to be more interested in producing an immanent critique of the texts of colonial authority. To say this is not, of course, to overlook the demystification of the colonial archive that was achieved within colonial discourse analysis – a process to which theoretically diverse scholars and critics contributed. Such powerful (and still indispensable) work disclosed how Western writings and disciplines had constructed versions of non-European worlds calculated to underpin the moral and utilitarian ground of the imperial project (Said 1978). These included the study of biomedical texts where the perceived difference of the "normal" African had been pathologized (Vaughan 1991); European representations of Africa's cognitive and cultural traditions as negative categories (Mudimbe 1988); and the spatial and temporal distance devised by Europe to remove the colonized from coevality (Fabian 1983). These early attempts to unmask the making and operation of colonial discourses were at pains to elucidate the contexts of political domination, economic exploitation, and cultural oppression. They thus shared a concern, for all their diversity, with the specific historical conditions and social purposes of ideological representation. Later work in this idiom, however, has been far less scrupulous in this regard. A consideration of what came to constitute the most influential positions within colonial discourse analysis, and subsequently postcolonial theory, will suggest the distance travelled from the initial conceptions.

Directions in postcolonial studies

When English and Cultural Studies departments took the lead in developing postcolonial criticism, the consequences were both significant and problematic. Whether by direct influence or osmosis the work of postcolonial studies has prompted the wider community of literary critics to recognize that signs of overseas empire, conspicuous or ghostly, were written across the body of both the canonical and popular British literature. This is an area more extensive than the "fictions of empire," a sub-genre for long regarded as the sole repository of colonialism's imprint on British literary consciousness. In the aftermath of decolonization these writings had attracted a singular form of criticism offering retrospects on empire that were sometimes infected by apologetics and often permeated by nostalgia. Notably lacking in skepticism about representation, and in large indifferent to stylistic considerations, the studies assumed these fictions to be a form of apprehending and reproducing already existing realities (Greenberger 1969; Meyers 1973; Mahood 1977).[4] Hence the fabrications were interpreted as transparent accounts of the Western experiences of empire and authoritative depictions of colonial culture. Furthermore the literature's veracity was validated in terms of approximations to the interested scholarship of Orientalists, Africanists, ethnographers, and anthropologists, or – worse – to the tendentious and disingenuous versions of foreign worlds construed by imperial spokesmen, missionaries, and travelers or the do-it-yourself hagiography of colonialism's agents and servants. Postcolonial studies has forced a move here, from a misconceived quest for the truths and degrees of empathy with the colonized offered by fictions of empire to a consideration of their invention, reiteration, or estrangement of colonialist perceptions and misconceptions. This has enabled a discussion of these writings as culturally constrained and ideologically inflected fabrications that were overwhelmingly received in the imperial homeland as authentic renderings of both distant geographical location social forms, and of the colonizer's deportment (Boehmer 1995; Brantlinger 1988; Chrisman 2000; Miller 1985; Parry 1997b, 1998b; Said 1993).

However, to understand the imperial imaginary of British literature, enquiry must extend beyond the manifest fictional presence of empire to those works where it impinges in cryptic or oblique or encoded ways. Such works had hitherto been read as narratives of an English condition sealed from and largely indifferent to the external world, even though it had for long been recognized by students of British history that the making of the domestic economy and state was inseparable from overseas empire, whether in the form of mercantile and plantation colonialism or of territorial rule. By bringing this understanding to the tangible and imaginary presence of empire in the imperial homeland, critics were able to draw attention to its place within everyday existence and to uncover its immanence in both high and popular culture (Arac and Ritvo 1991; Cheyfitz 1991; Coombes 1994; Cooper and Stoler 1997; David 1995; George 1996; Giddings 1991; Hulme 1992; Kabbani 1994; Krebs 1999; McClintock 1995; Mitchell 1991; Richards 1993; Spurr 1993). As part of this project, recent work, not all of it formally produced under the rubric of postcolonial studies but influenced by the discussion, has revealed the covert colonialist registers of such canonical and popular works as *The Tempest, Robinson Crusoe, Mansfield Park, Castle Rackrent, The Rime of the Ancient Mariner, Daniel Deronda, Jane Eyre, Wuthering Heights, The Moonstone, The Picture of Dorian Grey*, the Sherlock Holmes stories, *Tono-Bungay, Dracula*, and *The Waves* (see, for example, Bivona 1990; Boehmer 1995; Childs 1999; Eagleton, Jameson, and Said 1990; Ferguson 1991; Heller 1992; Heywood 1987; Hulme 1994; Lowe 1991; Meyer 1996; Miller 1985; Parry 1998a; Perera 1991; Plasa 1994; Said 1993; Sharpe 1993; Spivak 1985a; M. Wood 2002).[5]

At the same time as colonialist configurations were being re-viewed, and the traces of empire in the domestic imagination detected, the study of writings from the once-colonized world, as well as of literatures produced in the post-independence diasporas, expanded exponentially. Because proper critical attention was directed at "Third-World" writing through the generation of new reading paradigms, the existing purview of comparative literature was extended. Where older commentaries on "commonwealth" or "new" literatures had attempted to incorporate such texts into a common Anglophone tradition, postcolonial criticism was far more attentive to the politics of English, both as a language and as a corpus of texts (Talib 2002). The concept of "commonwealth literature" had by definition placed Britain and the colonial experience as its conceptual centerpiece (Rushdie 1991: 61–70). Similarly, the idea of "new" literatures had almost inevitably assumed the priority and modularity of the "old" European literatures (Sunder Rajan, 1992). More recent criticism (not necessarily postcolonialist in tenor) has extended the arena to Francophone, Lusophone, Hispanophone, and more localized languages (Bernabé, Chamoiseau, and Confiant 1990; Brathwaite 1993; Ngugi 1986; Osofisan 2001). Whereas previously only a narrow range of writings had been considered, and had been judged by approximation to the standards of the Western literary canon (Bhabha 1984), more recent criticism has demonstrated that far from being imitations of the dominant Western modes, works written or performed within other cultural contexts, or from the margins of the metropolitan centers, often comprised remarkable innovations. Such works, as scholars working within postcolonial studies have shown, not only incorporate, transgress, and redesign the forms, aesthetic conventions, and cognitive resources of the Western tradition, but also draw on traditional narrative forms and idioms (Irele 1981; Brennan 1989; Lazarus 1990; Boehmer 1995; Quayson 1997; Hallward 2001; Harrison 2003).

However, the new scholarship has not been without its own blind-spots. Already a canon of "Postcolonial Literature" is being formed, in which the "marvellous" or "magic" realisms of Latin American, Caribbean, African, and Asian writing (García Márquez, Chamoiseau, Okri, Rushdie, for instance) are given greater prominence than those closer to "realist" modes. At the same time, works written in the local languages of Asia and Africa (some of these with vast readerships and expansive literary histories, of course: Bengali, Chinese, Arabic, Urdu, etc.), that are deemed "uncongenial" to metropolitan taste, are seldom translated and largely overlooked within the academies, as are the traditions of testamentary and resistance literature (Harlow 1987; San Juan 1988; Lazarus forthcoming).[6]

The privileging of novelistic styles which animate a postcolonial identity as fissured, unstable, and multiply located can be related to the manifest preference in the postcolonial discussion for mestizo or creolized formations, the corollary of which is a tendency to scant the intelligibility, mutability, and inventiveness of the indigenous (Brennan 1997). Moreover, the rapt interest of Western academics in migration or exile has led to a neglect of developments and realities in post-independence nation-states, since, as has been argued, "diaspora" has swelled "to demarcate the entire experience of post-coloniality," and "the subject-position of the 'hybrid' is routinely expanded as the only political-conceptual space for revisionist enunciation" (Loomba and Kaul 1994: 4, 13, 14). The use of "diaspora" as a synonym for a new kind of cosmopolitanism is certainly relevant to émigré writers, artists, academics, intellectuals, and professionals; but it can entail forgetfulness about that other, economically enforced dispersal of the poor from Africa, Asia, Latin America, and the Caribbean – the vast numbers of contract workers, casual laborers, or domestic servants in Europe, North America, and the Gulf States, undocumented immigrants, refugees, asylum seekers, and victims of ethnic cleansing – whose passage is largely coerced and who encounter punitive barriers hindering the movement of populations from South and East to North and West (Cohen 1987, 1997; Smith, in this volume). This would suggest that the time has come for postcolonial studies both to promote empirical investigations of economic migrants, and to begin to attend to the substantive and experiential situations of the majoritarian settled populations of the nation-states of Asia, Africa, and Latin America. Due attention ought to be paid to the millions of people whose mobility is constrained; who are not part of the reservoir of cheap labor in either the home cities, the Gulf States, or the old and new metropolitan centers; who still engage in subsistence farming, or in extracting raw materials and producing goods for world-markets, often under pre-capitalist conditions; or who are economically redundant and constitute an underclass. The absence of such enquiries is an index of an insufficient engagement with the conditions and practices of actually existing imperialism.

Consequences of the linguistic turn in postcolonial studies

Having observed the new areas of enquiry enabled by postcolonial studies and indicated some attendant problems, I will now suggest that the location of the discussion within English and Cultural Studies faculties has had the effect of promoting an indifference to social explanation. The institutionalization of postcolonial studies took place at a time when the linguistic turn was in the ascendant within philosophy and literary theory, and at the moment when cultural studies was in the process of turning its back on its materialist beginnings, operating increasingly with "an essentially textualist account of culture" (Sparks 1996: 97–98). The stage was then set for the reign of theoretical tendencies which Edward Said, among others, has deplored for permitting intellectuals "an astonishing sense of weightlessness with regard to the gravity of history" (1993: 366–67). In the realm of postcolonial studies, where premises affording analytical priority to formations of discourse and signifying processes were already to the fore, discussion of the internal structures of texts, enunciations, and sign systems became detached from a concurrent examination of social and experiential contexts, situations, and circumstances.

A theoretical position wholly neglectful of political economy (see Dirlik 1994; Miyoshi 1993) has had the effect of disengaging colonialism from historical capitalism and re-presenting it for study as a cultural event. As the Marxist analysis of colonialism and imperialism was set aside, the economic impulses underlying territorial expansion, the military appropriation of geographical space and physical resources, the exploitation of human labor and institutional repression, all receded from view. The British historian, Eric Hobsbawn, once wrote that "[a]ll attempts to divorce the explanation of imperialism from the specific developments of capitalism in the late nineteenth century must be regarded as ideological exercises, though often learned and sometimes acute" (1987: 73). Hobsbawm's censure was directed against those established scholars who resolutely excluded discussion of capitalism from their narratives of the colonial project. However, there are many postcolonial critics who are susceptible to the same charge. For the effect of scholars' one-sided concern with the constitution of "otherness"/alterity/difference, or with the production of silenced subject positions, has been to cause matters of discourse undeniably to take precedence over the material and social conditions prevailing during colonialism and in the post-independence era.

The postcolonialist shift away from historical processes has meant that discursive or "epistemic" violence has tended to take precedence in analysis over the *institutional* practices of the violent social system of colonialism. Similarly, cultural resistance has been privileged in analysis over diverse oppositional political expressions, while the intrinsically *antagonistic* colonial encounter has been reconfigured as one of *ambivalence* and *negotiation*. In this context consider Sara Suleri, who interprets the texts written by English and Indian writers during the Raj as performing a *dialogue* across cultural boundaries, infers that this demonstrates the *complicity* linking colonized with colonizer, and urges therefore that "the critical field would be better served if it sought to break down the fixity of the dividing line between domination and subordination," since both were beset by anxiety (Suleri 1992a: 4). Nor is Suleri alone in using her interpretation of texts to assert that "a psychic disempowerment *underlay* 'the colonial *system of control*'" (115, my emphasis). Thus Gyan Prakash, espying the inner contradictions and vicissitudes in the *discourses* of colonialism, proposes that such *linguistic* uncertainties testify to insecurity in the exercise of colonial power (Prakash 1996: 199) – a move that deduces the substance of political practices from a theoretically informed reading of discursive equivocation, while ignoring textual evidence pertaining to the drafting and implementation of repressive laws and policies.

In yet another instance, the proposal that the colonial archive be re-read in ways which are attentive to "the more complex cultural and political boundaries that exist on the cusp of [the] . . . often opposed political spheres" of the colonizers and the colonized is directed at disrupting the customary epistemological and ideological divisions between colonizer and colonized so as to reveal colonialism as "a mode of authority that is agonistic (rather than antagonistic)" (Bhabha 1994: 173, 108). Significantly, "agonistic" relates to ancient Greek athletic contests, "agon" being derived from the word for "a gathering" and denoting "[a] public celebration of games, a contest for the prize at games," whereas "antagonistic" specifies "[t]he mutual resistance of two opposing forces, physical or mental; active opposition to a force" (*Shorter Oxford English Dictionary*). Thus is the conflictual nature of the colonial encounter occluded.

The theoretical ground of these revisions has been rehearsed by Stuart Hall in an essay in which he attempts to surmount the binary forms of representation evoked in anticolonial struggles by advocating a move "from one conception of difference to another . . . from difference to différance." Such a shift, he contends, is precisely what the serialized or staggered transition to the "postcolonial" marks, and it does so, moreover, not only in a "then" and "now" way but by obliging us "to re-read the very binary forms in which the colonial encounter has for so long itself been represented . . . as forms of transculturation, of cultural translation, destined to trouble the antagonistic model of colonialism for ever" (Hall 1996: 247).

In this late-breaking, revisionary narrative of empire, a historical project of invasion, expropriation, and exploitation has been reconstituted as a symbiotic encounter; the contradictory, volatile, but all the same *structural* positions occupied in analysis by the oppositional conceptual categories of colonizer and colonized have been displaced by categories of complicity, mutuality, and reciprocity; and the conflicting interests and aspirations immanent to colonial situations have been dissolved into a consensus. As Simon During has suggested, postcolonial thought, which "fused postcolonialism with postmodernism in [its] rejection of resistance along with any form of binarism, hierarchy or telos . . . came to signify something remote from self-determination and autonomy. By deploying categories such as hybridity, mimicry, ambivalence . . . all of which laced colonised into colonising cultures, postcolonialism effectively became a reconciliatory rather than a critical, anticolonialist category" (1998: 31–32).

The vaporizing of conflict in colonial situations by those preoccupied with uncovering agonistic relations rather than antagonistic ones has had little to do with acknowledging the necessary and often coerced "intimacies" between ruler and ruled, or with understanding the discrepant experiences of the parties as constituting one history. It has had everything to do with the dissemination of emollient retrospects, lacking in conceptual credibility and amenable to neither intertextual confirmation nor empirical validation. If the purpose of the revisionist endeavor is to construe colonialism as a complicated, overlapping, and entangled event, then this should not imply that its operations are to be understood as being conducted in an in-between space, or on middle ground.[7] The understanding that both interconnection and division are innate to the colonial encounter is addressed in the work of Nicholas Thomas (1991, 1994). When Thomas acknowledges that the sway of colonialism's power is never total, he attributes this to the fact that colonial discourse and rule always exist in unacknowledged traffic with native dissension and discontent; and are brought to crisis by virtue of challenges from without, and not only on the basis of their own internal contradictions. Because the history of colonialism is, for Thomas, shaped by resistance on the part of the colonized, and not just by accommodation, he dissociates himself from those paradigms within "the anthropology of exchange" which he considers to be "myopically liberal in their models of reciprocity and assumptions of consent" (1991: xi).

For what is relegated as mere external contingency, Thomas argues, is that this interchange took place in the "context of [the] illiberal domination" that was colonialism; and what is overlooked is that the centrality of exchange in everyday practice does not encompass "the larger field of power relations that constitutes the circumstances of colonized populations" (1991: xi, 8). This suggests the constraints on recovering accord within a coercive colonialism and hence the need to devise terms other than "dialogue" to describe transactions where the native was necessarily a participant, but rarely – and only in very special circumstances – an interlocutor recognized as an agent of knowledge. It is an irony that the story of mutuality now being composed by some postcolonial critics makes an inadvertent return to the narrative of benign colonialism once disseminated by British imperial historiography, and which in the metropolis continues to have a purchase on the official and popular memory of empire, especially of the Indian Raj.

The relationship of postcolonial studies to anticolonial theory

If the expectation of an interested student is to encounter discussion of colonial histories, of colonialism's socio-economic forms and institutions, of colonial resistance, and of the class alignments, international alliances, and ideological retreats of postcolonial regimes, s/he will soon learn that such enquiries are, in the main, not being conducted in the field of "postcolonial studies," but elsewhere, in specialist domains within the social sciences. Moreover, such a notional student will soon discover that the prevalent modes of postcolonial theory are not the progeny of Marxist-inspired anticolonialist thought, since postcolonial criticism typically evinces a hostility both to Marxism and to movements for national liberation. This standpoint both stems from an aversion to all nationalism, at all times (with nationalism being viewed as a tainted form of oppositional consciousness and with the site of the nation being viewed as a futile arena of resistance struggle), and rests on a misreading of anticolonialism as always nativist, essentialist, atavistic, and wedded to pre-modern ideologies.

One critic has disavowed struggles against colonialism as constituting "an anti-imperialist or black nationalist tradition 'in itself'" (Bhabha 1994: 241); another has attributed "the failure of decolonization" to "the ignoring of the subaltern" (Spivak 1995b: 146); while yet another has charged that when an anticolonial movement did incorporate "modern science and polity," these were represented "as the return of the indigenous and the archaic" (Prakash 1996: 194–95). There undoubtedly were movements against colonialism guilty of some or all of these defects. All the same the ringing assertions cited above signally fail to address the far-reaching political dimensions of many of the struggles against imperial domination. They also fail to attend to the differences between moderate nationalist movements for independence that aspired only to inherit the colonial state, and revolutionary programs animated by socialist goals. These matters are now increasingly engaging in the postcolonial discussion participants who are necessarily considering how the different postcolonial conditions came into being, the class compositions of the newer nation-states, and their places within the present global structure of late imperialism (see, for example, Ahmad 1992; Brennan 1997, 2002b; Chrisman 1995; Lazarus 1999a; Parry 1994, 2002; San Juan 1998, 2002; Sivanandan, in this volume; Sprinker 1993).

Amongst the numerous retrospects on the beginnings of postcolonial studies, and against the predominant trend, Robert Young's recent volume, *Postcolonialism: An Historical Introduction* (2001) is noteworthy. Young situates postcolonial criticism "within the historical legacy of Marxist critique on which it continues to draw but which it simultaneously transforms according to the precedents of the greatest tricontinental anticolonial intellectual politicians" (6). His designation of postcolonial criticism as "a form of activist writing that looks back to the political commitment of the anti-colonial liberation movements and draws its inspiration from them" (10), is still a rare statement in an intellectual environment where so many scholars are disposed either to ignore, relegate, or misconstrue this body of theory. However, Young goes on to modulate his account of the field's genesis by introducing poststructuralism as another and metropolitan begetter, contending that "the structure to which [poststructuralism] . . . is 'post' is the colonial apparatus, the imperial machine": the poststructuralist "deconstruction of the idea of totality," he avers, "was born out of the experience of, and forms of resistance to, the totalizing regimes of the late colonial state, particularly French Algeria" (415). According to Young, it was Derrida, the Algerian-born Jew, "neither French nor Algerian, always anti-nationalist and cosmopolitan, critical of western ethnocentrism from *Of Grammatology*'s very first page, preoccupied with justice and injustice, [who] developed deconstruction as a procedure for intellectual and cultural decolonization within the metropolis" (416).

If Young is not displacing Marxism with deconstruction in accounting for the ancestry of the postcolonial critique, then perhaps he is placing deconstruction among the tricontinental anticolonial intellectual traditions in terms of which the Marxist legacy was transformed within postcolonial studies – a reading supported by his description of his own work as an attempt to translate deconstruction's philosophical and literary strategies "into the more painful framework of colonial and postcolonial history" (412). Although he is sanguine about bringing the distinctive theoretical projects of poststructuralism, Marxism, and anticolonialism into alignment within postcolonial studies, the unambiguous rejection by so many poststructuralist thinkers of the Marxist categories that underpin leftist anticolonial thinking – the capitalist system, imperialism, class struggle, combined and uneven development, nationalism, an emancipatory narrative, universalism, for instance – suggests that the discrepancy between the informing premises cannot so readily be negotiated. This is a problem observed by Timothy Brennan when accounting for the paradoxical position of Marxism within a field where prominent theoretical tendencies have sought to suppress a parentage in anticolonial liberation movements: "If in the postcolonial discussion an undifferentiated Marxism has played a frequent role, it has done so usually as an example of how a certain brand of Eurocentrism promoted technological or disciplinary modernity, and therefore, by definition was antagonistic to non-Western forms of emergence" (Brennan 2002b: 188).

As histories of the field of postcolonial studies are being written, the various versions of its ancestry register the tensions between different methodologies and spheres of interest. Keya Ganguly has proposed the need for a project that will rescue the postcolonial critique "from being locked in an endless embrace of ideals of difference, deferral, and constitutive paraphrases that inform myriad readings in the literature about hybridity, liminality, mimicry, and so on." "If the time has come to move postcolonial scholarship beyond the now two-decade-old preoccupation with poststructuralist and deconstructive derivations of Freudian, Saussurean and Nietzchean ideas," she observes, "it may be worth casting another analytic look at the concepts and objects that were swept to the wayside on the march to 'self-reflexivity' by restoring the untranscendable horizon of truth and reality" (2002: 245). Only then will it be possible to examine the state apparatus, economic organization, social relationships, and cultural forms of different post-independence regimes and to understand that the "globalized" world order is structured such that the centers of economic, political, and cultural power remain entrenched in a small number of capitalist nation-states. The task facing postcolonial studies today is not, of course, to abandon the theoretical sophistication that has marked its engagement with Orientalist discourse, Eurocentrism, and the exegetics of representation, but to link such meta-critical speculations with studies of actually existing political, economic, and cultural conditions, past and present.

NOTES

1 The best-known Readers and Companions include Ashcroft, Griffiths, and Tiffin 1995; Castle 2001; Mongia 1996; Schwarz and Ray 2000; and Patrick Williams and Chrisman 1993. See also the inaugural issue of the journal, *Interventions* (1.1 [1998]), with its theme, "Ideologies of the Postcolonial."

2 Consider this statement, drawn from the editorial to the first issue of *Postcolonial Studies*, one of a number of dedicated journals in the field to have emerged since the mid-1990s: "Postcolonialism is what we employ to excavate the marginal, the magical, the erotic and the everyday . . . 'our' postcolonialism offers a new promiscuity which not only heads 'downmarket,' but . . . breaks through the cordon that separates the anthropological-based cultural studies practised in relation to non-western societies from the popular culture schools that focus on the popular in the West" (Seth, Gandhi, and Dutton 1998: 10)

3 Spivak maintains further that the task of postcolonial work is neither to recover signs of self-representation, of "the disenfranchised speaking for themselves," nor to address victimhood "by assertion of identity" (1990: 56).

4 An exception to this earlier criticism is Raskin 1971; see also Parry 1983, 1998c.

5 Whereas many of these readings situate the importation of colonial topoi to configure metropolitan dominations as paratactic – that is without narrative co-ordinates – they go on to re-articulate the *unsecured linkages* in the texts as constituting a critique of "the systematic operation of sexism and imperialism"; or as critically inscribing gender, race and class as intertwined or mutually reinforcing sub-sets (Ferguson 1991 on *Mansfield Park* and Heller 1992 on *The Moonstone*); or as demonstrating a historical alliance between the ideology of male domination and the ideology of colonial domination (Meyer 1996 on *Jane Eyre*).

6 An exception is the transcribed testament *I, Rigoberta Menchú: An Indian Woman in Guatemala* (Menchú 1984), which was a best-seller in the West.

7 Colonialism's histories are of course differential, because of which opportunities for discovering a "middle-ground" are greater, for example, in nineteenth century India than in the plantation colonies of the Caribbean, the genocidal settler regimes of Southern Africa, the Americas, and Australia, or the territorial expropriations in North and sub-Saharan Africa. However, even in the case of India it should be noted that the political and cultural traffic which occurred was between the rulers and India's regional and national élites, and not its overwhelmingly peasant populations.

2

THE SHAPE OF THE FIELD

5

JOHN MARX

Postcolonial literature and the Western literary canon

In this chapter, I describe how the novels, poems, and plays that scholars and common readers have come to recognize as postcolonial relate to texts likely to be included in a Western canon.[1] To be precise, I identify three sorts of relationships between postcolonial literature and this canon. Two of these have taken on the quality of scholarly common sense and will be familiar to non-specialists. First, postcolonial writing is held to *repudiate* the canon. Accordingly, readers have become well practiced in treating work from Europe's former colonies as the antithesis of canonical writing and as an instrumental component in efforts to recover oral and print traditions that imperialism threatened to obliterate. Second, postcolonial literature has been shown to *revise* canonical texts and concepts. Readers have learned to approach postcolonial literature as a critique of Western tradition involving the rewriting of specific works (*The Tempest* and *Heart of Darkness*, for instance) and the appropriation of entire genres (the *Bildungsroman*, for example, or the domestic romance).

Whether valued for its difference from the canon or for its reconstruction of canonical texts and concepts, postcolonial writing may also be credited with fundamentally altering how literature in general is thought of and how it is taught. It has become difficult for even the most recalcitrant critics to ignore imperialism when teaching European literary history, or to maintain that the canon is simply a record of what Matthew Arnold dubbed "the best that is known and thought in the world." Instead, postcolonial critics and creative writers have enabled educators and their students to re-examine the interaction between literature and history as well as to redefine the meaning of cultural literacy and literary culture.

In acknowledging that opposition to the canon and the revision of its contents have led to such changes, I take it as a given that these two relationships are far from mutually exclusive. It is not difficult to locate texts that define themselves through both their difference from the Western canon and their appropriation of its techniques. Chinua Achebe's *Arrow of God*, for instance, exemplifies both relationships. With a style Achebe attributes to habitual Igbo storytelling and a plot that features complex political struggle within and among the six villages of Umuaro, this novel's form and content work hand in hand to represent a local culture and history that colonialism tried to wipe out. At the same time, the fall of Achebe's protagonist Ezeulu might remind readers of the sublime tales of hubristic decline common throughout Western literary history and invite them to ask what it means to displace such a familiar narrative to such an unfamiliar locale.

Although *Arrow of God* facilitates both of these approaches, clearly a reader attends to different details when looking for evidence of cultural specificity, on the one hand, and cosmopolitan appropriation, on the other. Such divergent interest has important implications. When we treat Achebe's book as a documentation of Igbo politics and culture, we empower its writer to represent local life and imagine a readership that deems fiction an appropriate venue for such representation. Invariably, this procedure begs the question of who is authorized to write and who is the privileged reader for such a text. Is it necessary for the writer to grow up in a place like Umuaro, or would an attentive outsider be better equipped to write about Ezeulu and his fellows? Do "thick" descriptions of local culture presume a reader unfamiliar with the bond between the deity Ulu and his priest? Or does this novel expect that its readers will be able to notice where Achebe is taking liberties with a familiar ceremony or religious observance? We ask rather different questions if we emphasize Achebe's revision of Western material. Questions such as, "What does it mean for someone born on the African continent to write novels in English?"; and, "What other texts should be read alongside *Arrow of God*? Other Nigerian novels? African novels in general? Narratives of religious struggle and hubris no matter when and where they are produced?"

If the first set of questions presumes that *Arrow of God* provides a window onto the Igbo world and treats its writer as a native informant, the second set seeks to add Achebe to European literary history as an author more or less on par with writers ranging from Milton and Shakespeare to Jane Austen and Joseph Conrad. Indeed, Achebe is often credited with inventing modern African fiction and his *Things Fall Apart* has become a staple of high school and college curricula in the United States, Britain, and Europe (it has been translated into numerous European languages), as well as Africa itself. Again, we must remember that these two approaches often overlap despite the fact that they are logically at odds with one another. Paradoxical as it may seem, Achebe has earned a place in the Western canon at least in part as a representative of Nigeria and the Igbo. Nevertheless, when one argues that Achebe belongs alongside canonical stalwarts like Dickens and Woolf, it still matters whether we foreground his African roots or his literary genius.

How we read his work depends on whether we identify its unique qualities as particular to the novelist Achebe or to the Igbo people.

The fact that a writer's capacity to represent a place and its people is widely considered relevant to determining canonicity suggests how dramatically postcolonial literature has changed what we mean when we say "the canon." It is due, in part, to postcolonial literature that I can count on "the Western canon" to indicate an old-fashioned and suspect critical practice. This third sort of relationship between postcolonial literature and the Western canon becomes the focus of this chapter's final section, where I ask what happens to postcolonial writing as the ideal of a multicultural canon comes closer to reality. Every newly celebrated work that emerges from the former colonies or from the migrant populations engendered by imperialism helps to transform the canon into a more heterogeneous archive. Instead of opposing or revising it from outside, postcolonial literature increasingly *defines* a new sort of canon from an established position inside its boundaries. When I weigh this development, my largely descriptive chapter will become more analytic. I begin, however, by turning to the familiar contention that what postcolonial literature truly offers is a departure from the canon.

Repudiation

On 24 October 1968, the Kenyan novelist, Ngugi wa Thiong'o, called for the abolition of the English department at the University of Nairobi. Two colleagues, the poet and critic Taban Lo Liyong and the music scholar Henry Owuor-Anyumba joined his appeal. In their petition, these three professors proposed a new department of African Literature and Languages to replace that of English. They recommended marginalizing British writing in a European survey course, and encouraged students to attend instead to regional oral verse, Swahili narrative, and what Ngugi and company referred to as "Modern African Literature."

Behind this proposal lay the idea that literature is a privileged representative of that amalgam of custom and belief that anthropologists call culture. Such a thesis allowed Ngugi and his collaborators to marry their polemical message that "things must be seen from the African perspective" to a specifically literary medium (Ngugi, Owuor-Anyumba, and Lo Liyong 1978: 150). They maintained that reading African creative writing would help students at the University of Nairobi to recover distinctly African ways of seeing, which habituation to European texts had corrupted. "The dominant object in that perspective is African literature," the three professors explained, "the major branch of African Culture" (150). Ngugi has subsequently elaborated on this argument in his book *Decolonising the Mind*, wherein he describes literature as a "collective memory bank of a people's experience in history" (1986: 15). Literature creates a "whole conception of ourselves as a people" (15). It mediates our relationship to the world. If we read about that world in English fiction we will see it differently than if we read about it in fiction composed, for instance, in Gikuyu. For this reason, Ngugi argued not only that English departments should be abolished in Africa, but also that English itself ought to be avoided by African writers as a medium of literary expression. Language in this sense is not a passive object. In representing peoples and places, it has the capacity to make and remake them.

Ngugi was not the first writer from the colonial world to come to this conclusion. Some decades before his petition to abolish the Nairobi English department, the Senegalese poet and eventual President Léopold Senghor joined the Antillean writers Aimé Césaire and Léon Damas in an effort to establish a literature in French capable of defining a broadly comprehensive African cultural essence. With his neologism "*négritude*," Césaire identified a fellow feeling emerging less from a specific locale than from the "special geography" of the slave diaspora, a world map organized by "the geometry of my spilled blood" (Césaire 1983 [1956]: 77). A shared culture defined through documents of violence and the repressed memory of a rich African past resulted in the "fact of being black, and the acceptance of this fact, of our destiny as black people, or our history and our culture" (Irele 1981: 67–68). Appreciating the quality of creative writing was integral to such acceptance according to Senghor. He maintained that aesthetic creativity represented the essence of Africa, which he called one of the "mystical civilizations of the senses" (Senghor 1993: 33).[2]

Such salvage operations turned writers not only into cultural representatives but also into anticolonial activists. In the foreword to his pivotal 1938 novel *Kanthapura*, Raja Rao describes the Indian writer's responsibility to infuse prose with the "tempo of Indian life" (1963: vii). Rao was one of a trio of Indian novelists in the 1930s, including R. K. Narayan and Mulk Raj Anand, who used fiction to construct and endorse a model of Indian typicality. In *Kanthapura*, moreover, Rao's distillation of village existence serves as the foundation for national consciousness. The "quiet, generous" Moorthy is "our Gandhi," a local hero imprisoned by the British who publicly endorses Jawaharlal Nehru (5, 181). Doris Sommer documents a similar tendency to use fiction for nation building in Latin America (Sommer 1991). In nineteenth-century Latin American romance plots, lovers from antagonistic regions and classes evince affection for one another and thus allegorically demonstrate how to bridge the differences within an emerging state.[3] The conviction that literature can and ought to be understood as national makes allies of even antagonistic postcolonial writers and critics. Achebe disagrees with Ngugi over the use of European languages in African literature, for example, but both share a commitment to literary nationalism. Ngugi refers to local vernaculars as "our national languages," while Achebe contends that English is the only practical foundation for generating a literature equally accessible to all the members of a Nigerian citizenry that shares no other idiom (Ngugi 1986: 28; Achebe 1975: 75).[4]

Despite the evident success of these efforts to define postcolonial literature in opposition to the Western canon, it has been difficult for writers and critics to break entirely with the imperial past. The now-commonsensical notion that literary study connects a reader to the spirit of an age, to a people, and above all to a nation has its roots in eighteenth- and nineteenth-century colonial administration. It was disseminated by bureaucrats who looked to literature to educate their subjects in European language and culture. Gauri Viswanathan's foundational study of English instruction in India traces a history beginning with the Charter Act of 1813, which emphasized literary study as part of a campaign to Anglicize an élite portion of the sub-continent's population (1989: 23). Though Ngugi sought to avoid the heritage of such colonial schooling when he set out to abolish the English department in Kenya, the Victorian notion that literature expresses culture is precisely what underwrote his thesis that African poetry and prose would reconnect African readers to African traditions.

Similar influences haunt other models of repudiation. The contention that non-Western writing and art are collective and cultural rather than individual and personal derives as much from modernist primitivism as from *négritude* and Afrocentrism.[5] Though he coined the term *négritude*, Césaire himself noted the uncomfortable proximity between its presuppositions and racist stereotyping (A. J. Arnold 1981: 40–41). Similarly, if we have learned to credit literature with the capacity to reconnect the colonial dispossessed with their cultural heritage, it is difficult to know how to receive claims by Europeans like Graham Greene, who relished the way Narayan taught him "what it is like to be Indian" (Greene 1980: v).

If the wide variety of writing that critics and readers group under the label "postcolonial" has anything in common, it is an awkward reliance on imperial remainders. This observation provides a means for specifying the nature of its opposition to the canon. For instance, commentators have suggested that the sub-Saharan regions of Africa share a heritage of oral narrative. However, as Kwame Anthony Appiah contends, this inheritance makes itself felt in contemporary literature largely as a paradox. In African writing, "the authorial 'I' struggles to displace the 'we' of the oral narration" while, at the same time, claiming authority over the subject matter that the "we" of oral narration represents (Appiah 1992: 83). Césaire testifies to the complexity of this struggle in his "Notebook of a Return to the Native Land," a poem that features an infinitely capacious "I" narrator who "accept[s] . . . totally, without reservation . . . my race that no ablution of hyssop mixed with lilies could purify" (1983: 73). Césaire's narrator even accepts a whole catalogue of stereotypes. He responds to badgering questions – "The master of laughter? The master of ominous silence? The master of hope and despair? The master of laziness? Master of the dance?" – with an exclamatory "It is I!" (83).

The Zimbabwean author Tsitsi Dangarembga's *Nervous Conditions* also highlights the paradoxical quality of repudiation. In this novel, Tambudzai's mother relates local "history that could not be found in textbooks," while missionary schooling appears as a process of "assimilation" and "forget[ting] who you were" (Dangarembga 1988: 17, 178–79). Though this opposition seems designed to underscore the contention that postcolonial literature preserves a cultural alternative to the canonical materials circulated in colonial schools, readers trained in such schools surely recognize that *Nervous Conditions* presents its argument in the form of a *Bildungsroman*. Dangarembga's novel is an instance of this venerable Western genre, but one that alters the form in reproducing it. Tambudzai's life exceeds the bounds of the narrative, which concludes with the announcement that everything we have read is but a preamble to a more important – and as yet untold – story. Thus *Nervous Conditions* demonstrates the repudiation of the canon precisely through the feat of revising its familiar forms.

Unwriting

The appropriation and revision of Western form that one finds in Dangarembga's novel has a long history. We may discover it not only in her late-twentieth-century fiction but also in the nineteenth-century poetry of Michael Madhusudan Dutt. Dutt was born into the Bengali intelligentsia in 1824 and educated at imperial schools in Calcutta. There he began to compose verse, first in English and later in Bengali. Like Dangarembga's fiction, Dutt's poetry takes the Western canon as a starting point, but it does not treat its texts in isolation. Rather, Dutt dissects Western canonical and identifiably South Asian materials alike, chopping them into so many distinct parts which he cobbles together into something new.

His epic *Meghnad Badha Kabya*, for instance, borrows elements from Milton's *Paradise Lost* and welds them to content culled from an episode in the *Ramayana*. As Amit Chaudhuri explains, where Milton converts the origin myth of Christianity into a drama largely centering on Satan, Dutt turns Rama's adversary Ravana into a tragic leading man (Chaudhuri 2002: 94). Through such cutting and pasting, Dutt shows that to appropriate Western canonical literature one must first unwrite it, dismantle it, and come to see it less as an inviolate whole than as a collection of parts suitable for recycling. One's relationship to local tradition is no more nor less editorial. There is, thus, nothing entirely indigenous nor entirely imposed about Dutt's efforts to introduce the Shakespearean sonnet to Bengali literature. "Dutt used the sonnet's self-reflexivity," Chaudhuri observes, to create poems that were neither fully English nor fully Bengali (2002: 94).

Such acts of unwriting and rewriting had the effect of destabilizing the homology between colonial mastery and the mastery of European culture. Dutt and the host of writers who have since dissected canonical work demonstrate that learning the Western tradition in school does not necessarily equal obeisance. Ania Loomba remarks that Caribbean writers "wrestled with *The Tempest* not because they had their heads in academic clouds but because its dominant interpretations had the real effect of subordinating colonized peoples" (Loomba 1998b: 45). Given such reasoning, it is not surprising that the decades of the 1960s and 1970s saw not only the consolidation of regional liberation movements in the Caribbean but also a whole series of *Tempest* revisions.

Though such reworked versions tend to reinforce the centrality of Western writing by default, treating canonical texts as a source of raw material could not help but transform them. By adapting *The Tempest*, tropical playwrights turned Shakespeare into a means for questioning European accounts of colonization. In so doing, moreover, they estranged the canon for Western readers and uncovered complexity many had never noticed before. Before 1960, Peter Hulme notes, critics paid little attention to Prospero's allegation that Caliban raped Miranda and, further, tended to read right past Caliban's response: "Would't had been done! . . . I had peopled else / This isle with Calibans" (I.ii. 346–48; Hulme 2000: 231). As the play was being unwritten and appropriated by Caribbean writers, however, such passages became newly interesting. For instance, mulling over Prospero's fear of Caliban leads the Barbadian George Lamming to contemplate the "fusion" of dominant and dominated peoples and cultures that "Prospero needs and dreads" (Lamming 1984: 102).[6]

Perhaps the only work in English to rival *The Tempest*'s importance to postcolonial literature is Joseph Conrad's *Heart of Darkness* (1898). V. S. Naipaul's grim *A Bend in the River* (1979), Tayeb Salih's *Season of Migration to the North* (1969) – a *Heart of Darkness* in reverse that takes readers from the Sudan to London – and Arundhati Roy's *God of Small Things* (1997) are among the fictions to borrow from Conrad's tale. Like new *Tempests*, revisions of *Heart of Darkness* have served not only to reconfigure interpretations of a key work in the Western canon but also to provide a medium for exchange among writers and critics. Collating the various versions of this fiction is, in fact, an act tantamount to cataloguing and arranging the field of postcolonial prose as a whole. Criticism such as that by the Guyanese novelist Wilson Harris (1983, 1990) – himself the author of what might well be considered a *Heart of Darkness* rewrite, *Palace of the Peacock* (1985) – uncovers affiliations between figures as far-flung as the Nigerian Wole Soyinka and the American Jean Toomer.

Even as *Heart of Darkness* helps to underscore common textual interests among writings from Africa, Asia, the Antipodes, and South America, Conrad's novel also serves to demonstrate a profound ambivalence for an imperial literary inheritance. Achebe is far from alone in arguing that this book represents the most "thoroughgoing racist" tendencies of the European tradition (Achebe 1988: 11). Even as postcolonial writers have critiqued Conrad's account of life in the Congo, however, several notable figures have credited him as a model practitioner in the art of revision. In an early interview, Ngugi comments on Conrad's ability to "beat a language which was not his own into various shapes" and to use that language to interrogate English culture: "I'm impressed by the way he questions things," Ngugi explains (C. Pieterse and Duerden 1972: 126, 124).

Emphasizing interaction between the Western canon and postcolonial literature cries out for an explanation of how imperialism has connected the world's peoples and places. Edward Said singles out C. L. R. James interpretation of Césaire's "Notebook" as a prototype for criticism attuned to such interconnection. In *The Black Jacobins*, James highlights Césaire's attentive representations of the hardships of island life, and his dedication to uncovering the humanity colonialism has repressed. Then, suddenly, James shifts gears, and invokes T. S. Eliot in order to elucidate Césaire's work further (James 1963: 401–2). "By moving so unexpectedly from Césaire to Eliot's 'Dry Salvages,'" Said explains, "James rides the poetic force of Césaire's 'truth unto itself' as a vehicle for crossing over from the provincialism of one strand of history into an apprehension of all other histories, all of them animated by and actualized in an 'impossible union'" (Said 1993: 281). Reading Said as he reads James, we advance the project of connecting vernacular histories by following the argument of a Palestinian critic (who taught literature in New York and had a predilection for opera) commenting on an interpretation by a West Indian historian and novelist (who spent a large portion of his life in Britain and wrote on Melville and Marx and cricket) of another Caribbean writer (whose poetry appeared in French and who served as Martinique's deputy to the French Assembly) and an Anglophilic American (whose poetry was itself composed of multifarious and polyglot references). Though all of these figures might be equally (if differently) associated with cosmopolitanism or provincialism, taken together their work does not produce a homogeneous literary field. Rather, their local concerns and transnational affiliations suggest a network that may have been enabled by European imperialism but that no empire ever fully managed.

That postcolonial writing may be better positioned than Conrad or Shakespeare to describe this incipient network is the implication one might draw from Ahdaf Soueif's *The Map of Love* (1999), a novel that sets out to describe imperial history and geography from the perspective of both colonizer and colonized. Soueif chronicles the rise of Egyptian nationalism through the eyes of an Englishwoman who travels to Cairo and falls in love with a powerbroker in the anti-imperial movement. This is a fiction that avidly appropriates European narrative forms, among them the story of female exploration made popular by Mary Kingsley and Amelia Edwards before being parodied by E. M. Forster in *A Passage to India*. *The Map of Love* also revises the Orientalist tale of abduction and seduction as its heroine, Anna Winterbourne, finds herself kidnapped by two younger colleagues of the man who will soon become her lover, Sharif Pasha al-Baroudi.[7] By portraying colonial relations so thoroughly mediated by both English literary tradition and Egyptian nationalism, *The Map of Love* makes it possible to believe that only a novelist expert in each could come close to managing the complexity of empire and decolonization. Soueif hints at such a conclusion both in the form and the content of her novel, which takes shape less as a seamless narrative than as a baggy assemblage of journal entries and letters, diaries and stray notes left behind by Anna and Sharif Pasha.

The presumption that literature can organize what the disciplines of history and political science cannot leads Leela Gandhi to conclude that much of what circulates under the label "postcolonial" treats the "colonial encounter primarily as a textual contest, or a bibliographic battle, between oppressive and subversive books" (1998: 141). By emphasizing the importance of the canon, writers and critics pander to a Western audience, she alleges, a charge echoed by Ngugi, who wonders at the "lengths to which we were prepared to go in our mission of enriching foreign languages" (Gandhi 1998: 163; Ngugi 1986: 7). Aijaz Ahmad, meanwhile, helps us to see how turning the Western canon into the basis for linking together various postcolonial efforts effectively flattens the differences between them. It turns Nigerian and Sri Lankan, Dominican and Egyptian writers into variations on a colonial theme: "Calibans all," stuck revising the same self-reflexive fiction over and over "until the end of time" (1992: 102).

The most abiding criticism of those writers and readers who privilege revision is that their activity transforms postcolonial literature into a stridently élite category, one that presumes a thoroughly canonical education and that cannot help but be oriented towards Western – or "Westernized" – readers. Appiah has famously described postcoloniality as "the condition of what we might ungenerously call a comprador intelligentsia" (1992: 149). Organized by and around a global class that shares the "fairly homogeneous . . . intellectual formation of the . . . university-educated," nearly every text that gets called "postcolonial" – even work in regional languages that has not been translated – finds itself stamped as such by élite institutions, whether in London, New York, or Nairobi (Sunder Rajan 1997: 606). The interdependence between postcolonialism and the university is not only a sign of complicity, however. Postcolonial literature has become part and parcel of academic culture. However, we ought not to leap to the conclusion that such a development is inherently conservative. To acknowledge that postcolonial literature has entered the ivory tower, I contend, is not to negate its capacity to have widespread effects.

Going mainstream

Although he calls it an "extravagant claim," Simon Gikandi testifies to the influence that postcolonial literature can have when he argues, "Achebe is the person who invented African culture as it is now circulated within the institutions of interpretation" (2001: 7). Gikandi explains that from the moment of its appearance in 1958, *Things Fall Apart* has served as a counterpoint to representations of African life provided by major figures in British literature ranging from Haggard to Kipling to Conrad and Greene. As such, it has been instrumental in helping teachers and their students to imagine alternatives to those accounts. To remind ourselves why such alternatives continue to be necessary, we may turn to V. S. Naipaul's *The Enigma of Arrival* and to a passage in which the narrator relates the plot of a novel written by his English landlord. In it, a young European woman travelling through an unnamed part of Africa is kidnapped and then eaten by cannibals. The landlord draws this story from what Naipaul dubs "the joke knowledge of the world," invented but startlingly entrenched narratives of primitivism in "a fantasy Africa, a fantasy Peru or India" that continue to appear not only in bad fiction but also in the journals and published documents of travelers, administrators, journalists, and other more or less credible eyewitnesses (Naipaul 1987: 282). This is exactly the sort of knowledge, in other words, that Achebe's novel rebuts. Of course, *Things Fall Apart* only manages to refute joke knowledge about Africa if it is widely seen to contain a more authoritative report. It is, Gikandi confirms, seen in precisely this way. Since being published as the first volume in the Heinemann African Writers Series, this book has become a ubiquitous symbol for postcolonial literature's capacity to represent the local cultures of Europe's former colonies. As a result, it is no more surprising to discover *Things Fall Apart* on university syllabi in history, anthropology, or sociology, than in literature.

Postcolonial literature's interdisciplinary authority to identify and contest joke knowledge has enabled it to exert pressure on the canon, to "internationalize a field of study that has remained relatively insular in the West," incorporate new content in established surveys, and recognize the global scope of literary study in the various European languages (Ramazani 2001: 182–83). The fact that, as Rajeswari Sunder Rajan observes, "the academic study of English literature as a subject in Indian universities is . . . virtually indistinguishable from the curriculum shaped for it in the metropolitan university in the west," reminds us that the institutions of interpretation are now far-flung, and that what happens in one wing helps to shape and is shaped by what happens on the other side of the world (Sunder Rajan 1992: 7). While scholars in the US and the UK have recomposed their curricula with and against postcolonial work, teachers in Indian universities have established a broadly comparativist program that, Susie Tharu reports, takes for granted an "aesthetic that is universal and a humanism that is equally global in scope" (1998: 21). As a result, it may be possible to conclude that literary study is becoming less exclusively focused on the question of how fiction from the Maghreb and poetry from Indonesia repudiate or revise Western writing, and turning towards analysis of how they perform as part of a new and improved canon.

These developments have enabled a new set of literary critical questions. They have forced what Christopher Miller describes as "nothing less than a reconsideration of all the terms of literary analysis, starting with the word 'literature'" (1993: 217). In this vein Srinivas Aravamudan questions the very idea that "the literary" has a pre-eminently Western identity when he asks whether *All About H. Hatterr*, a novel by the Indian writer G. V. Desani that has been described as derivative of *Ulysses*, might not actually be a more fully accomplished version of its canonical predecessor. "Is Desani making good on the unkept promise of modernist iconoclasm made by an earlier Joyce/Stephen?" Aravamudan asks before answering, "It certainly seems so" (1998: 98). Appiah goes so far as to contend that postcolonial literature helps engender a new sort of humanism based not "as the older humanists imagined, [on] universal principles or values," but on the reading of postcolonial fictions like Dangarembga's *Nervous Conditions* (Appiah 2001: 224). "What is necessary to read novels across gaps of space, time, and experience," he argues, "is the capacity to follow a narrative and conjure a world: and that, it turns out, there are people everywhere more than willing to do" (224–25). Because it maintains an authority to mediate local culture, postcolonial literature reveals that cultural differences can be overcome, as demonstrated by what Appiah describes as a basic human capacity to read and understand literature (at least of the narrative sort). Without sacrificing its point of entry into literary curricula as the representative of cultures repressed by imperialism, therefore, postcolonial literature seems poised to acquire the responsibility once claimed by the Western canon of mediating and defining the essential elements of our humanity. As postcolonialist critiques of the West have taught us, this cannot be regarded as an apolitical stance. Nor does it seem inherently conservative, in the strict sense of the term.

Given this formula, it may seem puzzling that postcolonial writing so often questions the authenticity of the national, regional, and local cultures it describes. As Aravamudan observes, there is no claim in Desani's novel that Indian culture is in any way pure. Instead, *All About H. Hatterr* presents a region awash in recycled material and intellectual goods like the well-traveled theosophical notions that Desani seems as fond of as Joyce was at the beginning of the century. What Naipaul calls joke knowledge is also on display. "All probabilities are probable in India" is the "clichéd maxim," which Aravamudan notes in the introduction to Desani's fiction (1998: 111). *All About H. Hatterr* is far from the only novel to deprive local culture of an autonomous identity. Readers find similar heterogeneity in the town of Ayemenem that Arundhati Roy portrays in *The God of Small Things* – a novel that treats everything from the classical-dance drama of Kathakali to the late twentieth-century melodrama of the World Wrestling Federation as integral to life in one South Indian town.

By messing with local culture in this way, postcolonial literature does not forfeit authority so much as make the ability to describe the local into a special, specifically literary skill that can travel. Zadie Smith's *White Teeth* (2000) is one of the more celebrated examples of postcolonial literature's effort to teach readers to understand how local culture is messy everywhere, and especially in the former seat of the British Empire.[8] In contemporary London as in Ayemenem, autochthony is a pipe-dream. As Alsana pronounces in *White Teeth*, "you go back and back and back and it's still easier to find the correct Hoover bag than to find one pure person" (2000: 196). The challenge confronting visitors to Smith's London neighborhoods or Roy's Keralite homes is not one of distinguishing the colonizer's culture from that of the colonized in order to repudiate or rewrite it. The colonizer's culture,

Smith assures us, will prove just as impure in its origins as the colonial situation it creates elsewhere.

The mainstreaming of postcolonial literature confirms that such writing is equipped to represent the local cultures that imperialism has wrought as well as those it strove to demolish. If the Western canon formerly offered to archive the less-than-European places of the world as various examples of radical alterity, novels by Achebe, Smith, and others turn such administrative labor into a postcolonial privilege and thereby recast the problem of what it means to be "alter." We would do well, I believe, to treat the continued rivalry between postcolonial literature and the Western canon as competition within a shared field of operation. Doing so not only provides a new reason to read the two together, but also urges us to consider carefully the fact that each reproduces its authority through the international network of institutions of higher learning. It challenges us to describe what exactly it is that such institutions reproduce. Clearly, we need ways of approaching what it means for particular forms (the novel, the sonnet, and so forth) to be intelligible and adaptable on a global scale. To understand postcolonial literature and the canon as embattled allies within the academy is also to remember, as Sunder Rajan notes, that while "'Other' modes of thinking . . . as well as 'small' traditions . . . have an authentic existence . . . [it is] unlikely that anything can be considered unmediated by the protocols of knowledge we work with, except by idealization" (1997: 613). The mainstreaming of postcolonial literary writing and reading in the university, finally, becomes legible as less the limit than the enabling condition of literary expertise.

NOTES

1 For reasons of a purely practical nature, I concentrate largely on a British, English-language canon.

2 As Irele observes, critics and writers after Senghor and Césaire continue to focus their energy on defining a specifically African literature (Irele 1990: 49). See, for example, Asante 1990.

3 Chinweizu, Onwuchekwa Jemie, and Ihechukwu Madubuike treat "national criteria" as vital determinants of the authenticity of African creative work (1983: 13), while Sneja Gunew suggests that Australia might construct an identity through a multicultural literature that "could not easily be recuperated in the name of nostalgia or absorbed into an Anglo-Celtic canon" (Gunew 1990: 116).

4 English is often seen as serving a similar purpose in India (Sunder Rajan 1992: 15). In its very ubiquity, the national model may have become a too effective means of identifying postcolonial exemplarity. In what remains a controversial essay, Fredric Jameson argues that postcolonial texts "necessarily project a political dimension in the form of national allegory," but he also observes that the absolute quality

of such a claim tends to flatten the distinctions between, say, writing from the various places within South America or Africa (Jameson 1986: 69). In his well-publicized critique of Jameson, Aijaz Ahmad notes that singular "Third-World" literary models reiterate Western claims that what lies beyond Europe is simply alien even as they reassure Western readers that postcolonial literature can be contained in the familiar category of the national (Ahmad 1992: 98; see Jameson 1986: 77).

5 On primitivism and African artistry, see the catalogue to the Tom Phillips-curated "Africa: The Art of a Continent" exhibit that appeared at the Royal Academy of Arts and the Guggenheim Museum in New York (Phillips 1996). Two of the most important works on Western generalizations of non-Western culture are Said 1978 and Mudimbe 1988.

6 The term "fusion" usefully captures the breadth of *Tempest* revisions, which cut across linguistic and administrative boundaries. Lamming wrote of Caliban in English, Césaire's play *Une tempête* appeared in French, and Roberto Fernández Retamar published his influential account of Shakespeare's play in Havana's *Casa de las Américas*. Such revisions had earlier colonial models to draw on and to argue with, moreover, notably the Uruguayan José Enrique Rodó's 1900 *Ariel*. Decolonization has brought continued attention to the play. Raquel Carrió and Flora Lauten's 1998 *Otra Tempestad*, for example, advances interpretation of the play as an early account of the polymorphous quality of Caribbean culture by presenting a cast of characters that includes Afro-Cuban orisha deities as well as figures from other Shakespeare efforts, among them Othello and Desdemona. See Hulme 2000.

7 Soueif's characters know full well that they are embroiled in recycled narratives: her narrator Amal says of Anna at one point, "She has become as real to me as Dorothea Brooke" (1999: 26).

8 To refer to Smith's novel as postcolonial, I am fully aware, is to stretch the category to include work that might otherwise be sorted into the national categories of Black British or, simply, British fiction. If I call this a postcolonial novel, I do so because of its formal and thematic affinities with other books that less interestingly test the limits of the term.

6

SIMON GIKANDI

Poststructuralism and postcolonial discourse

I

Perhaps the most useful way to begin a discussion of the relationship between poststructuralist theory and postcolonial discourse is to call attention to the controversies and debates that have accompanied their rise as significant intellectual movements from the late 1960s and 1980s respectively. For one of the things these two movements have in common is that they have always generated heated questions about their political efficacy, their location within intellectual traditions informed by unequal relations of power, and their validity as theoretical categories that can provide us with useful knowledge about the cultures and literatures of previously colonized countries in Africa, Asia, and the Caribbean. These issues often divide scholars and critiques of formerly colonized societies into two broad groups: on one hand there are those critics who would like postcolonial theory to account for the specific conditions in which colonialism emerged and functioned and the role of decolonization as a specific narrative of liberation. For these critics, the pitfall of postcolonial theory inheres in its inability to periodize and historicize the colonial experience and to account for the role of colonized subjects as active agents in the making of culture and history. Aijaz Ahmad, for example, argues that the primary failure of postcolonial theory is to be found in its eagerness to foreground a set of questions – on historical agency, the production of colonial subjects, and even the history of modernity – or to consider "the question of cultural domination exercised by countries of advanced capital over imperialized countries" (Ahmad 1992: 2; see also Dirlik 1994; Bartolovich and Lazarus 2002). For such critics of postcolonial theory, its primary failure – its inability to account for the history and process of decolonization – arises from its close affinity to poststructural theory. If poststructuralism is seen as the source of the political or epistemological failure of postcolonial discourse, it is because it came to privilege the act of reading over politics, or, in Ahmad's terms, posited cultural hybridity "against the categories of nation and nationalism," or even situated culture and "the literary/aesthetic realm" at "a great remove from the economy" (1992: 3).[1]

On the other hand, however, many proponents of postcolonial discourse reject the claim that theory represents the separation of culture and political economy, or that acts of reading, especially ones informed by shifting theoretical notions of hybridity and difference, necessarily negate the categories of nation and nationalism. Indeed, for leading postcolonial critics such as Homi K. Bhabha, poststructuralism (and postmodernism) provides a powerful weapon against what they see as the prison-house of European humanism and the decolonized nation as a polity that has lost legitimacy in the age of migration and globalization. For these critics, rather than being ahistorical and apolitical, detached from the concerns of postcolonial subjects, a postcolonial discourse informed by poststructuralism provides a powerful vista into the modern world system at its moment of crisis. For example, Bhabha argues that postcolonial criticism "bears witness to the unequal and uneven forces of cultural representation involved in the contest for political and social authority within the modern world order" (1994: 271).[2]

Nevertheless, both sides in this debate are united by their recognition that postcolonial discourse emerged within the larger institutions of European, especially French, theory after structuralism. In this respect, a postcolonial discourse is unthinkable without poststructuralist theory. Locating postcolonial theory within this European genealogy, however, raises another set of questions or problems: why have theoretical questions that originally developed within French theory come to dominate debates about Anglophone postcolonial identities, cultures, and literatures? Is postcolonial discourse about how French theory plays out in the institutional practices of Anglophone intellectuals rather than a theoretical reflection on what Neil Larsen calls "the realities of cultural decolonization or the international division of labor" (2002: 205), or is it a technology for understanding the postcolonial condition? A different gloss on the same problem is presented well by Bhabha in a moment of self-interrogation in *The Location of Culture*: "Is the language of theory merely another power ploy of the culturally privileged Western élite to produce a discourse of the Other that reinforces its own power–knowledge equation?" (1994: 20–21).

It is difficult to respond to all these questions without accepting the basic fact that, unlike theories of the Third World, neocolonialism, or underdevelopment that were dominant in the 1960s, postcolonial theory was not a discourse produced in the postcolonial world by postcolonial intellectuals. Postcolonial discourse was produced by émigré postcolonial writers and intellectuals based in the West. Irrespective of the validity of its claims, this is a discourse marked by its sense of dislocation from what it considers to be one of its geographical references – the postcolony. At the same time, it is not enough to dismiss postcolonial discourse as French poststructuralism traveling in the imagination of the postcolonial intellectual class. For since the 1990s, the question of what postcolonial studies was, or was not, has come to revolve around the relation between theory as a category of thought and "Third-World" practices and experiences as its object of analysis. Even when it seems to be a discourse that is more important in the metropolitan centers than in the decolonized nation, postcolonial discourse is also an attempt to come to grips with the nature and meaning of colonial modernity from the dual vantage points of decolonization and migration (Hall 1996).

Let us note, however, that the apparent European identity of postcolonial discourse has been the source of some of the most heated debates in the field. At the center of these debates is the question of whether postcolonial theory, seen as a surrogate of poststructuralism, generates any new sets of questions. The boldest dismissal of postcolonial discourse's claim to originality is the one that sees it, to quote Ahmad's words again, as "a matter of catching up with many kinds of very diverse continental developments" while at the same time "reformulating much older and recalcitrant issues . . . as regards the archive of Western knowledges and the question of cultural domination exercised by countries of advanced capital over imperialized countries" (1992: 2). On the other side of this debate are critics like Robert Young who argued that the European identity of poststructural theory conceals its fundamental connection to "Third-World" debates on decolonization and its aftermath. Young's argument, first articulated in *White Mythologies* (1990), is that the historical roots of poststructuralism are to be found not in the crisis of European culture associated with the student revolts of 1968, but in the Algerian struggle against colonialism ten years earlier. In *Postcolonialism: An Historical Introduction*, Young goes as far as to present postcolonial theory as an extension of anticolonial movements in the "Third World," arguing that poststructuralism developed as an anti-Western strategy "directed against the hierarchical cultural and racial assumptions of European thought": "Though structuralism and poststructuralism were taken up and developed in Europe both were indeed alien, and fundamentally anti-western in strategy. Postcolonial thought has combined the radical heritage of such theory with further ideas and perspectives from tricontinental writers, together with other writers who have emigrated from decolonized tricontinental countries to the west" (2001: 67–68).

All these debates have taken place against what might best be described as an anxiety of influence: the major figures in postcolonial discourse, the symbols of its canon, are so closely identified with the dominant strands of poststructuralist theory that they have tended to be perceived as disciples of leading figures in European poststructuralist discourse. Thus, the works of Edward W. Said – especially *Orientalism* (1978), his pioneering study of the relationship between the representation of the "Orient" and Western systems of power – is indebted to Michel Foucault's work on discursive systems and power. Gayatri Chakravorty Spivak first came into prominence as the translator of Jacques Derrida's *Of Grammatology* and her work on a wide range of subjects from psychoanalysis to feminism can be considered to be a reinterpretation of Derridian deconstruction from the vantage point of colonialism and its subjects. Bhabha's work is a powerful echo of the revisionary theories of Jacques Lacan and Derrida on a set of subjects ranging from difference and split subjectivity to the indeterminate nature of meaning and representation. In the end, though, as I hope to show in this chapter, the real enigma of postcolonial discourse is not so much that it is embedded in Western theory but how a project so closely associated with European debates on questions such as representation, subjectivity, and historicism became central to the rethinking of the cultures and literatures of the postcolonial polity.

2

Still it is important to keep in mind that while the subjects who inhabit postcolonial theory and their historical experiences do originate from the colonial and postcolonial world, structuralism and poststructuralism were taken up and developed in France as responses to what were very localized moments of debate and crisis which, nevertheless, had a significant colonial dimension. These movements arose as a reaction against a European tradition of humanism whose most important proponent in the period after the Second World War was Jean-Paul Sartre. Sartre's humanism was central to the discourse of colonialism developed by anticolonial intellectuals such as Frantz Fanon, Aimé Césaire, and Léopold Sédar Senghor during this period. Because of this, the emergence of structuralism in the 1950s and 1960s as a critique of humanism could not leave the discourse of colonialism intact and unscathed. Similarly, if poststructuralism emerged as a critique of the residual humanism of structuralism, then it is important to conceive it as a critique of the central pillars of the discourse of colonialism. In this context, postcolonial discourse needs to be seen as a critique of an earlier discourse of colonialism anchored in the humanist tradition rather than as a continuation of what Young calls "tricontinental anticolonial intellectuals" (2001: 427). Rather than see postcolonial discourse as the continuation of the discourse of colonialism, we need to examine it as a radical break with this tradition, a break enabled by poststructuralist theory. However, this argument can only be clarified if we take the preceding terms or suffixes of postcolonial discourse and poststructural theory – namely, colonialism and structuralism – as key foundational terms rather than conceptual schemas that have been transcended. Indeed, postcolonial discourse and poststructural theory share an identity at a most basic level: they are haunted by their suffixes.

Thus if we are looking for a point of contact in the genealogy of poststructuralism and postcolonial discourse, the place to start is an unexpected one – in the existential phenomenology of Sartre. Here it is interesting to note that Sartre has come to be so closely associated with the discredited project of humanism, in the aftermath of poststructuralism, that critics have forgotten that in the period after the Second World War he represented the intellectual traditions against which others defined themselves. In addition, while the rejection of Sartre (in structuralism and poststructuralism) was premised on the claim that his theories of history and consciousness tended to reinforce ethnocentrism and universalism at the expense of "other" cultures and modes of knowledge, he was clearly the most important European philosopher involved in the struggle against colonialism. For this reason, his influence on the discourse of colonialism – the theoretical anticolonial project that emerged after the Second World War – cannot be underestimated. In addition to his well-known public stand and activism against French colonialism in Indochina and Algeria, Sartre's major works were preoccupied with the role of colonial violence and the colonial subject.[3] Indeed, a central goal of the Sartrean project was to overcome the gap between the European self and the colonial other by developing a theory of history – and an ethical practice – that would make the idea of a human culture *after* colonialism possible. It is in this sense that Sartre has come to be seen as the custodian of radical or syncretic humanism.[4]

It is now generally assumed that Sartre embodied the humanism which, as we will see below, structuralist and poststructuralist theorists set out to deconstruct in the 1960s and after. However, he appealed to colonized intellectuals of the 1940s and 1950s precisely *because of* his commitment to a radical form of humanism, not in spite of it. More specifically, he was the first major philosopher – perhaps the only one – to connect the colonial experience to both the limits of humanism and its utopian possibilities. Thus through Sartre's example, we can begin to understand how the critical terms that were to be discredited in poststructural and postcolonial theory because they were considered to be compromised by humanism – universalism, historicism, consciousness, and identity – were, implicitly and explicitly, cornerstones in the edifice of the discourse of anticolonialism constructed by

Césaire, Fanon, and Senghor. We hence need to consider the key terms in what has come to be known as radical humanism and then see how this directly impacted the discourse of anticolonialism.

At the top of the list was the question of history and historicism. The tradition of historicism, which had dominated French thought during the Hegelian revival of the 1930s associated with Jean Hyppolite and Alexandre Kojève, invested heavily in the idea of history, or rather the philosophy of history, as the "foundation for understanding the modern world and for providing insight into how that world might be changed for the better" (Roth 1988: ix). In most of its forms, argues Michael Roth, "French Hegelianism was a vehicle for confronting the historical, for thinking about the connection between history and knowing" (2). In Sartre, this investment in the philosophy of history as the foundation of knowledge went a step further: historicism was not simply about human consciousness; rather the historical process was one in which the human subject would come to conquer nature and discover the essential truth. This view of history was to be affirmed in Sartre's most important and controversial project, *Critique of Dialectical Reason*, in which his stated goal was nothing less than the establishment of what he called "the truth of history." The goal of his project, Sartre argued, was "to establish that there is one human history, with one truth and one intelligibility – not by considering the material content of this history, but by demonstrating that a practical multiplicity, whatever it may be, must unceasingly totalise itself through interiorising its multiplicity at all levels" (1976: 69; see also Young 1990: 28–47).

Closely aligned with this view of history as a process that would lead us towards the truth was the privileging of the subject. The humanist idea of history as either spiritual progress or the quest for truth was impossible without the centering of the human subject and its consciousness in the drama of social life. In fact, in his early works on existentialism, Sartre's goal was to pose the question of freedom as, in Mark Poster's apt phrase, "the ultimate question of the human condition" (1975: 80). Sartre's phenomenological philosophy, as presented in *Being and Nothingness*, was intended to affirm the centrality of the human subject in relation to the lived world and in the process to assert the distinctiveness of consciousness in relation to this experience, to prove that "[c]onsciousness is consciousness of something" (Poster 1975: 82). Consciousness was, of course, unthinkable without a knowing subject.

The third triad in this discourse of history and consciousness was the question of the other. Here, Sartre had an important Hegelian tradition to fall back on, for as is well known, one of the factors that had attracted French intellectuals to Hegel in the 1930s had been the "master/slave dialectic," seen as a powerful counter to Kantian rationalism and its insistence on the autonomy of an identity based on reason. Roth's summary of this dialectic is worth quoting in detail:

> The story of the master/slave dialectic is fairly straightforward . . . Hegel describes the confrontation of two persons, two "consciousnesses," who have forged their identities in isolation from other people. Upon meeting, each sees the other as a threat to his or her individual existence, and, more important, each seeks to dominate the other so as to be more certain of this existence. (Hegel speaks here of "self-certainty.") The two struggle for domination, for the recognition of the strength of their respective individualities. The loser of the struggle is the one who decides that life is more important than the recognition originally sought. This person abandons the fight and is made a slave who recognizes the sovereignty of the master. In other words, the loser allows the animal desire for self-preservation to take precedence over the human desire for recognition.
>   (1988: 100)

Perhaps the most important aspect of this dialectic was that, in the relation between the master and the slave, "it was the slave who moves humanity toward a higher level of self-realization . . . The slave is the secret of change in history and his desire for freedom from oppression is the ground of man's becoming more human" (Poster 1975: 13). The colonial situation presented the most dramatic modern example of the master/slave dialectic. The dialectic was, in turn, to become central to the discourse of anticolonialism precisely because of the agency invested in the enslaved within the humanistic project.

In general, Sartre's major contribution to colonial discourse was his projection of what might initially have been European issues – on identity, freedom, and consciousness – into the colonial sphere. He did so, not simply in his reflections on colonial violence in the *Critique of Dialectical Reason* but more poignantly in a series of introductions or prefaces he wrote for works by a group of colonial intellectuals – Senghor, Memmi, and Fanon – who were to become crucial in the anticolonial struggle. These prefaces opened important spaces for colonized intellectuals seeking to develop an anticolonial history as a first step to what they considered to be a decolonized truth. It is in these prefaces that Sartre – and his radical humanism – have to be seen as important interventions into the (anti)colonial process. For example, while Sartre used his preface to Albert Memmi's *The Colonizer and the Colonized* to reiterate his well-known claims for the centrality of experience and transcendence – the belief that self-consciousness of an experience was not enough in itself, that it needed to be transcended to the level of the universal – he also used the occasion to represent colonialism as a system defined by a totality.

Similarly, Sartre's famous preface to Fanon's *The Wretched of the Earth* enabled him both to return to the dialectic of violence that had been part of his philosophical project since the war and to recognize the crisis of humanism that had been exposed by a dying colonialism. Sartre's argument in this preface was that when they were located at the limits of the colonial system, the colonized exemplified the unhappy consciousness of history. In responding to Fanon's challenge – the insistence on the dialectic of violence as the enabling condition of colonialism – Sartre did not entirely give up the idea of the dialectic and the process of history as stages leading to reconciliation. Indeed, he located the significance of Fanon's project in what he saw as its clarification of the historical process, as constituting "step by step, the dialectic which liberal hypocrisy hides from you and which is as much responsible for our existence as for his" (Sartre 1968: 14). At the same time, in translating the colonial experience for European readers, Sartre was forced to come to terms with the fact that the dialectic of colonial history could not lead to reconciliation, as his dialectical sense of the historical process had assumed; the contradictory nature of colonialism, a system that claimed and denied the colonial condition at the same time, was explosive; it was out of this explosion that the Europeans themselves were becoming decolonized – confronted, as they were, with "that unexpected revelation, the strip tease of our humanism" (24).

Perhaps Sartre's most important intervention into the colonial debate, however, was in "Black Orpheus" ("Orphée Noir"), the 1948 preface he wrote for *Anthologie de la nouvelle poésie nègre et malgache de langage français* (Anthology of New Black and Malagasy Poetry in French), edited by Senghor. Sartre used the occasion of the "emergence" of a new black poetry in French to elaborate his view that language was a vehicle of consciousness and to oppose poetry, the art of a becoming consciousness, with other, objective forms of language use in science and technology. For Sartre, poetry had to remain subjective because it was only in its subjectivity that it could serve as a vehicle of consciousness. Whose consciousness, though? Sartre was not in doubt that what was at issue in the study of the new black poetry was both the lived experience of blackness and its connection to a larger humanistic project. The challenge confronting him was how to build a bridge between the lived experience of blackness (foreclosed to whites) and human consciousness (available to all).

The bridging function of this historic preface involved two stages. The first one was the illustration that "[T]hese blacks are addressing themselves to blacks about blacks; their poetry is neither satiric nor imprecatory; it is a *becoming consciousness*" (Sartre 2001b: 117). The second stage was to show that in coming to consciousness through a "poetic process," blacks had produced a poetry in French that had to be considered "the only great revolutionary poetry," the poetry through which they could come to a recognition of the truth about their lived experience through a process of "separation or negativity" while whites might come to a consciousness of themselves in the mirror held up by the other (117–18). For Sartre, however, *négritude* was ultimately part of a dialectic. Its function as a mode of knowledge was only possible through its transcendence:

> In fact, *négritude* appears as the minor moment of a dialectical progression: the theoretical and practical affirmation of white supremacy is the thesis; the position of *négritude* as an antithetical value is the moment of negativity. But this negative moment is not sufficient in itself, and these blacks who use it know this perfectly well; they know that it aims at preparing the synthesis or realization of the human in a raceless society. Thus *négritude* is for destroying itself, it is a passage and not an outcome, a means and not an ultimate end. At the moment that every black Orpheus most tightly embraces this Eurydice, they feel her vanish from between their arms. (137)

While colonial intellectuals were to reject this notion of *négritude* as a minor moment in the dialectic, Sartre's project had made them agents in the discourse of history and European identity.

3

Nowhere is Sartre's influence on anticolonial discourse more vivid than in Fanon's *Black Skin, White Masks*. For most readers Sartre enters Fanon's text through the famous section where the latter attacks the former's definition of *négritude* as a minor moment in the movement of the dialectic (Fanon 1967: 132–39). Yet almost every chapter of *Black Skin, White Masks* takes up the questions discussed above, elaborates upon or discards them. In this respect, Fanon's text needs to be located within the general project of European humanism, although this humanistic dimension has tended to be ignored by postcolonial critics (most notably Bhabha), who have been inclined to see *Black Skin, White Masks* as a text that either anticipated many of the central issues in poststructuralism – the role of the unconscious, the dislocation of subjectivity, otherness and desire – or that can be deployed against the general claims of humanism.[5] While Henry Louis Gates, Jr. was right to argue that the poststructuralist fascination with Fanon had "something to do with the convergence of the problematic of colonialism with that of subject-formation" (1991: 458), it is imperative to see this concern with subjectivity as a continuation of radical humanism rather than its negation.[6]

The clearest indication of Fanon's affinity with Sartrean humanism in *Black Skin, White Masks* is perhaps evident in his search for the truth about the black man imprisoned by his experience, "rooted at the core of a universe from which he must be extricated" (Fanon 1967: 8), and his almost stubborn search for a temporal structure in which this experience might become known and clarified.[7] It is paradoxical that what now appears to be Fanon's most postcolonial text is constructed around several basic (Sartrean) assumptions: that consciousness is "a process of transcendence," that understanding reality "requires a total understanding," that a psychoanalytic interpretation demands a temporal architecture, and that every human problem "must be considered from the standpoint of time" (8–11). Like Sartre, Fanon's primary concern was with the lived experience of blackness and his goal was to penetrate the morbid universe that imprisoned the black so that he could recover an authentic experience.[8] An authentic experience, however, was not conceived as a positive one; rather, what a psychoanalytic approach would reveal, Fanon hoped, were the forces of colonial domination and racism that had deprived the black man of his capacity for what he called "ontological resistance" (1967: 110).

Indeed, Fanon's primary complaint in *Black Skin, White Masks* was that French colonial policies in the Antilles had created black men who believed that they were white and hence had no imperative for demanding recognition through a dialectic of violence. Following Hegel and Sartre, then, Fanon argued that the black had no identity in himself; identity depended on recognition from the European; this recognition could not be granted; it had to be demanded through an act of resistance. It was only when it encountered resistance from the other that self-consciousness would undergo "the experience of *desire*"; and it was out of this experience that one would ask to be recognized: "As soon as I *desire* I am asking to be considered" (218). Conversely, without desire, there was no resistance, hence no recognition. It is in this context that Fanon turned to the black woman as a counterpoint to black men and located the experiences of black women in what has become the most controversial chapter in his book – "The Woman of Colour and the White Man."

Now, Fanon's misogyny has been the subject of many debates especially since the 1980s and it is a significant subject in itself. My concern here, however, is not Fanon's views on women, but the distinction he tried to make between the experiences of black men and women under colonialism. The simple, yet central, question here was: why did Fanon need the figure of the black woman in a discourse whose primary theme was the lack of ontological resistance in the black man? This is a vexed question, but as Rey Chow has shown, the figure of woman in Fanon's discourse is intimately connected to the problem of subject formation: like the little girl in Freud's theory of social formation who does not suffer from the anxiety of identity because she is already aware of what she lacks and what she needs, Fanon casts the black woman as a subject with agency but not unconscious desire (Chow 1999; see also Fuss 1994). If the existential anxiety of the black man arose from the realization that he was "overdetermined from without" (Fanon 1967: 116), the black woman was actively engaged in what Fanon calls "a bilateral process, an attempt to acquire – by internalising them – assets that were originally prohibited" (59–61).

In "Orphée Noir," Sartre needed the black in order to think through the possibility of a universal phenomenology; in *Black Skin, White Masks*, Fanon needed the black woman in order to think about the implications of the black man's failure to behave as "an actional person" (1967: 154). Most importantly, Fanon's goal was to restore the actional capacity of the black man so that he could demand recognition in an act of resistance with the understanding that the resulting consciousness only makes sense in its transcendence. In short, Fanon's hope was that the whole world could recognize the black man once his ontological resistance was restored. Hence his conclusion: "I want the world to recognize, with me, the open door of every consciousness" (232). Here and elsewhere, Fanon did not seek to negate humanism but to claim it for the colonized. In the opening of *Black Skin, White Masks*, he would bemoan the reduction of humanism to platitude. In his powerful conclusion (an epitaph written on his death bed) to *The Wretched of the Earth* he urged those committed to the advancement of humanity to seek the lesson of humanism elsewhere, away from Europe where it had failed (1968: 315–16).

4

What about structuralism, the other important suffix in the history of postcolonial discourse? Structuralism is important in any understanding of the history of postcolonial discourse because it represented the first major resistance to humanism and thus enabled the emergence of poststructuralism. The structuralist project had two sides to it: a technical or scientific side concerned with language (and especially generative grammar) as the key to understanding human society; and a philosophical side whose goal was to transcend humanism and its presumed ethnocentrism. In the first regard, structuralism was a program built on the revolutionary ideas of the Swiss linguist, Ferdinand de Saussure who, in a work called *Course in General Linguistics*, first published posthumously in 1915, had argued for the study of language as a science, insisting also that the study of language was quite distinct from the study of speech. While speech was historical or diachronic in nature, connected to the needs of individual speakers in a community, and hence able to change over time, language was "not a function of the speaker" but a product "that is passively assimilated by the individual" (Saussure 1966: 14). For Saussure, language was "a self contained whole and a principle of classification" (9) whose nature could not be explained by historical (diachronic) developments.

Having isolated language as an autonomous object of study, Saussure then sought to develop a science of signs – what he called "semiology". He did so by making two important claims: first, that the linguistic sign was "a double entity, one formed by the associating of two terms"; that this unit was not constituted by the relation between "a thing and a name, but a concept and a sound-image" (66). Put another way, a particular word did not naturally represent a particular concrete thing; rather, individual speakers had developed an association between this word and a particular concept which came to mind when the word was uttered. Words (Saussure gives the example of "tree") were sound-images that represented concepts. These words functioned as signifiers; the particular concept associated with them ("tree") was the signified. Brought together as a unit of speech, the signified and signifier constituted a sign. The fact that different languages deploy different signs for the same ideas or things –

> The idea of "sister" is not linked by any inner relationship to the succession of sounds s-ö-r which serves as its signifier in French; that it could be represented equally by just any other sequence is proved by differences among languages and by the very existence of different languages: the signified "ox" has as its signifier b-ö-f on one side of the border and o-k-s (*Ochs*) on the other.
>
> (Saussure 67–68)

– led to Saussure's second claim: that "the linguistic sign is arbitrary," that it has "no natural connection with the signified" (67, 69).

The most obvious influence of Saussure on structuralism was then on the linguistic level. In fact, influential structuralists like Claude Lévi-Strauss sought to turn language into an objective system of signs, one that would reveal the laws of social formation through a symbolic order that was autonomous of individual subjects and was hence collective in nature. For Lévi-Strauss, structuralism's ability to establish an order of signs autonomous of reality was important because, as Simon Clarke has shown, the symbolic order (the order of signs and linguistic relations) produced meanings that were not subject to the vagaries of individual interpretation (Clarke 1981). For phenomenologists like Sartre and Fanon, lived-experience (*Erlebnis*) was not the given or objective fact "but the process in which objects acquired their status as such for consciousness" (Judy 1996: 54). For the phenomenologists, reality was reality to the extent that it appeared as such to a subject. Against this privileging of individual perception, the structuralists argued that structures, because they were unconscious and collective, revealed objective experiences. Indeed, the linguistic structure would come to be regarded by the structuralists as "the only reality since knowledge can only be expressed and communicated in linguistic form" (Clarke 1981: 2). In addition, structuralists privileged structures (both social and linguistic) because they assumed these could clarify the relationship of things (the units that went into the making of the whole) while maintaining the natural or cultural differences that constituted these units.

On another level, the linguistic turn associated with structuralism seemed to be targeted against the humanistic project's faith in history. The structuralist critique of history and historicism was manifested in "History and Dialectic," the last chapter of Lévi-Strauss's *The Savage Mind*. In this essay, Lévi-Strauss sought to counter the humanistic project on several levels: concerning the nature of language in the representation of the human experience, history as a dialectical process, and the relation of the colonial or racial other and the European self. Sartre, for example, had argued that language was the vehicle for expressing Consciousness and Being; in contrast, Lévi-Strauss asserted that while language presented us with a dialectical and totalizing process, it existed "outside (or beneath) consciousness and will"; language was "an unreflecting totalization"; it was human reason "of which man knows nothing" (1966: 252; see also Poster 1975). Lévi-Strauss's conclusion was that language was not the property of subjects nor were subjects inherently bound by linguistic laws; it was possible for subjects to express their experiences outside language and for language to express human reason outside the will and consciousness of subjects. In effect, while Sartre and his colonial disciples had tended to privilege the subject and its consciousness, Lévi-Strauss's goal was nothing less than the displacement of the human subject from the position accorded to it in modern European thought.

In regard to the vexed question of historical consciousness, Sartre had, of course, been one of the major advocates of historicism. His goal, as Young has clearly shown, was to reconcile history and subjectivity, to show that history was made by individual actors who were, at the same time, products of the history they made (1990: 28–47). Sartre's ambition was to remove indetermination from the narrative of history, to establish what he considered to be the singular truth of history. By contrast, Lévi-Strauss was almost contemptuous of the "special prestige" which philosophers of history attached to "the temporal dimension," and especially the belief that a diachronic notion of time was "not merely superior to that provided by synchrony, but above all more specifically human" (1966: 256). His firm rebuttal was that historical facts were constituted by the historian not the subject, that history was a fragmented rather than continuous process, and that it was a point of departure not the end in the narrative of human experience. In regard to the question of the other, Lévi-Strauss was not convinced that Sartre's distinction between the savage and dialectical minds and his attempts to transcend this division through the invocation of "timeless consciousness" provided a way out of ethnocentrism (249).

What, then, was the relationship between these "internal" European debates and colonial and postcolonial experiences? To answer this question we need to underscore the point made earlier in this chapter: that the issues at stake here – history, language, consciousness – were at the center of the discourse of anticolonialism. For the major proponents of this discourse, "history" was an indispensable term; they believed that it was only under the rubric of historical consciousness that the alienating forces of colonialism could be overcome. In addition, Fanon and his compatriots were interested in the phenomenological dimension of language for two reasons: first, language mediated the violence of colonial relations; secondly, the narrative of nationalism took linguistic form (Fanon 1968). More significantly, within the discourse of anticolonialism, consciousness was posited as the way out of the prison-house of colonial representations. And as we have already seen, the critique was driven by an unrelenting commitment to radical humanism. Similarly, structuralism was committed to a critique of colonialism, especially its ethnocentrism, but it wanted to achieve this by connecting the phenomenological tradition itself – and its radical humanism – to ethnocentrism. The structuralists insisted that, contrary to its claims, a discourse built on consciousness and a privileging of history was ethnocentric. For this reason, if structuralism did not have an immediate impact on the politics of decolonization in the 1960s, it is not because it was not engaged in colonial questions. More likely, it was just historically belated to the extent that by the time the movement established itself as a major intellectual force in the early 1960s, colonialism was effectively over. Still, structuralism did generate significant debates on the nature of colonial society especially in the fields of history and anthropology.[9]

5

As in the cases discussed above, poststructuralist theory first emerged as a set of European debates on the nature of knowledge production in the so-called "human sciences" in the aftermath of colonialism and the student movements of the 1960s. The trauma of decolonization – like the student revolts that came in its wake – had thrown the European polity into a crisis of authority and legitimacy in the face of which the central claims of radical humanism and structuralism no longer seemed relevant. Indeed, poststructuralism announced its arrival on the intellectual scene in the form of Derrida's 1967 essay, "Structure, Sign, and Play in the Discourse of the Human Sciences," a systematic critique of structuralism as another failed antihumanist project.

In his critique of structuralism, Derrida approached his subject indirectly by arguing that, contrary to the view of Lévi-Strauss and others, the notion of structure was as old as the systems of Western thought itself, "as old as Western science and Western philosophy" (Derrida 1982: 278). What, then, was the difference between older notions of structuralism and the new one that became popular in the 1960s? Derrida argued that while structure had been the basis of Western systems of knowledge in earlier periods, in structuralism, the "structure's structurality" had been "neutralized or reduced" by being accorded a "center" or being referred to "a point of presence, a fixed origin" (278). The function of this center was "not only to orient, balance, and organize the structure . . . but above all to make sure that the organizing principle of the structure would limit what we might call the *play* of the structure" (278). In other words, what appeared to be autonomous structures were still subordinated to a center or explained by a presence outside themselves. Contrary to Lévi-Strauss's claim, structures were not free from metaphysical claims but were only explicable in terms of a point of reference that limited their free play. Structure could not escape metaphysics because it was part of it.

Derrida conceded that there had been various attempts to deconstruct this metaphysics in modern European philosophy. Modern European thinkers like Nietzsche, Freud, and Heidegger had sought to question or disrupt the notion of structure as a "transcendental signified"; but all these critiques were trapped in a unique circle – all the methods or categories used to deconstruct the history of metaphysics were borrowed from the tradition they sought to destroy (1982: 280). Derrida's argument, then, was that we did not have a language that was foreign to metaphysics. We could not even assume we had escaped metaphysics by concerning ourselves solely with linguistic signs (281). In Derrida's view, Lévi-Strauss's failure, the folly of structuralism as it were, was to believe that the concept of the sign could be liberated from systems of thought or even consciousness; on the contrary, the sign itself was imbricated in the thought it sought to deconstruct. Hence his conclusion that "the metaphysical reduction needed the opposition it was reducing . . . The opposition is systematic with the reduction" (281).

The second part of Derrida's essay sought to undermine the central claims of structuralism in several of its key areas: its deployment of anthropology or ethnography against ethnocentrism, its claim to have overcome the split between nature and culture, and its critical methods. Let us examine these critiques in turn. Both in his argument against Sartrean historicism in *The Savage Mind* and in laying out the case for ethnography in *Tristes Tropiques*, Lévi-Strauss had argued that structuralism promised a universalism without ethnocentrism because it privileged a discipline – anthropology – which allowed no limits (historical or social) except those of geography. Anthropology was able to link cultures across time and space (Lévi-Strauss 1992: 58). Freed from temporal constraints, anthropology was what Lévi-Strauss considered to be the ideal discipline of humanism without ethnocentrism. In response, Derrida argued that anthropology was a European science employing concepts embedded within the Western metaphysical tradition: "Consequently, whether he wants to or not – and this does not depend on a decision on his part – the ethnologist accepts into his discourse the premises of ethnocentrism at the very moment that he denounces them" (1982: 282).

However, if one was looking for the *raison d'être* of the ethnographic method in structuralism, it was its systematic elaboration of the opposition between nature and culture. Structuralist anthropology derived most of its authority from the claim that it was able to isolate aspects of cultural formation and to explain them in terms either of nature or of culture across time and space. In his major ethnographic works, such as *The Elementary Structures of Kinship*, Lévi-Strauss had separated elements of nature, which he considered to be spontaneous and universal, from those of culture, which depended on social norms and were hence particular and regulated. However, the opposition between nature and culture had come up against certain unusual phenomena, such as the incest prohibition which seemed to be both a natural phenomenon because it was universal in character and cultural because it was predicated on norms and regulations. This conflation of nature and culture was considered by Lévi-Strauss to be scandalous because it transversed the nature/culture opposition (1969: 8). However, Derrida refused to see the simultaneous location of the incest prohibition in nature and culture as scandalous. For him, the real scandal was "a system of concepts [structuralism] which accredits the difference between nature and culture" (1982: 283). In other words, the incest prohibition could be considered scandalous only if we accepted the validity of the nature/culture opposition itself. In this case, we were simply trying to fit the prohibition into a set of concepts that preceded it.

The final target of Derrida's critique was perhaps the most attractive aspect of Lévi-Strauss's structuralist project – "the discourse of his method" (Derrida 1982: 285). The centerpiece of the structuralist methodology, as sketched out in *The Savage Mind*, was what Lévi-Strauss called the art of the *bricoleur*, a person who used whatever methods or means were at hand rather than a set of engineered concepts. Derrida rejected the discourse of the *bricoleur* on two main grounds. First, he argued that, contrary to the view that the *bricoleur* was using the means at hand, *bricolage* assumed the existence of a center, a myth or mythology. Secondly, while structuralism claimed to be a critique of empiricism, the "structural schemata" were a series of hypotheses built on "a finite quantity of information" subjected to "the proof of experience" (1982: 288). Thus, Derrida was to present his critique of structuralism as "the beginning of a step outside of philosophy" (284). This stepping outside of philosophy is what has come to be known as poststructuralism.[10]

6

Poststructuralism didn't, of course, simply appeal to postcolonial discourse because of its critique of structuralism. Rather, it entered the institutions of literary study – and the public imagination – primarily as a method of deconstructing existing traditions of Western thought and culture and of reading literary texts differently. It was as a method of cultural analysis and as a mode of reading that poststructuralism became central to the post-colonial project. Indeed, it is when we view it as a method of reading – a deconstructive method – that poststructuralism reaches a point of con-juncture with postcolonial discourse. This conjuncture was perhaps best expressed in Derrida's most literary work, *Of Grammatology*, which was translated and introduced to the English-speaking world by Gayatri Spivak (Spivak 1976).

Of Grammatology is considered central to poststructuralism in general and postcolonial theory in particular for three closely related reasons. First, it was in this book that Derrida sought to overcome the traditional gap between the language of literature (based on rhetorical figures) and the lan-guage of philosophy (committed to truth and hence suspicious of rhetoric). Here his goal was to overcome the division between the languages of philos-ophy and literature by deconstructing the privileging of speech over writing in the Western tradition. In a section of the book called "That Dangerous Supplement," Derrida reminded his readers that speech had been privileged in Western thought all the way from Plato to Lévi-Strauss because it was associated with a metaphysical presence or truth. In a close and detailed analysis of Rousseau's philosophical and fictional works, however, Derrida detected another, often repressed, dimension in speech. Contrary to the view that speech promised presence, immediacy, and truth, it was also the form in which these factors were refused or repressed. The hidden law of language, argued Derrida, was that the linguistic process that inaugurated speech also deconstructed the speaking subject.

It was in the process of repressing or exorcising this law that Rousseau came to condemn writing "as destructive of presence and as a disease of speech" (Derrida 1976: 141). Yet, Derrida argued, speech could not be captured except in writing. In this context, writing was dangerous because it claimed to be what it is not – a form of "presence and the sign of the thing itself" (144). Rather than see writing as a sign of the thing itself, we needed to conceive of it as a surplus to nature, as "stand-in," rather than a representation of the thing itself: "The sign is always the supplement of the thing itself" (145). For Derrida, then, what other critics had considered to be the scandal of writing, that is, the claim that it pretended to represent the thing itself, was not a fact to be repressed; indeed, to consider writing as a supplement was not to see it as a pale imitation of what it sought to represent but to reconsider the nature of representation itself outside the bounds of nature and reason. Thus, the supplement – the subject of writing – was "what neither Nature nor Reason can tolerate" (148). This is how writing – or what has come to be known as textuality – came to dominate poststructural discourse and, by extension, postcolonial theory.

There was a second area in which *Of Grammatology* provided a philosophical program that was to prove crucial to postcolonial discourse. This was in its proposition that writing was a form of difference, one that defied categorization and appropriation. Derrida's main claim here was that to consider writing as a form of difference was to comprehend the nature of the sign as a form of both presence and absence. When he said that difference "produces what it forbids, makes possible the very thing that makes it impossible" (1976: 142), he was suggesting that the import of the sign, or even its meaning, depended on the opposition between what was present and what was absent; what was unstated was as important as what was stated. Nevertheless, difference was not merely the representation of a simple opposition between presence and absence; rather it was the simultaneous representation of what was and what was not, "the obliterated origin of absence and presence, major forms of the disappearing and the appearing of the entity"

(143). This rather complicated theory has come to be represented in the form of a word that exists on the page but is cancelled through by a mark: the word is present in front of us, but it is also erased; its significance hence lies in its simultaneous existence and erasure. Once again, postcolonial theory has come to adopt this notion of writing as difference and to extend it to the field of cultural politics in general.

The third area in which *Of Grammatology* came to influence an emerging postcolonial theory was that it proposed a method of reading. In fact, in order to consider writing to be a mode of either difference or supplement as discussed above, one had to rethink the nature of reading itself. For example, to stop thinking of the thing itself as something anchored in nature or reason, hence available for representation in writing, was to raise the question of signification and, by extension, textuality and reading, as alternatives to theories of interpretation based on an analogy between signs and signifiers. Since Derrida was claiming that writing was constituted by a series of substitutions, reversals, and repetitions whose meaning could not be authorized by a set of ideas outside the text itself, what was then needed was a new method for reading absences, aporiae, and gaps. In the circumstances, Derrida proposed the following "modest proposals" for reading. First, he proposed that we should start with the recognition that writing itself was governed by a set of laws that the writer's discourse could not absolutely dominate. Thus reading had to be aimed at a relationship, unperceived by the writer, between "what he commands and what he does not command of the pattern of language that he uses"; rather than uncovering a system at work in the text, one leading to another system outside the text, a critical reading produced its own "signifying structure" (1976: 158).

Secondly, Derrida proposed that the act of reading had the capacity to produce its signifying structure not by doubling (reading in the text a series of intelligible patterns, images, or symbols), nor by appealing to a referent or a "transcendental signifier" outside the text itself. We could not, for example, understand how colonial subjects were represented in the colonial text by comparing their representation with the real experience of colonialism since what we considered to be the real was only available to us through texts or discourses. This was the basis of Derrida's famous – or infamous – claim that "*There is nothing outside of the text*" (1976: 158). Thirdly, Derrida proposed that if we could not judge a literary sign by referring it to a fixed point of origin or presence, if we could not separate the signifier from the signified or privilege one over the other, then we had no choice but to see representation as the relationship between two entities that were both products of writing and reading rather than the process by which signs were made intelligible by being compared to the things they signified. In all these cases we had no choice but to rethink theories of representation, systems of meaning, and language as a manifest presence.

7

Why, though, should we consider the above claims important to postcolonial discourse in its moment of emergence? Because by the time Derrida's works from the late 1960s were translated into English in the late 1970s and early 1980s, the field of English studies, especially the sub-field known as "Commonwealth Literature," was in a state of crisis. By the early 1980s, students of Anglophone literature were already complaining that they were prisoners of a critical tradition that was unable to account for the production of colonial subjects (and their literature) because it was still imprisoned in a historicist and realist tradition. Traditional criticism, argued Homi Bhabha in a 1984 essay, was based on the assumption that the history of colonialism was given, that the subject that emerged out of the colonial experience was knowable, and that the forms of representing both this history and its subject were predicated on a stable relation between "the text and a given pre-constituted reality" (1984: 99). Bhabha's quest was for an alternative theory of reading designed both to deconstruct the mimetic assumptions of literary criticism and to question the unified (colonial) subject at the center of this criticism. In the first case, he proposed "raising the issue of the representation of the colonial subject" by questioning "the collusion between historicism and realism" (96). In regard to the question of subjectivity, Bhabha's categorical claim was that the representation of the colonial subject was nothing less than the conception of "the subject of difference, of an-other history and an-other culture" (98).

This alternative theory of representation was enabled by poststructuralism. Derrida's radical rethinking of the nature of signification came at a time when students of postcolonial literature were trying to liberate themselves from traditional theories of representation imprisoned in unquestioned theories of history as a progressive narrative, subjects as transcendental and unified, and forms of representation tied to realism and a consensual moral community. Indeed, Bhabha's operating premise in *The Location of Culture* was that poststructuralist theory contained within it a critique of Eurocentrism and provided us with models for recuperating "the cultural and historical hybridity of the postcolonial world" (1994: 21), for locating culture at the spaces of translations and difference, and for encountering the also "hybrid moment of political change" (28). In Bhabha's project, then, we have a vivid example of the theoretical assumptions that postcolonial discourse inherited from poststructuralism.

A few examples can help us illustrate the close affinity between some varieties of postcolonial theory and radical poststructuralism: in *Of Grammatology*, Derrida had argued that there was nothing outside the text; in *The Location of Culture*, Bhabha followed this with his desire to articulate a mode of critique without the regime of truth, insisting that there was no knowledge "outside representation" (1994: 25), even going as far as to collapse the distinction between "the political objective and its means of representation" (27). If the key term in Derrida's lexicon was "difference," then it is fair to say that Bhabha took this term to places that Derrida himself might not have contemplated. Indeed, if there is a certain skepticism towards difference as a social category in Derrida's work, it is not an exaggeration to say that the postcolonial project, as it was mapped out in Bhabha's early work, was built around radical theories of difference. At the beginning of *The Location of Culture*, for example, Bhabha's assumption was that difference and otherness simultaneously functioned in "the fantasy of a certain cultural space" and constituted "a form of theoretical knowledge" (31). His basic claim was that the revisionary force of poststructural theory was to be found in the invocation of the other, "the docile body of difference, that reproduces a relation of domination and is the most serious indictment of the institutions of power and knowledge" (33). In the works of leading European poststructuralists, Bhabha would recover the revisionary impulse that would impel him to make some controversial reinterpretations of Fanon such as the following: "In 1952, it was Fanon who suggested that an oppositional, differential reading of Lacan's Other might be more relevant for the colonial condition than the Marxist reading of the master–slave dialectic" (34).[11] From such examples, it is not difficult to present postcolonial theory, or certain varieties of it, as "the afterbirth" of poststructuralism.

Still, one final set of questions needs to be addressed: how and why did postcolonial theory come to concern itself with colonial and postcolonial questions? If postcolonial discourse is part of a "Western" theoretical project, as many of its critics have argued, why did it need the colonial space or postcolonial polity to carry out its work? The "how" part of the question is perhaps the easier to answer and Bhabha is exemplary here. The postcolonial project sought to go beyond poststructuralism by extending its theories and methods to the colonial space. After all, poststructuralism had come to posit itself as a critique of Eurocentrism in two main areas: in the tradition of humanism and its universalism, and in its theories of representation. Bhabha wanted to go a step further and argue that his theoretical project was intended to locate this critique of humanism and the sign in a specific referential and institutional moment, the moment of cultural difference whose genealogy was to be found in the culture of colonialism. This is how he put it in *The Location of Culture*:

> Such a reorientation may be found in the historical texts of the colonial moment in the late eighteenth and early nineteenth centuries. For at the same time as the question of cultural difference emerged in the colonial text, discourses of civility were defining the doubling moment of the emergence of Western modernity. Thus the political and theoretical genealogy of modernity lies not only in the origins of the *idea* of civility but in this history of the colonial moment. It is to be found in the resistance of the colonized populations to the Word of God and Man – Christianity and the English language.   (1994: 32)

Thus postcolonial theory came to posit its relationship to poststructuralism by insisting that the critique of Eurocentrism made famous by the "prophets" of difference and ambivalence was already implicit in the colonial moment and the discourse it produced (Spivak 1988b).

What, though, was the place of the postcolonial or decolonized nation in these debates? Here, it is interesting to note that, although postcolonial theory has provided us with some powerful critiques of the nation and nationalism, its engagement with the decolonized nation and its literature has been minimal. Indeed, it is precisely in relation to the decolonized space of the nation that major divergences in postcolonial discourse become pronounced even in the works of the most self-consciously poststructuralist theorists. In *The Location of Culture*, for example, Bhabha's work was focused primarily on the experience of migrant subjects and minorities within metropolitan cultures and their histories of cultural difference; it was in experiences and perspectives of subjects who exist outside the "foundational frames" (1994: 6) of cultural identity that the new temporality of postcoloniality would emerge and be reinforced. In contrast, Spivak was adamant that the minority or migrant subject could not be a substitute for the postcolonial subject. Her belief was that postcoloniality was not "the space of the colonization–decolonization reversal" in which nation was posited as the opposite of empire; rather, what was at stake in her project was "postcoloniality in the space of difference," a postcolonial space displaced from both empire and nation or excessive of both (1993: 78, 77). In the end, postcolonial discourse was caught – and is still caught – between its identity as an extension of poststructuralist theory and its desire to make the postcolonial space the center of its concerns and preoccupations.

NOTES

1 One of the most astute readings of postcolonial discourse as an extension of the poststructuralist project can be found in Larsen 2002.

2 However, not all postcolonial theory assumes that poststructural theory can account for the international division of labor and knowledge. For an alternative view, see Spivak 1988b.

3 Sartre's writings on colonialism are collected in Sartre 2001a. My discussion of Sartre here is indebted to Young 1990: 28–47.

4 For the influence of humanism over French intellectual life from 1945 to 1960 see Pavel 1989: 3. See also Young 1990: 21–47. According to Michael S. Roth, Sartrean existentialism would become "the guardian of a radical humanism" (Roth 1988: 1).

5 Bhabha's deployment of Fanon in the cause of postcoloniality can be found in Bhabha 1994: 40–65. However, postcolonial discourse and Marxism could be said to be involved in a continuous struggle to claim Fanon. In this regard see Taylor 1989: esp. 7–46; Sekyi-Otu 1996; and Lazarus 1999b.

6 For Fanon and the "new humanism," see Bernasconi 1996.

7 For reasons that are discussed below, Fanon's discourse is essentially gendered; his concern is the crisis of the black man in the Antilles.

8 Fanon's specific concern with the lived experience of blackness ("l'expérience vécue du noir") is meticulously discussed by Judy (1996) and Kruks (1996). In *Frantz Fanon: A Life*, David Macey insists that Charles Lam Markmann has served English readers very poorly in translating the title of the fifth chapter of *Peau noire, masques blancs* – namely, "l'expérience vécue du noir" – as "The Fact of Blackness." This translation, Macey argues, makes a mockery of Fanon's phenomenological framework, in terms of which "blackness" is precisely not a "fact" but a socio-biological schema which exists only to the extent that it is actualized (2000: 164–65).

9 In literary studies, the major proponent of structuralism in Africa was the Nigerian scholar Sunday Anozie (1984).

10 For an excellent discussion of poststructuralism as a post-philosophical moment see Dews 1987, especially the introduction.

11 For some of the debates on the "postcolonial Fanon" see Read 1996.

7

TIMOTHY BRENNAN

From development to globalization: postcolonial studies and globalization theory

Neither "globalization theory" nor "postcolonial studies" are terms that easily reveal their meanings. The areas of knowledge to which they refer are not what they seem, and a great deal of confusion surrounds their uses. Readers would be forgiven for thinking that "globalization theory" denoted an emergent body of writing called forth by inexorable recent developments in technology and communications, as well as radical shifts in the world economy and in geopolitics, all of them presaging the rise of a truly global culture – the obliteration of state sovereignty in a world marked by fluidity and border-crossing. In turn, these readers might suppose that "postcolonial studies" referred to an inaugural critique of Eurocentrism prompted by a new diasporic wave of intellectuals from the former colonies resident in metropolitan centers who – informed by postwar theories of language and representation – began in the late 1970s to cast older versions of "Western Man" in doubt in an act of writing back to Empire.

Actually, neither is the case. One has to begin by distinguishing between the study of global issues or colonial pasts *per se* and the fairly recent creation of schools of thought that retrospectively appropriate the more general cases fleetingly echoed in their names. When invoked in European or North American universities since the beginning of the 1990s, globalization theory and postcolonial studies turn out to be very specialized discursive formations passing for older and more varied types of enquiry. This slippage between connotation and code is one of the first things to understand about the conjunction of the two terms.

There have been many earlier traditions of investigating, on the one hand, globalizing features of world history and human societies and, on the other, colonial practices and anticolonial challenges in the cultural field. Indeed, these now separate foci were in earlier periods conjoined. The ancestors of both, as unified phenomena, include systemic analyses of colonization dating from the early years of the European conquest in the sixteenth century (Las Casas 1992; Raleigh 1997; Montaigne 1991), Enlightenment tracts protesting the ravages of imperial intervention in the late seventeenth, eighteenth, and early nineteenth centuries (Raynal 1991; Smith 1910; Bentham 1995; Voltaire 2001), studies in the nineteenth and early twentieth centuries of the origins and dynamics of capitalism as a global phenomenon (Marx and Engels 1988; Marx 1991; Melville 1988; Hobson 1902), comprehensive economic critiques of the division of the globe at the apex of European colonization prior to the First World War (Graham 1896; Morris 1901; Kautsky 1970; Lenin 1975), new forms of global or broadly regional historiographies associated with the *annales* school and other historical schools after the Second World War (Braudel 1992; McNeill 1963; Hodgson 1974), Marxist historiography based on the initiatives of the anticolonial movements (Kiernan 1969; Stavrianos 1981; Wolf 1982), dependency theory (Frank 1967; Rodney 1972; Santos 1978), and particularly – and very directly – world systems theory (Cox 1959, 1962, 1964; Wallerstein 1974; Samir Amin 1976). We will look at some of these efforts in more detail below.

In spite of reaching back several centuries, and despite being well developed, extensively documented, and self-conscious, these multiple and varied intellectual movements, with their own canons of texts and scholarly pantheons, are frequently discounted in contemporary globalization theory even as they are quietly accessed without acknowledgment. In a similar way, postcolonial studies – although in part resting on these same foundations – draws on more immediate precursors, especially the anticolonial intellectuals of the 1950s and 1960s, whose work was anticipated by, and directly inherited, interwar Marxist networks of anti-imperialism (Nehru 1946; Mao 1953; Fanon 1968; Lumumba 1972; Guevara 1969; Ho Chi Minh 1967; see Parry 2002; Brennan 2002b). Motifs of cultural difference, epistemological othering, colonial subjectivity, and social contradiction – all common in later postcolonial studies – were inaugurated by that earlier generation of politically engaged intellectuals, who were often members of actual governments following formal independence. These "independence intellectuals," if one can call them that, were in turn the inheritors of a tradition forged by intellectuals from Africa, Asia, and Latin America resident in Europe between the world wars, who in the communist milieux of those years had begun to forge a rhetorical and theoretical apparatus for studying colonialism as a comprehensive phenomenon, and even more importantly as a morally corrupt system of economic enrichment that could be defeated by organized counter-activity in which intellectuals from the colonies would play a prominent role.

The tendency of contemporary intellectual trends to supplant predecessors by erasing the history of their own making is not a chance occurrence, nor is it simply the work of uncharitable scholars. It is rather a characteristic feature of contemporary capitalist societies, which are at once *presentist* – that is, viewing each moment as the only reality while expunging the past in a gesture of calculated *anti*-historicism – and *modernist* in the technical sense of needing to judge every current discovery as an utterly new departure, an absolute rupture with all that went before. This intellectual reflex is, in fact, a central feature both of what globalization theory argues the world has become, and of what that theory unwittingly demonstrates about itself.

Contemporary modernism celebrates what earlier modernists greeted with suspicion or disparagement (as in those writers of the early twentieth century like Franz Kafka, Marcel Proust, or William Butler Yeats, who despised mass culture and the decline of the aristocratic sensibility of the refined patron of the arts). Today, by contrast, mass culture is enshrined in terms of obscure and refined aesthetic pleasure with populist pretensions that form the bedrock ideology of the most wealthy and the most privileged. Both versions are modernist in that they cast the new as the never-before-seen: in the first case, as a heroically constructed, formal experimentalism that preserves the unsurpassed intelligence and insight of the chosen few of the past, serving as a bulwark against the vulgarity of the masses; in the second case, as a radical break with a history considered to be heading in an unpredictable direction which is, then, valorized precisely for that reason. Although one speaks of *post*modernism today, the "post" does not connote a time after, but rather a heightening. What is meant by the term is less the supersession of modernity than *ultra*-modernity. The modernist does not merely express a neutral belief in the "year zero" of the now, as though dispassionately describing a fundamental historical fissure that evidence had forced him or her to accept. Instead, modernism (including its postmodern variant) is normative. The "now" is the new, and the new is rapturously and exuberantly embraced. Without ever questioning the fundamental self-contradiction of the move, the modernist then vigorously urges on a future that *should* unfold (because it is good) while simultaneously arguing that it *must* unfold (because it is inevitable). This style of thinking informs both globalization theory and postcolonial studies, and is another of the major links between them. Let us now develop in more detail the arguments outlined above.

I Globalization theory: five possible positions

As a term, "globalization" is marked by a fundamental ambiguity. On the one hand, it holds out hope for the creation of new communities and unforeseen solidarities; on the other hand, it appears merely to euphemize corporatization and imperial expansion. At its base, in other words, lies a tension between *process* and *policy*. Is globalization theory about describing a "process": that is, an amalgam of material shifts, spatial re-orderings, anonymous developments and movements, the inexorable concatenation of changes in communication, transportation, demographics, and the environment? Or does it describe a "policy" (and is it a part of that policy): that is, a myth-making operation whose purpose is to project a world order that a small group of national and/or financial interests ardently desires to be the future for the rest of us – a future that has happily not yet arrived? There is, as well, a normative dimension to this tension. Does globalization presage a new openness to the foreign and the out-of-reach, or is it rather (and paradoxically) just the opposite: a veiled way of alluding to the Americanization of foreignness in a world dominated by US power following the fall of the Soviet Union (Bourdieu 2001; Foster 2002; Friedman 1999)? As expected, given our observations above, a similar ambiguity – structurally identical, in fact – marks postcolonial studies, where various critics have wondered aloud whether assaults on "imperial discourse" or the "epistemic violence" of colonial mentalities are, as their authors claim, a more sophisticated way of battling Eurocentrism or merely a rendering of earlier radical positions of dissent in a form more accommodating to power by a professional diaspora to the imperial centers (Appiah 1991; Dirlik 1997; Huggan 2001). Questions such as these interrogate globalization, but are already outside "globalization theory," which does not typically open itself up to this kind of self-questioning. In particular, it would consider raising the issue of the *interestedness* of academic knowledge as being impertinent, for reasons we will describe.

Current globalization theory, in its restricted sense, cannot logically doubt itself in the manner I have suggested because it does not merely claim that economic or cultural integration is occurring on a global scale. The import of what is being said goes significantly beyond that. The intended point is rather that the world is being reconstituted *as a single social space*. One might interpret this to mean that the world is becoming more homogenized, that we are seeing the creation of a single, albeit hybridized, world culture whose pace of life, tastes, and customs – conditioned by a similar regime of commodities consisting of cars, computers, and cellular phones – has increasingly fewer local variations. It could also be taken to mean that we are on the road to global political integration. It is worth recognizing, however, that it does not necessarily stipulate either of these positions. To say "a single social space" still allows for complex and dynamic internal variations across an interconnected system of localities and regions. The key component is that there be a governing logic or social tendency that brings all these localities and regions into a unity unknown before.

The idea is further posited that globalization has become its own explanation: that is, not only has space/time been "distanciated" as a result of analyzable causal forces (that is, distances are less relevant to one's particular experience given the instant availability of images, objects, and information from afar); what is being claimed is rather that social theory itself has undergone a spatio-temporal reformulation in which the earlier modes of analysis are no longer tenable. Class antagonisms, geopolitical rivalries, the entrenched defense of privileges, imperial designs, the blunt arguments of war and profit-making – all of the earlier mechanisms of historical causation are, in globalization theory, implicitly downgraded into second-order explanations.

As these are cast as vestiges of a vanishing social logic, globalization theory looks rather to a "new" dynamic forged by the happy chaos of an infinitely mobile citizenry, a constantly self-defined subjectivity, a terrain of virtual space consisting of multi-faceted niches of an always malleable and morphing freedom. As such (the argument goes) the mandate of reliable definitions crumbles away; the researcher, in order not to be left behind, sprints frantically after a reality vastly more innovative on its own than earlier utopias had been in the imagination. Social sense-making is no longer determined by students of history or the organizers of thought known as philosophers; in the view of the globalization theorist, their structures of understanding only impede their ability to recognize the future unfolding before their eyes, which is being created by investors, technologists, managers, and organizers, not – thankfully not – working according to plan, but swept along in a process that is anarchic and autopoetic (Bauman 1998; Giddens 1991; Agamben 1993).

The paradigmatic tone and style of globalization theory is perhaps provided best by the sociologist, Anthony Giddens, who gives a clear indication of the type of argument found in the field in our restrictive sense. For Giddens, people in ultra-modernity live apocalyptically, experiencing levels of risk unknown before. As social institutions become more and more complex, they operate (and force us to operate) at increasing levels of abstraction, now built into the fabric of individual life. As a result, the subject is forced to *trust*, since abstract systems tend to "disembed" the subject from immediate experience, transforming intimacy from the previously anchored criteria of kinship and obligation to a "life politics" based on controlling one's own body. As deskilling renders most of us utterly dependent on expert systems whose functioning we simply have to trust, this bio-political control becomes more important as a response to the "runaway world" of modernity, and the unitary framework of experience of which we are constantly reminded. Doubt as a pervasive feature of modern critical reason now permeates everyday life, becoming part of its existential dimension. Time and space are separable and controllable by way of the technologies of clock and map. Although aspects of this vision sound threatening at first, our initial impressions are deliberately confounded by Giddens's jubilant conclusions. For him, our ability in ultra-modernity to outgrow providential reason produces an increasingly secular understanding of the nature of things, and so intrinsically leads to a safer and more rewarding existence (Giddens 1991).

Such an account is obviously at odds with a systematic account of financial forces or the impure motives of privileged agencies. By taking these conflicting approaches into consideration, one comes to recognize that globalization is not waiting to be found, discrete and safe, in the world of living social communities. There are no facts to be rehearsed in order to determine either whether the term "globalization" is merited, or whether (if so) this *thing* has not existed for many centuries without it being accompanied by the heraldic futuristic utterances that are now widely evident (utterances that often have the ring of a campaign). By themselves the facts, such as they are, are mute: for instance, the ownership patterns of transnational corporations (TNCs), the explosive rise in internet traffic, the radical breakdown of treaties governing international law, the increasing recourse to off-shore banking, the orchestrated planning imposed by the Bretton Woods institutions (International Monetary Fund, World Bank), or the flows of migrant labor in Southeast Asia.

To this extent, it is vital to grasp that debates over globalization are discursive. That is, they are debates over *theory*: over which explanatory mechanism makes the most sense given a body of (usually implicit) ethical and political objectives. The ensemble of theories of globalization invoked at the outset of this chapter – centuries-old critiques of capitalism, Enlightenment protests against colonial excesses, conscious attempts since 1945 to write a fully world history, and the more recent exuberant "globalization theory" that characterizes both poststructuralism and neoliberalism (often in similar terms) – all of these taken together have yielded five basic positions which again and again arise in various guises in the now massive literature on globalization. Heuristically, it might be useful to spell them out at this point.

The first position argues that globalization – however much it is the unintended result of economic logics, technical discoveries, and population growth – finds its only real significance as a *political promise*. Here, finally, the great Enlightenment program of Immanuel Kant for a single world government under universal law is perhaps realizable (Kant 1963 [1795], 1991 [1784]; Toulmin 1990; Kristeva 1993). Possibilities at last exist for either world citizenship under a single governmental entity (a new world state), or some flexible federalist structure allowing significant local autonomy. It is an exciting and welcome development, taking us beyond the petty factionalism, ethnic rivalries, and bloodletting of the past, associated with the ancient, premodern, and modern nationalist eras. Globalization, in this view, is welcome (Falk and Strauss 2000, 2001).

By contrast, the second position argues that globalization is not so much a matter of formal political outcomes as the development of *trade* and of *finance*, in which the pure freedom of exchange revolutionizes human contact along with the potential for understanding, leisure, and cultural sampling. It is not political actors but transnational corporations that are responsible for globalization, and therefore what is happening is happening deliberately *outside* political structures, and even in opposition to them (Sklair 1991). There is no clear local, or national, beneficiary of globalization since the TNCs are indifferent to nations (they are, after all, technically owned by people from many countries), and hostile to them (they naturally desire the permeability of borders). They supersede nations, which have therefore become obsolete. In this variant, globalization can be considered either welcome or unwelcome. A theorist such as Jagdish Bhagwati, for instance – an economist at Columbia University who celebrates capitalism – considers these developments the fruit of the marvelous rationality of market forces, while Félix Guattari and Toni Negri (post-Marxist intellectuals who describe themselves as "communists") share much the same view, considering the runaway market as unleashing powerful utopian energies (Bhagwati 2001; Guattari and Negri 1990). By contrast, the billionaire financier, George Soros, deems the unrestricted mobility of finance to be a human catastrophe (Soros 1998).

The third position combines the emphasis on politics and trade while shifting the criterion to *geopolitical motive*. In this variant, globalization is the result of developments in technology, transportation, and financial/corporate restructuring working in concert with an underlying *ideology* that is basically American (Valladao 1998; Bauman 1998). Thus globalization, although undoubtedly permeating the rest of the world and in some ways benefiting actors in several countries, is structurally American. It is the United States that primarily benefits, not only directly as a specific nation-state, but in the more ambitious sense that the United States is a mini-model of the future world – the world as it will appear when globalized. Were we to examine this recognizably American ideology as the dynamic contemporary expression of capitalism (the argument goes), we would see how important it has been in facilitating technological developments in media, travel, fashion, and entertainment in a wild and intrepid search for novelty without any thought for the consequences. In a more localized sense, however, it is the American twist on capitalism that has made globalization seem desirable, and has done so by making the following concepts widely believed in, either because they are thought inexorable or because they are thought attractive (the fusing of the two qualities, again, is paradigmatic): pragmatism, pluralism, individualism, and suspicion towards the "state." Here globalization can, again, be thought either good or bad, with Thomas Friedman offering perhaps the most outspoken and extreme views on behalf of an irrepressible American genius and beneficence, and Paul Krugman, the economist and op-ed columnist for *The New York Times*, tirelessly exposing the emptiness of neoliberal ideology, and the rampant corruption and cronyism at the heart of American profit-making (Friedman 1999; Krugman 1997).

A fourth variant is less evolutionary than the third while retaining its focus on the United States. It explicitly ties globalization to the problematics of the colonizing "West." Here, globalization is basically the form that imperialism takes in the late twentieth century (Lapham 1998; Blaut 1993; Samir Amin *et al.* 1990; Bourdieu 2001). It is a shibboleth whose emergence as a master-term coincided exactly with the fall of the Soviet Union and the Eastern bloc – that period, in other words, in which the last credible adversaries to US global hegemony were removed. Most of the features said to characterize globalization are American, and they are coercively imposed on others as a universal norm. Rather than the hybridity that is widely acclaimed as being on the rise, we are instead seeing the violent incorporation of global difference into a single national project that is importantly, even vitally, not perceived as such. Although the forms and styles of this imperialism are crucially different from those of the past, the intentions and effects are identical (conquest, occupation, and the stealing of resources continue, and enrich distinct national entities, but they are now performed not under the sign of "civilization" or "God" or "Britain" but in the name of "globalization" or simply the "new," which universalizes the interests of that distinct national entity). This analysis presents globalization as a largely fictive enterprise, either cynical or guilty of wishful thinking. Here, globalization is seen as a threat.

The fifth position is the most distinctive. It avers that globalization does not exist. Although it concedes that travel and communication are much easier and more accessible than previously, and although it readily agrees that this increased human contact has had profound effects on the way people see the world, nothing qualitatively has changed. The nation-state structure is still the international norm; ethnic, linguistic, and religious divisions have only intensified; most of the world's people are entirely localized, provincial, traditional, and cut-off from others, not only living outside this supposedly new globalized world, but outside modernity itself. Globalization is therefore not a description, but a projection; or more properly, it is a projection that passes itself off as a description. Once again, this is a mixed view, with globalization being thought either good or bad. As the self-styled Metternich of the late twentieth century, for instance, Henry Kissinger is not particularly happy to observe that globalization is an overweening fiction (Kissinger 1994). With grim pragmatism, therefore, he counsels his readers to be wary of obstacles still remaining to American supremacy, wishing in fact that globalization were more real than it is. In both Immanuel Wallerstein and Janet Abu-Lughod, by contrast, globalization collapses as a concept not because of wishful thinking, but from want of scholarship (Wallerstein 1984; Abu-Lughod 1989). An investigation of material relations makes it vain, in their opinion, to distinguish our own time from the high Renaissance (or even earlier); both eras are "global" in more or less the same ways, just as both equally fail to approximate the complete integration fancifully described in globalization theory.

These representative positions display more than different diagnoses or emphases; they are methodologically at odds as well. For instance, in his own primer on globalization, Anthony McGrew assumes that the claims to "global society" are uncontroversially real, seeking to introduce the topic only by discussing the conflicting explanations for this reality given by major voices in the field. He does not mention the fact, but his discussion reveals a paradox (McGrew 1996). His own argument is representative of only one of two major methodologies – which can be found throughout globalization discourse – that emerge as perfect dialectical opposites. A seesawing between the multiple and the unitary is highlighted in both, but the two elements play very different roles in each. On the one hand, the proponents of the view of an already achieved "global village" (McGrew's position combines the second and third variants above) often tend to see a multiplicity, randomness, and disconnectedness at the heart of an overall, fortuitous unity portrayed as the result of a progressive telos. By contrast, some of the critics of globalization – both those skeptical of its desirability and those doubtful of its presence – see behind "globalization" an underlying, comprehensive set of motives and related processes working on behalf of limited and localized interests: a symmetrically inverted position. Theirs is a *total* explanation based on the repetition of patterns of power-brokering from capitalism's past, whereas the former's is, as a matter of taste and principle, individual, separable, and "federal," if you will, at the same time that it resists the suggestion of familiarity.

The concept of "totality" employed by some critics of globalization theory is reminiscent of that theory, but, again, inverts it. It does not merely stipulate a unity, but suggests that any contingent or local problem is only clearly seen as being conditioned by its place in a total relationship of objects and events, all governed by a dominant logic. So, for example, the idea presented by a globalization enthusiast like McGrew that Immanuel Wallerstein, James Rosenau, and Robert Gilpin pose incompatible views on globalization because Wallerstein emphasizes historical capitalism, Rosenau the shift from industrial to postindustrial order, and Gilpin the power and legitimacy of a hegemonic liberal state would, from the vantage point of totality, be a crude way of seeing the matter. A theory that conceives of society as a totality would tend not to separate the economic, the political, the social, and the aesthetic in this way. These modes of societal interaction all devolve from interests and material conditionings such that, say, the preferred goals of historical capitalism could be said to *demand* at a certain point precisely a "hegemonic liberal state" to oversee its concerns, managing the vast division of labor that involves moving basic industry to the Third World while drawing on the highly trained citizens of the wealthier countries to set up information- and service-based businesses (the "postindustrial" ones). Capitalism is the logic in each phase of this operation, and there are not three explanations, but one.

In all of its variants, globalization theory presumes a knowledge of the following key terms.

- *Modernity* – apart from suggesting widely available technologies associated with "modern life" (televisions, cars, high-rises, computers), modernity more generally refers to a cast of mind, an attitude, and an approach to problems as much as to a period. Modernity begins with the Enlightenment and never ends (we are still in "modernity"). It centrally involves the idea of the "new," the break, the departure. Earlier, intellectuals (church clerics, for example) tended to base their arguments on Aristotle, Scripture, or the like. In modernity, legitimacy and authority are no longer based on principles derived from the past. Rather in modernity, the questioner (of law, of right, of religion, of truth) offers his/her own justification. Modernity means to create one's own normativity out of oneself.
- *The West* – a historical rather than a geographical construct. It means developed, industrialized, urbanized, capitalist, secular, and modern. Any society that shares these features is usually thought of as existing in the orbit of the "West". Derived originally from the division of the Roman Empire, and later by the division of the Christian churches in the eleventh century, it took on a new, ideological, coloring in the era of the Crusades, when the "Orient" (which referred at first only to Islam) was then allowed to stand in for everything east of it as well (China,

India, Persia, and so on). In the Cold War, a new binary opposition arose using the terms "East" and "West" with a slightly altered (but fundamentally similar) geopolitical significance (Lazarus 1991, 2002; Coronil 1997; Said 1993).

- *Space/Place* – the significance of the turn to space/place in globalization theory lies, first of all, in the overcoming of temporality. Time is supplanted by Space in a worldview that: a) perceives the conflicts of history as being decisively decided in favor of one of the warring parties; or (for exactly opposite reasons): b) allergically recoils from the Hegelian notion of a progressive telos to history, and is therefore drawn methodologically to a synchronic analysis, expressed in metaphors of spatiality (we identified these opposed, but complementary, features of globalization theory above in the terms "neoliberalism" and "post-structuralism"). In harmony with the assumption that globalization is an irrepressible unfolding, the logical issue is no longer what will happen, but when it will extend itself over a vast but finite territory. The optic logically shifts from pace to scale, and from the chronometric to the cartographic. As a matter of theory, the dual expression "space/place" means to suggest that a struggle over value is embedded in the way one thinks about spatiality (Sassen 1998). "Space" is more abstract and ubiquitous: it connotes capital, history, and activity, and gestures towards the meaningless of distance in a world of instantaneous communication and "virtuality"; "place" connotes, by contrast, the kernel or center of one's memory and experience – a dwelling, a familiar park or city street, one's family or community. An ambiguity of value is obviously contained in the pairing, since the former is both bloodless and forward-looking while the latter is both personally vital and static.

- *Cosmopolitanism* – colloquially associated with broad fellow-feeling, world-travel, openness to cultural otherness, and so on, cosmopolitanism discursively accompanies globalization as the political ethic of the humanities intellectual. It both describes and endorses (endorses *as* it describes) the creation of a singularity out of newness, a blending and merging of differences becoming one entity. Furthermore, it stipulates a theory of world government and world citizenship in which the term's cultural meaning is carried over to its political one. In that sense, it is distinct from internationalism, which sets out to establish a global network of respect and cooperation based on differences of polity as well as culture. Cosmopolitanism sprouts from an already existing culture of intellectuals and middle-class travelers, researchers, and businessmen. Internationalism, on the other hand – although based no less than cosmopolitanism on the facts of global interpenetration, the homogenization brought about by capitalist mass culture, and the cultural consequences of mass migration – is an ideology of the domestically restricted, the recently relocated, the exiled, and the temporarily weak (Hannerz 1990; Nussbaum 1996; Brennan 1997, 2002a).

- *Neoliberalism* – a position that became prominent in policy-making circles (and later in journalism and the academy) following the conservative electoral victories of Margaret Thatcher in Britain and Ronald Reagan in the United States. With the goal of dismantling the welfare state, neo-liberalism argues that an unrestrained market logic, freed from governmental constraints, will cure social ills and lead to general prosperity. As Pierre Bourdieu explains, it

> is not a discourse like others. Like psychiatric discourse in the asylum, as described by Erving Goffman, it is a 'strong discourse,' which is so strong and so hard to fight because it has behind it all the powers of a world of power relations which it helps to make as it is, in particular by orienting the economic choices of those who dominate economic relations and so adding its own – specifically symbolic – force to those power relations.
>
> (1998: 95)

It is a faith, rather than an analysis, which creates its own truth by imposing itself on the supposedly free agents of economic choice.

II Links to postcolonial studies

Globalization theory and postcolonial studies ambiguously evoke an ethical program while presenting themselves as iconoclastic departures from older modes of studying their fields of interest. A teleology of shared mores links them. On the one hand, postcolonial studies carries on the sensibilities formulated by anticolonial intellectuals who, given the conjunctures of foreign policy, caught the attention of metropolitan writers and thinkers at specific times (resistance intellectuals from Latin America throughout the nineteenth century, China of the 1920s, India of the 1940s, Algeria of the 1950s, Vietnam of the 1960s, Central America of the 1970s, and so on). Within the United States, many of the central motifs of postcolonial studies were formulated already in academia in the 1960s as a result of the anti-Vietnam War movement and the radicalizations that produced new Black Studies and Women's Studies departments. On the other hand, "postcolonial studies" is often taken to be something much more specific. It was less a discrete field than a collection of attitudes and styles of enquiry arising in a variety of disciplines more or less simultaneously in the early 1980s. Postcolonial studies in this sense alluded to its early parentage, but thought of itself as being more directly influenced by poststructuralism; indeed, the growth of "theory" in the late 1970s and the rise of postcolonial studies in this more restricted sense were virtually contemporaneous.

In the broadest sense, postcolonial studies is an intellectual movement driven by a critique of Eurocentrism and patriarchy. In its general arc, the work involves collecting and disseminating information, formulating arguments, or explaining concepts with the end of achieving emancipation for minority, marginal, or formerly colonized peoples. However, it is also and at the same time involved in questioning value – that is, it seeks to reorient cultural values attendant upon learning to understand and appreciate aesthetically the cultural achievements of those outside the European sphere. It seeks to show how earlier scholars in the West have been narrowly obsessed, culturally limited, and tendentiously ignorant of many of the world's most consequential artistic and intellectual creations. Many trace the origins of the field to the publication of Edward W. Said's *Orientalism* in 1978, and the elaborations later provided (in a very different vein) by Gayatri Chakravorty Spivak, Homi K. Bhabha, and others. In practice, these later elaborations (unlike Said's) tended to merge colonial or non-Western themes with deconstruction, discourse-analysis, and Lacanian psychoanalysis, whereas Said was more consciously drawing on an earlier philological and social democratic tradition of historians and activists.

There has been a good deal of argument about the term "postcolonial" since it suggests that colonies no longer exist (a suggestion that does not bear scrutiny). The term, however, survived in part because it successfully euphemized harsher terms like imperialism or racism in professionally respectable academic environments, but also because many of the field's practitioners believed the fight over the independence of sovereign states (over which the colonial struggle had once been fought) was no longer the issue. In an age of globalization the issue was about Eurocentric assumptions rather than military occupations: hence, the "post."

As a matter of intellectual precedent, however, one clearly sees the ties of globalization to the problems of imperial practices, and so can appreciate a rather different kind of bond between them as well. "World systems theory" is often cited as the most obvious forerunner of globalization theory, and either Immanuel Wallerstein or Samir Amin is usually considered its most commanding presence, if not its founder. Who came first is of less importance than that a leftist critique of development ideology arose in the 1950s and 1960s, creating the basis for much of what later became known as the theory of "globalization." Amin was formulating its basic tenets in his dissertation in 1957 (published in 1970 as *L'Accumulation à l'échelle mondiale* [*Accumulation on a World Scale*, 1974]). For his part, Marshall Hodgson was publicly using the term "world system" already in 1965, and that was a year *after* Oliver Cromwell Cox had completed the third volume of his neglected trilogy on the foundations of capitalism as a world system (Hodgson 1974; Cox 1959). The central arguments of world systems theory are: (a) that intricately organized systems of trade, cultural contact, and borrowing are extraordinarily old, even ancient; (b) that capital accumulation is the motor force for such contact; (c) that history must be founded on a rejection of Eurocentric assumptions or by the artificial separation of cultural and economic questions; and, (d) that world systems have a center/periphery structure, and alternate between hegemony and rivalry marked by economic cycles of ascending and descending phases.

A related predecessor would be "dependency theory." If the colonial era's naively ethnocentric evolutionary argument of European superiority gave way after the Second World War to "modernization theory," the latter nevertheless adapted many of the former's assumptions: for example, Europe entered history in a dominant posture by way of the "European miracle," its unique mastery of reason, freedom, and individualism. These cultural traits distinguish it among world civilizations (Landes 1998; McNeill 1963). Hence, the rest of the world is on the way to "modernizing" itself, but cannot do so without the diffusion of European traits. The dependency theorists, primarily based in Latin America and the Caribbean, arose to contest this narrative. They argued by contrast that the dominant countries deliberately "underdeveloped" the Third World, and that First-World wealth was derived not only from the theft of resources from the periphery, but from pressing home the artificial advantages won in an earlier period of conquest (Santos 1978; Frank 1967; Frank and Gills 1996; Rodney 1972).

Theories of globalization, then – as Justin Rosenberg points out – are not necessarily "globalization theory," just as studies of colonialism, anticolonialism, and imperialism are not necessarily "postcolonial studies" (Rosenberg 2000; see also Ahmad 1992; Lazarus 1999a; San Juan 1998; Brennan 2000). In the university at least, both were driven by a set of *ethical* postulates popularized by poststructuralist theory: the striving for ambivalence as a matter of principle; the ardent belief that answering a question "forecloses" it; the elision of meaning in pursuit of epistemological doubt; and, most of all, the deployment of a variety of tropes such as "migrancy," "nomadism," "hybridity," and "decentering" which are marshalled in order to make the case that mobility and mixedness – not as contingent historical experiences but as modes of being – are states of virtue. What is implied is that these conditions are *ontologically* superior, and that political life should be based today on approximating them. It is important not to confuse this ethical program with theories of globalization, since many critics believe such a program to be precisely an adjunct to the very corporate (and American) globalization being analyzed. To its predecessors, as well as to its critics, globalization theory shares with postcolonial studies a dubious relationship to the power it purportedly questions. In these circles, one would want to emphasize not ethics but the large-scale structural determinants of both fields of inquiry: namely, *capitalism* and *the West*. What both are really attempting to do is expose the tyrannies of value lying behind the creation of the myth of "the West" – a myth continually reinvented in each subsequent era in order to outmaneuver the disrepute into which the older discrimination had fallen (Blaut 1993; Stokes 2001). If globalization is a continuation of colonialism, however, what exactly is colonialism?

Both colonialism and imperialism entail the subjugation of one people by another. Traditionally, neither term refers to individuals within one society subjugating others within that same society. What is meant, rather, is that people who live in one region of the world – not just living together, but acting as organized members of a recognizable political territory such as a nation-state – subjugate those of another part of the world. So the concept suggests not only the largeness of the operation, or the ethnic, racial, or cultural differences of the parties, but the global scale upon which it is carried out. When we say "subjugation," we mean forcible, often violent, control over others: the rendering of people "subjects," which is to say placing them in a situation where their freedom is contingent upon the will of the dominant group.

Colonialism and imperialism, unlike other forms of subjugation, are not based on rank or privilege alone – as, for instance, in the inequalities experienced by people of different social classes in eighteenth-century France. That is, the dominant group is not composed only of the rich and powerful, or the generals who did the conquering, or the businessmen who profited from the conquest. On the contrary, the key idea that motivates colonialism and imperialism is that *everyone* from the conquering country is civilizationally superior to the conquered people. One can feel that one belongs to the dominant group simply by virtue of one's race (the racial identity that is preponderant in the home territory), one's nationality (whether one is a citizen of the conquering country), or one's cultural identity. In this way, the poor, the subservient, or the discriminated-against within a given country often support imperialism because in *that* relationship they are considered members of the superior group.

What prompts this form of subjugation? Historically, several different factors exist, at times in combination: the desire to acquire new territory for expansion or settlement; to acquire raw materials needed in production (ones that cannot be found in the home territory); to acquire labor by enlisting laborers who can be forced to work for free or for less money than in the home country; to set up businesses that either could not exist in the home territory (because of the climate or the distances from essential commodities) or would not be tolerated at home (given the cruelty of the operation, or the amount of pollution the business generates, or other legal or moral reasons). Other motives are less immediately linked to the extraction of wealth: to have a place for expelling unruly social elements (criminals, religious dissidents, unwanted racial populations, the diseased, or the insane); to have a place to flee persecution and so to become the persecutors in turn; or, simply, to create new markets. Here the point is not to *take* things from the colony, or make things in the colony less expensively, but to create a new culture that will be receptive to the things one makes in the home territory so they can be more readily sold there. This last point often entails the export of ideas and values: the setting up of new educational systems; the establishment of new local customs; the dissemination of books, dress, musical performances, and other artistic and broadly cultural practices, as well as religious indoctrination, in order to transform the local population into a "familiar" one.

There were many ancient and modern *empires* – that is, attempts by a people to conquer the known world and bring it under a single jurisdiction: the Persians, Macedonians, Romans, Mongols, Mughals, Ottomans (Turks), and Spanish all had extensive empires. When one uses the word "imperialist" today, however, it does not refer to these empires. This is rather a modern, and more specific, term for a system that grew out of European colonial expansion between the fifteenth and nineteenth centuries, and involves a comprehensive interconnected economic system, as well as an accompanying cultural penetration and unification rather than simply a conquest as in the ancient empires. Coined in the late nineteenth century by critics of empire who saw the global system as an organic outgrowth of capitalist expansion, the term "imperialism" in practice refers to the French, Dutch, Spanish, Portuguese, and especially British empires, but also to the US empire, which after the Second World War inherited the system these European countries created (Chilcote 2000; Tabb 2000; Brewer 1980).

The basic difference between colonialism and imperialism (for they vary greatly from case to case) is that imperialism is a later and more systematic organization of the foreign exploitation pioneered by colonialism. Another way of expressing this idea is this: imperialism makes the process begun by colonialism more efficient and generalized, and often (although not always) reduces the need for a bald, direct confrontation of peoples from two different cultures. In general, colonialism characterized the period before imperialism: roughly the fifteenth to the nineteenth centuries (it is, in this sense, a chronological term). Although widespread and even concerted, it tended to be pragmatic, occasional, and unsystematic. Colonies, especially in their origins, were often run by private ventures or holding companies rather than states. Colonization was carried out either for purposes of settlement or for economic exploitation; it was largely conducted in terms of a confrontation between the "White" and the "Dark" races; it often involved direct military occupation, and the setting up of alternative cultural institutions for the purpose of creating a native caste that shared the same culture as those in the home country. Imperialism, by contrast, grows out of colonialism, both by extending its logic but also by responding more subtly to the demands for political independence launched by the freedom movements within the colonies during the twentieth century. It tends to be comprehensive and systematic, ruled by a central authority like a state or decisive financial or political institutions effectively controlled by a state or an alliance of states. Imperialism can and does involve military invasion and/or occupation, but usually not for the purpose of settlement.

Under imperialism, conquest is often maintained from afar, by the *threat* of military invasion or by means of economic coercion. In its classical sense, imperialism is above all a structured system of economic disparity that places certain countries of the world in a position of dependence on those states whose economies are strongest, and whose strength is artificially (and coercively) maintained by unequal rates of exchange, punitive lending laws, and by other financial and commercial means. One of imperialism's classic definitions, therefore, is simply "the export of capital." Under imperialism, the cultural institutions in a foreign country that serve the imperial center are no longer run by the imperial center itself (at least directly). A whole sector of "native" intellectuals and élites, inherited from the colonial era, identify with the imperial center, and carry out its wishes either out of conviction or through pay-offs, bribery, personal networks of affiliation, and so on. The ideology of civilizational superiority incipient under colonialism becomes under imperialism a given, and is used by the imperial center as a natural justification for all its actions. There is no open enlistment, as under colonialism, of the rhetoric of a righteous cause, or a confrontation of the enlightened versus the benighted. These categories are rather fully internationalized, bureaucratized, and no longer controversial.

One can appreciate, then, why globalization theory so carefully dissociates the process of globalization from *national* identifications, ethnocentric attitudes, forcible inclusion, or the discourse of civilizational superiority, since unless it does so the continuities between its purportedly "new" and liberatory panorama and older exploitative arrangements would be obvious and uncomfortable. Taking globalization theory at its word, the classic features of colonialism seem not only alien to globalization, but its very opposite, since the latter is relentlessly cast as popularly willed, anonymous, permeating, and unplanned. Can this assumption be confidently maintained, however? One notices, for instance, that colonialism always worked by playing cultural differences off against one another in the name of acquiring material advantages. Differences, as such, were critical to a strategy of profit-making that relied upon the *dissemination* of local values in the guise of global ones. If it is obvious that cultural differences were greeted negatively in earlier centuries whereas they now stand at the very core of the universal ethic of global pluralism, the stark contrast is perhaps a little too easy to misinterpret. Rather than being opposites, these positions are complementary. In each case, a carefully nurtured separability of locality, political knowledge, and cultural practice allows the perpetuation of an educated caste with means to manipulate sectoralism, benefitting from the disparities that keep them in competition while calling forth a unifying force whose "inevitability" renders it both invisible and benevolent.

What we are seeing today under the banner of globalization repeats a process, with some changes, that we saw over two centuries ago with the emergence of *national* markets (Polanyi 1957). The significant development today is only the larger scale on which the process occurs, and the smaller number of beneficiaries. Much has been made in recent years of the need for nations to create artificially a sense of belonging via print media and invented traditions – a distinct culture perceived as national (B. Anderson 1991; Hobsbawm 1987; Hobsbawm and Ranger 1983). In globalization – often portrayed as the *transcendence* of nationalism – the same dynamic pertains: homogenization takes place as a concentration of power on the road to monopoly. Samir Amin's account of the rise of finance capital demonstrates from another angle this parallelism between globalization and national state-formation. Via immense deficit spending, the United States dictates terms of structural readjustment to other countries, just as the Bretton Woods institutions (under US tutelage) form the nucleus of a new global megastate (Bourdieu 1998; Amin 1997). Capitalism, Amin argues, has been falsely associated by many commentators with "development" and "the market" whereas it is actually hostile to both. It thrives, rather, in the zero-sum contest of mobile finance drifting around the globe in search of investment, victimized by its own victorious monopolization, hungering for new worlds to conquer.

The underlying logic linking globalization theory and postcolonial studies has, in at least one respect, a perverse cast. The mutual hostility of both to the nation form (particularly as nation-*state*) is projected as an irrepressible ultra-modernism. In turn, this ultra-modernism in its contemporary variant is given an almost aesthetic accent in which *mobility* as an ontological condition is portrayed as the exciting play of an infinite self-fashioning. The cast is "perverse" because in accordance with such a logic one is forced to revile contemptuously, even while resonating with, a specific and conjunctural national-statist project (that of the United States) which in a vigorously broadcast system of images and slogans embraces the same hybridity, modernity, and mobility as globalization theory. Like that theory, it depicts the world as having moved *past* colonialism and imperialism.

It would be an enormous irony, of course, if this shared logic were purely and neatly self-contradictory. In fact, both discursive formations have helped generate, often in spite of themselves, a more complicated and internally riven set of theories. Even in their restrictive senses, both are institutional arenas where a welcome intellectual generalism has lately begun to flourish, pushing researchers into a rudimentary knowledge of sociology, economics, and social history. Particularly in the last few years, cultural theorists have moved past interrogations of methodology and epistemology (however important these gestures always were on their own terms, and however admirable when contrasted with the relative methodological complacency of the natural and social sciences). The globalization theorist him/herself has at last become part of the object of inquiry, placed in a field of interests and seen as functioning in a larger division of intellectual labor. In the shift in academic fashions, which has driven many postcolonial theorists to retool themselves as globalization theorists, this "economics" of the cultural intellectual may be the most consequential future field of action.

8

PRIYAMVADA GOPAL

Reading subaltern history

"My mother picked up the bloody foetus with some straw and threw it away. Even after that the pain in Chandra's belly continued to increase and she died when it was still 4 or 5 *dondoes* left of the night . . . I administered the medicine in the belief that it would terminate her pregnancy and did not realize that it would kill her."

(Qtd. Guha 1987: 136)

In the Bengali year 1255 (1849 CE), a young widow becomes pregnant during an (illicit) affair with her brother-in-law; he demands that her natal family eliminate the problem. During the abortion arranged by her mother and sister, Chandra dies. Her relatives are arrested and their statements are taken down. The depositions are later archived and anthologized with other documents at Viswabharati University.

"How is one to reclaim this document for history?" (Guha 1987: 138). In his compelling essay, "Chandra's Death," Ranajit Guha poses the question integral to Subaltern Studies, the influential school of Indian historiography he helped to found in the early 1980s. The question encapsulates the collective's contestatory framework: *how* is Indian history to be written outside the historically dominant frameworks, first of colonialism and, later, of élite nationalism? *Who* is the "one" who interprets historical events and how does the mediation of that "investigative consciousness" influence the writing of history? What *documents* and *archives* have been overlooked? When documents and archives have been consulted, how have they been *read*? What does it mean to *reclaim*? Last but not least, what is *history* and to what ends is it *written*? In trying to interpret the events around Chandra's death, Guha re-states the Subalternist position:

The ordinary apparatus of historiography has little to offer us here. Designed for big events and institutions, it is most at ease when made to operate on those larger phenomena which visibly stick out of the debris of the past. As a result, historical scholarship has developed . . . a tradition that tends to ignore the small drama and fine detail of social existence, especially at its lower depths.   (138)

"[Bending] closer to the ground," Subaltern scholars have cobbled together gripping stories out of the "untamed fragments" that constitute the "residuum of a dismembered past" (139). This attention to the "exceptional-normal" (Sarkar 2000: 308) has brought forth a memorable cast of characters, local legends, and village scandals: unruly peasants attacking landlords and police-stations much to the chagrin of national leaders like Gandhi and Nehru (Shahid Amin 1988); a "tribal" leader who calls himself Gandhi and declares the end of the British Raj (D. Arnold 1984); a *sadhu*, or mendicant, prosecuted for "murder, arson and 'affront to feminine modesty'" claiming "to be the Kalki avatar, the tenth incarnation of Vishnu" (Sarkar 1989b); and a Devi or goddess who possesses *adivasis* (indigenous inhabitants) and commands entire villages to give up meat and "boycott Parsi liquor dealers and landlords" (Hardiman 1984). Like Michel Foucault (1987), whose work influenced them, the Subalternists have pursued a consistent interest in the staging of violence and the narrative construction of crime or *récit de crime*.

Using the tools of narratology which had been developed in linguistics and literary studies, the new historiography has given critical attention to plot, character, authority, language, voice, and time: "the narrative in the document violates the actual sequence of what happened in order to conform to the logic of a legal intervention which made death into a murder, a caring sister into a murderess, all the actants in this tragedy into defendants, and what they said in a state of grief into *ekrars* [depositions]" (Guha 1987: 140–41). In reconstructing on the basis of the fragment available to him a family "tragedy" and "death" out of what had been archived as "crime" and "murder," Guha appeals to concepts which would later come to be interrogated by other Subalternists: the "actual sequence of what happened," and the "real historical experience" which had been narrowed by the vocabulary of crime and abstract legalism. If historical events are only available to us through narrative, Guha states the case for the historian's responsibility to write contextualized and full narratives. By "registering" "the humble peasant voices which speak here in sobs and whispers," the historian defies the "stentorian voice of the state" that has made a univocal "case" out of the "many sided and complex tissue of human predicament" (141). Guha's discourse is simultaneously sharply anticolonial and profoundly humanist, attentive to the human suffering that is the consequence of domination and oppression at various intersecting levels, including class, caste, gender, and enforced criminality. History, like literature, has the capability to produce postpositivist knowledges which would not detach "an experience from its living context," denuding it of a range of significances.

Drawing attention to "the small voice of history," Subaltern Studies emerged as a corrective to both colonialist and "bourgeois-nationalist" historiography, under whose auspices nationalism had been "written up as a sort of spiritual biography of the nationalist élite" (Guha 1982b: 2). Missing from that biography had been "the contribution made by the people on their own, that is, independently of the élite, to the making and development of [nationalism]." This "un-historical historiography" had paid no attention to "the politics of the people" who had acted "in the course of nationalist campaigns in defiance or absence of élite control" (2–4). Subaltern Studies was to interrogate some of the privileged emphases of Marxist intellectual work while retaining "a broad socialist and Marxist horizon" (Sarkar 2000: 300). The category of the "subaltern" was intended to shed light on the practices of dominance and resistance outside the framework of class struggle, but without ignoring class itself: "'Subaltern' would be of help in avoiding the pitfalls of economic reductionism, while at the same time retaining a necessary emphasis on domination and exploitation" (301). While in recent years the Subaltern Studies school has expanded to include work on other regions and has inspired Subaltern Studies initiatives in other historical and geographical contexts,[1] its purview has largely been "South Asian" (or strictly speaking, *Indian*) history. Bourgeois-nationalist historiography of the sort that Subaltern Studies challenges is, Guha argues, "primarily an Indian practice" (1982b: 1).

Who or what is a subaltern? In the early work of the Subaltern Studies collective, the term was often interchangeable with the category of "peasant," marking the project's debt to the Italian communist, Antonio Gramsci. The Italian term "subalterno," as used by Gramsci, translates roughly as "subordinate" or "dependent" (Arnold 2000: 30; Gramsci 1971: 52–120). Gramsci used "subaltern" to question the received Marxist emphasis on the urban proletariat and economy, arguing that questions of culture and consciousness needed to be taken seriously.[2] The peasantry was dynamic and numerically predominant in Gramsci's Italy and they had to be brought into alliance with revolutionary forces in the city "if communism were to survive as an active political force" (Arnold 2000: 26). To that end, their grievances, aspirations, and consciousness must have a central place in Marxist revolutionary thinking; peasants "were not the doomed breed they so often appear as in the pages of Marx" (27). The intellectual had a specific responsibility to engage with the complexities and contradictions of peasant thought and "to search out signs of subaltern initiative and incipient class identity that could be nurtured and educated into true class consciousness and effective political action" (28). In theory, "subalternity" as a category was to be extended to "the general attribute of subordination in South Asian society whether this is expressed in terms of class, caste, age, gender and office or in any other way" (Guha 1982a: vii, see also 1997).

Reading "power"

Drawing on structuralist narratology, Barthesian semiology, and Foucauldian discourse analysis, some early Subalternist work examined the rhetorical and linguistic strategies employed by those in power, in particular colonial administrators. Guha's "The Prose of Counter-Insurgency" argues powerfully that, by emphasizing spontaneity and instinctuality, all the major historiographic schools have tended to disengage peasant *action* from peasant *consciousness*. For Guha, however, it is important to understand rebellion as "motivated and conscious":

> To rebel was indeed to destroy many of those familiar signs which [the peasant] . . . had learned to read and manipulate in order to extract a meaning out of the harsh world around him and live with it. The risk in "turning things upside down" under these conditions was indeed so great that he could hardly afford to engage in such a project in a state of absent-mindedness.
>
> (1988: 45)[3]

While élite discourse has always held a curiously prominent place in Subaltern Studies, the aim of some of this inaugural work was to show how the archives themselves were skewed and led to certain blind spots in historiography. In the case of peasant insurgency, Guha suggested, there are three kinds of discourse which, curiously, end up sharing similar assumptions: primary discourse (e.g. official communiqués) which conveys immediacy; secondary discourse (e.g. memoirs) which is "shorn of contemporaneity" and makes claims to impartiality; and tertiary discourse (historiography), which is "removed in time from the events it has for its theme" and is under no constraint to represent official viewpoints (47–48, 50–53, 71–74). The first two of these kinds of discourse "do nothing to illuminate that consciousness which is called insurgency," but "[t]here is nothing in tertiary discourse to make up for this absence" (71). Though the idioms of historiography vary from colonialist to liberal to left on the political spectrum, Guha argues that even left-wing historiography, which "adopts the insurgent's point of view," has typically been guilty of "an act of appropriation which excludes the rebel as the conscious subject of his own history" (72, 77). Thus where colonial historiographers had annexed peasant rebellion to the triumphal progress of the Raj, Marxist historians had tended to "arrange it along the alternative axis of a protracted campaign for freedom and socialism" (77).

This, then, is the argument for a Subaltern Studies that will distinguish itself from hitherto existing Marxist historiography by avoiding "assimilative thinking" in its attempts to make the subaltern the subject of his own history (Guha 1988: 76). Guha is careful to acknowledge that appropriation is inevitable in the construction of revolutionary traditions, and that while "the mediation of the insurgent consciousness by the historian's" is problematic, historiography can do nothing to "eliminate such distortion altogether, for the latter is built into its optics" (77). To acknowledge the insurgent as "the conscious subject of his [sic] own history" is to take a greater interest in questions of consciousness; Guha stresses here a "specific" (or particular) rather than "transcendental" (or general) consciousness (77). In its study of "specific" peasant consciousness, Subaltern Studies distinguishes itself from most Marxist historiography by paying particular attention to what Guha calls "religiosity" (77). For by appropriating peasant action to larger histories of revolutionary action whose "Ideal" subject has a deeply secular consciousness, Marxist historiography had generally either evaded "religiosity" or explained it away as "clever but well-intentioned fraud"; this inclination had rendered the received Marxist historiography "ill-equipped to cope with contradictions which are indeed the stuff of which history is made" (83).

While the point about the dangers of assimilative thinking with regard to an ideally secular revolutionary subject is well taken, the alternative emphasis on "religiosity" is less persuasive. If the problem is that Marxist historians had simplified a complex historical subject by imposing a desirable "secular consciousness" on it, then it seems merely a reverse reductionism to argue, as Guha does, that "religiosity" constitutes *the central modality* of peasant consciousness in colonial India" (1988: 81; my emphasis). As we shall see later, while specific aspects of "religiosity" were unquestionably important – even determinative – to some rebellions and movements on the part of subaltern groups, the Subalternists have tended to deploy this category (along with "peasant-communal") in increasingly diffuse and abstract ways. Indeed, their anthropologizing term "religiosity" has never itself been subjected to scrutiny by them as, for instance, the term "historicity" has been; instead, it has been taken as self-explanatory, unambiguously expressive of states of being or belief.

The best Subalternist writing on élite/colonial discourse includes David Arnold's work on the Indian body, disease, and medicine (1993); Gyanendra Pandey's critique of the "construction of communalism in colonial India" (1989, 1992); and Bernard Cohn's essay on language and colonial command

(1985). Arnold examines Western medicine in relation to the body "as a site of colonizing power and of contestation between colonized and colonizer" (1993: 7–8). Pandey addresses the making of a "master narrative" which entailed "compulsive thinking in stereotypes," arguing that "[c]ommunal strife, or conflict between people of different religious persuasions was represented by the British colonial regime in India as one of the most distinctive features of Indian society, past and present" (1989: 132). Within this discourse, "the Indian character" is understood to be fractious and prone to spontaneous violence. Accordingly, descriptions of conflict contain an abundance of terms such as "frenzy," "sudden outbreak," "tumult," "disorder," "friction," and "turbulence." "This tradition of 'strife,'" which is given a prominent place in colonialist Indian history, "becomes, indeed, the justification of colonial rule" (151). Unlike more standard readings of "colonial discourse," Cohn's essay on the "language of command" undertakes to look at the relationship between "complicated and complex forms of knowledge created by Indians, but codified and transmitted by Europeans" (1985: 276). To contemporary readers familiar with Edward W. Said's *Orientalism* and the large corpus of writing spawned by its power/knowledge paradigm, Cohn's essay makes few unusual claims, perhaps. While much has been written about English education in India,[4] however – the "Anglicist" project – far less attention has been paid to the acquisition of "native" languages as instruments of commerce and rule – in particular, the creation of "Hindustani" as "the British language of command" in South Asia. It is something of a commonplace in postcolonial literary studies that, like Shakespeare's Caliban, colonized peoples were able to appropriate a language that was imposed on them and use it to their own ends. Cohn suggests that the reverse process was also taking place and that the colonizer's profits were literally linked to the acquisition of the languages of the colonized. At the most trivial level, this resulted in the writing of grammar books that stressed the use of the imperative; in a more profound way, the enterprise is evidence of the construction of a system to "classify, bound and control variety and difference" (1985: 327).

Reading the Subaltern

"There was a lad of a Barai (betel-leaf grower) in that gathering as well. It is said that he had asked a Mishrain (wife of Misr, a high-caste Brahman) for a wrapper to come to the station. She reprimanded him and refused to give him the blanket. The poor soul came shivering to the station, had darshan of the Mahatma and went back home. In the morning I heard a rumour in the village that she had suffered the same fate as befell the household of Babu Bhagavan

Prasad . . . [i.e. shit rained all over . . .] In the end, only when she kept a fast, not
even touching water for a day and a night and did *aradhana* (ritual praying)
of the Mahatma, did peace finally return to her."
　　　　　(Sri Murlidhar Gupt, qtd. Shahid Amin 1988: 319)

In a fascinating study of rumors around the figure of Mahatma Gandhi,
Shahid Amin describes "an incipient political consciousness called upon, for
the very first time, to reflect – albeit vaguely and intermittently – on the
possibility of an inversion of many of those power relations deemed invi-
olable until then, such as British/Indian, landlord/peasant, high-caste/low-
caste etc." (1988: 312). The rumors – which were printed in a regional newspaper – reflect, on the one hand, apparent devotion to a figure invested with
miraculous ("thaumaturgical") powers and, on the other, a subaltern inter-
pretive ability that exceeds and subverts the singular logic of nationalism.
"Mahatma Gandhi" became a polysemic text and there were "distinctly independent" interpretations of his message that could not be explained away
by theories of manipulation or incitement by *agents provocateurs* (294).
Subaltern "readings" of Gandhian injunctions appropriated and pluralized
the basic framework of resistance to colonialism and nation-building. The
Gandhian call to "purify" and build moral character was extended to an
awareness of other kinds of oppression and liberation: "The movement for
'self-reform' now revealed 'a tendency to forsake hereditary callings as well'"
(300). Contemporary writings remarked on a "growing restlessness . . . arising out of the general spirit of revolt" among the most marginalized castes
(300). Crucially, there was a disjuncture between the ways in which the subaltern masses "read" Gandhi and the ways in which subaltern actions were
read by the local leadership. For the élite leadership, the "task of the *janta*
[masses] is to congregate in large numbers, 'feast their eyes on the Mahatma,'
count themselves lucky, and after such a brief taste of bliss return to their inert
and oppressed existence" (305). That this is not quite what happened is clear
from Gandhi's own speeches which reflect anxiety about loss of control; he
condemns peasant violence and insists that no action should be undertaken
that he has not directly called for.

　　Amin's argument is, to some extent, a speculative one, albeit powerfully and persuasively so. He reads élite texts (newspaper reports, Gandhi's
speeches and his secretaries' diaries) symptomatically – as much for what they
do not say as for what they make evident – and attempts to reconstruct the
history of subaltern action through the warnings and silences of these texts.
Amin makes a thoughtful and convincing case for the awakening of "bhav"
or "urge to action" which then exceeds the nationalist paradigm in which
it was engendered. He contends that the occurrences giving rise to rumors

"were being read in a *familiar way*, that is according to the conventions of reading the episodes in a sacred text but with their religiosity overdetermined by an incipient political consciousness" (317; my emphasis). The argument is, then, that it is new *content* rather than altered *form* which makes for insurgency. Belief in the miraculous power of Gandhi "accorded with existing beliefs about marvels and miracles, right and wrong" (335). What does not get addressed in Amin's otherwise nuanced analysis, however, is the question of what happens to religious beliefs themselves when they are "overdetermined" by political consciousness – assuming that the relationship between political and religious consciousness is necessarily a dynamic one. If dominant political discourse is subverted through religiosity, in what ways are hegemonic religious discourses reshaped by political consciousness? Without such considerations, "religiosity" becomes something of a static master category, one which is deployed for subversive political ends but which does not itself seem to change.

The strategic Subaltern

Subaltern Studies was transformed from a somewhat provincial, albeit interventionary, "area studies" enterprise into a cutting edge "theoretical" (hence, portable) one with the publication in 1988 of the volume, *Selected Subaltern Studies*, edited by Ranajit Guha and Gayatri Chakravorty Spivak, with a foreword by Edward W. Said. Published and, more crucially, *distributed* by Oxford University Press, New York, rather than its Indian branch (which continued to publish the annual volumes in the series), this selection marked the official incorporation of Subaltern Studies into the fast-growing corpus of writings that came under the rubric of "postcolonial theory."[5] This necessitated a critical evaluation of the *theoretical* scope of the project, which was undertaken by Spivak in an introductory essay entitled "Subaltern Studies: Deconstructing Historiography." Veering, sometimes patronizingly, between the defensive and the corrective, Spivak's essay makes three claims for the "theoretical" nature of the Subalternist project (emphases below are mine):

1. Subaltern Studies breaks out of the standard Marxist "modes-of-production narrative," in terms of which the history of colonialism in India is read as a particular instance of the transition from feudalism to capitalism. Subaltern Studies plots change under the rubric of "confrontations rather than transition." It does so by tracking changes in "sign-systems." Subaltern Studies is "a *theory of reading* in the strongest possible general sense" (Spivak 1988a: 4).

2. Subaltern historians "perceive their task as making *a theory of consciousness or culture* rather than specifically a theory of change" (4). Though

they are "self-professed dialecticians," interested in the engagement of oppo-sites, their "actual practice . . . is closer to deconstruction," which questions oppositions such as "history and structure" or "spontaneity and conscious-ness" (4).

3. Their work shows us that (colonial) society, like a text, is a *"continuous sign-chain."* What we call "action" emerges out of the constant breaking and relinking of this chain – or "discursive displacements" (5). Conscious-ness itself is part of this semiotic chain and the work of the Subalternists would seem to acknowledge this. As such, their desire to find subaltern consciousness in a pure state constitutes a "discrepancy" in their general methodology which deals with "signs" rather than "things."

This reconstellation tells us something about the ways in which "theory" itself was increasingly coming to be defined and deployed in postcolo-nial studies as the field consolidated itself in the late 1980s. To make the Subalternists "properly" theoretical (and, therefore, properly postcolonial), Spivak "hope[s] to *align them with deconstruction*" (8; my emphasis). The historian must be rescued by the literary theorist from the pitfalls of his-torical explanation and – despite the stated interest of scholars like Guha in the layered complexity of human predicaments – from their own radical humanism. "The critical force of anti-humanism" must mark Subalternist–postcolonial work, Spivak declares (13). Today we should ask what the implications were of claiming that scholars whose ambitious and explicit intentions were to read texts for suppressed or elided human voices – to examine the myriad contours of oppression beyond the colonizer–colonized dyad – were, *despite themselves*, antihumanist. We might note here a theo-retical sleight-of-hand, whereby concepts with quite different constituencies and philosophical resonances are brought into such close proximity that they can be folded into each other. These include "positivism" (reality consists of "things" which can be discovered through sense-experience); "metaphysics" (there is knowledge beyond quantifiable sense-experience); "essentialism" (things have a knowable essence which is homogeneous and unchanging); and "humanism" (human beings have the ability and the right to shape their existence and to give meaning to it).

"Deconstructing Historiography" made another influential contribution to Subaltern and postcolonial studies. For scholars caught between the desire to deconstruct concepts such as "the individual subject" and a political imperative to recover the histories of actual subjects – social and historical agents capable of initiating or undertaking action – who had been marginal-ized by history, Spivak offered a helpful way out. Acknowledging a certain commitment to representing the subaltern, she advocated "a *strategic* use of positivist essentialism in a scrupulously visible political interest" (1988a: 13;

original emphasis). In other words, even when we might believe that such things as "consciousness" or "will" are fictions, we will need – in order to undo the wrongs of history – to posit the actuality of their existence provisionally. In Spivak's reading, what Subaltern historians *really* ("unwittingly") meant when they used terms such as "subject" or "will" to describe the agency of peasants was "what in post-structuralist language would be called the subaltern subject-effect" (12). "Subjects" are in fact *texts*, "part of an immense discontinuous network . . . of strands that may be termed politics, ideology, economics, history, sexuality, language and so on" (12–13). Subaltern "will" is, therefore, an effect made by an effect. Strategic essentialism makes it possible for "the radical intellectual in the West" to avoid "granting to the oppressed either that very expressive subjectivity which s/he criticizes or, instead, a total unrepresentability" (17). The problem with this otherwise compelling "resolution" is that while "strategic essentialism" itself may allow for action rather than paralysis, it is dogged by the persistence of the very binary thinking it deplores and seeks to counter. The opposition of "text" and "essence" in describing consciousness is something of a red herring, a false opposition that evades the complexities of the ways in which consciousness operates. Inasmuch as it is always open to change, consciousness cannot be "essence" (broadly understood as an unchanging quality that defines something). It is always mediated by language and inflected by the specificities of social and historical location. "Strategizing" in this manner, *resorting* to admittedly discredited concepts like essentialism and positivism, can become, "in spite of the best possible personal politics," an unwitting act of bad faith.[6] It evades the far more difficult but necessary work of examining the complicated engagement of selves, societies, bodies, histories, events, memories, interests, and desires that goes into the making of both consciousness and action.

Interestingly, the subaltern became a spectacular presence in cultural theory and postcolonial studies through Spivak's *negative* answer to the famous question she posed in her essay "Can the Subaltern Speak?" This dense and lexically convoluted essay takes issue with those branches of poststructuralism which, after undoing the idea of the subject through theories of subject-effects, come to the conclusion that "[t]here is no more representation; there is nothing but action" (1988b: 275). Spivak argues here that poststructuralist philosophers like Foucault and Deleuze, who valorize "concrete experience," make the mistake (an essentialism) of assuming that subjects are coherent and undivided. (It is not entirely clear whether this same critique could be applied to "strategic" essentialism as well.) Spivak argues that the Foucault–Deleuze claim that oppressed subjects can "speak, act, and know *for themselves*" (276, original emphasis) is problematic because it presumes an unchanging, homogeneous subject ("essentialist") and suggests that the world can be changed for the better through the actions of this subject without intervention from elsewhere. A more "developed theory of ideology" would recognize, apparently drawing on Marx, that the subaltern is "a divided and dislocated subject whose parts are not continuous or coherent with each other" (276, 280). Therefore, and this is Spivak's leap of logic: "The subaltern cannot speak . . . Representation has not withered away" (308).

There can be no quarrel with Spivak's insistence that "the intellectual's solution is not to abstain from representation" (1988b: 285). The problem, however, is that both subaltern history and Marxism are granted interventionary value by Spivak only as *necessarily* deconstructive projects that emphasize "the *mechanics* of the constitution of the Other [rather] than invocations of the *authenticity* of the Other" (294, original emphasis). This emphasis on discourse analysis nudges Subaltern Studies, on Spivak's reading of it, towards an embrace of the very thing the project had originally sought to rectify: the "primacy assigned to [the élite] by the long-standing tradition of elitism in South Asian studies" (Guha 1982a: vii). It should be noted that Spivak offers us something of a false choice again between "authenticity" and "constitution." Despite her own apparent preference for such analysis, missing from Spivak's argument is precisely what "a developed theory of ideology" would offer us: the possibility that the subaltern may have a mediated (rather than incoherent) relationship to both consciousness (of her condition) and agency (to resist). Neil Larsen observes that Spivak's essay, "in its haste to make of Marx a precursor for the deconstruction of the subject-as-agent, excludes entirely from consideration *The Eighteenth Brumaire*'s richly elaborated, differential analysis of class agency" (Larsen 2002: 209). Since agency, like class itself, emerges out of specific historical conditions, crises of self-representation and self-knowledge cannot become the stuff of generalizable proclamation. If Spivak is right to take issue with "unrepresentability," then it must also be asked what is at stake in suggesting that it is only a specific kind of (postcolonial) intellectual who can read and then represent the mute subaltern's actions. What are the implications of the attempt, as Larsen puts it, "to equate the abstract, textualist notion of deconstruction with a principle of anticolonialist/anti-imperialist subversion" (2002: 214)? Within such a schema, almost anything can be read as a "displacing gesture." Spivak gives us the example of Bhuvaneswari Bhaduri, a young woman who hanged herself in 1926: "[As] Bhuvaneswari was menstruating at the time it was clearly not a case of illicit pregnancy" (1988b: 307). Bhuvaneswari's suicide remained a puzzle until it was revealed about a decade later that she had been an armed independence fighter entrusted with a political assassination she felt unable to carry through. Spivak argues that the young woman had deliberately waited to menstruate so that her death would not be read as "the outcome of illegitimate passion." In doing so, she had displaced "the sanctioned motive for female suicide" (308). What is remarkable about this authoritative reading is the complete elision of Bhuvaneswari's life and agency *as a nationalist revolutionary* with an anguished relationship to the assassination mission she was asked – and found herself unable – to carry out. In Spivak's reading, the young woman's consciousness and interests are reduced – as might well be the case in any non-feminist interpretation, ironically enough – to a gesture within the *singular* discourse of female sexuality. Bhuvaneswari's agency is restricted, once again, to affirming or denying/displacing "the physiological inscription of her body" in relation to male passion (308).

The literary subaltern

If "the narrativizations of history are structured or textured like what is called literature" (as Spivak has suggested with regard to literary representations of the subaltern [1988c: 243]), the productive relationship of the two disciplines, between real and imagined events, is powerfully brought out by the novelist Amitav Ghosh's work on "the Slave of MS. H.6," included in *Subaltern Studies* VII. Ghosh's article is inspired by the mention, in letters written by Middle Eastern Jewish traders in the twelfth century, of a South Indian man indentured to one of them – Ben Yiju – who spent several years in the Indian port-city of Mangalore. Ghosh undertakes symptomatic readings of these letters, which had been kept for centuries in a Geniza, a special depository in synagogues intended to safeguard from desecration "any written token of the name of God." "[M]ore a prompter's whisper than a recognisable face in the cast" (1992a: 159), the slave is almost a paradigmatic subaltern – one whose "voice-consciousness" is absent and whose life must be read out of the fragments available to the historian–writer:

> It is an ordinary trader's letter, the mention of the slave is so brief as to be hardly worth notice. But it happens to come to us from a time when the only people for whom we can even begin to imagine a properly individual human existence are the literate and the consequential: those who have the means to inscribe themselves upon history. (161)

Ghosh's book, *In an Antique Land*, elaborates this reconstructed history of the slave alongside an account of Ghosh's fieldwork as a researcher in twentieth-century Egypt. Brilliantly conceived, the book juxtaposes in all their productive dissonance, past and present, history and fiction, archive and imagination, personal insights and academic commentary. The wry allusive-ness of its Orientalist title marks the location of the anthropologist Ghosh, a postcolonial Indian citizen undertaking "fieldwork" in postcolonial Egypt. The text is sharply attentive to the relationship between power and the writing of history – in particular, the institutional legacy of imperialism, which enables a young Indian studying at Oxford to access hoards of documents that had "found their way" from synagogues in North Africa and the Middle East to the powerful private collections and academic libraries of Britain and North America. Even as it critiques the institutional violence that underlies colonialist disciplinary formations, however, Ghosh's book retains a power-ful interest in the possibility of reconfiguring those disciplinary tools in the service of greater knowledge. The slave is both heuristic device and elusive subject – irrecoverable as a whole, yet an affirmative means of challenging the "univocality" of historiography. Even Ghosh's attempt to figure out the slave's name, with only the three Judaeo-Arabic consonants B-M-H avail-able to hand, becomes a "peg . . . on which to hang a history" (1992a: 167). It is a quest that generates glimpses of other marginalized histories: that of the Tulu-speaking peoples of South India, for instance – "a different ecolog-ical, linguistic and cultural world" (though "no culture is an island") – and of Bhuta-worship, a reminder of communities that once existed outside the Sanskritic Hindu fold which constructs itself as pan-Indian and threatens to engulf the heterogeneous cultures of contemporary India (173). The move-ments of the archives themselves – none left in Egypt, for instance, "not a single scrap or shred of paper to remind" the country of its richly heteroge-neous past – speak to the historical excisions and amnesias that mark our present: "It was as though the borders that were to divide Palestine several decades later had already been drawn, through time rather than territory, to allocate a choice of Histories" (1992b: 95).

While the disciplinary optics of anthropology and historiography – the colonial imprints of which seem ever-present – are subjected to scrutiny, as is the location of the investigator (Ghosh himself), the end result is neither intellectual paralysis nor the repudiation of the ideas of truth or history. The fact that the subaltern does not speak in any unmediated or imme-diately accessible ways, far from foreclosing the possibility of knowledge, invests the search for better understanding with greater urgency. Taking us to the Malabar coast with its precolonial history of the trading cultures of "accommodation and compromise," the quest to find the slave's lost ori-gins also helps to recover textured histories and political possibilities out-side the singular paradigm of colonial conquest and postcolonial resistance. Ghosh invokes the unassuming tolerance of a time when the Indian Ocean "had always been open to anyone who wished to trade there" and when the

Portuguese demand to a Hindu ruler that all Muslims be expelled was "met with a blank refusal":

> Within the Western historiographical record the unarmed character of the Indian ocean trade is often represented as a lack, as failure, one that invited the intervention of Europe, with its increasing proficiency in war. When a defeat is so complete as that of the trading cultures of the Indian ocean, it is hard to allow the vanquished the dignity of nuances of choice and preference. Yet it is worth allowing for the possibility that the peaceful traditions of the oceanic trade may have been, in a quiet and inarticulate way, the product of a rare cultural choice – one that may have owed a great deal to the pacifist customs of the Gujarati Jains and Vanias who played such an important part in it.
>
> (1992b: 288)

An impossible romanticism seems to mark this passage as we read it in the context of the violence that continues to maul the lives of many in the Indian sub-continent today, not least that unleashed by Hindu majoritarianism in the very Gujarat of which Ghosh writes. Even as we might wonder what (hi)stories of violence or exploitation get left out of his account, it is important to recognize that Ghosh's project is precisely one of excavating hope, of imagining utopian possibilities in a world prior to the violent rupture of European imperialism. As such, the subaltern – the slave – is a real and imagined means of coming to an understanding of human commonalities that have been excised by the marginalizing sweep of large historical processes and systems (such as colonialism, militarism, pan-Hinduism, and Brahminism).

Nowhere is this more evident than in Ghosh's discussion of the idea of slavery in medieval Vachanakara and Sufi poetry, where despite significant differences (pantheism versus monotheism, for instance), there is a "commonality in the nature of their quest" for perfect devotion and ennobling human commitment. For Ghosh, Sufism, Bhakti, and other such spiritual practices are the "subversive counter-image[s]" of orthodox religions – Hinduism, Islam, and Judaism – and hold out the possibility of human connection in the face of cultural difference: "It was probably those inarticulate counter-beliefs, rather than the formal conversion that Bomma probably had to undergo while in Ben Yiju's service, that eventually became a small patch of level ground between them: the matrilineally descended Tulu and the patriarchal Jew who would otherwise seem to stand on different sides of an unbridgeable chasm" (1992b: 263). Language itself offers surprising points of convergence in the face of seeming untranslatability. Thus, even as Ghosh notes the difficulty of reading a language like Judaeo-Arabic, which is no longer in use, he finds inspiring and enabling similarities between the colloquial speech of the Egyptian peasants whose lives he studies and the language of his archives: "it would never have occurred to me that this simple, rustic dialectic could be of any use in so rarefied a domain of erudition as the reading of twelfth-century Judaeo-Arabic manuscripts . . . that far from being useless, the dialect of Lataifa and Nashawy had given me an invaluable skill" (103–4). Indeed, even the story of the evolution of Judaeo-Arabic, "a colloquial dialect of medieval Arabic, written in the Hebrew script" is one of "odd smeltings" and tells us something about the dynamism of culture itself:

> At the same time, everyone who wrote Judaeo-Arabic had thorough knowledge of the Hebrew scriptures, and though they were not usually able to use Hebrew as a language of expression, they were well able to quote in it. Thus their prose is studded with Hebrew proverbs and long passages from the Bible, as well as legal and religious terms from the archaic language Aramaic. (102–3).

In an Antique Land attempts a cultural history of cosmopolitanism in the Indian Ocean before the advent of European colonialism which erased "virtualy every trace of this extraordinary past" (245). It is an era characterized by a "diverse network of associations" where it would not have been unusual for the Jewish trader's closest connections in Mangalore to have been expatriate Muslim Arabs and where, poignantly, a fleet hastily put together by "the Muslim potentate of Gujarat, the Hindu ruler of Calicut, and the Sultan of Egypt" is decisively vanquished by the Portuguese (277, 288). Only traces remain of that richly cosmopolitan culture; to this day "throughout North India, crystallized sugar is still known as *misri* in commemoration of traders like Ben Yiju and the tastes they imported from Masr" (269).

Nation, community, and modernity

Where Ghosh embarks on a search for communities, cultural encounters, and even an "India" prior to the rupture of imperialism, Subalternist theorists of nation and modernity such as Partha Chatterjee, Sudipta Kaviraj, and Dipesh Chakrabarty maintain that "the Indian nation" is "not an object of discovery but of invention" (Kaviraj 1992: 1). Narratives of nation separate "out of the chaos of varying ideological events, a single thread, and [show] nationalism arising and moving to its destiny" (2). This homogenizing narrative intersects with another grand narrative, that of the inevitable historical triumph of modernity. Kaviraj argues that the nation itself was an "unprecedented" institution which attempted to replace premodern communities marked by "fuzzy" boundaries and intense emotional ties with an "enumerated" and modern national community. The latter is territorially specific, has clear boundaries and must "enumerate" what belongs to it; hence, "the endless counting of citizens, territories, resources, majorities, minorities, institutions, activities, import, export, incomes, projects, births, deaths, diseases" (30–31). For Kaviraj, colonialism in India created a rupture out of which the nation emerged as an entirely new – and alien – historical institution. Unlike premodern communities, the nation is conceived as a contract between *individuals* based on the "purely rational calculation of advantages," but it must also deal with the paradoxical imperative to speak the language of *community* (31). It must hide its newness and rationality by presenting itself as "an immemorially ancient community" based on "a mystic unity of sentiments" rather than interests (31). In order to do this, it makes use of "narrative contracts" where stories about nation define who belongs to it and how. Addressing the further paradoxes of nationalism in colonial contexts, Partha Chatterjee argues that there was "an inherent contradictoriness in nationalist thinking" in India (1986: 38). Put simply, Indian nationalism relied on a concept of nation whose legitimizing framework (the "thematic") was Western modernity. Yet, anticolonial nationalism also needed to justify its claims to independence by asserting radical difference (the "problematic") from the colonizer. In wrestling with this tension, Indian nationalism "succeeds in producing a *different* discourse . . . yet one that is dominated by another"; it resolves the paradox by coming up with a specifically *Indian* interpretation of nationalist thought (42). Elsewhere, Chatterjee elaborates this insight in terms of Indian nationalism's separation of spheres into the material and the spiritual: Western civilization and modernity were allowed to dominate in the sphere of the material / the outer / the world while the East retained its sovereignty, its distinctive essence, in the sphere of the spiritual / the inner / the home. This meant that in such areas as technology, statecraft, and economic organization, European techniques were to be adopted so that the colonizer could be overthrown on his own terms; in the sphere of the home, Eastern traditions would be preserved and allowed to "strengthen the inner core of the national culture" (1993: 121). Women, of course, would play a key role in the latter enterprise.

Both Kaviraj and Chatterjee point out, rightly, that the nation (as we know it, one might add) is a fundamentally modern concept. It has its own narratives and these narratives necessitate the elision of some notions of community (the delineation of communism as un-American, for instance); the appropriation of others (nations are often depicted as "families" or "clans"); and the creation of particular kinds of triumphal Histories (doctrines such as the "Manifest Destiny" of the United States to expand and possess the North American continent, or Nehru's description of India's independence as a "tryst with Destiny" and the redemption of a "pledge" [1997]). What is unconvincing in the theories advanced by Kaviraj and Chatterjee is the claim that premodern, apparently "fuzzy," communities enabled a wider network of solidarities than does the nation. In what appears like a resurrection of the Foucault–Deleuze valorization of "desire" over "interest," which Spivak, as we have seen, had rightly critiqued, Kaviraj argues that in these premodern (they seem almost prelapsarian) formations, "a strong sense of community" prevailed over "interest-actuated" decisions to belong (1992: 20). While "the imaginative possibilities afforded by the fuzziness of community" are seductive in the face of the homogenizing drive of global capitalism, neither political theorist makes a *historically* nuanced case for the existence of such communities. It should be noted here also that some influential Subalternist work on Indian nationalism often makes unproblematized general claims for nationalism or community based on readings of select Bengali texts, often literary works by élite men. The generically "premodern" community then becomes what Spivak calls an "irreducible methodological presupposition" or an axiom without origin or history. If capitalism has obviously generated its own forms of what constitutes "rational interest," the reverse assumption that precapitalist societies relied on simple notions of identity/difference for their "intense solidarity and belongingness" rather than a "convergence of interest" does not follow (nor is it clear that abandoning a notion of "interest" is in and of itself a liberatory move).

Chatterjee also offers us a somewhat constrained choice between "the grand *narrative of capital* as the history of freedom, modernity and progress" and "the *narrative of community* . . . persistent in its invocation of the rhetoric of love and kinship against the homogenizing sway of the individual" (1993: 238–39; my emphasis). He dismisses any doubts about the political implications of insisting on "'natural' affiliation to a community"; these necessarily arise, he claims, from a flawed liberal individualism which does not recognize that "people are not free to choose the social locus of their birth" (232). Any suggestion that "natural" connections to community might be limiting for certain subjects and groups is, for Chatterjee, of a piece with the most retrograde "European" social theory which, "fed . . . on large doses of Orientalist literature and colonial anthropology," sees precapitalist social formations as zones of subjugation (232). Given these terms, there can be no standpoint for critique outside this binary; any critique is already irrevocably tainted by the heritage of an undifferentiated European liberalism. (Chatterjee's own "strenuous reading" of Hegel to arrive at these conclusions is presumably exempt from the dangers of "the provincialism of the European experience" [238]!) Even if one were to concede freedom, history, and modernity to the narrative of capital (and such a concession is far from inevitable), it would be necessary to ask how the narrative of community would distinguish itself from the narratives of élite *post*colonial (far from revolutionary) nationalisms. These, like discourses around "Bharatiyata"/Indian-ness, or the Pledge of Allegiance in the United States, also "speak in the language of love and of self-recognition through the free surrender of the individual will to others in the community" (232). The fundamental distinction being made by Chatterjee, it would seem, is that the narratives of "nation" have a contractual character and are authored by the nation-state while the narratives of "community" have no apparent author (and are, therefore, by a sleight-of-hand, not authoritarian). The narrative of community seems to have a sacramental character (with the accompanying connotations of "mystical" and "primordial") and, like subaltern action itself, is figured as "raising its irrepressible head" through the "contractually regulated structure of civil society" (233). If Chatterjee and Kaviraj are right to critique the conversion of particular interests into universal rights in capitalist civil society, there are also obvious unaddressed problems with the "fuzzy" alternative Chatterjee offers – i.e., "subjective rights [which] must be negotiated within the 'ascribed' field of the ethical life of the community" (232). Who ascribes the "field" of community life? On what and whose terms do the "negotiations" occur? Who determines what is ethical? What happens when potentially non-negotiable conflicts take place – say, when the subjective right of a woman to bear a child she wants to keep clashes with the patriarch's will to have it "eliminated"? What other narratives might have emerged out of "Chandra's Death," for instance?

Beyond reason

The question of "community" in relation to "modernity" and "reason" has now come to constitute the most significant faultline within Subaltern Studies. Theorists like Chatterjee are critical of both modernity and nation as instruments of reason, itself – in their opinion – a brainchild of the European Enlightenment. Others, like the eminent historian of India, Sumit Sarkar, have now dissociated themselves from Subaltern Studies, arguing that the new emphasis on critiquing an undifferentiated post-Enlightenment rationality undermines the original Subalternist project of tracking resistance rather than domination. Sarkar also finds the valorization of premodern communities questionable. Referring to Chatterjee's delineation of the Gandhian peasant-communal idyll as an example of a community which was "violently *interrupted* by the postcolonial national state," Sarkar points to the ironic fact that a "project that had started with a trenchant attack on élite nationalist historiography had now chosen as its hero the principal iconic figure of official Indian nationalism" (1997: 92). (Chatterjee shifts, we should note, from claiming that Gandhian thought enabled the evolving political structures of the Indian state to *appropriate* subaltern communities to arguing that the state actually *disrupted* the Gandhian-subaltern community.) In the privileging of community over state, Sarkar points out, there is an assumption that "power within communities matters very much less" than the exercise of state power (101). Sarkar also critiques the "folding back of all history into the single problematic of Western colonial cultural domination"; the same point has been made by the critic Aijaz Ahmad who points out in his book, *In Theory*, that colonial discourse analysis in literary studies can, paradoxically, reinscribe a fixation on the colonizer (Sarkar 1997: 106; Ahmad 1992: 73–94). At the same time, Sarkar contends, late Subaltern Studies manages to ignore the flourishing *new* imperialisms entirely: the "rationality" of the "free market," "globalization," and "structural adjustment" (1997: 107–8).

In response, scholars like Dipesh Chakrabarty maintain that there can be no "wholesale rejection of the tradition of rational argumentation" out of which Subaltern Studies itself emerged and that his object of critique is, in fact, the "hyper-rationalism" of Indian Marxists who continue to fail to understand the "place of the 'religious'" in Indian life (2000b: 259). Yet Chakrabarty's own compelling work, articulated as the provocative project of "provincializing Europe" – which points out that ideas that pass for universal are, in fact, culturally specific to Europe – takes two somewhat distinct forms. The first analyzes the Enlightenment origins of colonial reason and the violence with which it was applied to colonized subjects through institutions such as schools or hospitals. The other thrust of the project is to interrogate "rationality" itself as a criterion for the writing of history. Chakrabarty argues that even Subaltern Studies is trapped in historicism which prevents it from taking the subaltern's own interpretation of her actions seriously. Such historicism imposes a rationally defensible, democratizing, and secular framework on subaltern action by reading such things as divine commands to rebel as "evidence" of subaltern agency. Since history as a discipline still requires "a certain minimum involvement in rationality," Chakrabarty asserts, there will always be "an irreducible gap" between the voice of the historian and that of the subaltern (2000a: 99). To understand the subaltern truly and make him our contemporary would be to concede him complete alterity – an entirely different "way of being in the world . . . a disjuncture of the present within itself" (109).

Chakrabarty's most important and provocative claim concerns the persistent assumption that concepts are, ultimately, translatable. He points out that words such as "labor," "culture," or "religion" are treated as universally applicable categories when there are many "life-worlds" in which these concepts do not exist as such. One consequence of this assumption of translatability is the way in which "diverse and enchanted worlds," or worlds in which gods, spirits, and other supernatural forces have agency, get forcibly secularized in the "disenchanted language of sociology" (Chakrabarty 2000a: 89). To provincialize Europe is to remind ourselves that not all notions of time are "godless, continuous . . . empty and homogeneous," that "other temporalities, other forms of worlding, coexist and are possible" (73, 95). The "strong opposition between the rational and the affective, or between reason and emotion" which Chakrabarty critiques in Indian Marxism was discussed several years ago by the Marxist scholar, Terry Eagleton, in an essay on Irish nationalism that warned the left against surrendering "the particular," the "sensuous," and the "aesthetic" to the right (Chakrabarty 2000b: 263; Eagleton Jameson, and Said 1990: 34). Curiously, Chakrabarty himself resurrects this polarity in the form of a division between the "analytical" and "the lived," and between "our" world (rational) and the subaltern's (constitutively non-rational). What if the subaltern upset our generous expectation of "complete alterity" by articulating "rational" or even merely non-religious views of her own, however? What if she told us of things other than ghosts and spirits? Would she cease forthwith to be subaltern (enough)? One might invert Guha's formulation concurring the Marxist evasion of religiosity and ask Chakrabarty: "Since the Ideal is supposed to be one hundred percent non-rational in character would the devotee look away when confronted with evidence of reason?" Chakrabarty gives us the peculiar example of Rushdie's "Reverend Mother" (from *Midnight's Children*) as the paradigmatic subaltern confronting the violence of patriarchal modernity. (While it is true that she is subjected to the emancipatory rationalism of her doctor-husband, it seems odd to valorize "an ironclad citadel of traditions and certainties" for whom tradition is not "a system of self-defence . . . but a means of defence against herself" [Rushdie 1995: 40–41].) Acknowledging that such subaltern characters are mediated by an élite literary consciousness, let us note that the insurgent subalterns of Mahasweta Devi's fiction are quite clear that it is their common *humanity* that has been repeatedly denied by a state whose interests masquerade as universal even as it justifies marginalizing them as spirit-worshiping Others. In the powerful story, "Shishu," the *adivasis'* literally "altered" and dehumanized bodies are a source of insurgent rage, not spectral Difference: "'Can your "no" make it all a No? Then how have our organs come to be so shrunken? Have a good look and take in the fact that we are not children, we are adults.' . . .

They rubbed their organs against him and told him they were adult citizens of India" (Mahasweta 1993: 250).

Insisting that he is not advocating "incommensurability" (absence of common ground) or cultural relativism, Chakrabarty concedes "the demonstrable and documentable permeability of cultures and language" (2000a: 83). However, where Ghosh strives to undertake this documentation in *In an Antique Land*, Chakrabarty's emphasis is undoubtedly on the impossibility, in the final instance, of mediation between the voice of the historian and that of the subaltern (108). Secular history then becomes a strategic enterprise, like the essentialism advocated by Spivak, politically necessary even where it is philosophically suspect: "We need universals to produce critical readings of social injustices" (Chakrabarty 2000a: 254). If universals (presumably such things as democracy, egalitarianism, and tolerance) are to be strategically rather than wholeheartedly deployed by "moderns desirous of social justice," then questions once again arise as to who is empowered to "desire" this justice and why. Who decides what constitutes a legitimate "universal"? How would one differentiate between the "ethical" and "unethical" or define "social justice" itself? Chakrabarty's answer would be that these, their own narratives, are the only grounds on which capital or nation-state could adequately be challenged. Even this is doubtful, however; as Amitav Ghosh points out in a conversation with Chakrabarty, "anti-hierarchical thought in India goes back through the *bhakti* period to the Buddha and Mahavira . . . Why should we assume also that the egalitarian impulse in 19th century India derived its power primarily from the Enlightenment (when indeed, all the exegetical material goes against this)?" (Ghosh 2001). Though *Provincializing Europe* remains, in many regards, an engaging and truly provocative project, it is dogged by a persistent tension between "incommensurability" and "heterogeneity." Chakrabarty attempts to juxtapose the analytical (e.g., Marxist ideological critique that looks towards social justice by deploying universals) and the hermeneutic (e.g., Heideggerian thought with its attention to the diversity of life-worlds and an emphasis on the particular) productively; in the final analysis, he seems to me unable to clarify whether the two poles are necessarily connected to or constitutively exclusive of each other.

While few scholars are likely to have problems with "heterogeneity" (the complex variations of human and cultural lives), it is "infinite incommensurabilities" (Chakrabarty 2000a: 254) that pose a political and methodological problem. This becomes abundantly clear in Gyan Prakash's advocacy of "post-Orientalist histories" (2000) (the call for which seems oddly dated given the large body of work that had already been produced in the wake of Said's critique of "Orientalism" by the time that Prakash was writing in 1990) where heterogeneity is conflated with "unrepresentability" and the impossibility of "historicizing." One of the more serious problems in Prakash's work, as in the Spivak essay discussed earlier, is the series of slippages whereby very different terms are collapsed into each other as variations on an overarchingly rationalist theme. These include "real," "essential," "objectivist," "Orientalist," "modernist," "developmentalist," "historicist," and "foundationalist." What is termed "post-Orientalist history" is not then, as one might hope, the production of richer modes of understanding selves and societies, but a panoply of rhetorical flourishes. "Unsettling," "disrupting," "decentring," "displacing," "resisting" become the only possible way of opposing "modes-of-production" narratives. The grandest, though surprisingly definitive, act of them all is that of "refusal" – not just to write foundationalist histories, it would seem, but to write history at all; for at the end of the day, any act of knowledge production or historiography becomes, by definition, damningly "foundational."

Conclusion

Rather than attempt to cover all aspects of twenty-odd years of Subaltern Studies, the aim of this chapter has been to lay out the broad contours of the debates this body of work has generated in relation to postcolonial cultural studies. It might be appropriate to end now with Frantz Fanon who, Chakrabarty writes, "struggle[d] to hold on to the Enlightenment idea of the human – even when he knew that European imperialism had reduced that idea to the figure of the settler-colonial white man" (2000a: 5). While Chakrabarty rightly identifies the complicated relationship to Enlightenment reason and modernity that is the "global heritage of all postcolonial thinkers" (2000a: 5), Fanon's own point about the real tragedy of the colonial situation had been more specific. By imposing its values with such violence, it is not just that colonialism displaces indigenous intellectual traditions but that it "distorts the very relations that the colonized maintains with his *own* culture" which under other circumstances would be in a *continuously* dialogic relationship with itself and with other cultures (Fanon 1965: 130; my emphasis). Fanon wrote as a European-trained anticolonial doctor, anguished about the complicit role of the medical institution under colonialism which leads to an unhappy "opposition of exclusive worlds . . . a vehement confrontation of values" (1965: 131). In Fanon's speculative narrative of pre- and non-colonial situations, not without its own tinge of idealization, there are no obvious "precolonial" values or communities; what is violently disrupted by colonialism is precisely the fundamental ability of cultures and communities to change continuously and self-critically. It is this feature that colonial modernity freezes into suspension; to then valorize the "premodern" or the "precolonial" would be, ironically, to endorse the worse effects of colonization and the kind of modernity it seeks to impose: "The colonial situation standardizes relations, for it dichotomizes the colonial society in a marked way" (126). For Fanon, incommensurability is a *consequence* of the alienation from self wrought by colonialism and not an adequate response to or resolution of it. Fanon defined the challenges he faced in terms of "the impossibility of finding a meeting ground in any colonial situation" (125). Perhaps it is this task – to search for a *defiant and difficult* (rather than merely strategic) commensurability of human concerns in the face of the legacy of colonialism – that lies ahead for a truly decolonized subaltern and postcolonial studies.

NOTES

I thank Neil Lazarus and Kavita Philip for helpful critical readings of this chapter, and my students, Sameer Rahim and Polly Stokes, for asking useful and difficult questions of this material.

1 Outside South Asia, Subaltern Studies has been particularly influential in Latin American scholarship. For a general overview of that field, see Rodriguez 2001 and Coronil, in this volume.

2 For a fuller discussion, see Brennan 2001.

3 Guha alludes here to the work of radical English historians such as Christopher Hill whose famous account of the English revolution is called *The World Turned Upside Down*. In its early days, the Subaltern Studies project was influenced by the work of Hill and other scholars such as E. P. Thompson who undertook to produce a "history from below." See Hill 1972; Thompson 1968.

4 See for instance Viswanathan 1989; Joshi 1991; Sunder Rajan 1992.

5 See also the subsequent volumes edited by Chaturvedi (2000) and Ludden (2001).

6 A phrase used by Spivak in her discussion of the inadequacies of Mahasweta Devi's reading of her own story, "Draupadi," in Spivak 1988c: 245.

9

KEYA GANGULY

Temporality and postcolonial critique

How does time signify in postcolonial analysis? This question has occasionally been taken up as a matter of deciding the status of the prefix "post." Theorists who approach the question in this way have answered it by periodizing the postcolonial – that is, by situating it in epochal terms, relative to such other putative eras as the colonial, the modern, the postmodern, and so on (Appiah 1991; Hutcheon 1994). Since the attempt here has been to separate the postcolonial from these other epochs or eras (to specify when it emerges and its distinctive constituent features as an epoch), this approach has usually emphasized nominal and categorical rather than conceptual or epistemological issues.

The periodizing approach to the question of time in postcolonial analysis has generated some thought-provoking insights. Its weakness, however, is that it has tended to eschew larger philosophical meditations on what makes epochal pronouncements intelligible in the first place (e.g., explorations of *how* time has figured in the analysis of the postcolonial). Temporality has been explored rather more fruitfully in postcolonial studies by approaches that regard the postcolonial not as an epoch or age but as *a particular mode of historical emergence*. Here, the issues have entailed characterizing the "alterity" associated with postcolonial forms of being; in other words, the focus has been on the ways in which, and the degree to which, the postcolonial has been taken to represent an "other" time whose logic and historical expression are incommensurable with the normative temporality of clock and calendar associated with Western modernity. What follows is a discussion of such lines of enquiry into time.

One must begin by recognizing that although postcolonial scholarship has gained an independent and influential position within the humanities and related social sciences, its own precepts and perspectives borrow heavily from philosophical and theoretical sources that are not themselves specifically of postcolonial provenance. Knowledge never appears in a vacuum and, for all its avowed antagonism to Eurocentric thought, postcolonial critique cannot of course entirely defy conceptual models associated with the West. Consequently, the idea of time as giving particular shape to experiences and histories must be seen as at least in part produced by existing conceptions of temporality within the philosophical heritage of European thought. To speak of time-consciousness in relation to postcolonial understanding, then, is itself to mark the recursive nature of temporal influence – as it recedes from the present to the past and back into contemporary focus. Put differently, emphasizing time-consciousness in both the constitution of the postcolonial predicament as well as in our analytic approaches to it has to do with recognizing not only that time is a fundamental dimension *of* all thought (as the Enlightenment philosopher, Immanuel Kant argued) but also that ideas ebb and flow *in* time. Accordingly, preoccupations that today seem urgent and unprecedented, and that are declared as the novel province of postcolonial scholarship, need to be historicized, and their novelty interrogated rather than presumed.

From this perspective, if the discourse of postcolonial criticism evinces a concern with problematizing the issue of time, this is in turn shaped by questions of historicity, modernity, and temporality that constitute the broader horizon of present approaches to knowledge. In other words, there is no *special* postcolonial theory of time, nor any reason to assume that postcolonial studies has contributed *uniquely* to our understanding of time by virtue of its foci, range of experience, or methodological insights. Hence, to conceive of time as an objective constituent of postcolonial forms of consciousness is not to suggest that we can say something about time in ways that were previously unthought or unthinkable. To imagine that we could do so would be to reflect an attitude in which knowledge was rendered abstract, an outcome of the putative singularities of postcolonial experience (as a time *outside* time and beyond the patterning of material reality). Thinking about time as a key element in shaping and understanding the present instead requires submitting the convergences and divergences of colonial histories and postcolonial cultures to a more reflexive understanding about the constitutive effects of history on consciousness. This, it should be understood, is not the same as idealizing the newness or asserting the ineffability of postcolonial temporality.

Perhaps the most useful way to provide concrete form to the abstract issue of temporality is by looking at the central position given to the problem of being modern within the general purview of postcolonial analysis. This emphasis is itself born of nineteenth-century notions regarding subjectivity and consciousness. For it is only with G. W. F. Hegel's arguments that modernity, as a specific configuration of historical understanding (*viz.*, to be modern is to be contemporary) as well as a mode of social existence (belonging to rational, law-abiding, citizen-subjects), becomes intelligible. In his *Philosophy of Right* (in German, *Recht*, meaning both "right" and "law"), Hegel famously deployed the trope of Minerva's owl – as the figure of both philosophical wisdom and historical understanding – to propose that, "When philosophy paints its grey in grey, then has a shape of life grown old. By philosophy's grey in grey it cannot be rejuvenated but only understood. The owl of Minerva spreads its wings only with the falling of the dusk" (1967: 13). In other words, the paradox of historical self-understanding is that it emerges belatedly, at the dusk of an age rather than at its dawn. The irony here is that while celebrating the philosophical wisdom he attached to European thought, Hegel regarded the history of Europe as belated if not decadent.

This irony has been lost on many postcolonial scholars, who have seen in Hegel *only* the celebration of European thought, as though for him the owl of Minerva spread its wings in broad daylight, under the noonday sun. For it is a commonplace within postcolonial writing to portray Hegel as simplistically linear in his vision of history, myopically holding out for the superiority of Europe. Despite his status as the philosopher of modernity *par excellence*, he has come under heavy attack for being teleological in his vision of historical progress, totalizing in his attempts to build systems of thought, as well as Eurocentric in his normative focus. A more nuanced reading of his propositions about history would permit us to realize that for Hegel, *the end of history* (when Minerva's owl figuratively takes flight) actually signals *the beginning of historical understanding*. Thus, according to him, philosophy can only come to terms with its own time-boundedness, its epochal status, when belatedness is subsumed – through self-consciousness – into the project of a future, experiencing in this way its *Aufhebung* or sublation. This is to view the end of history not as a triumphant moment, as has sometimes been rendered (Fukuyama 1992; Bell 1960), but as melancholy or, at least, uncertain.

Accordingly, closer scrutiny of Hegel's writings reveals that the passage of time is a double-edged proposition within his system. Even though he viewed time and history as unfolding in stages that ended with the moment of European modernity, he suggested (as I have indicated above) that historical understanding is constitutively belated and becomes significant only when "the form of life" associated with it is past or on the verge of extinction. Moreover, if we also take into account the fact that from Hegel's standpoint philosophy was nothing other than the philosophy of history, we can take his historical vision as our point of departure – rather than as the fixed point of arrival into which all attempts at systematic history are supposedly locked.[1] Paradoxically, but in keeping with the dialectical framework of his thinking (and despite his cultural biases which were exclusively European and, even more narrowly, Prussian), Hegel advanced the idea that history only comes into focus when the mode of consciousness attached to it is in decline. By this light, even if his own conception and historical delineation of modernity took Europe as their center, Hegel made it possible, theoretically, to prefigure forms of cultural and social emergence that though chronologically late are not yet tarnished by age. The progress of history may be nothing other than, as Hegel put it in his Introduction to *The Philosophy of History*, "the progress of the consciousness of Freedom," but also – and more tellingly – this freedom "is an indefinite and incalculably ambiguous term . . . liable to an infinity of misunderstandings, confusions, and errors, and to become the occasion for all imaginable excesses" (1956: 19).

This, however, is not the way of reading Hegel that has gained currency in postcolonial theory. Indeed, to regard Hegel as I have been suggesting runs counter to some of the most commonly asserted positions in the field, which offer themselves as critiques of Hegelian "historicism" (if, more typically, by force of repetition rather than argument). In his influential *White Mythologies*, Robert Young, for example, takes his lead on evaluating Hegel from the French feminist critic, Hélène Cixous (Young 1990: 2–4). Launching his denunciation of "the Hegelian dialectic" – on whose basis he condemns all dialectics, including that of Marx – Young contends that when it comes to the role of understanding history in the construction of knowledge, "poststructuralism challenges not only just the politics and institutions of the right but also the politics and theoretical systems of the left" (2). Young champions Cixous as a compelling example of poststructuralist critique and begins the introductory, eponymous chapter of his book by avowing that Cixous demonstrates not only how poststructuralism's politics are superior albeit "difficult to place" but also how "Marxism, as a body of knowledge itself remains complicit with, and even extends, the system to which it is opposed" (2–3). Young implicates in such complicity "the entire Hegelian machinery . . . whether it be Marxism's History, Europe's colonial annexations and accompanying racism or orientalist scholarship, or, in a typical conflation of patriarchy and colonialism, Freud's characterisation of femininity as the dark unexplored continent" (3).

Cixous's political efficacy and the sharpness of her critique of Hegelian racism are granted mostly by citing phrases in which, for instance, she disparages "annihilating dialectical magic" and the "commonplace gesture of History." Young then quotes her as follows:

[I]n History, of course, what is called "other" is an alterity that does not settle down, that falls into the dialectical circle . . . With the dreadful simplicity that orders the movement Hegel erected as a system, society trots along before my eyes reproducing to perfection the mechanism of the death struggle: the reduction of a "person" to a "nobody" to the position of "other" – the inexorable plot of racism.   (1990: 2)

As readers, however, we may ourselves want to pause before trotting alongside Cixous and Young from Hegel to Marx and from dialectics to colonial racism. In poststructuralist criticism as they represent it, the rhetoric of "otherness" turns out to be the main culprit in the history of European colonization; the material appetites of an emergent European bourgeoisie are largely ignored, as are its imperial ambitions and sense of civilizational supremacy. Yet the indictment of Marxism's allegedly "collusive" Eurocentrism hardly seems effective given in such unspecific terms; nor is the philosophical apparatus of Hegelian critique undermined simply by positing the abstract complicity of "capitalist economic exploitation, racism, colonialism, sexism, together with (and somewhat unexpectedly) 'History' and the structure of the Hegelian dialectic" (Young 1990: 1).

Beyond this, the issue is whether it is at all productive to flatten out the role of Hegelian and Marxist traditions (the two are not the same despite Young's attempt to conflate them) in the very foundation of postcolonial thought – e.g., in the writings of Amilcar Cabral, Frantz Fanon, C. L. R. James, Eric Williams, Manabendranath Roy, Aimé Césaire, and so on. In many poststructuralist approaches such as Young's (but not limited to him alone), the antipathy towards dialectical thought has more to do with writing off the question of historical *process* as (bad) "History" and (worse) "totalization" than it does with finding substantive ways to overcome the insights produced within the Hegelian lineage (see for instance Prakash 2000). This lineage would of course begin with Hegel and move forward in time to include Ludwig Feuerbach, Marx, Lenin, Antonio Gramsci, Rosa Luxemburg, Georg Lukács, Theodor W. Adorno, Ernst Bloch, Guy Debord, Henri Lefebvre, and other figures whose work anchors, sometimes in paraphrased and unacknowledged ways, the corpus of postcolonial theory (see Brennan 2002b). In the decade or so since the publication of *White Mythologies*, Young has shifted to a different position with regard to the utility of various Marxist arguments for postcolonial thought. In *Postcolonialism: An Historical Introduction* (2001), for example, he revises many of his earlier, formulaic propositions about poststructuralism's alleged novelty in thinking beyond Marxism's apparently narrow frames of reference. In this later work, he begins to credit earlier traditions of philosophy and political movements for their legacies to postcolonial theory, although for him the telos of revolutionary postcolonial thinking still resides in Jacques Derrida. Young's assertions of the early 1990s can be located within a 1968-ist faith in antihistoricism that now, in his latest writings, reveals its own historical assumptions – taking as it did most, if not all, of its cues from the declared priority of Louis Althusser's and Michel Foucault's ideas. Nonetheless, his current attempts to re-value the role of Hegelian modes of thinking associated with the likes of Lukács or Luxemburg, though welcome, have as yet to mark their impact on the antihistorical trends still prevalent in postcolonial criticism. For most postcolonial critics remain lagging behind, still touting the virtues of reading history "against the grain," against the declared "white mythologies" of totality and causality, asserting the priority of "non-white" aporias and fragments (see the critical discussions in Hogan 2001; Brennan 2002b).

To insist that Hegel's ideas continue to have great value for thinking about the temporal dimensions of postcoloniality is not to disregard the flaws in his vision of history. On the contrary, it is to underscore that in so far as postcolonial discussions center on problems of experience, consciousness, understanding, these terms are not the same. In fact, they must be seen as temporally dynamic as well as acting on each other in mutually self-cancelling ways, rather than as "disjunct" or "differential." In much postcolonial scholarship, the rhetoric, premised as it is on the synchronic and static terms of structuralism, seeks to dissimulate an interest in the diachronic (i.e., the historical) by compacting the dynamism of experience and understanding into conceptual conceits about "differentials," "disjunctions," "singularities," and so on – with the implication that theorizing postcoloniality requires the language of mathematics or set theory (as opposed to the language of dialectics). But since it is to Hegel's dialecticization of Kant's ideas that we owe our systematic understanding of the time lag between experience and understanding, outright rejection of his influence on the grounds that his system is too "totalizing" does not automatically result in the production of anti-Eurocentric accounts of postcolonial history or theory. The rhetoric of fragments, fractals, and incommensurables ushers in its own totalizations; it also risks evading the very history it purports to recover. The alternative to totalizing history – a history "for use" – may be an appealing idea but it often tends towards functionalism, relativizing the problems of force and scale that describe colonial apparatuses (such as slavery and settlements) and which therefore remain key to understanding postcolonial history as a mode of coming to terms with the past as well as of narrating it.

The disciplinary production and separation of knowledge has made it well nigh impossible to explore the impact of Enlightenment thought in general, and Hegel in particular, on the ways that Western philosophical narratives about human freedom were directly influenced by the practices of slavery and colonization. In an important corrective, Susan Buck-Morss places before us the paradigmatic example of Haiti to demonstrate the links between Hegel's ideas about the logic of freedom and the social context of his writing: "The Haitian Revolution was the crucible, the trial by fire for the ideals of the French Enlightenment. And every European who was part of the bourgeois reading public knew it" (2000: 837). This mode of reading Hegel's philosophy (particularly his highly self-conscious arguments about the dialectic of bondage and lordship), however, defies an accepted and authorized view of postcolonial scholarship, which is based on mounting a critique of Hegel and sees itself as providing an alternate and antidialectical route to the discussion of subjective freedom. Buck-Morss's counter-intuitive suggestion is that "the arguments of several black scholars, which they believe to be *in opposition* to Hegel, are in fact close to Hegel's original intent" (848, n. 85; original emphasis).[2]

A more thorough confrontation of Hegel's shortcomings makes it necessary to address the specificities of the colonial archive in its myriad effects: as a system of thought (e.g., demonstrated early in Edward W. Said's *Orientalism* [1978] and more recently in Gayatri Chakravorty Spivak's *A Critique of Postcolonial Reason* [1999]); as a set of administrative logics (e.g., Ranajit Guha's *A Rule of Property for Bengal* [1996] or W. E. B. Du Bois's *Black Reconstruction in America* [1977]); and, perhaps most foundationally, as a mode of critique (Aimé Césaire's *Discourse on Colonialism* [1972], C. L. R. James's *The Black Jacobins* [1963], and Frantz Fanon's *The Wretched of the Earth* [1968]). At the heart of these critics' important formulations is the insight that the moment of colonial hegemony (beginning in the eighteenth century and reaching its peak in the next one) is also the moment that produces the contradictory formulation of Enlightenment ideals of freedom and reason. In other words, these markers of our present – the Enlightenment no less than imperialism, colonialism, and postcoloniality – belong to the same time and are embedded in the same historical process (which does not have to be seen as governed by inexorable laws but only by the actual contingencies and contradictions of historical emergence). Such an argument is not inimical to Hegel, but generatively a part of his thinking in both the *Philosophy of Right* and the *Phenomenology of Mind*. By the same token, neither does this argument counteract the overall Eurocentrism of the Western tradition to which Hegel belonged. As Marx himself pointed out in *The German Ideology*, this tradition was ideological precisely because it was caught up in contemplative views of the world that denied their social, historical, and geographical circumstances. In the context of our discussion of temporality, what is at stake is the somewhat discontinuous task of accounting for the exclusions through which European thought silences the role of non-European actors and events in its narrative of self-becoming. This requires acknowledging that Europe's historical self-understanding has depended at a very deep level upon the action and events in its colonies. Thus in the example of Hegel and Haiti, much of what Hegel had to say about the problematic of "lordship and bondage" was formulated exactly in the context of German newspaper reports about the Haitian revolution (which he is known to have read avidly). The time of philosophy is, we might say, the time of the colonized (as the post-1968 effusion of French philosophical thought also demonstrates in its relation to the Algerian struggle for independence), even if the latter is subsumed into Europe's sense of intellectual and political sovereignty. The larger point is that the shared and universal – albeit unequal – narrative of the present depends upon the dialectic of Europe and its others, given the simultaneity of ideals of freedom and realities of colonization and slavery that together make up the past (see E. Williams 1966).

One of the means of disavowing the mutual embeddedness of European and "non-Western" history has been the denial of what Johannes Fabian has called "co-evalness" or the sharing of time (1983: 31). In *Time and the Other*, Fabian offers a thoroughgoing critique of anthropological thinking by means of a careful scrutiny of its epistemological blind-spots and its construction of the "other" as object. Fabian is acutely mindful of the fact that if Hegelian historicism idealized the progress of time in its accounts of "civilization," then structuralism – a paradigm whose overwhelming influence can be felt not only in anthropology but also in semiotics and cultural theory – has been more than equally guilty of placing a functionalist faith in the synchronic, reinforced by talk of history's discontinuities handed down by Ferdinand de Saussure's followers and made into an axiom by Michel Foucault.[3] Fabian criticizes the ways that anthropologists, in their very efforts to privilege otherness and difference, are disposed to construct their objects as "culture gardens" whose boundaries (whether they place the anthropologist within or without) have the effect of distancing and relativizing the culture under investigation.

Referring to this as the problem of *allochronism* – that is, the denial of co-evalness – Fabian's study lays out a typology of the "uses of time" in various socio-cultural and historical approaches. According to Fabian, anthropological discourse in particular, but also other forms of cultural study that depend on the construction of relations between the self and the other, conceive the object of knowledge as existing in a distant place – further down the stream of time from the anthropologist or analyst. He argues that this tic of Western modes of thinking – to project social differences in covertly developmental ways – resides in putatively non- and anti-developmentalist theories as well; that is, those that purport to value synchrony and structure. Accordingly, within the sphere of linguistics and semiotics, thinking about language in the immaterial terms of language-as-such (Saussure, Emile Benveniste), or of the object as the *monde commenté*, as the givenness of the world in the present, results in the failure to recognize that all human societies are, in Fabian's words, "of the same age." It is only these conceptual maneuvers, however, that allow forms of synchronic analysis – depending upon the "abbreviation of sequences in such a way that order [meaning] can be perceived at a glance" (1983: 4) – to advance their celebratory claims regarding discontinuity and difference. Privileging the "now" of writing (as well as the "here" of thinking) is, in fact, the reverse coin of claiming to speak for *all* times. In either case, coevalness is circumvented or pre-empted. Consequently, while historicism may be guilty of a false universalism and of producing accounts of other times and places that are in the end banal, Fabian's harshest criticism is reserved for relativistic cultural perspectives that, under cover of valorizing the distinctiveness of the "other," end up unable to reckon with the sameness of the "one history that leads from the slingshot to the megabomb" (a phrase he quotes from Adorno).[4]

Fabian's charges against anthropological modes of thinking can be read productively alongside Benedict Anderson's arguments about temporal consciousness in *Imagined Communities*, by now one of the most frequently cited texts in postcolonial studies as well as in the wider fields of literary, cultural, and historical study. Anderson's wide-ranging and influential theses on nationalism represent an attempt to account for the kind of "anomaly," as he puts it, that nationalism has proved for Marxist theory. For him, the world-historical significance of the problems of "nation, nationality, nationalism" (1991: 3) only emerges once there is both an imagined and invented but also limited and sovereign sense of the nation as a political community. First published in the same year (1983) as *Time and the Other*, Anderson's book shares its understanding that all nations are not only geographically delimited and physically demarcated but also the products of "chronic" forms of thinking: those religious modes of thought attached to temporal ideas about mortality and continuity, fatality and the contingencies of life. According to Anderson, "If nation-states are widely conceded to be 'new' and 'historical,' the nations to which they give political expression always loom out of an immemorial past, and still more important, glide into a limitless future" (1991: 11–12). Instead of elaborating the problem of nationalism as a political ideology, Anderson specifies it in the light of the "cultural systems" underpinning nationalist thought and practice. Time emerges as a cortical issue in cultural understanding because it is the exemplar of "a fundamental change . . . taking place in modes of apprehending the world, which, more than anything else, made it possible to 'think' the nation" (22). What is thus unprecedented about nationalism as a discourse, Anderson proposes, is that it reflects a profoundly modern sensibility about the passage of time that was, by the eighteenth century, quite distinct from the "mediaeval Christian mind [which] had no conception of history as an endless chain of cause and effect or of radical separations of past and present" (23).

The most provocative line of thought in *Imagined Communities* turns on this shift in sensibility that its author associates with a modern conception of temporality: a particular consciousness about the meaningfulness of time that has far-reaching consequences in defining the nature of nations not only in Europe but also elsewhere in the world (as he elaborates in later chapters of the book). A new idea of "simultaneity" is at the crux of the reorganized sense of past and present in modern times, an idea whose importance Anderson derives from Erich Auerbach and Walter Benjamin. He adapts Auerbach's and Benjamin's diverse propositions to argue that the prevailing form of consciousness in modernity is attached to a profoundly different notion of temporal simultaneity from that which stretched across biblical to medieval times.[5] In those earlier historical periods, simultaneity related to the convergence of past and future in an instantaneous present, in a prophetic notion of scriptural eternity. By contrast, Anderson states, "[w]hat has come to take the place of the mediaeval conception of simultaneity-along-time is, to borrow . . . from Benjamin, an idea of 'homogeneous, empty time,' in which simultaneity is, as it were, transverse, cross-time, marked not by prefiguring and fulfilment, but by temporal coincidence, and measured by clock and calendar" (1991: 24). To cast this another way, homogeneous empty time is a kind of time in which multiple actors perform minute tasks in a vast arena without cognizance of each other, creating a world that evolves inexorably but by inches (like worker bees performing their individual roles). Simultaneity is a product not of the immortality of time but of its insignificance, expressing itself haphazardly, inconsequentially. Equally, however, within the regime of simultaneity the cataclysmic sense of the Middle Ages is removed, as time is already numbered; marked out as taking place in an enormous chamber with rooms in which things unfold incrementally.

Of crucial importance to discussions of postcolonial emergence – which of course are premised on the assumption of nationhood in formerly colonized societies – is Anderson's further argument that "[t]he idea of a sociological organism moving calendrically through homogeneous, empty time is a precise analogue of the idea of the nation, which also is conceived as a solid community moving steadily down (or up) history" (1991: 26). More than any other single factor, this transformation in temporal thinking is the basis for the articulation of nationalist consciousness; it leads, as well, to the emergence of particular kinds of culture and technology that require the kind of productive order possible only by way of time-management (such as that of print and piracy, along with latter-day re-inventions of imperialist ideology from the nineteenth century onwards into its present-day avatars).

If Anderson's genealogy of the origins of nationalism represents a concrete focus on the material historical effects of temporal simultaneity on the "imagined communities" of modern nations, more associative ruminations on the discursive and semiotic aspects of the time of the postcolonial have been offered by Homi K. Bhabha in his routinely cited volume of essays, *The Location of Culture* (1994). Bhabha's ideas, often suggestive though always elusive in terms of precision or rigor, have come to be associated with the deconstructive bent of much postcolonial criticism (especially within literary-critical analysis). For him, the postcolonial functions as a supplementary element in the text of colonial modernity – as a sort of "contra-modernity" that is both contemporaneous with the present yet manages to re-stage the past and introduce "other, incommensurable cultural temporalities into the invention of tradition" (1994: 2). Mostly, these acts of staging and re-staging the postcolonial are premised on readerly strategies of interpretation which, according to Bhabha, illuminate the "*metaphoricity* of the peoples of imagined communities" (141; author's emphasis). His attempt, in various ways, is to elucidate this "metaphoricity" by invoking the ideas not only of Derrida (on whom he relies for his conceptions of writing the nation), but also of feminist theorist Julia Kristeva, novelist Toni Morrison, historians such as Eric Hobsbawm, Ernest Gellner, and Partha Chatterjee, and, on the question of temporality, the propositions of Benjamin.

"The sign temporalizes the iterative difference that circulates within language, of which meaning is made, but cannot be represented thematically within narrative as a homogeneous empty time. Such a temporality is antithetical to the alterity of the sign which, in keeping with my account of the 'supplementary question' of cultural signification, alienates the synchronicity of the imagined community" (1994: 158). Dense formulations like these have made it popular to think of the temporal dimension as another potentiality that signifies difference, although both syntactically and semantically Bhabha's proposition is hard to pin down. For instance, if all signs are constitutively non-synchronous (given the deferral of language and reality and the "supplementarity" attaching to all signification), why or how is it the case that the imagined community of the nation is seen as both homogeneous and synchronous – against which "minority discourses" become the locus of "a more instantaneous and subaltern voice of the people" (158)? The problem is that if signification betokens the deferral of meaning *tout court*, then all signs are non-synchronous, not only those that one wishes to privilege on account of their postcolonial or subaltern provenance. The desire to escape "Western epistemologies," as postcolonial studies is wont to put it, is salutary. However, what Benita Parry has called the "exorbitation of discourse" in Bhabha (Parry 1987: 43) merely replicates the epistemological fixation on the language of the subject and on speculative concepts. The point is that the objective domain of the postcolonial extends beyond epistemology and cannot be willed out of existence by asserting a rupture or break with past ideas alone. Bhabha's position displays complexity, although it may do no more than reproduce an old-fashioned nativism about the so-called "alterity" of postcolonial cultural practices, couched in terms of non-synchronousness. Moreover, it may be said that he disguises a fairly reductive set of binarisms about the homogeneity of "the nation" as opposed to the anarchist sublime of "the people" in hypostatic statements about textuality.

Nonetheless, Bhabha's deconstructive translation of more materialist configurations of ideas about non-synchronism has acquired the patina not only of respectability but indeed of novelty – through the elegance and skill with which historical problematics are by him reduced to wordplays about time and narrative. The essays in *The Location of Culture* serve as vehicles for exploring the ways that "difference" can be conceptualized as simultaneously ontological and performative, mimetic and alteristic, uncanny and antagonistic, colonial and postcolonial. In the process of this translation, the very substantiality of the non-synchronous as a contradiction *within* modernity gets lost, to return in Bhabha's retelling as the aporetic, marginal, and oppositional arenas of postcolonial incommensurability. For him, at the heart of postcolonial agency – which is almost exclusively understood in terms of utterance and enunciation rather than action, force, or revolution – is the notion that there is a "discursive time-lag" which he also regards as a "contingent tension between the social order of symbols and the 'desubjected' scansion of the sign" (1994: 198). According to him, this is the realm of the sign deprived of the subject – an idea deriving much of its impetus from the work of Jacques Lacan on the production of subjectivity within the symbolic order. Bhabha grafts his reading of Lacan onto the vastly different and dissimilar terrain of arguments about historical materialism that Benjamin, echoing Ernst Bloch's arguments about temporal discontinuity, proffered in his "Theses on the Philosophy of History" (Benjamin 1969b). The result is a dizzying mélange of constructions whose power to explain the postcolonial predicament is compelling only if one accepts Bhabha's eclectic deployment of concepts taken from sources whose political and intellectual energies have little in common. For this reason, it may be instructive to recall the import of Benjamin's, and perhaps more pertinently, Bloch's ideas about non-synchronism in so far as they bear on postcolonial considerations of time.

If, in Bhabha's writing, non-synchronousness is seen as a matter of the "temporal split" that purportedly characterizes postcolonial subjectivity (in opposition to what he regards as the homogeneity of national culture), the problem of non-synchronism or non-simultaneity is formulated in completely different, even opposing terms in Bloch's highly suggestive essay, "Non-synchronism and the Obligation to Its Dialectics," first published in 1932. Bhabha (mis-)reads non-synchronousness as an argument about *agency*, making it appear oppositional, even subversive, whereas Bloch's point was that it represented a blockage against social mobilization. Moreover, non-synchronousness (*Ungleichzeitigkeit*) – or the presence of distempered worldviews and modes of existence within the present – was, Bloch argued, produced by the derangements of class society and the distances that separate certain classes and groups of people (such as youth, the peasantry, and the bourgeoisie) from the mode of production, making them non-contemporaneous with the present. "One has one's times" he said, "according to where one stands corporeally, above all in terms of classes" (Bloch 1977: 22). Thus, from a materialist standpoint – which must seek, as Marx said in the famous eleventh of his "Theses on Feuerbach," not merely to describe the world but to change it (Marx 1981: 123) – the problem is to figure out how to eliminate non-simultaneity so that people can be wrested away from the grip of the past, from an "ascetic contemplation of the unresolved myth of dark old being or of nature" (Bloch 1977: 35). On this reading, to come into the present – that is, to be synchronous with it – is less about ideological or cultural homogeneity than about the ways that consciousness can be transformed: "the liberation," as Bloch put it, "of the still *possible future* from the *past* . . . by putting both in the present" (33; original emphases).

Needless to say, there is no reason why Bloch's arguments cannot be adapted to theorize postcolonial situations. It is worth pointing out, however, that the hypostatization of cultural identity in Bhabha's work (and in scholarship inspired by him) comes at the expense of the analysis of class and class consciousness. The resources bequeathed to us by the thinkers of the Frankfurt School, who had offered a class-inflected reading of non-synchronous being, are firmly disavowed by Bhabha's approach. Within the social philosophy of the Frankfurt School, the question of temporality was never settled by referring to metaphysical conceptions of identity; Bhabha, however, poses it in exactly such terms: of the "disjunction" between "modern times and colonial and slave histories," a disjunctiveness that permits him to enlarge on the "reinvention of the self" (1994: 244). Whether his misreadings are intentional or unwitting is, ultimately, less consequential than the possibilities that exist for exploring the problem of non-synchronousness as yet another modality of alienation under capital. At this level, Bhabha has little to contribute.

By contrast, many of Benjamin's writings reveal exactly this concern with how capitalist modernity effects the destruction of experience (although it has become something of a pattern within cultural studies to quote selectively and exclusively from his "Theses on the Philosophy of History," despite the fact that the "Theses" as a whole represent unfinished meditations on the dilemma of co-ordinating the relationship of the past to the present and future). Given the diverse, incomplete, and sometimes inconsistent nature of his arguments, it is difficult to ascribe to Benjamin's positions anything resembling a unity. In fact, Jürgen Habermas, in a famous essay written in 1972, suggested that Benjamin's interpretation of the past entailed "a conservative-revolutionary hermeneutics" whose "position relative to political praxis" was "highly mediated" (Habermas 1983: 159, 153). The open question here is whether the prevailing politics of postcolonial criticism are themselves conservative (notwithstanding avowals to the contrary); this would account for the allure of an idealist and aestheticist version of Benjamin for the likes of Bhabha. Regardless, the aspect of Benjamin's writings centering on the problem of non-synchronism as opposed to the homogeneity or simultaneity of time is relatively easy to decipher.

For example, one of Benjamin's earliest utterances on the subject, "The Life of Students" (written in 1914–15), bears witness to a theory of temporal complexity that has marked similarities with what he says later, in 1939, in the "Theses on the Philosophy of History." Commenting on the experience of temporality in "The Life of Students," he declared: "The historical task is to disclose this immanent state of perfection and make it absolute, to make it visible and dominant in the present" (Benjamin 1996: 15). In saying this, Benjamin was not simply contending – in terms compatible with Hegel's speculative philosophy – that the future is immanently available in the present; nor was he monumentalizing it. He preferred, instead, to locate the potentiality of the future in the insignificant, rejected, and unwanted elements of the present. His was a more radical, if counter-intuitive, proposal that we need to grasp the metaphysical structure of the future in order to enable us to correct what is distorted in the present. Ultimately, the sole object of critique for Benjamin was, as Howard Caygill quotes him, "to recognise and free the future from its disfigured form in the present" (Caygill 1998: 9).

Benjamin's early ideas about the immanent totality of experience understood in terms of time also inflect the specification of "homogeneous empty time" in the "Theses on the Philosophy of History," his last text. Bhabha misses the dialectical tension in which Benjamin held this proposition, rendering it into a dogmatism about subaltern presence and agency with the imputation that "homogeneity" is the province of metropolitan nationalism, whereas "heterogeneity" can be celebrated as the preserve of the so-called "subaltern collective." However, Benjamin's original idea is both very different from Bhabha's rendition of it and still very powerful. Written as a harsh critique of rationalized societies (in both their capitalist and socialist variants), Benjamin concluded that the concept of progress implied by what he called "historicism" was complicit in reproducing past power structures and forms of thinking because it reduced historical time to an instrumental matter of moving through the continuum of history – from barbarism to civilization, from the primitive to the modern, from the bad old days to the good new ones. Against this "historicism," Benjamin formulated his conception of historical materialism in which time was seen not as homogeneous, simultaneous, or continuous, but shot through with the "shards" of the past and redirected to the future of a "redeemed humanity" (Benjamin 1969b). Debate over the status of "redemption" in Benjamin's thought marks a significant point of contention between idealist and materialist readings of his work, making it difficult to gauge the exact status of this proposition within the project of materialist history. Nonetheless, it would be extremely one-sided to assert that the idea of a "redeemed humanity" represents a purely messianic conception – not least because, as a dialectical thinker, Benjamin was profoundly committed to the critical cancellation of propositions; which is to say, to their transformation into new constellations and possibilities. His resort to the trope of redemption, while perhaps vague and unsatisfying, emblematizes the doubling of his thought – which he himself characterized as "surviv[ing] suspended over this abyss" separating human from spiritual reality (Benjamin, qtd. in Caygill 1998: 17; see also 1–33).

For Benjamin, the task of redemption lies in the hands of the materialist historian – who, by undertaking to overcome the failures of historical representation, could and should contribute to the transformation of human society from its alienation in the present. In his scheme, the homogeneous present of modernity is not just counterposed to the heterogeneity of the past (and future) in which things either were (or will be) infinitely better; this would make his view fairly simplistic and undialectical. Rather both past and present are constituted by the collective temporal catastrophe that betokens the predicament of modernity. Accordingly, the materialist historian should neither empathize naively with the past – "the good tidings which the historian of the past brings with throbbing heart" (Benjamin 1969b: 255) – nor valorize the present "in the name of progress" (257), but recognize the failure of modernity as well as of himself (or herself) as historian. What is required is the restoration of the task of *revolutionary* history in the interests of keeping faith with a truly classless society and a future world that gives an inkling of itself in the "attentiveness" of the materialist historian to the multifaceted nature of time. Benjamin captures this restoration with his image of a "leap in the open air of history," adding that this "is how Marx understood the revolution" (261). The conception of "homogeneous empty time," which for Benjamin "cannot be sundered" from the empty concept of progress, is deployed to augur its negation. Of great importance to Benjamin, though, is that this negation is not simply to be taken as the non-synchronous – this continues to be the error of historicism enthralled by the past, not liberated by it – but the as-yet-unexploded course of the present itself.

The importance of these considerations for conceptualizing time in postcoloniality should be abundantly clear if we think about the myriad ways that the past and present impinge upon our understanding of the problems and possibilities attached to emerging out of colonial conquest and attaining cultural and political sovereignty. Moreover, our own implication as scholars in these narratives of history, experience, and subjectivity also embeds the question of temporality as untranscendable. To adapt the lyrics of the popular song, time is on our side – in the sense that the conditions of possibility for thinking historically require us to conceptualize time as an integral and structuring principle of experience and understanding, rather than as a valueless or *a priori* horizon against which the meaning of being postcolonial is articulated. Space and time have, since Kant, been conceived within the Continental philosophical tradition as constituting the subjective and objective dimensions of thought and experience. However, the dearth of rigorous theorizations of time within mainstream postcolonial criticism has made it difficult to separate the wheat of substantial arguments from the chaff of readymade pronouncements about the "double consciousness" that not only defines postcolonial subjectivity but supposedly also attends the experience of time;[6] about the "incommensurability" of postcolonial difference which makes it unassimilable to the "teleology" of the modern nation (see, for instance, Ashcroft 2001; Chow 1993; Seyhan 2001; Trinh 1989); and other formulations that mystify how time matters in understanding the postcolonial present.

The metaphoric possibilities of thinking about time in the free-falling terms of postcolonial discourse notwithstanding, the fact is that as social formations, postcolonial nations are (like any others) subject to the dictates of capitalist modernity. So, in contrast to the culturalist hypostatization of the "otherness" of time itself, the above discussion has tried to demonstrate the texture and depth of theoretical formulations in which capitalist modernity serves as the *de facto* referent for any understanding of postcolonial culture (see Lazarus 1999a: 6–9). Fredric Jameson has been the most influential voice in pressing for such a perspective, and in his most recent book, *A Singular Modernity*, he argues against sloppy conceptions that seek to promote ineffable portraits of postcolonial culture through the voguish assertion of "alternative modernities."[7] Against this current touted, as he puts it, by "ideologues of modernity" to forward the reassuring notion "that you can fashion your own modernity differently," he re-emphasizes the fundamental meaning of modernity and modern times as the system of world-wide capitalism itself (2002: 12). In Marx's writing, at least, this was never about the "normative" status of Europe or England, but rather about the contingent and determined roads taken by capital under unique national circumstances. Certainly, until present conditions of historical and social existence have been transformed, a vocabulary that accounts for our collective experience of time as constrained by the rationalizing imperatives of clock and calendar seems to be preferable to approaches in which the discussion of temporality provides one more opportunity for insubstantial position-taking about "postcolonial" futures.

NOTES

1 This point will be explored and contested in greater detail below, but for now let me flag it as the nub of a certain line within postcolonial historiography which sees itself as an improvement on supposedly "historicist" versions associated with various Marxist traditions of history writing such as that of E. P. Thompson, Christopher Hill, and their followers (see Chakrabarty 2000a; Prakash 1993, 2000).

2 In particular, Buck-Morss cites Paul Gilroy and Orlando Patterson as guilty of such misunderstanding in their desire to pit minoritarian histories against the perceived dogma of Enlightenment thought.

3 See, for instance, Fabian's reference to Claude Lévi-Strauss's "temerity" in arguing for the discontinuous nature of historical knowledge. According to Fabian, Lévi-Strauss falls into "metaphysics of the worst sort, the one which is mixed with moralism" (1983: 58). Fabian is equally harsh about claims on behalf of discontinuity advanced within anthropological studies inspired not only by Lévi-Strauss, but also by Althusser and Foucault.

4 Fabian's point in citing this trope from Theodor Adorno's *Negative Dialectics* [1987] relates to his agreement with Adorno that critics of the idea of universal history (criticism of which is in itself to be recommended) often forget that a simple rejection of historicism is itself trapped by it, and unable to recognize the catastrophes of history (Fabian 1983: 159).

5 Although Anderson does not cite R. G. Collingwood, some of his key proposals are similar to, and bear comparison with, Collingwood's *The Idea of History* (1961, first published in 1946).

6 The phrase itself, taken from W. E. B. Du Bois, has undergone substantial distortion. Du Bois intended it to refer to the experience of people subject to apartheid

for whom he wished a complete *inclusion* into modernity; in latter-day postcolonial usage (for example, in Paul Gilroy's *The Black Atlantic* [1993]), it has taken on the inflection of bifocality, a form of double vision that is seen as both produced by and providing the privilege of racialized otherness.

7 In postcolonial studies, the discussion of "alternative" or "counter" modernities – for and against – has been most intensively and sustainedly undertaken in the work of Appadurai 1996; Dussel 1998; García Canclini 1995; Gilroy 1993; Harootunian 2000; Mignolo 2000; and Nandy 2003. See also Gaonkar 2001; Kang 1998.

3

SITES OF ENGAGEMENT

10

LAURA CHRISMAN

Nationalism and postcolonial studies

Postcolonial studies emerged in the 1980s. By this time, the great era of Third-World anticolonial nationalism was at an end, and violent ethnic communalism was beginning to assume global dimensions. Such political shifts fed the tendency of postcolonial studies to regard nationalism as inherently dominatory, absolutist, essentialist, and destructive. The 1980s additionally witnessed the global expansion and intensification of capitalism. This led to the popular academic view that the era of nation-states was itself nearing a close and that nationalism was therefore redundant (Hobsbawm 1993). These tendencies were further fueled by developments in critical theory. The culturalist turn of social and literary theory, poststructuralist critiques of Enlightenment rationality and modernity – these encouraged postcolonial studies to view nationalism as a primarily cultural and epistemological, rather than socio-political, formation. This accompanied the view that nationalism was, as Gayatri Chakravorty Spivak suggested, "a reverse or displaced legitimation of colonialism," doomed to repeat the "epistemic violence" of the colonialism it had rejected (1999: 62). Less antagonistic are the approaches associated with Benedict Anderson's *Imagined Communities* (1991, first published 1983). In these, nationalism is construed as Janus-faced, paradoxical in its cultural, temporal modernity and simultaneous reliance on the past to define and legitimate itself.

This chapter outlines and explores these tendencies, under the subheadings of "nationalism as a derivative discourse"; "nationalism as a cultural/temporal paradox"; "nationalism as a dominatory formation"; "nationalism as a nativist projection"; "nationalism and narrative"; and "nationalism as a failed historical project." The critical emphasis falls on postcolonial constructions of anticolonial nationalism.

Nationalism as a derivative discourse

This view sees anticolonial nationalism as derivative of, and imprisoned within, the mental framework of "the West." Depending on the particular critic concerned, the "Western" conceptual apparatus from which anticolonialism allegedly derives is "the Enlightenment" (Lowe and Lloyd 1997), colonialism (Spivak 1999), or European nationalism (Miller 1990). At times the critique of anticolonial nationalism's "discourse" extends to the political structure of the nation-state. The concept and political practice of the nation-state are, accordingly, seen as "Western" inventions that colonialism has imposed on colonized peoples. By adopting the nation-state as the object and medium of social liberation, anticolonial nationalism dooms itself to conceptual self-contradiction (Lowe and Lloyd), cultural inauthenticity (Miller), political failure (Spivak), and, inevitably, repetition of the dominatory modes of thought that led to its imposition in the first place.

These perspectives are open to conceptual, historical, and political contestation. Historically, neither the political unit of the nation-state nor the concept of nationalism was necessarily alien to colonized countries. As Kenneth Harrow points out,

> Europeans did not export state formation to Africa, they imposed an administration upon populations already accustomed to being ruled by some state entity, or else cognizant of such entities in the form of neighboring states . . . State formation could be traced back to the kingdoms of Ghana and Mali in the first millennium and the start of the second, to take the Sudanic region alone. In all the territories where the terrain was favorable to settlement, trade, and population growth, states both large and small developed.   (2001: 33)

The same may be said of the ideology of nationalism. Timothy Brennan, like Anderson, observes that "the first nationalists are not Frenchmen, Spaniards, or Englishmen, but the creole middle classes of the New World – people like Simon Bolívar, Toussaint L'Ouverture, and Ben Franklin" (1990: 58–59).

It is important to recognize, as do Basil Davidson and Mahmood Mamdani, that the particular administrative regimes and national boundaries that European colonialism created in its colonies were imposed, inorganic, and designed to serve the interests of imperial, colonial, and metropolitan domination (Davidson 1992; Mamdani 1996). Moreover, the political legacy of these particular structures and boundaries has often been disastrous. However, this does not mean that the concept of the nation-state itself demands categorical rejection. The challenge, as Mamdani has argued, is to reinvent the nation-state radically to serve the needs of its own population. Indeed numerous anticolonial nationalists have remarked on the danger of simply adopting the political structures created by colonialism.

Aimé Césaire, for example, contrasted "good decolonization" with "less good," contending that the latter "thinks only of utilizing colonial structures which have been adapted to a new reality, whereas true decolonization understands that its task is to make a definitive break with colonial structures" (1970: 156).

The effect of presenting the nation-state, and the practice of nationalism, as a permanently "derivative discourse" is to deny the capacity of colonized and formerly colonized peoples to transform structures of thought and governance. Some of the most influential scholars in postcolonial studies have made this mistake. In doing so they have also risked essentializing thought itself in an implicit striving for a form of "pure" alterity, an autonomous epistemological space for non-Western "discourse" to inhabit. Even if nationalist ideology *were* the invention of Europe, however, it does not follow that it must *remain* a European monopoly. As Edward W. Said argues, "A confused and limiting notion of priority allows that only the original proponents of an idea can understand and use it. But the history of all cultures is the history of cultural borrowings" (1993: 217).

Another problematic element of the "derivative discourse" approach is its generalization about "the Enlightenment" and "the West," as if these were monolithic formations. There were many different political and intellectual tendencies at work in the Enlightenment: revolutionary, conservative, and liberal. The readiness to equate *liberalism* with the Enlightenment is evident in Lowe and Lloyd's contention that anticolonial "ideology is in large part structured in terms of liberal discourses and for liberal state institutions: it speaks of rights and the citizen, of equality, fraternity, and liberty, makes its claims to self-determination on the basis of enlightenment universality, and asserts the cultural if not economic and military equivalence of its nation-people to that of the imperial power" (1997: 9).

In fact, the Enlightenment ideology that structured nationalism was as likely to be revolutionary as to be liberal; claims to self-determination were as likely to be made on the basis of land ownership as on the basis of universal reason. If we look, for example, at the Irish Republic's Provisional Government 1916 declaration, we see the discourse of rights and citizenship, but also the nationalist self-articulation invoking the radical discourse of freedom rather than "liberty"; resistance to foreign domination rather than "equality"; and land, not Enlightenment universality:

> We declare the right of the people of Ireland to the ownership of Ireland, and to the unfettered control of Irish destinies, to be sovereign and indefeasible. The long usurpation of that right by a foreign people and government has not extinguished the right, nor can it ever be extinguished except by the destruction

of the Irish people. In every generation the Irish people have asserted their right to national freedom and sovereignty: six times during the past three hundred years they have asserted it in arms. Standing on that fundamental right and again asserting it in arms in the face of the world, we hereby proclaim the Irish Republic as a Sovereign Independent State, and we pledge our lives and the lives of our comrades-in-arms to the cause of its freedom, of its welfare, and of its exaltation among the nations.

Nationalism as a cultural/temporal paradox

Many postcolonial scholars – among them Partha Chatterjee (1986) and Anne McClintock (1995) – have followed Benedict Anderson's characterization of nationalism as a constitutively paradoxical formation. The paradox arises from the historical rupture of capitalist modernity. Nationalism is the product of modern, secular consciousness; it views the emergence of nations as part of the forward march of history. At the same time, nationalism's imagined community stretches back to antiquity; the nation's identity and credibility depend upon the assertion of unbroken cultural tradition. Nationalism is thus the paradoxical expression of a historical and cultural rupture that must assert itself as a historical continuity.

These approaches are concerned with the cultural or ontological dimensions of nationalism, rather than its directly political concerns. If one looks at anticolonial nationalist writings, however, it becomes difficult to maintain this distinction between cultural and political spheres systematically. Likewise the dichotomy between modernity and tradition becomes much less formulaic than these postcolonial critics maintain. Chatterjee (1986) convincingly argues that Indian bourgeois nationalism was historically structured upon the cultural contradiction of British modernity and tradition. He contends that the contradiction was resolved through the production of a bifurcated "discourse" in which nationalism posited an "inner" space of traditional cultural and spiritual essence, gendered feminine, and an "outer" space of "Western" progress and secular modernity. However, this formula does not characterize all anticolonial nationalism, and should not be seen as anything other than a historically specific case study.

For all its undeniable modernity as a political practice and an ideology, anticolonial nationalism does not, in fact, dictate a set of attitudes to modernity or to tradition but articulates a range of perspectives. These are generated through particular contexts and contingencies, and have mobilization as their immediate aim; their ultimate objective is national self-determination.

Some nationalisms have appealed to precolonial cultural traditions in order to sanction or define their nationalist project. Others have construed "native culture" as an arena of heterogeneous practices, measuring these practices not according to their "traditionalism" or "modernity," but according to their ability to contribute to human freedom. Amilcar Cabral, for example, argued for a nationalism that selected what was emancipatory and useful from "precolonial" and from "modern" cultures, combining these in new and creative ways (1973: 39–56).

For nationalists like Frantz Fanon, the notion of traditional culture was, on occasion, nothing other than a contradiction in terms. Arguing that colonialism had destroyed precolonial culture and history, to the point of irrecoverability, Fanon insisted that nationalism ought not to preserve or synthesize "the past" but rather to invent a qualitatively new cultural consciousness, one that could only begin to be engendered through the political creation of struggle itself (1968: 206–48). Elsewhere, however – including in some of the other essays in *The Wretched of the Earth* (1968; see also Fanon 1965) – Fanon posited the ongoing existence and utility of precolonial cultural formations. In other words, there is no schematic polarization of traditional and modern cultures in his nationalism; instead there is a sustained emphasis on nationalism as an activity that transforms human subjects in new and unimaginable ways.

Scholars in postcolonial studies would benefit from looking more closely at political and economic sovereignty over a finite landmass – a specific and delimited geopolitical terrain – rather than cultural/temporal paradox, as foundational elements to nationalist ideology. The Irish nationalist James Connolly, seeking to define "what is a free nation?" came up with a set of definitions which foregrounded these material concerns: a free nation would be one that has "absolute control over all internal resources and powers, and which has no restriction upon its intercourse with all other nations"; "complete control over its own harbours, to open or close them at will, or shut out any commodity, or allow it to enter in, just as it seemed best to suit the well-being of its own people, and in obedience to their wishes"; "full power to nurse industries to health"; "full power to alter, amend, or abolish or modify the laws under which the property of its citizens is held in obedience to the demand of its own citizens" (1997a). Fanon, likewise, emphasizes the central significance of political sovereignty and the origins of national community in a physical landmass: "the mass of the country people have never ceased to think of the problem of their liberation except in terms of violence, in terms of taking back the land from the foreigners, in terms of national struggle, and of armed insurrection" (1968: 127).

Nationalism as a dominatory formation

Scholars in postcolonial studies frequently characterize nationalism as a movement that promotes the interests of a particular group while claiming to represent the whole. It is the élitist interests of the bourgeoisie that nationalism is alleged to serve, necessarily sacrificing or "ignoring" the interests of "subaltern" groups (Spivak 1995b: 146). Similarly nationalism has been defined as a patriarchal project that opposes the needs of women and the goals of gender equality (McClintock 1995; Parker *et al.* 1992; Spivak 1995b). Many intellectual elements feed these tendencies. One is a Nietzschean conception of the "will-to-power," which is held to animate human activity; thus all action stems from self-interest and an irrepressible urge to dominate, be it through direct or indirect (ostensibly egalitarian) expression. This Nietzschean conception is based on conviction, and as such it is not open to argument. Alternative, materialist explanations can, however, be found for human practices.

In fact, anticolonial nationalists such as Cabral, Césaire, and Fanon could not have been more concerned about the dangers of élite nationalism, a nationalism that they anticipated and also witnessed coming into postcolonial power in a number of states. Fanon's classic analysis of "The Pitfalls of Nationalist Consciousness" gives a trenchant account of the means by which bourgeois élites assume anticolonial leadership and then governmental power, resulting in neocolonial puppet states that maintain economic servitude to Europe or the US (1968: 148–205). Fanon's prescient discussion identifies the neocolonial élite's "prostitution" of their country through tourism; their taste for conspicuous consumption; their creation of political autocracy; their instrumentalization of nationalist rhetoric to disguise their corruption and to stifle dissent; their failure to diversify national industries and develop economic self-sufficiency; their reliance on outside loans. Fanon also outlines the neocolonial revival and intensification of ethnic identities that were created by colonial rule, and the tendency of an economically and politically frustrated population to push these identities into xenophobic conflict. Kwame Nkrumah dedicated a book-length analysis to the phenomenon of neocolonialism (1965). Thus it is important to credit nationalism – in particular, socialist forms of nationalism – with the capacity to generate a class-conscious, critical analysis of nationalist élites. It is also important to credit nationalism with the ability to envision and attempt liberatory government and wealth redistribution.

This is not to suggest that the heterogeneous elements of the population historically involved in socialist nationalist struggles were always united in their motivations, values, and understandings of the goals of struggle themselves. Nor is it to suggest that nationalist activists and theorists always correctly interpreted the class and social dynamics of the struggles to which they belonged. Discussing Algeria, for example, Neil Lazarus points to Fanon's failure to grasp just how different the peasantry's conception of nationalist struggle was from that of the urban proletariat (1999a: 68–143; see also Clegg 1979; Ageron 1991). It would, however, be problematic to conclude that subalterns, leaders, women, and men are necessarily fixed in their identities, needs, and interests, and that these necessarily conflict with those of others involved in nationalist liberation. There are two, interconnected, questions involved here: the transformability of subjects through political action; the positive value of "unification" over "difference." The most influential voices in postcolonial studies have been inclined to deny the possibility of the first and to reject the second.

The transformability of subjects is assumed and theorized by the majority of anticolonial movements and theorists. I have already suggested that Fanon's conception of nationalist struggle is based upon an understanding of the reciprocal transformability of leaders and masses (an argument developed also by Parry [2002] and Premnath [2000]). We need to take seriously the thrust of such passages as: "Decolonization . . . transforms spectators crushed with their inessentiality into privileged actors, with the grandiose glare of history's floodlights upon them. It brings a natural rhythm into existence, introduced by new men, and with it a new language and a new humanity" (Fanon 1968: 36). To emphasize human transformability, however, is to go against the categorical, antidialectical, foundations of much postcolonial theory. The latter, fed by postmodern conceptions of the politics of difference, and poststructuralist conceptions of *différance*, has also shown itself opposed to the principles of *unity*, which are seen as a kind of violence upon the principle of "difference" itself. (Such valorization of difference often leaves unexamined the question of who is responsible for defining and controlling that difference.)

It needs to be observed that the nationalist drive for unification is not an attempt to deny the legitimacy of difference in certain spheres of human identity and activity. Again, anticolonial theorists and activists supply a corrective to such misconceptions. Cabral, for example, acknowledges the cultural diversity of Cape Verde and Guinea-Bissau populations (1973: 39–56). Equally, though, he stresses the need for a nationalist mobilization that is based upon *political* unification. Unification, in other words, is a necessary condition for accomplishing the political goal of collective autonomy, expressed (in the first instance) through control of the nation-state. We can see such arguments in Fanon's critique of "Spontaneity":

The taking on of nationhood involves a growth of awareness. The national unity is first the unity of a group, the disappearance of old quarrels and the final liquidation of unspoken grievances . . . In undertaking this onward march, the people legislates, finds itself, and wills itself to sovereignty . . . The leaders of the rebellion come to see that even very large-scale peasant risings need to be controlled and directed into certain channels . . . They discover that the success of the struggle presupposes clear objectives, a definite methodology and above all the need for the mass of the people to realize that their unorganized efforts can only be a temporary dynamic.   (1968: 135–36)

Fanon emphasizes the necessity of co-ordinating discrete struggles, under a disciplined leadership, in order to create effective resistance and national sovereignty. All the key words of his activist discourse here – "control," "direction," "channel," "objectives," "definite methodology" – may sound alarms for a postcolonial studies that is inclined to associate such terms with authoritarianism and dangerous teleological tendencies. To be alarmed, however, is to miss the force of the argument itself: the only way a systematically disempowered people can become an empowered people is through a united and systematic struggle under strong leadership.

About the relations of gender and nationalism, scholars in postcolonial studies have written much. The editors' introduction to *Nationalisms and Sexualities* succinctly summarizes the prevailing postcolonial understanding that "[i]n anticolonial struggles . . . feminist programmes have been sacrificed to the cause of national liberation" (Parker *et al.* 1992: 7). Perhaps the most often-cited schema for classifying gender and nationalism is by Nira Yuval-Davis and Floya Anthias in *Woman-Nation-State*. Women, they argue, serve five fundamental (and patriarchally restrictive) functions for the nation:

1. as biological reproducers of members of ethnic collectivities;
2. as reproducers of the boundaries of ethnic/national groups;
3. as participating centrally in the ideological reproduction of the collectivity and as transmitters of its culture;
4. as signifiers of ethnic/national differences – as a focus and symbol in ideological discourses;
5. as participants in national, economic, political and military struggles (1989: 7).

This is an extremely useful list, but it is by no means exhaustive. As Sylvia Walby (1996) notes, the weighting is heavily towards ethnic, ideological, or cultural spheres; only in the last item does the agency of women in economic, military, and political spheres receive recognition, and the recognition rather problematically conflates these three spheres. More extensive approaches are to be found in works by Kumari Jayawardena (1986) and Valentine

Moghadam (1994), which take as their starting point the historical range of women's involvement in nationalist struggles, and illuminate a variety of articulations between gender, feminism, and national culture (see also Randall 1981; Urdang 1989; Walker 1991).

There is no necessary antagonism between feminist and nationalist agendas, even if, in practice, there has frequently been tension between them. Male nationalists themselves were, on occasion, very much aware of the injustice that is patriarchy, and dedicated to its overcoming as an integral element of their liberatory nationalism. One might cite James Connolly here (1997b). Alternatively, one might cite Fanon himself, whose sexual politics Madhu Dubey (1998) has persuasively demonstrated to be less patriarchal than are often alleged. Just how irreducible nationalism is to the schematic charge of patriarchal determinism is suggested by Cabral's response, in interview, when asked about the "nature of women's transformation from the old system under imperialism." He begins his answer by explaining the national co-existence of a large variety of gender structures:

> In our country you find many societies with different traditions and rules on the role of women. For example, in the Fula society a woman is like a piece of property of the man, the owner of the home. This is the typical patriarchal society . . . In the Balante society all that is produced belongs to the people that work and women work very hard so they are free . . . You know that in our country there were even matriarchal societies where women were the most important elements. On the Bijagos Islands they had queens. They were not queens because they were the daughters of kings. They had queens succeeding queens. The religious leaders were women too.   (1973: 85)

In itself this refutes the widespread tendency in postcolonial studies to generalize a singular patriarchy as defining all precolonial traditions. Cabral continues by addressing the question of women's social transformation through nationalist struggle (a struggle that was ongoing at the time the interview took place):

> But during the fight the important thing is the political role of women. Yes, we have made great achievements, but not enough. We are very far from what we want to do, but this is not a problem that can be solved by Cabral signing a decree. It is all a part of the process of transformation, of change in the material conditions of the existence of our people, but also in the minds of the women, because sometimes the greatest difficulty is not only in the men but in the women too.   (85)

There is no premature optimism here, but an emphasis on the interconnectedness of material and subjective struggles, together with a recognition of the limitations of a purely legislative mode of intervention, and a conviction that humans can and do achieve social transformation through collective action. Above all, Cabral signals his commitment to the political liberation of women; this is a fundamental component of his nationalist vision (75–92).

Nationalism as a nativist projection

"Nativist" nationalism may be what a majority of cultural and literary critics associate with nationalism itself; it is certainly among the most heavily vilified forms of nationalism. (By "nativism" I refer to a politics whose authority rests primarily upon the claims of, and to, "native" cultural identity or ethnicity.) Paul Gilroy, for example, criticizes contemporary First-World black nationalism as incorrigibly nativist; this renders it necessarily "ethnically absolutist," "cultural insiderist," and, ultimately, fascistic (1993, 2000). For Gilroy, black nationalism expresses and exposes the essentialist, violent basis of all nationalisms. It is important, however, to resist the urge to view all nationalisms, past and present, from the vantage point of present-day ethnic fundamentalisms. Equally, postcolonial criticism needs to examine the strategic elements of "nativist" ideologies. Discussing the nativism of Aimé Césaire's poetic articulation of *négritude*, for example, Benita Parry (1994) uncovers its strategic provisionality and mutability. She provides a more intellectually nuanced approach than blanket condemnation, and considers nativism within the broader historical and political contexts of its emergence.

Nativism, like nationalism more broadly, can be used for progressive or reactionary ends. Fanon, in "On National Culture," offers a far-ranging discussion of nativism that suggests it to be both useful and limited for nationalist political movements (1968: 206–48). It is the subjective function of nativism for Third-World intellectuals and petty bourgeoisie that particularly engages him – a concern that Cabral shares (1973: 57–74). Both thinkers analyze the "return to the source" as an impulse of an élite that has become alienated from its community through its assimilation of European cultural and intellectual values. The move to embrace and promote native culture marks the beginning of anticolonialist identification, for these intellectual élites and individuals, and as such is of both psychological and political value: the intellectuals begin to overcome the self-hatred and alienation that colonialism has created. For Fanon and Cabral, however, the "native culture" that is claimed and proclaimed by this élite is intrinsically dynamic, and nativist intellectuals who do not recognize this fact construct a static image of the culture they seek to rejoin. Rather than fully joining the people whose culture this is, they connect themselves to an anachronistic idea.

The danger of this nativist move is that it risks reifying culture and substituting cultural for political activity. Cabral goes further and suggests that

"The 'return to the source' is of no historical importance unless it brings complete . . . identification with the hopes of the mass of the people, who contest not only the foreign culture but also the foreign domination as a whole. Otherwise, [it] is nothing more than . . . a kind of political opportunism" (1973: 63). It is as *nationalists* that Cabral and Fanon develop their critiques of nativism; it is as *socialist nationalists* that they are led to examine and to differentiate the class dynamics at work in élite formulations of nativist ideology. The same Cabral who dissects intellectuals' "return to the source" affirms the paramountcy of "native" culture within nationalist struggles. This attentiveness to class specificity in the analysis of nativism is something from which postcolonial studies could learn.

Nationalism and narrative

Benedict Anderson's *Imagined Communities*, first published in 1983, initiated postcolonial literary analysis of nationalism's relationship to narrative forms such as the novel. Perhaps the best-known summation of this movement is Homi Bhabha's edited volume *Nation and Narration* (1990a). For Anderson, the practices of nationalism and of narratives are benign; his emphasis falls upon the inclusive community that is imagined through the narrative form of a novel, the synchronized daily reading of a newspaper, and the idea of nationalism itself. However, postcolonial studies have demonstrated much greater skepticism towards narrative forms. Narrative is now seen to proceed by imposing unity on heterogeneity, excluding and subordinating multiple discourses in order to produce coherent and comprehensible form. In other words, narrative seeks to banish "difference" in the interests of promoting "identity" and teleology.

In Gayatri Spivak's formulations, the conditions of possibility of narrative representation are inextricable from imperialism. The narrative project proceeds through the production of "self-consolidating others" (1999: 112–97). The task of the postcolonial critic is, accordingly, to deconstruct that procedure. Domination, exclusion, and instrumentalization are thus regarded as integral to the operations of textual representation itself. In hegemonic postcolonial studies, societies are construed as texts. This leads to skepticism towards all socio-political representation. Nationalist claims to representativeness, and to representation, are allegedly implicated in these same narrative "laws" or "logics" of domination, identity, exclusion, and instrumentalization. Nationalism, accordingly, is always-already doomed to fail as a project of human liberation. This formalist approach is found in (among others) the work of Bhabha (1990b) and David Lloyd (1991).

Such an approach fails to differentiate between nationalisms of the dominator and those of the oppressed – it cannot make such a differentiation, in fact, because it is based upon a structuralist, as opposed to a historical, understanding of social formation. If it is structuralist in its understanding, it is poststructuralist in its values, giving absolute valorization to difference as a (metaphysical) good in itself, and refusing to recognize that people may share needs, values, interests that override their differences. Bhabha's celebrated essay "DissemiNation: Time, Narrative and the Margins of the Modern Nation," first published in *Nation and Narration*, exemplifies these tenets. Inspired as it is by Anderson's work, the essay is simultaneously an expansion, distortion, and critique of Anderson. Bhabha recasts the core ingredients of Anderson's nationalism as oppressive elements that restrain the national population: "The people will no longer be contained in that national discourse of the teleology of progress; the anonymity of individuals; the spatial horizontality of community; the homogeneous time of social narratives" (1990b: 302).

Bhabha classifies nationalism as a dominatory force that is expressed through the discursive mode of "pedagogy." Challenging it – through the contradictions of national "discourse" itself – are the operations of the "performative" mode. Thus "the people" operate as performative subject and as pedagogical object of "the nation," generating "counter-narratives" that "continually evoke and erase its totalizing boundaries" (299). The "narrative" of the nation, that is, tends to self-deconstruction. What is significant, here, is the way that Bhabha's language casually characterizes nationalism as an essentializing, absolutist, and authoritarian power. Thus, the boundaries of the nation are referred to as "totalizing," which is far from Anderson's nuanced account of the nation's boundaries as both open and closed, depending on whether linguistic, legal, cultural, or biological definitions of nationality are used.

Bhabha continues that the deconstructive counter-narratives "disturb those ideological manoeuvres through which 'imagined communities' are given essentialist identities. For the political unity of the nation consists in a continual displacement of the anxiety of its irredeemably plural modern space" (1990b: 300). Anderson's materialist characterization of "imagined communities" (as historically constructed) is quietly replaced here by an account that alleges "essentialism" to be foundational to national identity-formation. Political unity is reduced to a psychological reaction, rather than a foundational and enabling social action, and is presumed to be antithetical to "pluralism." This account is both historically and conceptually contestable. In *The Necessary Nation* Gregory Jusdanis (2001) has, indeed, contested this construction of nationalism as a cultural narrative grounded upon authoritarian principles. A major problem, as Jusdanis points out, lies in the textualist premise itself; to construct nations primarily, or exclusively, as aesthetic structures is to impose the very "monologic" mentality for which nationalism is indicted.

Nationalism as a failed historical project

Another strand of postcolonial studies constructs the political, social, and economic problems of post-independent countries as a consequence of nationalism itself. For example, Spivak refers to "the problem that has been my major life experience: the failure of decolonization through the ignoring of the subaltern" (1995b: 146). That many postcolonial countries have not succeeded in ending the socio-economic inequities and political unfreedom created by colonialism is undeniable. Spivak, however, casts this as a categorical feature of all nationalist decolonization. Her choice of the verb "ignore" is striking: it inflates the subjective sphere and *itself* ignores all the material forces that affect or determine the operations of society. It excludes from acknowledgment the role played by extrinsic factors such as international capitalism in the "failure" of decolonizing countries to achieve their liberatory goals. Instead, postcolonial countries are doubly condemned through a contradictory formula that assumes them both to be preprogramed for, and to voluntarily exercise, subaltern neglect. Casual determinism informs, too, the editors' introduction to *Nationalisms and Sexualities*, which alleges as a foregone conclusion that the needs of women will be sacrificed both during nationalist struggle and after independence, when "women have been reconsigned to their formerly 'domestic' roles" (Parker *et al.* 1992: 7).

M. Jacqui Alexander (2000) provides a more expansive framework for the analysis of post-independent states that have introduced repressive sexual legislation. Focusing on Trinidad and Tobago, and the Bahamas, she argues that capitalist globalization has helped to create a crisis of political authority for these independent states, and has destabilized the "ideological moorings of nationalism." In such a context, state criminalization of same-sex sexualities (in the name of "nationalism") becomes a means to reconstitute weakened political authority. At the same time that the state aggressively (hetero-)sexualizes the nation, it continues to *internationalize* the nation, further subjecting it to the very economic processes – structural adjustment programs, the expansion of tourism and other service industries, the reduction of agrarian production – that have compromised its own authority. The result is national immiseration. Women constitute the majority of the super-exploited workforce within the official and unofficial (sex trade) service industries.

Alexander's approach does not exonerate state nationalism from responsibility for the situation. Rather than blanket condemnation, however, she creates a class- and gender-specific critique, charting the region's historical development of a bourgeois class of nationalist politicians whose masculinity has been defined, policed, and problematized by colonial regimes. This class's preoccupation with the spheres of sexuality and gender identity is thus, she reveals, historically overdetermined. Her analysis conceptually connects the national with the global, the ideological with the political-economic, the historical with the contemporary. It is also meticulous in examining the particular configurations of two Caribbean states, eschewing generalities about "nationalism" to focus on *state* nationalism of Trinidad/Tobago and the Bahamas. Through this example Alexander highlights the complexities of determination and agency that operate to create neocolonial injustice.

Such work as Alexander's, that extends Fanon's analysis of neocolonialism, is rare in postcolonial cultural studies. Instead hegemonic postcolonial discussion characterizes nationalism *per se* as a failed attempt at human liberation, and holds nationalism alone responsible for the horrors of contemporary globalization. Postcolonial studies would be wise to follow Fanon's and Alexander's lead and examine the global structural forces, historical and contemporary, that seek to block the realization of liberatory, socialist nationalism. They would also do well to follow Fanon and Alexander in looking more closely at the ways in which particular state agents (ab)use nationalist rhetoric to serve particular political and economic ends. Instead of abandoning the nation and its discourses to those who dominate and exploit them, postcolonial critics might provide alternative national visions of collective identity, culture, and power.

At the same time it is important to acknowledge the important gains made by nationalist struggles, past and present. The fundamental political value of citizenship and of state self-determination is unarguable. So is the infrastructural development, and the fundamental improvements in health and literacy struggled for and won, however partially, by nationalist movements. Amilcar Cabral, addressing the United Nations while Guinea-Bissau and Cape Verde, led by the PAIGC, were still struggling against Portuguese colonialism, observed:

> What fills us with pride is our ever-increasing national consciousness, our unity . . . which has been forged in war . . . We take pride in the fact that thousands of adults have been taught to read and write, that the rural inhabitants are receiving medicines that were never available to them before . . . This is the greatest victory of the people of Guinea and Cape Verde over the Portuguese

colonialists, for it is a victory over ignorance, fear and disease – evils imposed on the African inhabitants for more than a century by Portuguese colonialism.

(1973: 25)

Nkrumah, in a speech delivered in February 1957, also signaled the material goals and priorities of a Ghana on the threshold of liberation:

Development of water and electricity services, construction of more feeder roads, provision of more mail and telephone facilities and more and more houses for the people are some of our next objectives . . . The emphasis of the struggle has now shifted from the anti-imperialist phase to the internal one of the struggle against the enemies of social progress; that is, against poverty, hunger, illiteracy, disease, ignorance, squalor and low productivity.

(1973: 91–92)

Such statements might provide postcolonial studies with a reality check – and with constructive critical ammunition also. For in cases where decolonizing nations have not adequately delivered on their own founding promises, these nationalist promises themselves supply a basis for renewed social mobilization. National governments can be held accountable, through this very same liberatory nationalism, to their own populations. (See, for example, the critical discussions of the African National Congress's performance in power in post-apartheid South Africa in Marais 1998; Saul 2001; Desai 2002.) Through the unit of the nation-state, claims for legislative, political-economic transformation can effectively be made, and social justice measures implemented.

Another alleged failure of nationalism is the narrowness of its liberatory horizons: to prioritize the category of the nation is, necessarily, to neglect the international dimensions of human liberation. Such a view cannot be sustained by a postcolonial studies that actually engages with anticolonial nationalism. Edward Said suggests that nationalism and global humanism have been crucially inter-linked projects for a number of liberation movements: "There is . . . a consistent intellectual trend within the nationalist consensus that is vitally critical, that refuses the short-term blandishments of separatist and triumphalist slogans in favour of the larger, more generous human realities of community *among* cultures, peoples, and societies. This community is the real human liberation portended by the resistance to imperialism" (1993: 217). This is borne out by the most cursory glance at a range of nationalist writings. For Césaire, the struggle against colonialism is in itself a contribution to global emancipation: "by articulating our effort in the colonized peoples' effort for freedom, by fighting for the dignity of our peoples, for their truth, and their *recognition*, we are by definition fighting for the entire world, to free it from tyranny, hate, and fanaticism" (1970: 161).

For Fanon, nationalism generates, and is dialectically related to, internationalism: "It is at the heart of national consciousness that international consciousness lives and grows" (1968: 52). There is, then, no necessary antagonism between the values of nationalism and global liberation, between the politics of international solidarity and nationalist mobilization. These theorists insist that global struggles against imperialism need to work through, and alongside, nationalist expressions for self-determination. Theirs is at once a pragmatic and an intellectual argument.

This chapter has outlined a number of directions for future research on nationalism in postcolonial studies. Such research needs to pay more attention to a range of historic anticolonial theorists, activists, and struggles; it needs to develop a more rigorous conceptualization of nationalism, that differentiates between élite and popular, patriarchal and pro-feminist, anticolonial and European, civic and cultural, secular and ethnic nationalisms; it needs to engage with politics and economics as they generate or mediate nationalist ideology; it needs to broaden its theoretical foundations to include materialist alongside poststructuralist perspectives.

Any future research needs also to read existing "postnationalist" formulations against the grain (see Dubey 2002). One has to consider how far these critical practices uphold their own arguments. Does the critic who chastises nationalist intellectuals for assuming the right to represent subalterns also problematize her own representational claims? Does the critic who criticizes nationalism for essentialism himself essentialize, romanticize, or reify a model of national community? In the particular context in and for which the postcolonial critic writes, does the promotion of a politics of difference serve socially emancipatory or disabling ends?

11

DEEPIKA BAHRI

Feminism in/and postcolonialism

[T]here are no women in the third world.
Suleri, 1989: 20

Introduction

In her influential and controversial essay "Can the Subaltern Speak?" Gayatri Chakravorty Spivak recounts the tale of a mysterious suicide: "A young woman of sixteen or seventeen, Bhubaneswari Bhaduri, hanged herself in her father's modest apartment in North Calcutta in 1926. The suicide was a puzzle since, as Bhubaneswari was menstruating at the time, it was clearly not a case of illicit pregnancy" (1988b: 307). Because Bhubaneswari "had known that her death would be diagnosed as the outcome of illegitimate passion," we are told, "[s]he had . . . waited for the onset of menstruation" (307). Some years later, when Bhubaneswari's nieces are asked about the suicide, they say that "it was a case of illicit love" (308).

Spivak confesses in *A Critique of Postcolonial Reason* that contemplation of "this failure of communication" had "so unnerved" her that, in her initial discussions of Bhaduri's suicide she had been led to write, "in the accents of passionate lament: the subaltern cannot speak!" (1999: 308; see also 1988b, 1985b). The lament arose from her realization that the subaltern in general, and the "historically muted subject of the subaltern woman" in particular, was inevitably consigned to being either misunderstood or misrepresented through the self-interest of those with the power to represent (1988b: 295). Spivak's various meditations on the female subaltern have spawned a series of critiques and responses that raise certain central questions in any discussion of feminism in/and postcolonialism: "Who can speak and for whom?" "Who listens?" "How does one represent the self and others?" Such questions point to heated issues concerning representation and essentialism; the relationship between the First-World intellectual and the Third-World object of scrutiny; the embattled and conflicted position of the Third-World intellectual within the West ("questions of positionality and location," as Lata Mani calls them [1990: 25]); and the possibility of a coherent, cohesive feminist movement.

The topic of feminism in/and postcolonialism is integrally tied to the
project of literary postcoloniality and its concerns with the critical reading
and interpretation of colonial and postcolonial texts. A postcolonial feminist perspective requires that one learn to read literary representations of
women with attention both to the subject and to the medium of representation. It also requires a general critical literacy, that is, the capacity to read
the *world* (specifically, in this context, gender relations) with a critical eye.
Thus Bhaduri's suicide, described by Spivak through the trope of "speaking," functions as a letter from the past which may be read and interpreted
variously by different "readers" with multiple motivations in different locations and in various times. The etymological links between "literary" and
"literacy," stemming from the Latin *littera* for "letter," reinforce the idea
that communication comprises not only the act of "speaking" but also that
of reception, listening, and interpretation. It could be argued, in fact, that
nearly all the issues central to postcolonial feminism are concerned with the
various ways of reading gender: in the world, the word, and the text.

As one might expect, feminist criticism emphasizes the significance of gender issues in history, politics, and culture. Inherently interdisciplinary, feminism examines the relationships between men and women and the consequences of power differentials for the economic, social, and cultural status
of women (and men) in different locations and periods of history. Feminist perspectives have been central to postcolonial studies from its inaugural
moment, sharing many of the broad concerns of postcolonialism, but also
revising, interrogating, and supplementing them. As Edward W. Said's mag-
isterial study *Orientalism* details, the characterization of the oriental in fem-
inized terms – and by extension that of all native, colonized peoples in mainstream colonial discourses – marks the prominence and constitutive quality
of gender in the colonial project. Hence colonial fears of native rebellion, as
Jenny Sharpe has argued in *Allegories of Empire*, find expression in the figure of the violated European woman. Interracial rape, Sharpe contends, must
thus be "understood as a highly charged trope that is implicated in the management of rebellion" (1993: 2). No less significant is the way in which the
status of native women was used to justify the colonial project as a civilizing
mission. Spivak has famously described British intervention in the Sati practice in India as "white men saving brown women from brown men" (1988b:
297). Partha Chatterjee explains that the colonizers were thus able to "transform this figure of the Indian woman into a sign of the inherently oppressive
and unfree nature of the entire cultural tradition of a country" (1995: 118);
and Mrinalini Sinha adds in this context that colonial women were complicit
with the colonizing mission inasmuch as Indian women "provided an opportunity for British women to exert their influence in India through . . . maternal

imperialism" (1995: 60; see also Jayawardena 1995). Not surprisingly, many anticolonial struggles for nationalism in turn used the figure of woman to symbolize the nation, and exerted themselves to articulate a significant role for women in the nation-building and decolonization processes. Sinha notes that in India "the Anglo-Indian strategy of using women's subordination in India as a handy stick with which to beat back Indian demands for political equality had converted the 'woman-question' into a battleground over the political rights of Indians" (1995: 45). Anne McClintock observes that "[n]ationalism is . . . constituted from the very beginning as a gendered discourse and cannot be understood without a theory of gender power" (1995: 355), a view shared by other feminist critics, notably Elleke Boehmer (1992) and Naila Kabeer (1991). Numerous critics have elaborated the relationship between feminism and nationalism (McClintock, Mufti, and Shohat 1997; West 1997). In the postcolonial phase, the status of women continues to preoccupy many critics. Under contemporary circumstances of globalization and the almost complete sway of capitalism world-wide, the condition of women has become a more urgent issue than ever. Gender issues are thus inseparable from the project of postcolonial criticism.

Discord and concord

Feminist theory and postcolonial theory are occupied with similar questions of representation, voice, marginalization, and the relation between politics and literature. Given that both critical projections employ multidisciplinary perspectives, they are each attentive, at least in principle, to historical context and the geopolitical co-ordinates of the subject in question. While there is obvious harmony and overlap between the two projections, however, tension and divergence are no less in evidence. Feminist studies and postcolonial studies sometimes find themselves in a mutually investigative and interactive relation with each other, especially when either becomes too narrowly focused, i.e., when feminist perspectives are blind to issues pertaining to colonialism and the international division of labor and when postcolonial studies fails to include gender in its analysis. On the one hand, thus, feminists sometimes complain that analyses of colonial or postcolonial texts fail to consider gender issues adequately, bracketing them in favor of attention to supposedly more significant issues, such as empire building, decolonization, and liberation struggle (in the colonial context), and nation-building (in the postcolonial context). McClintock notes that "male nationalists frequently argue that colonialism or capitalism has been women's ruin, with patriarchy merely a nasty second cousin destined to wither away when the real villain expires" (1995: 386). "Nowhere," she ruefully observes, "has feminism in its own right been allowed to be more than the maidservant to nationalism" (see also Peterson 1984). bell hooks, too, complains that "for contemporary critics to condemn the imperialism of the white colonizer without critiquing patriarchy is a tactic that seeks to minimize the particular ways gender determines the specific forms oppression may take within a specific group" (1994: 203). On the other hand, postcolonialists are apt to be critical of mainstream (Western) feminism, focusing on its failure or inability to incorporate issues of race, or its propensity to stereotype or over-generalize the case of the "Third-World woman." Writing in 1984, hooks bemoaned the fact that "white women who dominate feminist discourse today rarely question whether or not their perspective on women's reality is true to the lived experiences of women as a collective group" (1984: 3). In postcolonial feminism, by contrast – that is, feminism congruent with broad postcolonial perspectives, simultaneously "postcolonial" and "feminist" in temper and commitment – emphasis tends to be placed on the *collusion of patriarchy and colonialism.*

There are thus tensions between feminism and postcolonialism, and between "Western" and "postcolonial" feminisms. (Within postcolonial feminist theory, there are even misgivings about relative racism and "colorism" *among* women of color.) The implications of these tensions are many. A feminist position *within* postcolonialism must confront the dilemma of seeming divisive while the projects of decolonization and nation-building are still under way. Outside postcolonial studies, within the broader framework of mainstream feminism, postcolonial perspectives that focus on race and ethnicity may be perceived as forces that fragment the global feminist alliance. Differences between postcolonial feminist theorists surface repeatedly as the category of "women of color" is fractured by the politics of location, strife between minority communities in the First World, women in diasporic communities, and women in the Third World. Critics working on gender and race are sometimes susceptible to internal and external criticism for insufficiently addressing class as a crucial factor in relations between people, whether the relationship is one between men and women, North and South, or within groups that have been bifurcated not by gender or race but by economic status. Postcolonial feminism touches on many of these issues, and is thus a dynamic discursive field. It interrogates the premises of postcolonialism as much as those of feminism, supplementing them with its own particular concerns and perspectives, while in turn being subject to criticism and revision by them. Internal critique within the field is no less in evidence, with consistent interrogation of tokenization and the usurpation of the subaltern perspective. Characterized by debate, dialogue, and diversity, postcolonial feminism consistently calls for sustained and instructive examination of its major premises, methods, and tensions.

Key concepts

Postcolonial feminism is often perceived as an academic construction inextricably allied with the rise of postcolonial literary studies in the Western academy. A survey of major thematic concerns and key concepts in the field of what we might call "postcolonial feminist studies" clearly indicates the relational identity of the field, suggesting that it exists as a discursive configuration in dialogue with dominant First-World academic constructions even when it is in tension with them. This dialogic and interactive relationship obliges us to ask questions about who speaks for (or in the voice of) postcolonial feminism? Who listens and why? What is the content of postcolonial feminist work? When and where does postcolonial feminist work take place? Finally, what are the likely future directions of feminist work within postcolonial literary studies? The relational identity of the field and its evolution in the context of globalization also oblige us to recast the broad question of critical literacy in terms of transnationality and transculturality. "Transnational literacy," as Spivak explains it, is "a sense of the political, economic, *and* cultural position of the various national origin places in the financialization of the globe" (1996: 295). It is not necessary, for instance, that immigrants to the United States consider their national origin simply in terms of their position as minorities; as Americans, they can try to influence American policies that adversely impact the fortunes of their countries of origin (295). Similarly, a study of the position of women in any given location may have global or international ramifications and determinations; one need no longer assume that the issues are neatly bounded by national boundaries. Although an understanding of women in globality is "an immense field of study," as Spivak notes elsewhere, a committed comparative global perspective can gradually help us understand how our multiple identities function in different situations (1995a: 12).

The major conceptual categories evoked by these questions are reflected in the discussion below. "Representation," "Third-World woman," "essentialism," and "identity" are key conceptual constructs for many of the debates and discussions arising from feminist perspectives within postcolonial literary studies. Discussion of these concepts in the work of various critics reveals the struggle in postcolonial feminist studies to establish identity as relational and historical rather than essential or fixed, even as it attempts to retain gender as a meaningful category of analysis. For instance, Alexander and Mohanty pithily note in their introduction to *Feminist Genealogies*,

Colonial Legacies, Democratic Futures: "We both moved to the United States of North America over fifteen years ago . . . We were not born women of color, but became women of color here" (1997: xiv). Debates about the ways in which identity is produced within particular contexts and the operation of power relations between various groups inform the discussion of several of the concepts described below.

Representation

"Representation" is a term with multiple and sometimes confusing connotations. Meaning presence as much as reproduction, likeness, the formation of an idea in the mind, or even proxy presence in the sense of a political "speaking for," the term is at the heart of many debates in postcolonial and/or feminist theory. The manifold resonances of the term "representation" are skilfully summarized and brought into focus by Ella Shohat in her essay, "The Struggle over Representation: Casting, Coalitions, and the Politics of Identification": "What all these instances share is the semiotic principle that something is 'standing for' something else, or that some person or group is speaking on behalf of some other persons or groups" (1995: 166). Understanding the various nuances of the term can help us better conceive of the uses to which it is put in the specific argumentative positions taken up by critics. Spivak suggests that there are two principal ways of representing: the first, *Vertreten*, is "to tread in someone's shoes . . . Your congressional person, if you are talking about the United States, actually puts on your shoes when he or she represents you" (1990: 108). *Vertretung* is thus closest in connotation to "political representation." The other mode of representation, Spivak suggests, is *Darstellung*. As she explains, "*Dar*, there, same cognate. *Stellen*, is to place, so 'placing there.'" Representing is thus done in two ways: by "proxy and portrait" (108). The relation between these two modes of representation, as we will see later, is the ground of much contestation in postcolonial debates.

Fields such as women's studies and postcolonial studies have arisen in part in response to the absence or unavailability of the perspectives of women, racial minorities, and marginalized cultures or communities in historical accounts or literary annals. This lack of representation is paralleled in the political, economic, and legal spheres. Those "other" to the dominant discourse have no voice or say in their portrayal; they are consigned to be "spoken for" by those who command the authority and means to speak. When minorities and others are represented, as Said argues in *Orientalism*, the representation may effectively exist instead of rather than in correspondence to any "real" thing. Thus, Said claims,

In any instance of at least written language, there is no such thing as a delivered presence, but a re-presence, or a representation. The value, efficacy, strength, apparent veracity of a written statement about the Orient therefore relies very little, and cannot instrumentally depend, on the Orient as such. On the contrary, the written statement is a presence to the reader by virtue of its having excluded, displaced, made supererogatory any such real thing as "the Orient." (1978: 21)

Said's work demonstrates that it is possible to generate a largely fictitious account, without meaningful reference or compatibility with anything real, to create the idea of a place and people in the minds of readers. Moreover, it has proven possible, historically, to formulate policies based on these representations, that impact the lives of real people in tremendously significant ways. A similar history characterizes the position of women within patriarchal systems. The celebrated Foucauldian nexus between knowledge and power becomes clear in the arenas of both colonial relations and gender relations.

Those with the power to represent and describe others clearly control how these others will be seen. The power of representation as an ideological tool has traditionally rendered it a contested terrain. The narrator of J. Nozipo Maraire's epistolary novel, *Zenzele*, reminds her daughter that "until the lions learn to write, tales of hunting will always glorify the hunter" (1996: 78–79; see also Busia 1989). Once feminist critics commenced their interventions, women's perspectives and stories began to find voice, even as some critics, such as Ketu Katrak (1989), began to ask if we had yet found an appropriate model for studying women's writing. The development of critical ways of *reading* is just as important as the use of writing to represent women. Reading Charlotte Brontë's *Jane Eyre*, Spivak makes the necessary point that speaking for women does not always entail speaking for the marginalized or silenced in general. Her well-known essay, "Three Women's Texts and a Critique of Imperialism," demonstrates that Brontë's project of installing a feminist ideal subject in the figure of Jane Eyre necessarily proceeds through a demonization of Bertha, Rochester's abject, insane, Creole bride who functions as dutiful other (Spivak 1985a). Even within the feminist project, then, there is no guarantee that the perspective of the Third-World woman will be represented or honored. There is even the danger that the mechanism of "othering" that characterizes colonial hegemonic discourse will become instrumental in the project of producing the individual and individualist feminist self *against* its other. To pose the question of the subject "while postponing a theory of gender," McClintock wryly notes, "presumes that subjectivity itself is neutral with respect to gender" (1995: 363). By the same token, one might ask whether it is possible to tackle the question of feminist subjectivity in the woman writer's colonial novel without broaching the question of race.

It is important that the questions of race and location be considered alongside the question of gender. Answering the question, "why do we have to be concerned with the question of Third World women? After all, it is only one issue among many others," Trinh T. Minh-ha replies as follows: "delete the phrase Third World and the sentence immediately unveils its value-loaded clichés" (1987: 17). If it is important that one be sensitive to sexism in literary and other representations, it is no less incumbent upon the critic to remain alert to racism.

Curricular and theoretical discussions in the Western academy hail writing by postcolonial women as a salutary counter to the problems noted above. The resulting expansion of the traditional canon allows readers to explore postcolonial issues through the specific contexts of Third-World women's lives. Collections such as *Interventions: Feminist Dialogues on Third World Women's Literature and Film* (B. Ghosh and Bose 1997) have exposed readers to literary and filmic representations of and by women. Said's incisive warning, however, calls the enterprise of representation, whether by others or by the self, into question. In the first place, a particular representation may be misread as representative of an entire culture. In her reading of Chinua Achebe's *Things Fall Apart*, for instance, Florence Stratton makes the following observation: "while women are excluded from the male domain of community power, men are permitted to intrude into the domestic domain. Moreover, if Okonkwo is representative, the intrusion is often violent" (1994: 27). Stratton's willingness to consider Okonkwo as representative of Igbo culture is not unusual for many readers of Third-World fiction. Moreover, aesthetic representations in literature can be reduced to informal sociology, as the literary context is elided by the political status of the text as a representation of Third-World women. In the above reading, Stratton goes on to generalize about gender power dynamics in Igbo culture by reading Okonkwo as representative, while also assuming that literary representations of a society need not be too carefully distinguished from sociological studies. Lastly, it is possible to take available representations – literary, political, or theoretical – as having met the need to represent the subaltern. Said's statement about representation and the real clearly indicates the inherent difficulties of representation. Many critics share the concern that representation can be fraught with the potential for misreading even when the motives are benevolent or supposedly in the self-interest of those finally able to represent themselves.

Spivak's explanation of the two forms of representation exposes quite clearly some of the problems of essentialism and usurpation mentioned above. To represent politically, Spivak argues, is inevitably also to "represent yourself and your constituency in the portrait sense" (1990: 108). Identity is thus not a predetermined quality but one that must be adopted. As Spivak puts it, the

> question of "speaking as" involves a distancing from oneself. The moment I have to think of the ways in which I will speak as an Indian, or as a feminist, the ways in which I will speak as a woman, what I am doing is trying to generalize myself, making myself a representative, trying to distance myself from some kind of inchoate speaking as such. There are many subject positions which one must inhabit; one is not just one thing. (60)

Spivak and many other postcolonial and feminist critics alert us to the ways in which a subject position is constructed within discourse, rather than pre-existing the discourse. Hence her cautionary reminder that "[i]t is not a solution, the idea of the disenfranchised speaking for themselves, or the radical critics speaking for them; this question of representation, self-representation, representing others, is a problem" (63). Spivak advocates "persistent critique" to guard against "constructing the Other simply as an object of knowledge, leaving out the real Others because of the ones who are getting access into public places due to these waves of benevolence and so on" (63).

Representation is always fictional or partial because it must imaginatively construct its constituency (as a portrait or a "fiction") and because it can inadvertently usurp the space of those who are incapable of representing themselves. The problems outlined above have led to considerable dissatisfaction on at least two fronts. Both point to the complexities of the First-World/Third-World relationship: one is the monolithic construction of non-Western women and the other is the usurpation of the space of representation by Third-World women in the West (Narayan 1997). Before we turn to these, however, a brief introduction to the idea of essentialism will thicken our understanding of the complexities involved.

Essentialism

An explicit indictment of the practice of essentialism seems evident in Pnina Werbner's description of it below: "to essentialize is to impute a fundamental, basic, absolutely necessary constitutive quality to a person, social category, ethnic group, religious community, or nation. It is to posit falsely a timeless continuity, a discreteness or boundedness in space, and an organic unity. It is to imply an internal sameness and external difference or otherness" (1997: 228). Werbner goes on, however, to add that:

[a]ttempts to avoid essentializing the social collectivities we study lead . . .
to a series of conundrums. If to name is to re-present, to imply a continuity
and discreteness in time and place, then it follows that all collective namings
or labellings are essentialist, and that all discursive constructions of social
collectivities – whether of community, class, nation, race or gender – are essentializing.   (228–29)

The study of any identity-based collectivity must contend with the problem
of essentialism, first as it has operated or continues to operate in the portrayal of that collectivity by others and subsequently as it is used to describe,
distinguish, and assist the collectivity in question.

Given the stress on identity and culture in both postcolonial and feminist studies, it is not surprising that discussions on essentialism loom large
within them. Colonial practices of Orientalism or exoticism rely on a variety of essentialisms that can persist in the postcolonial or neocolonial phase
through collectivist groupings that ghettoize and separate. Protesting the category of "commonwealth literature," for instance, Salman Rushdie describes
essentialism as "the respectable child of old-fashioned exoticism. It demands
that sources, forms, style, language and symbol all derive from a supposedly
homogeneous and unbroken tradition. Or else" (1995: 67). The essential-
ized concept is marked by expectations of formulaic fixity and invariability.
The reduction of differences in such grouping is irksome to many a writer
unwilling to be read and understood solely through the exclusive and confining lens implied by essentialist terminology. Spivak notes that tokenization
which allows individuals space to speak because they are thought to represent
a certain essential category "goes with ghettoization," such that "when you
are perceived as a token, you are also silenced in a certain way" (1990: 61).

As Diana Fuss elaborates, essentialism

is most commonly understood as a belief in the real, true essence of things,
the invariable and fixed properties which define the "whatness" of a given
entity . . . Importantly, essentialism is typically defined in opposition to difference . . . The opposition is a helpful one in that it reminds us that a complex
system of cultural, social, psychical, and historical differences, and not a set
of pre-existent human essences, position and constitute the subject. However,
the binary articulation of essentialism and difference can also be restrictive,
even obfuscating, in that it allows us to ignore or deny the differences within
essentialism.   (1990: xi–xii)

Fuss's nuanced treatment of essentialism as itself marked by difference allows
us to understand that difference and essentialism may operate as two sides
of the same coin. The strategy of essentialism can be used to stereotype and

characterize individuals or groups with any of a number of motivations and consequences. Essentialist stereotypes can be and have been used to demean and disenfranchise, to create racial hierarchies, and to exploit. In her study of European travel and exploration writing, for instance, Mary Louise Pratt points out the comparative and hierarchical categorization of the varieties of *Homo sapiens* in early natural history; essentialist descriptions of the Asiatic type as "sooty, melancholy, rigid . . . governed by opinions" and of the African as "black, phlegmatic, relaxed . . . governed by caprice," stand against the supposedly scientific description of the European as "gentle, acute, inventive . . . governed by laws" to "naturalise the myth of European superiority" (1992: 33). At the same time, essentialist typology is also used to justify agendas of development and uplift, or indeed to redress historical wrongs done to individuals and groups. It may be useful to remember that essentialism of one sort or another may be unavoidable. In fact, identitarian grouping of any sort demands acceptance of essentialist typology, even as the group itself may be struggling against it.

It is possible to avoid the pitfalls of biological determinism or formulaic fixity while continuing to use essentialism in a self-conscious and meditated fashion. Spivak describes the tactical and deliberate use of essentialist typology as "strategic essentialism": "a strategic use of positivist essentialism in a scrupulously visible political interest" (1996: 214). Although it is undesirable to accept any positivist or deterministic notion of identity, Spivak nevertheless allows for its contingent use in a specific and well-defined context for the work being undertaken. During a struggle with targeted and specific goals, it is thus justified to posit a group identity with common features in order to advance its interests while continuing to debate and contest the hegemony of essential identity. In this context, Lisa Lowe positively identifies the work of the Subaltern Studies group which "suggests that it is possible to posit specific signifiers such as Indianness, for the purpose of disrupting discourses that exclude Indians as Other while simultaneously revealing the internal contradictions and slippages of 'Indianness' so as to ensure that the signifier *Indianness* will not be reappropriated by the very efforts to criticize its use" (1991: 198). The formation of fields such as African American studies and Women's Studies might be considered examples of strategic essentialism to counter erasure or oversight in the mainstream academy.

Postcolonial feminist critics nevertheless protest when the use of essentialist strategies by identity-based groups begins to succumb to naturalization of essential categories or when they are used to describe a group as an undifferentiated totality. Some years ago, Julia Kristeva's book, *About Chinese Women*, generated a great deal of controversy and debate because some

critics found its essentialist characterization of Chinese women problematic.
In her study of Kristeva's writings, Kelly Oliver described *About Chinese
Women* as a "most questionable and often offensive text" (1993: 7). Spivak
chides the author for "the most stupendous generalizations about Chinese
writing" and her text's tendency to "authorize . . . the definition of the essentially feminine and essentially masculine as non-logical and logical" (1988d:
138). Rey Chow contends that for Kristeva,

> China exists as an "other," feminized space to the West, a space where
> utopianism and eroticism come into play for various purposes of "critique."
> Kristeva's book about Chinese women shows us how the alluring tactic of
> "feminizing" another culture in the attempt to criticize Western discourse actu-
> ally repeats the mechanisms of the discourse and hence cannot be an alternative
> to it.   (1991: 32)

Elsewhere Chow notes Kristeva's move "to revere them [the natives] as silent
objects" and likens it to other European engagements with the East as subject
that make "this other an utterly incomprehensible, terrifying, and fascinating
spectacle" (1993: 33). In a nuanced reading that acknowledges Kristeva's use
of Orientalist essentialisms, Lisa Lowe nevertheless insists that "[t]he principal manner in which Kristeva's 'China' differs from the orientalist texts
of the eighteenth and nineteenth centuries is that its various deployments of
orientalist tropes are meant to represent breaks with colonialist ideology"
(1993: 150). The debates about Kristeva's depiction of Chinese women suggest the difficulties of speaking about any group as a whole, even if it is to
identify the group's inscrutability. Speaking across difference is a challenge
to which all critics, no matter where they are located, must remain sensitive
(John 1996).

Concerns about the depiction of people as members of groups intensify
within the context of cultural diversity within the First-World academy. Rey
Chow concedes that the desire to accommodate difference is laudable, but
she also warns that this desire can take the form of mass-producing images
of otherness, thus reducing the complexity of the other. The category of
"Third-World woman" is one such depiction of the other that sometimes
belies its status as constructed by the desire for otherness rather than being
naturally available (1993: 69).

In response to the reductive construction of the category of "Third-World
woman" – discussed in detail below – Sara Suleri famously issues the following pronouncement in her fictional autobiography, *Meatless Days*: "[T]here
are no women in the third world" (1989: 20). Categories of gender and race
derive partially from biology and rather more from culture and social constructions. Suleri refuses the naturalization of these categories in hegemonic

discourses as she scrupulously exposes the categories of "woman" and "Third-World woman" as constructed by discourse. Such categories may well be identified with certain stereotypical attributes that may prematurely curtail further methodical exploration. Suleri refers to this process dismissively when she says that "contemporary critical theory names the other in order that it need not be further known" (1992a: 13). Since critical theory is concerned with examining the premises, concepts, and categories used in various disciplines, it is a matter of some concern for Suleri that it should not produce formulaic sorts of otherness. Irked by the unwritten requirement that she function as an "otherness machine," in *Meatless Days* she carefully shows how the categories of "woman" and "Third-World woman" are constructed as one might a text or a story. In doing so, Suleri is unravelling a prior text that might be said to characterize Third-World women in stereotypical ways. Even as she acknowledges the biological identity of women as "a hugely practical joke . . . hidden somewhere among our clothes," she nevertheless insists that women live in language as much as with other people (1989: 1). There is thus no authentic Third-World womanly self that lies (let the pun be noted) awaiting discovery, just that which inhabits the language games, plots, and discursive regimes of the social world.

Third-World woman

The slippage between "postcolonial" and "Third-World" is so common as to be scarcely remarked. In at least some of its usages, the "postcolonial is simply a polite way of saying not-white, not-Europe, or perhaps not-Europe-but-inside-Europe" as Aijaz Ahmad bluntly puts it (1995b: 30). Even though one assumes that the term "postcolonial" will refer to societies and states that were once colonized, its use for such countries as Ireland or Australia is always seen as a debatable rather than an evident choice in postcolonial studies. Instead the term is more readily used for societies and states identified as of the "Third-World." The implications of this unacknowledged slippage are too numerous and wide-ranging to be discussed here, except to note that the term "postcolonial feminism" is often used interchangeably with "Third-World feminism." This overlap is significant in that it signals the particular relationship of both formulations, "postcolonial" and "Third World," to the "*First* World." Invested with suggestions of "lack," "underdevelopment," and "difference," the Third World, by virtue of nomenclature if nothing else, stands in a clearly hierarchical relationship to the West. Kumkum Sangari argues that the term "Third World" not only designates specific geographical areas, but imaginary spaces. According to Sangari, it is "a term that both signifies and blurs the functioning of an economic, political, and imaginary geography able to unite vast and vastly differentiated areas of the world into a single 'underdeveloped' terrain" (1990: 217). Ahmad's and Sangari's formulations may imply the dubiousness (or even nullity) of the term, but the objections of these and other critics have not prevented its use in academic discussions. The category is not useless for many critics, who nevertheless insist that it must be used very carefully.

"What happens," asks Chandra Talpade Mohanty, "when an assumption of women as an oppressed group is situated in the context of Western feminist writing about *Third World* Women?" (1991: 71; my emphasis). The answer is a chilling indictment: "Western feminists alone become the true 'subjects' of this counter-history. Third world women, on the other hand, never rise above the debilitating generality of their 'object' status" (71). The article from which this citation is drawn, "Under Western Eyes: Feminist Scholarship and Colonial Discourses," first published in 1982, is frequently acknowledged as a significant postcolonial challenge to mainstream Western feminism. Mohanty's piece has also been credited with challenging traditional understandings of the Third World as confined to predictable geographical areas such as formerly colonized nations. She points to structures that place women in an exploitative relationship to the state and the economic system in the First World as well. In her formulation, the term "the Third World" should be extended to include oppressed or exploited women within what we think of monolithically as the First World (see also Johnson-Odim 1991). The bulk of Mohanty's piece identifies key features in particular Western feminist anthropological texts that attempt to explain the lives of Third-World women. Mohanty charges that Western feminists typically "homogenize and systematize" Third-World women, creating a composite, singular picture. The problem lies not in the use of geography-based terminology but in the collapsing of difference on the basis of this terminology. There is nothing wrong, obviously, with describing women from the continent of Africa as "African women" or "women of Africa." However, "[i]t is when 'women of Africa' becomes a homogeneous sociological grouping characterized by common dependencies or powerlessness (or even strengths) that problems arise – we say too little and too much at the same time" (1991: 59). Drawn in broad strokes within a global framework, "Third-World women" are typically seen as an undifferentiated group uncomplicated by the heterogeneity that characterizes their conceptual counterpart ("First-World women") in the more developed world. Oppression is then seen as a "Third-World" preserve, and "Third-World women" reduced to objects of consumption for a developed world which can implicitly and complacently reaffirm its superiority to the rest as the "norm or referent" (56).

Likening the discursive moves in such analyses to the project of colonial-ism, Mohanty argues that "it is in the production of this 'third world dif-ference' that Western feminisms appropriate and 'colonize' the fundamental complexities and conflicts which characterize the lives of women of different classes, religions, cultures, races and castes in these countries" (1991: 54). She argues that the representation of the "third world woman as a singu-lar monolithic subject" within Western feminist theory enacts a "discursive colonization" (51):

> in the context of the hegemony of the Western scholarly establishment in the production and dissemination of texts, and the context of the legitimating imperative of humanistic and scientific discourse, the definition of the "third world woman" as a monolith might well tie into the larger cultural and eco-nomic praxis of "disinterested" scientific inquiry and pluralism which are the surface manifestations of a latent economic and cultural colonization of the "non-Western" world. (74)

If Western feminism reproduces imperialism in the act of reading colonial and postcolonial texts, research into the status of Third-World women can some-times also reproduce imperialist assumptions as to their inferiority, through the production of "the image of 'the average third world woman,'" who leads "an essentially truncated life based on her feminine gender (read: sexually constrained) and her being 'third world' (read: ignorant, poor, uneducated, tradition-bound, domestic, family-oriented, victimized, etc.)" (56). Implicit in these representations of Third-World women as an aggregate category is the "self-representation of Western women as educated, as modern, as hav-ing control over their bodies and sexualities, and the freedom to make their own decisions" (56).

Insisting on the heterogeneity of the lives of "Third-World" women, Mohanty pleads for an inter-relational analysis that does not limit the defini-tion of the female subject to gender and does not bypass the social, class, and ethnic co-ordinates of those analyzed. Mohanty is not alone in agitating for a more nuanced understanding of the status of "Third-World" – indeed, of *all* – women. The Egyptian writer, Nawal El Saadawi, had earlier argued that "the oppression of women, the exploitation and social pressures to which they are exposed, are not characteristic of Arab or Middle Eastern societies, or countries of the 'Third World' alone" (1980: i). Instead, a universalist the-ory of women's oppression should note that such oppressions "constitute an integral part of the political, economic and cultural system, preponderant in most of the world – whether that system is backward and feudal in nature, or a modern industrial society that has been submitted to the far reach-ing influence of a scientific and technological revolution" (i). Saadawi links women's oppression to the global capitalist system and warns that under expanding capitalism and ensuing globalization, "working women not only grow in numbers but they face a whole range of new problems resulting from the social changes to which they are exposed. They are deprived of the support, assistance and numerous functions that were previously afforded by the extended family system" (xii).

Saadawi is responding not merely to the characterization of "Third-World" women as a monolithic group of victims, but also to the particular fetishization of Arab Muslim women for whom the veil serves as a supersaturated symbol of oppression. Declaring that she is "against female circumcision and other similar retrograde and cruel practices," Saadawi nevertheless opposes "all attempts to deal with such problems in isolation, or to sever their links with the general economic and social pressures to which women everywhere are exposed" (1980: xiv). She concludes that "it is Arab women alone who can formulate the theory, the ideas and the modes of struggle needed to liberate themselves from all oppression" (xvi). In this context it may be necessary to pay attention to the ways in which other "Third-World" women resist oppression; Haleh Ashfar's edited volume, *Women and Politics in the Third World* (1996) explores the variety of strategies of resistance used by women in Latin America, Southeast Asia, China, and the Middle East (see also Basu 1995; Jayawardena 1986; Wilford and Miller 1998).

Third-World woman in the West

In *The Rhetoric of English India*, Sara Suleri rejects the anxious "collusion between postcolonial and feminist theories, in which each term serves to reify the potential pietism of the other" (1992a: 274). The production of an idealized marginal subjectivity has occasioned a good deal of critical comment in postcolonial feminist work. In her essay, "The Fascist Longings in our Midst," Rey Chow even compares "the new 'desire for our others'" which emerges in postcoloniality with the "positive, projectional symptoms of fascism" that also grew from "a longing for a transparent, idealized image and identifying submission to such an image" (1995: 44–45). In her editorial introduction to a special edition of the journal *Discourse*, Trinh T. Minh-ha makes a wry reference to difference as a special Third-World women issue in the title of her essay, thereby drawing attention to the exoticism of otherness and the "Third-World woman's" participation in the production of this otherness. Amplifying Suleri's and Chow's reservations, she observes that

[n]o uprooted person is invited to participate in this "special" Third World wo/man's issue unless s/he MAKES UP her/his mind and paints her/himself thick with authenticity. Eager not to disappoint, I try my best to offer my benefactors and benefactresses what they most anxiously yearn for: the possibility of a difference, yet, a difference or an otherness that will not go so far as to question the foundation of their beings and makings.   (1987: 22)

In "Woman Skin Deep: Feminism and the Postcolonial Condition," Suleri criticizes the moves made by "Third-World" feminist scholars in the Western academy in response to a climate of receptiveness to representations of "marginal" subjectivity. By a strange twist, the very tendencies that are decried in the monolithic definition of "Third-World woman" in terms of powerlessness become the engines for the production of an iconic and politically untouchable position of Third-World womanhood. This position then provides a space from which Third-World feminist critics can speak, ironically with the very privilege whose lack is thought to characterize the status of Third-World women. Some critics in the West take on the persona of "Third-World women" to disarm criticism, since to criticize somebody from the "Third World" might seem to breach the etiquette of political correctness. "The coupling of postcolonial with woman," Suleri reiterates, "almost inevitably leads to the simplicities that underlie unthinking celebration of oppression, elevating the racially female voice into a metaphor for 'the good'" (1992b: 758–59). Criticizing the work of Mohanty and Trinh as well as that of bell hooks, Suleri argues that

rather than extending an inquiry into the discursive possibilities represented by the intersection of gender and race, feminist intellectuals like hooks misuse their status as minority voices by enacting strategies of belligerence that at this time are more divisive than informative. Such claims to radical revisionism take refuge in the political untouchability that is accorded the category of Third world Woman, and in the process sully the crucial knowledge that such a category has still to offer to the dialogue of feminism today.   (765)

Identifying two feminist moves – the claim to authenticity on the basis of national or racial origin, and the recourse to narratives or stories – Suleri takes well-known postcolonial and minority feminist critics writing in the West to task. Of Mohanty she says that her "[C]laim to authenticity – only a black can speak for a black; only a postcolonial subcontinental feminist can adequately represent the lived experience of that culture – points to the great difficulty posited by the 'authenticity' of female racial voices in the great game which claims to be the first narrative of what the ethnically constructed woman is deemed to want" (760). Suleri condemns the specious and untenably "literal ethic that underlies such a dichotomy [Western feminist Third-World women]" (760).

Similarly, Suleri attacks hooks and Trinh for claiming that "personal narrative is the only salve to the rude abrasions that Western feminist theory has inflicted on the body of ethnicity" (1992b: 764). The manipulative appropriation of the concept of "lived experience" to justify the use of personal narrative, she objects, is mystifying at best, and dangerous at its worst in its propensity to take subjective experience and to attempt to turn it into some sort of objective truth: "Realism . . . is too dangerous a term for an idiom that seeks to raise identity to the power of theory" (762). If anything, Suleri protests, "lived experience," through such uses, "serves as fodder for the continuation of another's epistemology, even when it is recorded in a 'contestatory' position in its relation to realism and to the overarching structure of the profession" (765).

If lived experience and realism are to be the relevant categories for a feminist critique, Suleri suggests, it is necessary to examine how "realism locates its language within the postcolonial condition." She insists that "lived experience does not achieve its articulation through autobiography, but through that other third-person narrative known as the law" (1992b: 766). In the institutional context, Suleri's work is extremely significant in that she is willing to retain the category of "Third-World woman", but is scrupulously clear that it must be activated through a materially located feminist theory. To instantiate the arena of such work, she offers "life in Pakistan as an example of such a postcolonial and lived experience" (766). Pakistani laws, she argues, "pertain more to the discourse of a petrifying realism than do any of the feminist critics whom I have cited thus far" (766). Analysis of the discourses of the law and the state can provide the text for examining the lived experience of those whose bodies are directly implicated by them. Citing Zina (fornication) laws in Pakistan as an example, Suleri goes on to give the example of "a fifteen-year-old woman, Jehan Mina, who, after her father's death, was raped by her aunt's husband and son" and was then "convicted for fornication and sentenced to one hundred public lashes" on her own testimony (768).

Rather than confine such examination to the "local" and provincial preserve of the "Third World," Suleri, in fact, relocates the issue multiculturally. She explains the connection thus:

I cite these alternative realisms and constructions of identity in order to reiterate the problem endemic to postcolonial feminist criticism. It is not the terrors of Islam that have unleashed the Hudood Ordinances on Pakistan, but more probably the U.S. government's economic and ideological support of a military regime during that bloody but eminently forgotten decade marked by the "liberation" of Afghanistan.   (1992b: 768)

She then asks us to consider the following question: "in what ways does her [Jehan Mina's] testimony force postcolonial and feminist discourse into an acknowledgement of the inherent parochialism and professionalism of our claims?" (768). Any effort by "Third-World" feminist critics to examine the question of what it means to be multicultural in the West must confront not only their own position in the West as minorities but also the experience of "Third-World women" within a carefully examined socio-historical context. In the absence of this ability to cede the role of "Third-World woman", Suleri fears that postcolonial feminism in the West – reliant on duality and the politics of authenticity – risks being narrowly absorbed with the experiences of postcolonial feminists in the West.

In implicit rejoinder to Suleri's critique, Mohanty has insisted in her recent work that the category of "Third-World woman," even if it is reliant on a dualistic politics, retains an heuristic value, particularly under globalization. In "Women Workers and Capitalist Scripts," Mohanty draws attention to the ways in which "issues of spatial economy – the manner by which capital utilizes particular spaces for differential production and the accumulation of capital and, in the process, transforms these spaces (and peoples) – gain fundamental importance for feminist analysis" (1997: 5). "Third-World" women workers, defined by Mohanty "as both women from the geographical Third World and immigrant and indigenous women of color in the U.S. and Western Europe," are seen to "occupy a specific social location in the international division of labor which illuminates and explains crucial features of the capitalist processes of exploitation and domination" (7). Mohanty's implicit denunciation of an unequal power dynamics which favors the First World is amply in evidence in her writings on women in globalization.

In recent years there has been a shift of focus away from cultural issues to the status of women in an international arena defined by globalization. Decrying the "First-World" preoccupation with questions of tokenism, identity politics, and the politics of location, Rajeswari Sunder Rajan and You-me Park extol those "feminist scholars, in both the First World and the Third, [who] are producing a more dialectical and praxis-oriented understanding of postcolonial feminism that links labor sites in the First and Third worlds and emphasizes the international division of labor as a major concern" (2000: 57). Sunder Rajan and Park remind us that "many transnational feminists identify the international division of labor – rather than cultural conflicts

or transactions – as the most important defining feature of postcoloniality" (58). The growing importance of the global as the context for feminist
scholarship has given new vitality and often new shape to debates about
representation, location, and the category of "Third-World woman."

Globalization

The above discussion leads us to the issue of international and comparative work in the area of feminist studies even as it requires us to review
the importance of the politics of location. The emergence of these issues is
only to be expected in a period marked by the massive movement of people
across global boundaries, by the development of an international market
of goods and ideas, and by the growing power of publishing houses with
a global reach. The title of an article by Lata Mani, "Multiple Mediations:
Feminist Scholarship in the Age of Multinational Reception," captures in its
phraseology the challenges and opportunities for feminist scholarship at this
unprecedented juncture. The asymmetries of power, registered in differential funding opportunities, institutional links, and barriers, uneven access to
publishing and circulation of information – all the "multiple mediations" –
bear directly on the production and reception of knowledge in different parts
of the world (Mani 1990; see also Amireh and Majaj 2000).

Each location carries its own history and its markings in the present. In the
context of her work on Sati, for instance, Mani explains that in Britain and
the US, where elements of nineteenth-century colonial discourse still circulate
"in service of British racism and US cultural imperialism," the recuperation
"of the colonial prehistory of such ideas" might be considered a political
gesture. Conversely, however, unlike "many nations in the Caribbean or in
Central America, in India it is not the boot of imperialism that is felt as
an identifiable weight upon one's neck," but rather the pressure "of the
nation state, dominant social and political institutions, and religious 'fundamentalisms' of various kinds" (1990: 29). In the Indian context, in these
terms, a politically engaged criticism must direct itself to "the limited parameters within which nationalists posed the question of women's status, the
marginality of women to nineteenth-century discussions supposedly about
them, and the legacy of colonialism in contemporary discussion of women's
issues" (29–30). The concept of "significant scholarship" is thus dependent
on the context in which it will be received and used as it articulates with
local concerns.

Mani's discussion of the salience of location in the production and reception of knowledge harks back to some of the issues raised above: the presence of "Third-World" postcolonial feminist scholars in the West and their

responsibility to represent the various constituencies with which they are associated, while remaining alert to the provisionality and social construction of their own identities in the precise contexts of their scholarly practice. It is also necessary to look at the degree to which a metropolitan location (and outlook) frame research agendas everywhere, not least because the number of sources of funding and outlets for publishing are greater in the West.

Inderpal Grewal and Caren Kaplan have been working collaboratively to develop the concept of "transnational feminist practices" in response to the challenges and opportunities occasioned by globalization or what David Harvey has referred to as "time–space compression" (Grewal and Kaplan 1994; Harvey 1989). For Grewal and Kaplan (2000), "the relationship between postcolonial and transnational studies is one of a specific feminist trajectory that has always focused on the inequalities generated by capitalist patriarchies in various eras of globalization." The structure of a transnational feminist responsibility is indicated in Caren Kaplan's remarks below:

> Examining the politics of location in the production and reception of theory can turn the terms of inquiry from desiring, inviting, and granting space to others to becoming accountable for one's own investments in cultural metaphors and values. Such accountability can begin to shift the ground of feminist practice from magisterial relativism (as if diversified cultural production simply occurs in a social vacuum) to the complex interpretive practices that acknowledge the historical roles of mediation, betrayal, and alliance in the relationships between women in diverse location. (Kaplan 1994: 139)

Kaplan's flexible grid for a transnational feminist politics begins to sketch out the terms of transnational engagement without the grandiose project of erasing inequalities or the prospect of being paralyzed by them.

In the arena of global theory, Carla Freeman has made a notable intervention in the usual understanding of the global and local. Freeman rejects the untenable dichotomy between "masculinist grand theories of globalization that ignore gender as an analytical lens and local empirical studies of globalization in which gender takes center stage" (2001: 1008). On the basis of her examination of market-women in the contemporary Caribbean, Freeman concludes that "local processes and small-scale actors might be seen as the very fabric of globalization" (1009). Refusing to sunder the local (signed as feminine) from the global (signed as masculine), Freeman alerts us to the ways in which a properly developed transnational literacy would enable us to read both in a continuum. Another explanation of the importance of transnational literacy can be found in Spivak's essay "Feminism and Critical Theory." In this essay, Spivak draws our attention to a *Ms.* magazine article extolling the

Control Data Management corporation's benevolent "social-service leaves" and other family-friendly policies (1988e: 91). Spivak bemoans the fact that bourgeois feminists' "blindness to the *multi*national theatre" prevents them from recognizing the company's repressive practices in its factory in Korea and its use of the local male labor force to divide women and undermine their organization as a collective. Cynthia Enloe's pathbreaking work, *Bananas, Beaches and Bases: Making Feminist Sense of International Politics* (1989), shows how gender and international politics are vitally intertwined, reminding us that a feminist lens can reveal a great deal about the ways in which the global, the local, and gender are mutually constitutive (see also Mitter and Rowbotham 1995).

Globalization offers unprecedented opportunities for transnational feminist activism, but seizing these opportunities will depend upon feminists' ability to read sameness and difference on a global scale. For Mohanty, "experience must be historically interpreted and theorized if it is to become the basis of feminist solidarity and struggle, and it is at this moment that an understanding of the politics of location proves crucial" (1995: 89). When capital and manufacturing no longer take account of national boundaries, when ideas and literatures are transacted globally, the ability to read and to translate becomes ever more crucial. A meaningful transnational literacy will require recognition of the location of readers and of reading as a socialized activity within a particular context. It will require that we learn to read literature by and about "Third-World" women as more than informal sociology, even as it will enjoin upon us the need to read global experiences and events as complex, intricately interwoven social texts. In other words, it will oblige us to recognize the complexities of subject construction everywhere and to learn to read the world through what I would refer to as the "logic of adjacence." We would then read women in the world not as the same but as neighbors, as "near dwellers" whose adjacence can become more meaningful. Through this logic – a logic that might usefully be applied to the general orientation of postcolonialism – we would read the world, not as one (in the sense of being already united), but as belonging together.

12

FERNANDO CORONIL

Latin American postcolonial studies and global decolonization

Given the curiously rapid rise to prominence of "postcolonial studies" as an academic field in Western metropolitan centers since the late 1980s, it is to be expected that its further development would involve efforts, like this one, to take stock of its regional expressions. Yet, while the rubric "Latin American postcolonial studies" suggests the existence of a regional body of knowledge under that name, in reality it points to a problem: there is no corpus of work on Latin America commonly recognized as "postcolonial." This problem is magnified by the multiple and often diverging meanings attributed to the signifier "postcolonial," by the heterogeneity of nations and peoples encompassed by the problematical term "Latin America," by the thoughtful critiques that have questioned the relevance of postcolonial studies for Latin America, and by the diversity and richness of reflections on Latin America's colonial and postcolonial history, many of which, like most nations in this region, long predate the field of postcolonial studies as it was developed in the 1980s. How then to identify and examine a body of work that in reality does not appear to exist? How to define it without arbitrarily inventing or confining it? How to treat it as "postcolonial" without framing it in terms of the existing postcolonial canon and thus inevitably colonizing it?

These challenging questions do not yield easy answers. Yet they call attention to the character of "postcolonial studies" as one among a diverse set of regional reflections on the forms and legacies of colonialism, or rather, *colonialisms*. In light of the world-wide diversity of critical thought on colonialism and its ongoing aftermath, the absence of a corpus of Latin American postcolonial studies is a problem not *of* studies on Latin America, but *between* postcolonial and Latin American studies. I thus approach this discussion of Latin American postcolonial studies – or, as I prefer to see it, of postcolonial studies in the Americas – by reflecting on the relationship between these two bodies of knowledge.

While its indisputable achievements have turned postcolonial studies into an indispensable point of reference in discussions about old and new colonialisms, this field can be seen as a general standard or canon only if one forgets that it is a regional corpus of knowledge whose global influence cannot be separated from its grounding in powerful metropolitan universities; difference, not deference, orients this discussion. Rather than subordinating Latin American studies to postcolonial studies and selecting texts and authors that may meet its standards and qualify as "postcolonial," I seek to establish a dialogue between them on the basis of their shared concerns and distinctive contributions. This dialogue, as with any genuine exchange even among unequal partners, should serve not just to add participants to the "postcolonial discussion," but also to clarify its assumptions and transform its terms.

My discussion is divided into four sections: (a) the formation of the field of postcolonial studies; (b) the place of Latin America in postcolonial studies; (c) responses to postcolonial studies from Latin Americanists; and (d) open-ended suggestions for deepening the dialogue between postcolonial and Latin American studies. By focusing on exchanges between these fields, I have traded the option of offering close readings of selected texts and problems for the option of engaging texts that have addressed the postcolonial debate in terms of how they shape or define the fields of postcolonial and Latin American studies.

Postcolonial studies

Despite a long history of critical reflections on modern colonialism originating in reactions to the conquest and colonization of the Americas, "postcolonialism" as a term and as a conceptual category originates in discussions about the decolonization of African and Asian colonies after the Second World War. At that time, "postcolonial" was used mostly as an adjective by sociologists and political scientists to characterize changes in the states and economies of ex-colonies of the "Third World," a category that was also created at that time. This regional focus was already present in French sociologist George Balandier's analysis of "the colonial situation" (1951) as well as in later debates about the "colonial" and "postcolonial state" (Alavi 1972; Chandra 1981), the "colonial mode of production" (Alavi et al. 1982), or the "articulation of modes of production" (Wolpe 1980; Berman and Londsdale 1992). Although Latin America was considered part of the Third World, because most of its nations had achieved political independence during the first quarter of the nineteenth century, it was only tangentially addressed in these discussions about decolonization that centered on the newly independent nations of Africa and Asia.

As "old" postcolonial nations that had faced the problem of national development for a long time, the key word in Latin American social thought during this period was not colonialism or postcolonialism, but "dependency." This term identified a formidable body of work developed by leftist scholars in the 1960s, designed to understand Latin America's distinct historical trajectory and to counter modernization theory. Riding atop the wave of economic growth that followed the Second World War, modernization theory presented capitalism as an alternative to socialism and argued than achieving modernity would overcome obstacles inhering in the economies, cultures, and subjective motivations of the peoples of the "traditional" societies of the Third World. W. W. Rostow's *The Stages of Economic Growth* (1960), revealingly subtitled *A Non-Communist Manifesto*, was a particularly clear example of modernization theory's unilinear historicism, ideological investment in capitalism, and teleological view of progress.

In sharp contrast, dependency theorists argued that development and underdevelopment are the mutually dependent outcomes of capitalist accumulation on a world scale. In their view, since underdevelopment is the product of development, the periphery cannot be modernized by unregulated capitalism but through an alteration of its polarizing dynamics. This basic insight into the mutual constitution of centers and peripheries was rooted in Argentinian economist Raúl Prebisch's demonstration that unequal trade among nations leads to their unequal development. Formulated in the 1940s, Prebisch's critique of unequal exchange has been considered "the most influential idea about economy and society ever to come out of Latin America" (Love 1980: 46). His insights were integrated into "structural" reinterpretations of social and historical transformation in Latin America by Fernando Enrique Cardoso, Enzo Faletto, Anibal Quijano, Theotonio Dos Santos, Rui Mauro Marini, and many other "dependency" theorists; as Cardoso (1977) noted, their work was "consumed" in the United States as "dependency theory" associated with the work of Andre Gunder Frank.

The world-wide influence of dependency declined after the 1970s. Dependency theory was criticized for its one-dimensional structuralism and displaced by the postmodern emphasis on the textual, fragmentary and indeterminate; its Eurocentric focus on state-centered development and disregard of racial and ethnic divisions in Latin American nations has been a focus of a recent critique (Grosfoguel 2000). Despite its shortcomings, in my view the dependency school represents one of Latin America's most significant contributions to postcolonial thought within this period, auguring the postcolonial critique of historicism, and providing conceptual tools for a much needed postcolonial critique of contemporary imperialism. As a fundamental critique of Eurocentric conceptions of history and of capitalist development, dependency theory undermined historicist narratives of the "traditional," "transitional," and "modern," making it necessary to examine postcolonial and metropolitan nations in relation to each other through categories appropriate to specific situations of dependency.

Starting around three decades after the Second World War, the second usage of the term "postcolonial" developed in the Anglophone world in connection with critical studies of colonialism and colonial literature under the influence of postmodern perspectives. This change took place during a historical juncture formed by four intertwined world-wide processes: the increasingly evident shortcomings of Third-World national development projects; the breakdown of really existing socialism; the ascendance of conservative politics in Britain (Thatcherism) and the United States (Reaganism); and the overwhelming appearance of neoliberal capitalism as the only visible, or at least seemingly viable, historical horizon. During this period, postcolonial studies acquired a distinctive identity as an academic field, marked by the unusual marriage between the metropolitan location of its production and the anti-imperial stance of its authors, many of whom were linked to the Third World by personal ties and political choice.

In this second phase, while historical work has centered on British colonialism, literary criticism has focused on Anglophone texts, including those from Australia and the English-speaking Caribbean. The use of postmodern and poststructuralist perspectives in these works became so intimately associated with postcolonialism that the "post" of postcolonialism has become identified with the "post" of postmodernism and poststructuralism. For instance, a major postcolonial Reader argues that "postcolonial studies is a decidedly new field of scholarship arising in Western universities as the application of post-modern thought to the long history of colonising practices" (Schwarz 2000: 6).

In my view, equally central to postcolonialism has been the critical application of Marxism to a broad spectrum of practices of social and cultural domination not reducible to the category of "class." While marked by idiosyncratic traces, its identifying signature has been the convergence of these theoretical currents – Marxist and postmodern/poststructuralist – in studies that address the complicity between knowledge and power. Edward W. Said's integration of Gramscian and Foucauldian perspectives in his pathbreaking critique of Orientalism (1978) has been widely recognized as foundational for the field. A similar tension between Marxism and poststructuralism animates the evolving work of the South Asian group of historians associated with Subaltern Studies, the strongest historiographical current of postcolonial studies.

Postcolonial critique now encompasses problems as different as the formation of minorities in the United States and African philosophy. But while it has expanded to new areas, it has retreated from analyzing their relations within a unified field; the fragmentary study of parts has taken precedence over the systemic analysis of wholes. Its critique of the grand narratives of modernity has led to skepticism towards any grand narrative, not always discriminating between Eurocentric claims to universality and the necessary universalism arising from struggles against world-wide capitalist domination (Amin 1989; Lazarus 1999a).

As the offspring of a tense marriage between anti-imperial critique and metropolitan privilege, postcolonial studies is permeated by tensions that also affect its reception, provoking sharply different evaluations of its significance and political implications. While some analysts see it as an academic commodity that serves the interests of global capital and benefits its privileged practitioners (Dirlik 1994), others regard it as a paradigmatic intellectual shift that redefines the relationship between knowledge and emancipatory politics (Young 2001). This debate helps identify what in my view is the central intellectual challenge postcolonial studies has raised: to develop a bifocal perspective that allows one, on the one hand, to view colonialism as a fundamental process in the formation of the modern world without reducing history to colonialism as an all-encompassing process and, on the other hand, to contest modernity and its Eurocentric forms of knowledge without presuming to view history from a privileged epistemological standpoint.

In this light, the apparently simple grammatical juxtaposition of "post" and "colonial" in "postcolonial studies" serves as a sign to address the murky entanglement of knowledge and power. The "post" functions both as a temporal marker to refer to the problem of classifying societies in historical time and as an epistemological sign to evoke the problem of producing knowledge of history and society in the context of imperial relations.

Postcolonial studies and Latin America

Given this genealogy, it is remarkable but understandable that debates and texts on or from Latin America do not figure significantly in the field of postcolonial studies as it has been defined since the 1980s. As Peter Hulme (1996) has noted, Said's canonical *Culture and Imperialism* (1993) is emblematic of this tendency: it centers on British and French imperialism from the late nineteenth century to the present; its geographical focus is limited to an area stretching from Algeria to India; and the role of the United States is restricted to the post Second World War period, disregarding this nation's origin as a colonial settlement of Britain, Spain, and France, the processes of internal colonialism through which Native Americans were subjected within its territory, and its imperial designs in the Americas and elsewhere from the nineteenth century to the present.

The major Readers and discussions on postcolonial studies barely take Latin America into account. One of the earliest attempts to discuss post-colonial literatures as a comprehensive field, *The Empire Writes Back: Theory and Practice in Post-Colonial Literatures* (Aschroft, Griffiths, and Tiffin 1989), acknowledges a focus on Anglophone literatures. Even so, its extensive sixteen-page bibliography, including "all the works cited in the text, and some additional useful publications" (224), fails to mention even a single text written on Latin America or by a Latin American author. The book treats Anglophone literatures, including those produced in the Caribbean, as if these literatures were not cross-fertilized by the travel of ideas and authors across regions and cultures – or at least as if the literatures resulting from the Iberian colonization of the Americas had not participated in this exchange.

This exclusion of Latin America was clearly reflected in the first general anthology of postcolonial texts, *Colonial Discourse and Postcolonial Theory* (P. Williams and Chrisman 1993), whose thirty-one articles include no author from Iberoamerica. Published two years later, *The Post-colonial Studies Reader* (Aschroft, Griffiths and Tiffin 1995), reproduces the Anglo-centric perspective that characterizes their earlier *The Empires Writes Back*, but this time without the justification of a topical focus on English literatures. The Reader features eighty-six texts divided into fourteen thematic sections, including topics such as nationalism and hybridity, which have long concerned Latin American thinkers. While some authors are repeated under different topics (Bhabha appears three times, Spivak twice), the only author associated with Latin America is José Rabasa, whose contribution is a critical reading of Mercator's *Atlas*, a topic relevant but not specific to Latin America.

The marginalization of Latin America is reproduced in most works on postcolonialism published since then. For example, Leela Gandhi's *Postcolonial Theory: A Critical Introduction* (1998) does not discuss Latin American critical reflections or include even a single reference to Latin American thinkers in its extensive bibliography. While *Relocating Postcolonialism* (Goldberg and Quayson 2002) "relocates" the postcolonial through the inclusion of such topics as the cultural politics of the French radical right and the construction of Korean-American identities, it maintains the exclusion of Latin America by having no articles or authors associated with this area. This taken-for-granted exclusion appears as well in a dialogue between John Comaroff and Homi Bhabha that introduces the book. Following Comaroff's suggestion, they provide a historical frame for "postcoloniality" in terms of two periods: the decolonization of the Third World marked by India's independence in 1947; and the hegemony of neoliberal capitalism signaled by the end of the Cold War in 1989 (Goldberg and Quayson 2002: 15).

In contrast, two recent works on postcolonialism include Latin America within the postcolonial field, yet their sharply different criteria highlight the problem of discerning the boundaries of this field. In an article for a book on the postcolonial debate in Latin America, Bill Aschroft (whose co-edited book, as has been mentioned above, basically excludes Latin America) presents Latin America as "modernity's first born" and thus as a region that has participated since its inception in the production of postcolonial discourses (1999). He defines postcolonial discourse comprehensively as "the discourse of the colonized" produced in colonial contexts; as such, it does not have be "anticolonial" (14–15). He presents Menchú's *I, Rigoberta Menchú* and Juan Rulfo's *Pedro Páramo* as examples that reveal that "the transformative strategies of postcolonial discourse, strategies which engage the deepest disruptions of modernity, are not limited to the recent colonized" (28). While his comprehensive definition of the field includes Latin American discourses from the conquest onwards, his examples suggest a narrower field defined by more discriminating but unexamined criteria.

The second text is Robert Young's *Postcolonialism: An Historical Introduction* (2001). While Young (like Aschcroft) had not discussed Latin America in a previous work (*White Mythologies*, 1990) that had served to sacralize Said, Bhabha, and Spivak as the foundational trinity of postcolonial studies, in his new book he gives such foundational importance to Latin America and to the Third World that he prefers to name the field "tricontinentalism," after the Tricontinental conference held in Havana in 1966 (2001: 57). Young recognizes that postcolonialism has long and varied genealogies, but he finds it necessary to restrict it to anticolonial thought developed after formal political independence has been achieved: "Many of the problems raised can be resolved if the postcolonial is defined as coming after colonialism and imperialism, in their original meaning of direct-rule domination" (57). Yet Young distinguishes further between the anticolonial thought of the periphery and the more theoretical thought formed at the heart of empires "when the political and cultural experience of the marginalised periphery developed into a more general theoretical position that could be set against western political, intellectual and academic hegemony and its protocols of objective knowledge" (65). Thus, even successful anticolonial movements "did not fully establish the equal value of the cultures of the decolonised nations." "To do that," Young argues, "it was necessary to take the struggle into the heartlands of the former colonial powers" (65).

Young's suggestive discussion of Latin American postcolonial thought leaves unclear the extent to which its anticolonialism is also "critical" in the sense he ascribes to metropolitan reflections. Young discusses Latin American postcolonial thought in two brief chapters. The first, "Latin America I: Mariátegui, Transculturation and Cultural Dependency," is divided into four sections: "Marxism in Latin America," an account of the development of communist parties and Marxist thinkers in the twentieth century, leading to the Cuban revolution; "Mexico 1910," a presentation of the Mexican revolution as precursor of tricontinental insurrections against colonial or neocolonial exploitation; "Mariátegui," a discussion of Mariátegui's role as one of Latin America's most original thinkers, highlighting his innovative interpretation of Peruvian reality; and "Cultural Dependency," an overview of the ideas of some cultural critics which, for brevity's sake, I will reduce to a few names and to the key concepts associated with their work: Brazilian Oswald de Andrade's "anthropophagy" (the formation of Latin American identity through the "digestion" of world-wide cultural formations); Cuban Fernando Ortíz's "transculturation" (the transformative creation of cultures out of colonial confrontations); Brazilian Roberto Schwarz's "misplaced ideas" (the juxtaposition in the Americas of ideas from different times and societies); and Argentinian Nestor García Canclini's "hybrid cultures" (the negotiation of the traditional and the modern in Latin American cultural formations).

Young's second chapter, "Latin America II: Cuba–Guevara, Castro, and the Tricontinental," organized around the centrality of Cuba in the development of postcolonial thought, is divided into three sections: "Compañero: Che Guevara," focuses on Guevara's antiracism and radical humanism; "New Man" relates Guevara's concept of "the new man" to José Martí's proposal of cultural and political independence for "Our America" and to Roberto Fernández Retamar's Calibanesque vision of *mestizaje*; and the "Tricontinental," which presents the "Tricontinental Conference of Solidarity of the Peoples of Africa, Asia and Latin America" held in Havana in 1966 as the founding moment of postcolonial thought; in Young's words, "Postcolonialism was born with the *Tricontinental*" (2001: 213).

While Young's selection is comprehensive and reasonable, its organizing criteria are not sufficiently clear; one can easily imagine a different selection involving other thinkers and anticolonial struggles in Latin America. Despite the significance he attaches to theoretical reflections from metropolitan centers, Young makes no mention of the many Latin Americanists who, working from those centers or from shifting locations between them and Latin America, have produced monumental critiques of colonialism during the same period as Said, Bhabha, and Spivak – for example, Enrique Dussel, Anibal Quijano, and Walter Mignolo, among others.

The contrasting positions of Ashcroft and Young reveal the difficulty of defining postcolonial studies in Latin America. At one extreme, we encounter a comprehensive discursive field whose virtue is also its failing, for it must be subdivided to be useful. At the other extreme, we encounter a restricted domain that includes an appreciative and impressive selection of authors, but that needs to be organized through less discretionary criteria. Whether one adopts an open or a restricted definition of Latin American postcolonial studies, however, what is fundamental is to treat alike, with the same intellectual earnestness, all the thinkers and discourses included in the general field of postcolonial studies, whether they are produced in the metropolitan centers or in the various peripheries, writing or speaking in English or in other imperial and subaltern languages. Otherwise, the evaluation of postcolonial thought risks reproducing within its midst the subalternization of peoples and cultures it claims to oppose.

Latin American studies and postcolonial studies

It is understandable that the reception of postcolonial studies among Latin Americanists should have been mixed. Many thinkers have doubted the appropriateness of postcolonial studies to Latin America, claiming that postcolonial studies responds to the academic concerns of metropolitan universities, to the specific realities of Asia and Africa, or to the position of academics who write about, not from, Latin America, and disregard its own cultural traditions (Achúgar 1998; Colás 1995; Klor de Alva 1992, 1995; Moraña 1997; Pérez 1999; and Yúdice 1996). Klor de Alva has presented the most extreme critique, arguing that colonialism and postcolonialism are "(Latin) American mirages," for these terms, "as they are used in the relevant literature," or "as commonly understood today," properly apply only to marginal populations of indigenes, not to the major non-Indian core that has formed the largely European and Christian societies of the American territories since the sixteenth century. For him, its wars of independence were not anticolonial wars, but élite struggles inspired in European models that maintained colonial inequalities.

This argument, in my view, has several problems: it takes as given the standard set by discussions of the Asian and African colonial and postcolonial experiences; it assumes too sharp a separation between indigenous and non-indigenous peoples in America; it adopts a restricted conception of colonialism derived from a homogenized reading of Northern European colonialism and an idealized image of the effectiveness of its rule; it disregards the importance of the colonial control of territories in Iberian colonialism; it pays insufficient attention to the colonial control of populations in the high-density indigenous societies of Mexico, Peru, and Central America and in plantations run by imported slave labor in the Caribbean and Brazil; and it fails to see the similarity between the wars of independence and the decolonizing processes of Asia and Africa, which also involved the preservation of élite privilege and the reproduction of internal inequalities (what Pablo González Casanova [1965] and Rodolfo Stavenhagen [1965] have theorized for Latin America as "internal colonialism"). Rather than presenting one set of colonial experiences as its exclusive standard, a more productive option would be to pluralize colonialism – to recognize its multiple forms as the product of a common historical process of Western expansion.

An influential debate on colonial and postcolonial studies in a major journal of Latin American studies was initiated by Patricia Seed, a historian of colonial Latin America, who presented the methods and concepts of colonial and postcolonial discourse as a significant breakthrough in social analysis. According to Seed (1991), postcolonial studies' critique of conceptions of the subject as unitary and sovereign, and of meaning as transparently expressed through language, recasts discussions of colonial domination that are simplistically polarized as resistance versus accommodation by autonomous subjects. Two years later in the same journal, three literary critics questioned her argument from different angles. Hernán Vidal expressed misgivings about "the presumption that when a new analytic and interpretative approach is being introduced, the accumulation of similar efforts in the past is left superseded and nullified," which he called "technocratic literary criticism" (1993: 117). Rolena Adorno (1993), echoing Klor de Alva's argument, argued for the need to recognize the distinctiveness of Latin America's historical experience, suggesting that colonial and postcolonial discourse may more properly apply to the historical experience of Asia and Africa. Walter Mignolo (1993), for his part, argued for the need to distinguish among three critiques of modernity: postmodernism (its internal expression), postcolonialism (its Asian and African modality), and postoccidentalism (its Latin American manifestation). Yet far from regarding postcolonialism as irrelevant for Latin America, he suggested that we treat the former as liminal space for developing knowledge from our various loci of enunciation. Mignolo has developed his ideas of "postoccidentalism" (building on its original conception by Fernandez Retamar [1974], and on my own critique of "occidentalism" [Coronil 1996]) in his pathbreaking *Local Histories / Global Designs* (2000), a discussion of the production of non-imperial knowledge that draws on wide-ranging Latin American reflections, in particular Quijano's notion of the "coloniality of power" (2000) and Enrique Dussel's critique of Eurocentrism (1995).

Subaltern Studies has been widely recognized as a major current in the postcolonial field. While historians developed Subaltern Studies in South

Asia, literary theorists have played a major role in the formation of Subaltern Studies in the Latin American context. Around the time of the Seed debate, the Latin American Subaltern Studies Group was founded at a meeting of the Latin American Studies Association in 1992. Unlike its South Asian counterpart, after which it was named, it was initially composed of literary critics, with the exception of Seed and two anthropologists who soon thereafter left the group. Its "Founding Statement" offered a sweeping overview of major stages of Latin American studies, rejecting their common modernist foundations and celebrating the South Asian critique of élitist representations of the subaltern. However, unlike the South Asian Group, formed by a small group of historians organized around a coherent historiographical and editorial project centered on rewriting the history of India, this group, mostly composed of literary critics, was characterized by its diverse and shifting membership and the heterogeneity of their disciplinary concerns and research agendas. While the publications of its members have not fitted within traditional disciplinary boundaries, they have privileged the interpretation of texts over the analysis of historical transformations. The group's attempt to represent the subaltern has typically taken the form of readings of texts produced by authors considered subaltern or dealing with the issue of subalternity. In its decade-long life (I myself participated in the second half of it), the group stimulated efforts to rethink the intellectual and political engagements that had defined the field of Latin American studies.

While centered on literary studies, Subaltern Studies has been considered a major source of postcolonial historiography in Latin America. In a thoughtful discussion entitled "The Promise and Dilemma of Subaltern Studies: Perspectives from Latin American History" published in a forum on Subaltern Studies in a major history journal, historian Florencia Mallon (1994) examines the consumption and production of Subaltern Studies in Latin America and evaluates the tensions and prospects of this field. Her account focuses on historical works, making explicit reference to the contributions of scholars based in the United States who have made significant use of the categories or methods associated with Subaltern Studies. She highlights Gil Joseph's pioneering use of Guha's work on India's peasantry in his examination of banditry in Latin America (Joseph 1990), noting that it moved discussion beyond simplistic oppositions that reduced bandits to either resisters or reproducers of given social orders.

In her review Mallon does not address Subaltern Studies in literary and cultural criticism (perhaps because she does not find this work properly historical), but she does offer a critique of the Latin American Subaltern Studies Group's "Founding Statement," noting its ungrounded dismissal of historiographical work on subaltern sectors in Latin America. She makes a similar critique of the more substantial article by Seed, the one historian of the group (already discussed here). Objecting to Seed's presentation of members of the "subaltern studies movement" as leaders of the "postcolonial discourse movement," Mallon offers ample references to recent historical work on politics, ethnicity, and the state from the early colonial period to the twentieth century that "had begun to show that all subaltern communities were internally differentiated and conflictual and that subalterns forged political unity or consensus in painfully contingent ways" (1994: 1500).

Mallon's erudite discussion expands the scope of Subaltern Studies, but it does not sufficiently clarify why certain historical works should be considered part of the "subaltern" or "postcolonial" movement. Since studies on the social and cultural history of subaltern sectors ("history from below") and subaltern/postcolonial studies share subalternity as a subject matter and employ similar theories and methods, the lines separating them are sometimes difficult to define. Yet South Asian subaltern historiography has sought to distinguish itself from social and cultural history by attaching singular significance to the critique of historicist and Eurocentric assumptions, problematizing the role of power in fieldwork and in the construction of archives, and interrogating such central historiographic categories as the "nation," the "state," "consciousness," and "social actors." The historiographical subaltern project has been marked by the tension between its constructivist aim, which necessarily involves the use of representational strategies not unlike those of social and cultural history, and its deconstructivist strategy, which entails questioning the central categories of historical research and interrupting the narratives of the powerful with those expressed by subaltern actors.

Mallon casts the "dilemma" of Latin American Subaltern Studies in terms of the tension between (Gramscian) Marxist and postmodern perspectives (a tension frequently noted in discussions about South Asian Subaltern Studies). She proposes to solve this dilemma by placing the Foucauldian and Derridean currents of postmodern criticism "at the service of a Gramscian project" (1994: 1515). Perhaps her subordination of deconstruction – so central to subaltern history – to the Gramscian project – so fundamental to social and cultural history – helps account for her insufficient attention to the difference between these fields.

This difference is central for John Beverley, one of the founders of the Latin American Subaltern Studies Group, who in his writings argues for the superiority of subaltern perspectives over non-subalternist ones of the subaltern (1993, 1999, 2000). Deploying criteria that for him define a subalternist perspective, he criticizes Mallon's *Peasant and Nation. The Making of Postcolonial Mexico and Peru* (1995), arguing that, despite her intentions, she appears as an omniscient narrator engaged in a positivist representational project that uses subaltern accounts to consolidate rather than interrupt the biographies of the nation, re-inscribing rather than deconstructing the official biographies of these nations.

In a sophisticated discussion of Subaltern Studies and Latin American history, Ecuadorian historian Guillermo Bustos (2002) uses Mallon and Beverley as a focal point to assess the relation between these two bodies of knowledge. While sympathetic to Mallon's discussion of this topic in "The Promise and Dilemma of Subaltern Studies" (1994), Bustos notes the Anglocentric and metropolitan focus of her discussion, and suggests the inclusion of a more representative sample of work produced in Latin America; her only reference is to Andeanist historian Flores Galindo, which Bustos complements by mentioning three related Andeanists: Assadourian, Colmenares, and Rivera Cusicanqui. Like Beverley, Bustos recognizes the need to distinguish between social history and subalternist perspectives. While Beverley, however, uses this distinction to evaluate Mallon's work in terms of the standards of Subaltern Studies, Bustos uses it to caution against assuming the superiority of a subaltern perspective, recalling Vidal's critique of "technocratic literary criticism" (1993).

Bustos's proposal is to turn claims about the theoretical and political superiority of any perspective into questions answerable through concrete analysis. He exemplifies this option through a subtle reading of Mallon's *Peasant and Nation* (1995) that demonstrates the complexity of her narrative, including her attempt to engage in dialogical relation with her informants and fellow historians. While distancing himself from Beverley's critique, Bustos endorses Tulio Halperin Donghi's observation that Mallon's presentation of other perspectives does not prevent her from assuming (as in common practice) the superiority of her own professional account. His point is thus neither to criticize nor to defend Mallon's work, but to refine the dialogue between Subaltern Studies and Latin American historiography. He develops his argument by discussing other texts, including related attempts to break away from accounts organized as "the biography of the nation-state," based on the critical use of multiple voices and sources (Chiaramonti 1997; Coronil 1997; Thurner 1997). In agreement with Italian historian Carlo Ginzburg, Bustos proposes that we meet the postmodern challenge not by making "evidence" impossibly suspect, but by following, as Paul Ricoeur suggests, the "traces that left from the past, take its place and represent it" (Bustos 2002: 15). Needless to say, the challenge remains how to retrieve and interpret these traces.

Postcolonial historical studies also received attention in Latin America in a book published in Bolivia, *Debates Post Coloniales. Una Introducción a los Estudios de la Subalternidad* (1999) ("Postcolonial Debates. An Introduction to Studies of Subalternity"), edited by historians Silvia Rivera Cusicanqui and Rossana Barragán and composed of translations of a selection of nine essays by South Asian authors. In their introduction Rivera Cusicanqui and Barragán make only tangential reference to the Latin American Subaltern Studies Group, and none to the work of its members. They are critical of its "Founding Statement" for reducing the contributions of the South Asian group to an assortment of ethnographic cases that "exemplify from the South the theory and the broad conceptual guidelines produced in the North" (1997: 13). They also criticize Mallon's article on Subaltern Studies both for its inattention to a long Latin American tradition of critical work on colonialism and postcolonialism, and for reducing South Asian Subaltern Studies "to a questionable Gramscian project on behalf of which one should place the whole postmodern and poststructuralist debate" (13).

Their own interpretative effort is centered on underlining the significance of South Asian Subaltern Studies for Latin American historiography, emphasizing the innovative importance of the poststructuralist perspectives informing the South Asian scholarship. Their brief discussion of Latin American work highlights three critical currents: the Argentinian school of economic history represented by Enrique Tandeter, Carlos Sempat Assadourian, and Juan Carlos Garavaglia, distinguished by its transformation of Marxist and Gramscian categories through a confrontation with the specificities of Indian labor in the Potosí area; the studies of peasant insurgency and oligarchic rule carried out by the Taller de Historia Oral Andina (Workshop of Andean Oral History) and by such influential scholars as Alberto Flores Galindo and Rene Zavaleta; and the studies of "internal colonialism" initiated by Mexican sociologist Pablo González Casanova in the 1960s (and, I should add, Rodolfo Stavenhagen). Their call for a "South/South" dialogue at the same time avoids a dismissal of the "North," warning against the danger present in "certain academic Latin American circles" of adopting new theories and discarding "our own intellectual traditions – and Marxism is one of them – for this impoverishes and fragments the Latin American debate" (Rivera Cusicanqui and Barragán 1999: 19). Their horizontal dialogue establishes a common ground between postcolonial studies and Latin American historiography on colonialism and postcolonialism, yet presents Subaltern Studies as the product of an "epistemological and methodological rupture" (17). If Subaltern Studies is postcolonial, its "post" is the post of postmodernism and poststructuralism.

A variant of this view is presented by philosophers Santiago Castro-Gómez and Eduardo Mendieta in their thoughtful introduction to an important book of essays written by Latin Americanists published in Mexico under the title *Teorías sin disciplina. Latinoamericanismo, postcolonialidad y global-ización en debate* (1998) ("Theories without Discipline. Latino American-ism, Postcoloniality and Globalization in Debate"). Focusing on the rela-tionship between critical thought and the historical context of its produc-tion, Castro-Gómez and Mendieta seek to determine the specific charac-ter of postcolonial studies. They draw a distinction between "anticolonial discourse," as produced in Latin America by Las Casas, Guamán Poma de Ayala, Francisco Bilbao, and José Enrique Rodó, and "postcolonial dis-course," as articulated by Said, Spivak, and Bhabha. For them, anticolonial discourse is produced in "traditional spaces of action," that is, "in situa-tions where subjects formed their identities in predominantly local contexts not yet subjected to intensive processes of rationalization" (as described by Weber and Habermas). They argue that postcolonial theories, in contrast, are produced in "post-traditional contexts of action," that is, "in locali-ties where social subjects configure their identities interacting with processes of global rationality and where, for this reason, cultural borders become porous" (16–17). For them, this distinction has political implications: while anticolonialist discourse claims to speak for others and seeks to dismantle colonialism deploying colonial categories, postcolonial discourse historicizes its own position, not to discover a truth outside interpretation, but to pro-duce truth effects that unsettle the field of political action. It follows that radical politics lies not in anticolonial work that defines struggles with the categories at hand, thus confirming the established order, but in intellec-tual work that deconstructs them in order to broaden the scope of politics. From this perspective, the "post" of postcolonialism turns out to be an anti-anticolonial "post" at the service of decolonizing decolonization.

This position has the merit of offering a clear definition of postcolonial-ism. In my view, it raises several questions. Its distinction between anticolo-nial and postcolonial discourse risks reproducing the tradition/modernity dichotomy of modernization theory, turning the convulsed and rapidly changing social worlds of Las Casas, Guamán Poma, or Bilbao into stable "traditional" societies of limited rationality, in contrast to the globally ratio-nal worlds that engender postcolonial theorists and their superior discourses. By treating deconstruction as a theoretical breakthrough that supersedes pre-vious critical efforts – now relegated to less rational traditional contexts – this position also risks becoming an expression of Vidal's "technocratic lit-erary criticism." Spivak's dictum that "Latin America has *not* participated in decolonization" (1993: 57) is perhaps an extreme expression of this risk. While Castro-Gómez and Mendieta acknowledge the "irritation" of those who recognize that Latin American thinkers have "long shown interest in the examination of colonialism," they seem to accept this risk as an inevitable consequence of the radical theoretical and methodological novelty of postcolonial studies (1998: 20).

By contrast, Cuban public intellectual Roberto Fernández Retamar's discussion of Latin American decolonizing struggles, originally offered as a lecture for a course on Latin American thought in Havana, can be seen in part as a response to Spivak's dictum, which, according to him, wins the prize for epitomizing the problem of Latin America's exclusion from postcolonial studies (1996). It is impossible to summarize his already tight synthesis, organized around thirteen interrelated themes identified by key phrases or ideas that embody political and intellectual movements, such as "Independence or death." Suffice it here to indicate that his presentation links together political struggles and intellectual reflections as part of a single process of decolonization. Thus he joins the Haitian revolution, wars of independence, the Mexican revolution, the Cuban revolution, and the movements of the Zapatistas and the "Madres de la Plaza de Mayo" with such diverse intellectual struggles as literary modernism, theology and philosophy of liberation, dependency theory, pedagogy of the oppressed, Latin American historiography, and *testimonio*. His wide selection of authors and texts celebrates the originality and heterogeneous sources informing self-critical reflections from the Americas. His examples are too numerous to mention here, but they include Venezuelans Simón Rodríguez and Andrés Bello, Mexicans Leopoldo Zea and Octavio Paz, Brazilians Oswald de Andrade and Darcy Ribeiro, and Cubans José Martí and Fernando Ortíz. He highlights the contemporary importance of Rigoberta Menchú and Subcomandante Marcos as articulating in new ways the decolonizing projects of indigenous and national sectors in Guatemala and Mexico. Fernández Retamar is not concerned with defining or erasing the boundaries between Latin American and postcolonial critical thought, but with appreciating their shared engagement with decolonization.

The difference between Mendieta/Castro-Gómez and Fernández Retamar, like that between Ashcroft and Young, reveals the difficulty of defining the relation between postcolonial and Latin American reflections on colonialism and its aftermath. As in Bustos's discussion of the Mallon/Beverley exchange, a dialogue between these intellectual traditions requires not only clearer classificatory efforts, but also closer reading of texts, in order to refine the criteria that define these fields. A treatment of authors who are not considered part of the postcolonial canon as postcolonial thinkers may help us appreciate different modalities of critical reflexivity, as Castro-Klarén has done through her subtle reading of Guamán Poma and of the Inca Garcilaso de la Vega (1999, 2001). Or perhaps, as Hulme suggests, "the real advantage of considering distant figures like Ralph Waldo Emerson or Andrés Bello as postcolonial writers is that this leads us to read them as if they were new" (1996: 6). A particularly productive option is to engage the postcolonial debate through studies of specific postcolonial encounters, as in the pioneering integration of theoretical reflection and detailed historical case studies of US – Latin American relations in the collection edited by Joseph, LeGrand, and Salvatore (1999).

Elephants in the Americas?

This discussion has made evident how difficult it is to define "Latin American poscolonial studies." As in the well-known parable of the elephant and the wise blind scholars (each of whom visualizes the elephant as a different creature by the part he or she feels), this field, like the wider field of postcolonial studies itself, can be represented in as varied a manner as there are different perspectives from which it can be "seen." If this parable shows that knowledge of reality is always partial and inconclusive, its use to reflect on Latin American postcolonial studies raises two more fundamental points.

First, the peculiar object of postcolonial studies is not a natural entity, like an elephant, or even a social subject regarded as sharing the cultural world of the observer, but one formed as a colonized object, an inferior and alien "Other" to be studied by a superior and central "Self." Since the "elephant" can speak, the problem is not just to represent it but to create conditions that would enable it to represent itself. From the perspective of postcolonial studies, analysis should involve not just self-reflection (an inherent dimension of any serious intellectual enterprise), or granting subjectivity to the social subject studied (as anthropologists and cultural historians have typically sought to do), but the integration of these two analytical endeavors into one unified intellectual project directed at countering this unequal, colonizing relationship. Its epistemology is not just representational but transformative; it uses representational strategies to counter the hierarchies and assumptions that turn some subjects into objects of knowledge for allegedly superior subjects.

Second, insofar as postcolonial studies appears as the most evolved critique of colonialism, it tends to invalidate or diminish the significance of reflections on colonialism developed from other locations and perspectives. If the wise scholars were to act wisely, they would not privilege their respective views of the elephant or isolate it from other creatures. As a reflection on the relationship between postcolonial and Latin American studies, the parable appears as a literal story, the absence of indigenous elephants in the Americas justifying the identification of postcolonial studies with scholarship on Africa and Asia.

If we take the parable literally, since the only elephants that exist in the Americas are imported ones, artificially confined in zoos or circuses so as to protect them from an inhospitable terrain, we may have the desire to see only those rare creatures who have managed to mimic their Asian or African counterparts – our Latin American "elephants." Refusal is another option. Following thinkers who justifiably object to the ease with which metropolitan ideas become dominant in Latin America, or who unjustifiably see Latin America as a self-fashioned and bounded region and argue in defense of its autochthonous intellectual productions (but doing so typically in metropolitan languages and with arguments supported by theories which were once considered "foreign"), one could reject the attempt to define Latin American postcolonial studies, restricting postcolonial studies to other continents and regarding it as an imperial "import" that devalues "local" Latin American knowledge.

In my opinion, the view that restricts postcolonial reflexivity to certain currents of Western intellectual theory, as well as the position that treats postcolonial studies as another foreign fad that undermines local knowledge, reinforces both the field's theoretical and ethnographic provincialism and its *de facto* exclusion of Latin America. These two sides of a protected parochial coin prevent us from taking advantage of the global circulation of postcolonial studies as a potent intellectual currency for the exchange and development of perspectives on colonialism and its legacies from different regions and intellectual traditions.

The problem is not simply, as some Latin American critics of postcolonialism have suggested, that Latin Americanists should be drawing on Kusch or Jorge Luis Borges as much as on Said or Derrida, but that knowledge should be global and acknowledge the world-wide conditions of its production. Just as Kusch drew on Heidegger, and Derrida was inspired by Jorge Luis Borges, Said and Ortíz developed independently of each other, fifty years apart, a contrapuntal view of the historical formation of cultures and identities that disrupts the West/rest dichotomy (Coronil 1995). Critical responses to colonialism from different locations take different but complementary forms. While from an Asian perspective it has become necessary to "provincialize" European thought (Chakrabarty 2000a), from a Latin American perspective it has become indispensable to globalize the periphery: to recognize the world-wide formation of what appear to be self-generated modern metropolitan centers and backward peripheries.

As it has been defined so far, the field of postcolonial studies tends to neglect the study of contemporary forms of political domination and economic exploitation. Recognized by many as one of the field's founders, Edward Said has distanced himself from it, saying that he does not "belong to that," and arguing that "postcolonialism is really a misnomer" that does not sufficiently recognize the persistence of neocolonialism, imperialism, and "structures of dependency" (2002: 2). Said's concerns, so central to Latin American thought, highlight the importance of expanding postcolonial studies by building on Latin American critical traditions.

If the relationship between colonialism and modernity is the core problem for both postcolonial and Latin American studies, the fundamental contribution of Latin American studies is to recast this problem by setting it in a wider historical context. The inclusion of Latin America in the field of postcolonial studies expands its geographical scope and also its temporal depth. A wider focus, spanning from Asia and Africa to the Americas, yields a deeper view, revealing the links between the development of modern colonialism by Northern European powers and its foundation in the colonization of the Americas by Spain and Portugal. This larger frame modifies prevailing understandings of modern history. Capitalism and modernity, so often assumed both in mainstream and in postcolonial studies to be a European process marked by the Enlightenment, the dawning of industrialization, and the forging of nations in the eighteenth century, can be seen instead as a global process involving the expansion of Christendom, the formation of a global market, and the creation of transcontinental empires since the sixteenth century. A dialogue between Latin American and postcolonial studies ought not to be polarizing, and might range over local histories and global designs, texts and their material contexts, and subjective formations and structures of domination.

This dialogue should bring to the forefront two interrelated areas of significant political relevance today: the study of postcolonialism itself, strictly understood as historical transformations after political independence, and the analysis of contemporary imperialism. Ironically, these two areas, so central to Latin American thought, have been neglected by postcolonial studies. At the juncture of colonialism's historical dusk and the dawn of new forms of imperial domination, the field tends to recollect colonialism rather than its eventualities. Building on a long tradition of work on post-independence Latin America, I have argued for the need to distinguish "global" from "national" and "colonial" imperialism as a phase characterized by the growing abstraction and generalization of imperial modes of political and economic control (Coronil 2003). Drawing on postcolonial studies, I have proposed to understand what I call "occidentalist" representations of cultural difference under global imperialism as involving a shift from "eurocentrism" to "globalcentrism." I see globalcentrism as entailing representational operations that: (a) dissolve the "West" into the market and crystallize it in less visible transnational nodules of concentrated financial and political power; (b) lessen cultural antagonisms through the integration of distant cultures into a common global space; and (c) emphasize subalternity rather than alterity in the construction of cultural difference. In an increasingly globalized world, US and European dominance is achieved through the occlusion rather than the affirmation of radical differences between the West and its others (Coronil 2000: 354).

This dialogue should also redefine the terms of postcolonial studies. Postcolonialism is a fluid and polysemic category, whose power derives in part from its ability to condense multiple meanings and refer to different locations. Rather than fix its meaning through formal definitions, I have argued that it is more productive to develop its significance through research into and analysis of the historical trajectory of societies and populations subjected to diverse modalities of imperial power (Coronil 1992: 101). In the spirit of a long tradition of Latin American transcultural responses to colonialism and "digestive" appropriation of imperial cultures, I thus opt for what I call "tactical postcolonialism." While Spivak's notion of "strategic essentialism" serves to fix socially constructed identities in order to advance political ends, tactical postcolonialism serves to open up established academic knowledge towards open-ended liberatory possibilities. It conceives "postcolonialism" not as a fenced territory but as an expanding field for struggles against colonial and other forms of subjection. We may then work not so much *within* this field, as *with it*, treating it with Ortíz as a "transcultural" zone of creative engagements, "digesting it" as Andrade may playfully do, approaching it as a liminal locus of enunciation as Mignolo suggests, in order to decolonize knowledge and build a genuinely democratic world, "a world which would include many worlds," as Subcomandante Marcos and the Zapatistas propose.

NOTE

This chapter reflects the lively discussions of a postgraduate seminar on postcolonialism and Latin American thought that I taught during the summer of 2002 at the Universidad Andina Simón Bolívar, Ecuador. My gratitude to all. Thanks also to Genese Sodikoff and Julie Skurski for help with the editing of this chapter.

13

ANDREW SMITH

Migrancy, hybridity, and postcolonial literary studies

Introduction: damning the vessel

This chapter deals with the relationship between migration and postcolonial literary studies. It seems appropriate, therefore, to begin with an incident from a story that is about exile and travel in the colonial world. This event occurs in February 1767, on board a ship sailing from Montserrat, in the east Caribbean, towards Savannah, Georgia, passing the Bahamas *en route*. The cargo of the vessel in question includes "above twenty" slaves. Our narrator, by his own account, had been born in West Africa, captured as a child, and sold to white slave-traders. Unlike many others he had survived both the horror of the middle passage and the brutalities of plantation life and had managed, a year previously, to buy himself back from his owner as a formally, if precariously, free individual. His name is Olaudah Equiano and he writes:

> [T]he next evening, it being my watch below, I was pumping the vessel a little after eight o'clock, just before I went off the deck, as is the custom; and being weary with the duty of the day, and tired at the pump, (for we made a good deal of water) I began to express my impatience, and I uttered with an oath, "Damn the vessel's bottom out." But my conscience instantly smote me for the expression. (Edwards 1988: 106)

Sure enough, that evening, sometime after midnight and while the Welsh captain refuses to leave his bed, the vessel is driven against rocks and begins to founder. Equiano, remembering his previous utterance, is beset with guilt: "I thought that God had hurled his direful vengeance on my guilty head for cursing the vessel on which my life depended" (107–8). The response of the captain is immediately to order the sealing of the hatches leading to the hold so that the slaves on board cannot swamp the ship's boat. Equiano is infuriated: "I could no longer restrain my emotion, and I told him he deserved drowning for not knowing how to navigate the vessel . . . However the hatches were not nailed down" (108). In the end, working with "three black men and a Dutch creole sailor," Equiano manages to ferry the crew and the slaves to "a small key or island, about five or six miles off" (109), while the white sailors "abandoned all care of the ship and themselves, and fell to drinking" (108). After some time they are rescued and Equiano arrives, eventually, in Savannah.

Human beings have presumably always traveled, and they have presumably always recounted and imagined tales on the basis of their traveling. As Walter Benjamin suggested in a famous essay (1969a), the tradition of telling stories has a historical link to social figures such as the journeyman apprentice, the pilgrim, the merchant sailor: all those who were able to leave their homes and return with narratives, straightforward and embellished, of the places and people they had seen in their wanderings. We might say then, most simply, that the fascination in postcolonial literary studies with migration derives from the fact that the human acts of storytelling and travel are tangled together. However, things are not quite so simple. "Postcolonialism," in common with other fields of academic inquiry today, is happier to focus on what makes it *new*, what distinguishes it from previous endeavors, than on what it shares with them. In this respect, postcolonial studies stakes its claim in the idea that the relationship between narrative and movement takes on a new and qualitatively different significance in the context and aftermath of colonialism.

History

Firstly, and most obviously, such a claim has as its background the sense that the modern world is marked by greater numbers of people, moving more often and travelling greater distances, than ever before. Not all journeys, of course, entail the same experience or involve the same risks; nor are all journeys equally a matter of unconstrained free choice. Nevertheless, there is at the most general level a consensus among commentators in the social sciences and humanities that "migration seems likely to go on growing into the new millennium, and may be one of the most important factors in global change" (Castles 1998: 4; see also Appadurai 1996; Clifford 1992; Cohen 1997; Papastergiadis 2000; Vertovec and Cohen 1999).

There is not sufficient space for detailed historical background here, but we can say that in many respects this new migratory and interlinked global order is the culmination of a history that begins with the emergence of capitalism and its outward expansion from Europe, firstly in search of new trade routes, later for the manpower and raw materials that fed the Industrial Revolution, and contemporarily in the development of a new international division of labor (Rodney 1972; Hoogvelt 1997). In a much-quoted passage from their 1848 *Manifesto of the Communist Party*, Marx and Engels registered the actuality and tendential thrust of this new world order:

> The need of a constantly expanding market for its products chases the bourgeoisie over the whole surface of the globe. It must nestle everywhere, settle everywhere, establish connexions everywhere.
>
> The bourgeoisie has through its exploitation of the world market given a cosmopolitan character to production and consumption in every country . . . In place of the old wants, satisfied by the productions of the country, we find new wants, requiring for their satisfaction the products of distant lands and climes. In place of the old local and national seclusion and self-sufficiency, we have intercourse in every direction, universal inter-dependence of nations. *And as in material, so also in intellectual production. The intellectual creations of individual nations become common property. National one-sidedness and narrow-mindedness become more and more impossible, and from the numerous national and local literatures there arises a world literature.*
>
> (1988: 37–38; emphasis added)

The prescience of this account of globalization is well noted, even though Marx's and Engels's recognition that this process would also threaten the existence of insular national literary traditions is more rarely commented upon. It is precisely this history of impelled *cultural* meeting, however, that has been of so much interest to the literary branch of postcolonial studies.

Maps of the 1400s show the extent to which Africa and the Americas appeared in European eyes as *terra incognita*, as worlds without names, waiting like Eden for words and history to envelop them. In the various and often sensationalized accounts of early European travelers these supposedly pristine lands were reported, fictionalized, and imagined for the domestic audience. Such travelogues feature prominently in Edward Said's extraordinarily influential study of *Orientalism* (1978). In this book, from which so much of postcolonial critical writing takes its cue, Said argues that it was *in and through* travel writings and other forms of literature that Europeans learned to think of themselves as fundamentally different from the rest of the world. Of course, many of the accounts that Europeans gave of Africa, Asia, and the Americas were made in the prelude to or in the context of colonial rule. Descriptions of local practices and beliefs often sanctioned European governance as a moral force, or what is now called a "humanitarian intervention." This project of describing the colonized (or the soon-to-be-colonized) had the effect of fixing local traditions which had historically been fluid and adaptable. One of Said's achievements was to point up this link between the narratives made in and about human movement and the historical development of forms of political and economic domination.

Writing back

This brief history reminds us of how long and in how many different ways narratives have been formed in the experience of human movement. We still have to explain exactly what it is that constitutes postcolonial literary studies as a discrete field of investigation and why migrancy is such a central trope within it. The primary and overriding concern of this field has been with those works which straddle the borders between the colonized and colonizing nations. Generally, this means work written or filmed in European languages which adopts, adapts, and often rejects the established European models. As the authors of an early and seminal study put it, "the perspective brought . . . by post-colonial literatures is their accentuation of this phenomenon of *distance*: they present us with readers and writers far more 'absent' from each other than they would be if located in the same culture" (Ashcroft, Griffiths, and Tiffin 1989: 186).

The quote catches neatly the dizzy feeling that a new and unexpected gap has opened up beneath the feet of the metropolitan cultural consumer. It is here, of course, that migration comes in. Fundamental to postcolonial criticism has been the puzzle of how aspects of life and experience in one social context are impacting on worlds that are geographically and culturally distant. This is not simply an abstract concern. Many of the most prominent writers and artists on the lists of Western-based publishing houses were born, or live, or have connections with, the world beyond Europe and America. Gabriel García Márquez, Carlos Fuentes, Wole Soyinka, Derek Walcott, Vikram Seth are a few familiar and fairly random names. The history of imperialism has been imagined in Europe, at least in official culture, as civilization taking an outward journey. The dominant image is that of the intrepid administrator or explorer sailing down the river into the dark hinterland. From the middle of the twentieth century, however, there has been a rise in the prominence of "figures who address the metropolis using the techniques, the discourses, the very weapons of scholarship and criticism once reserved exclusively for the European, now adapted for insurgency or revisionism at the very heart of the Western centre" (Said 1990: 29). Although, as Said says, there has been a conservative backlash against this "voyage in," contemporary attempts to insist on the self-containment and purity of "Western" culture or civilization – as in Samuel Huntington's *The Clash of Civilizations and the Remaking of World Order* (1998; see Said 2000: 569–90), for instance, or (in the context of the debate over literary canonicity) in "the effort to restate the ten, twenty, or thirty essential Western books without which one could not be educated" (Said 1990: 48) – seem increasingly forlorn. Thus Chris Ofili and Meera Syal, Asian Dub Foundation and

Cornershop are all central to the cultural map of contemporary Britain, and contribute significantly to the definition of what it is to be British today. What makes them "British" cannot be referred to essentialist or absolutist notions of nation or culture, race or ethnicity. At the very least it is clear that we can no longer hold comfortably on to the notion of a closed national culture, complete within and for itself. Postcolonial literary studies claims its novelty and its authority, therefore, in the idea that as people move, the cultural center also moves, not in any specific direction, but in a diffusing, outward spread. Suddenly Marx's and Engels's comments seem absolutely on the mark. Not least because of the social changes that have occurred as a result of migration, the idea of a self-contained national literary tradition seems anomalous, time-bound, and hopelessly nostalgic. Increasingly, cultural products are exposed as hybrid, as tying together influences from many traditions, as existing not so much *in* a specific place and time as *between* different places at once.

We might note that there is something of a paradox here. If the project of postcolonial literary studies begins with the sense that "other" places and stories are suddenly visible and vocal in the heart of the metropolis, courtesy of mass migration and new forms of communication, it has also led to the recognition that those "other" places have been there from the very beginning of the modern Western literary tradition. There, for example, when Marvell imagines his mistress picking rubies by the Ganges; or in Donne's "Indias of spice and myne"; or as the setting of *The Tempest*; or as the escape-route for Moll Flanders in Defoe's novel. Although postcolonial literary studies has a pragmatic investment in describing the *newness* of the world of migration and the late-breaking prominence of mixed-up cultural forms, it has tended increasingly to disclose the hybridity of *all* cultural traditions *at all times*, their repeated summoning up of the place that is not here, the people who are not us.

Despite this, the rhetorical gesture in postcolonial literary theory is to celebrate the opening up of things that are said to have been closed, especially the protected arenas of national culture. It is often the migrant writer who is taken to be the figure of this new liberation, prising the lid from locked histories and self-centered stories. Said, for example, argues that the migrant individual's refusal to remain "in place" is not only indicative, but constitutes an inherently radical gesture (Said 1993: 239–61, 326–36; 1994). By becoming mobile and by making narratives out of this mobility, people escape the control of states and national borders *and* the limited, linear ways of understanding themselves which states promote in their citizens. There is a flip-side to the "free-air-miles" sentiment in postcolonial theory, however: namely that, for most people in the modern world, migration is a terrifying option. Without the right circumstances of birth or bank account the majority of the world's population remain intractably in place and very distant from the celebration of a newly mobile, hybrid order (Cohen 1987). Because our world is marked by such disparities – because travel is price-tagged like any other commodity – migration can involve forms of domination as well as liberation and can give rise to blinkered vision as well as epiphanies.

This point takes us to the ambiguous heart of the relationship between postcolonial literary theory and migration. Said describes the birth of postcolonial theory as the sudden "extension into the metropolis of large-scale mass movements" (Said 1990: 30). However, this "journey in" is not without complicated, ambivalent repercussions. Let us return, for a moment, to the point at which we started, with Equiano the ex-slave, fully aware of the brutalities of slave life, working on board a slave ship in order to survive. Working as he did, indeed, in order to buy his own freedom, in order to get to London. Everything in Equiano's story is rife with the tension of having no choice other than to labor *inside* the very system to which he wants to see an end. So it is a very powerful, although probably unintentional, symbol of his situation when he shouts out in frustration, damning the very vessel "on which my life depended."

This is also, of course, a neat figure for the situation of a great deal of postcolonial theorizing and of the position of its practitioners. The bulk of postcolonial literary criticism, and the writing with which it works, is produced within the middle-class enclaves of the Western or Northern world even as it is critical of this world and of its cultural assumptions. For these reasons, Benita Parry has argued that what mainly distinguishes postcolonial theory is that it is a form of "immanent critique": criticism from the *inside out* (Parry 1997a: 11). Postcolonial cultural work has often involved, we might say, the damning of a necessary vessel. Migrant writing in particular has been read in postcolonial theory as revealing the fact that no act of criticism is entirely free of complicity in that which it criticizes. More often, however, this body of theory has celebrated the idea that the migrant is in a position of peculiar insight, blessed with a specific awareness of the relativity of cultural rules and forms.

Migration as a new way of being

To examine this a little further, and in keeping with our sea-bound analogy, we will step back on-board ship, only this time in the company of Ben Okri, one of the most celebrated of recent postcolonial migrant writers. Okri is on a voyage somewhere in the mid-Atlantic and together with his fellow passengers he is watching a magician perform. He tells us that the scene brings to his mind another image, that of the traditional oral African storyteller. A realization dawns on him that "the old storytellers were the first real explorers and frontierspeople of the abyss" (39). They were, in other words, the first to expand and challenge the horizons of their communities, imaginatively and conceptually. Okri, the modern-day novelist, summons up this ancestral figure precisely because he believes that we live in a world in which there are no longer set centers, definite horizons, or clear limits on things. By settling his readers with him on-board ship, mid-ocean, Okri places us as common dwellers in this in-between space. He goes on to argue, quite deliberately, that it falls to the contemporary migrant writer to rediscover the role of the cultural frontiersperson. Now more than ever, he suggests, we need the individual who can explore, in writing and art, what life is like in a world where everything is becoming borderspace. For Okri, and for many who work in postcolonial studies, this fluid cultural landscape seems an inviting prospect. He goes as far as to discern in it the glimmerings of a "first universal golden age" (31). Here *migrancy* becomes the name for the condition of human beings *as such*, a name for how we exist and understand ourselves in the twenty-first century.

Such a vision would not always have been plausible; the idea of migrancy as a name for human being is sustainable only because of specific historical or ideological shifts which we need to understand. A first key alteration is a growing uncertainty over nationalism. In the ex-colonial world, the hopes invested in formal sovereignty – political independence – have been brutally trampled upon by new formations of Euro-American hegemony and the tenacious hold on power of parasitic local élites. There is a link between the loss of hope in anticolonial nationalism and migration. There is, of course, a direct causal connection between the two, as people from bereft postcolonial nations – the Philippines, Sri Lanka, Somalia, Algeria, Haiti, for instance – struggle to find a space and livelihood in the centers of economic control. In addition, however, there is also a theoretical link. As we can infer from Okri, much of the hope and optimism that *had* been invested in the new nations at decolonization is being transferred to a traveling cosmopolitan position in which the nation no longer seems to be a vehicle for any kind of social or historical progress.

Hand in hand with the disappointments of the post-independence era there emerges a crisis of confidence in oppositional political movements generally. We should draw a distinction here between the position of writers and intellectuals associated with postcolonial studies and the majority of the impoverished population of the world. National strikes, uprisings against the effects of free-market reforms, religious and ethnic insurgencies, both progressive and regressive in form, are evident in many areas of the world. Direct political opposition remains as assertive on the streets of the world as it has become absent from the textbooks of the academic humanities. Nor does migrancy necessarily relate to a detachment from political struggle. Nevertheless, in the writing of a Salman Rushdie or a Homi K. Bhabha, migration and exile are associated with the establishment of the truth that truth is relative, that no knowledge can ever be certain. Rushdie himself is in many respects the archetype of those who have, in his own words, "been forced by cultural displacement to accept the provisional nature of all truths, all certainties" (1991: 12). Scholars in postcolonial studies have been fascinated by the idea that cultural facts and values are mutable, contested, and shaped in and through storytelling. As Rushdie makes clear, and as we have seen Okri suggest, it is the "double perspective" of the migrant that is taken to expose this "relativity." Political action becomes awkward in this situation, partly because it would be hard to find the basis on which to judge the validity of any particular stance. For some recent theorists, class- or race- or sex-based anti-systemic movements are seen to have lost their authority: oppositionality is now seen to consist most sharply in an individualist cosmopolitanism (Chambers 1994; Hannerz 1990, 1996).

To understand all of this a little more clearly, it might be helpful if we were to look briefly at the arguments of Homi Bhabha, which begin with the recognition that there is "no necessary or eternal belongingness" (Bhabha 1994: 179). In an intuitive and everyday sense we think of our identities, whether ethnic or national or of any other form, as pre-given and stable facts of our lives. For Bhabha, however, this comfortable feeling of the self-sufficiency of traditions, or of national or personal identity, masks the much more tangled and ambiguous processes by which these constructions come to have "cultural compulsion" (1990a: 1): "[C]ultures come to be represented by virtue of processes of iteration and translation through which their meanings are vicariously addressed to – *through* – an Other. This erases any essentialist claims for the inherent authenticity or purity of cultures" (1994: 59). What interests Bhabha about this is *not* the existence of dialectical pairs which appear to confirm each other in distinct, separate identities – colonialist/colonized, for example, or local/immigrant. Such pairings are usually, he argues, ruses of the powerful, attempts to create unequal structures of order. Such strategies and hierarchies are threatened when we look closely at the borderline between communities, at the threshold of what we call "cultural difference," and realize how implicated different identities are in and with each other: "[I]t is the 'inter' – the cutting edge of translation and negotiation, the *in-between* space – that carries the burden of the meaning of culture" (38).

It is in respect of this aspect of culture, the fact that it is constituted from the edges rather than by virtue of a closed and coherent center, that the position of the migrant is peculiarly symptomatic. For Bhabha, the "newness" or "untranslatability" of immigrant communities dramatizes the flaw in the pluralist dream of a multicultural society where difference is smoothly assimilated. The migrant represents the "signifying position of the minority that resists totalization" (1994: 162), undermining the liberal dream of a single national body under command from the center and marking up in its stead the "menacing agonistic boundary of cultural difference that never quite adds up, always less than one nation and double" (168). The presence of the migrant, or what he calls elsewhere the "borderline community," shows us how, despite the attempt to fix others (and ourselves) with stereotypes of sameness and essence, cultures are not closed and complete in themselves, but split, anxious, and contradictory. Like Okri, Bhabha implies that the migrant (especially the migrant intellectual and writer) is therefore a forerunner of a new type of politics in which groups no longer mobilize on the basis of the old dichotomies of opposition, but move together in and through hybridity and difference.

Postcolonial literary studies, I began by saying, has posited a new relationship between narrative and migration. If human beings have tended to understand themselves as citizens of nations or as blood members of ethnic groupings, migration increasingly exposes the insufficiency of these ways of identifying ourselves. It reveals these identities as stories which are acted out in life but which are not unchangeable. It also shows how they often smother and silence other competing stories. Migrants become emblematic figures in postcolonial literary studies precisely because they represent a removal from "old" foundations and from previous "grounded" ways of thinking about identity (Krishnaswamy 1995). An earlier generation of migrants living in the diaspora promoted the idea of a search for lost "roots." Postcolonial literary studies, however, is very suspicious of this type of language. As Gayatri Chakravorty Spivak has put it, in an interview: "If there's one thing I distrust, in fact more than distrust, despise and have contempt for, it is people looking for roots. Because anyone who can conceive of looking for roots, should already, you know, be growing rutabagas [turnips]" (1990: 93). Whatever older formations of identity were based in – ancestry, passport, or geography – it is their apparent fixity that migrancy calls into question. If there is a space left for unity and political action it is an awkward one in which what we share is, as it were, a strangeness, the common fact of having little definite in common. To quote Bhabha again: "it is by living on the borderline of history and language, on the limits of race and gender, that we are in a position to translate *the differences between them* into a kind of solidarity" (1994: 170). Migration, therefore, is central to what is grouped as postcolonial literature and to its analysis both thematically and concretely. It is also a kind of metaphor, a symbol that catches many of the shared understandings and assumptions which give postcolonial studies its parameters and shape.

Connected to this conception of migration are a whole cluster of other concepts. I shall now move on briefly to discuss two of these further concepts: hybridity and diaspora – which are central to debates in postcolonial literary studies.

Hybridity

"Hybrid" was originally, as Robert Young's very important history of the idea explains, a term of denigration – literally so: the blackening or sullying of a thing. Hybridity as a concept came to prominence in the context of supremacist Eurocentric accounts of racial origins and racial distinction. In particular, colonialism presented the proponents of racial separation with the disturbing scenario of racial interbreeding and intermarriage. A whole discourse arose alerting a European audience to the dangers of this mis-cegenation, warning of a dissolution of the blood of the higher races and suggesting that the resulting mulattos, cross-bred humans, would prove to be sterile or retarded. At the same time, this fascination with the mainte-nance of racial purity, Young argues, had its flip-side in a covert, repressed desire. Colonial racialism operated in terms of separated categories whose borders its proponents both sought to maintain *and* wanted to transgress. In the possibility of the "hybrid" the categories through which racial theory conceived the world were upheld and, tantalizingly, collapsed (Young 1995).

Young's intention, therefore, is to recall for his readers the prehistory of the term "hybridity." He wants to demonstrate how "hybridity" has slipped from being a metaphor about *racial* intermingling or purity to one of *cultural* mixture or separateness: "Hybridity . . . shows the connections between the racial categories of the past and contemporary cultural discourse" (1995: 27). As the discourse of "race" became invalid, the focus shifted onto the less contentious ground of "culture" but with the same fears of collapse, dissolution, and entropy held in place. More importantly, there remained the same impossible but tacitly asserted sense that there are or were dis-tinct, wholly separate, wholly "other" or incommensurable human cultures existing in unpolluted isolation across the globe.

The fact that "hybridity" has become a progressive term is another exam-ple of that familiar historical pattern in which a derogatory label, connoting regression and disintegration, is recuperated and used to disrupt the very patterns of categorization and control which first gave rise to it. Broadly speaking we can distinguish two different ways in which the term "hybridity" is used contemporarily, especially in relation to questions of culture. The first is the everyday sense of the word; the second is the way in which "hybridity" has tended to be deployed in contemporary critical theory. In everyday usage, in which Britain or Australia or the United States – for example – are seen as increasingly *multicultural* societies, "hybridity" implies the mingling of once separate and discrete ways of living. In the idealized liberal view this *hybridization* occurs on a level ground of equality, mutual respect, and open-mindedness – a vision whose selectivity seems obvious as soon as we hold it up against the harsher material and institutional realities of social life, even in the most ostensibly tolerant of societies. At the theoretical level, we can note that this idea of "hybridity" as a synonym for diversity or multiculturalism continues to rely on the assumption that there were primeval, separate, and distinct cultural orders which are only now beginning to meet in the context of global migration. Although the language of blood and racial descent has been precluded, this conception of culture is thus still shaded by essentialist assumptions about people and their lives, while the language of diversity and integration, so evident in policy documents and institutional press releases, masks continuing structural inequality. As Abdul JanMohamed and David Lloyd argue in their introduction to a volume of critical essays on "minority discourse,"

> [t]he semblance of pluralism disguises the perpetuation of exclusion insofar as it is enjoyed only by those who have already assimilated the values of the dominant culture. For this pluralism, ethnic or cultural difference is merely an exoticism, an indulgence that can be relished without significantly modifying the individual who is securely embedded in the protective body of dominant ideology. Such pluralism tolerates the existence of salsa, it even enjoys Mexican restaurants, but it bans Spanish as a medium of instruction in American schools. Above all, it refuses to acknowledge the class basis of discrimination and the systematic economic exploitation of minorities that underlie postmodern culture.   (1990: 8)

It is precisely this residually essentialist, multiculturalist conception that is challenged by the leading theorists of hybridity in postcolonial studies (see Brah and Coombes 2000).We have already seen Homi Bhabha arguing that culture is never essential or innate, but is always something whose apparent closure is performed and learnt – in fiction and drama, classrooms and lecture halls. Néstor García Canclini (1995) argues similarly that the ideal of a fixed and pure national culture – what he refers to as "a patrimony" – has to be staged in a very selective manner in institutions such as national museums, where competing accounts of a national history appear to be unified. If a culture is a thing learnt, created, and staged, however, then it is also profoundly susceptible to the possibility of being aped, copied, or appropriated, in a fashion that disrupts the claim that it is the specific property or the unique expression of a single community. The history of the cultural relations of colonialism makes this very apparent. Terence Ranger (1983), for example, has shown how much of the classic conception of upper-class British identity was the product of expatriate life in the colonies and how many of these practices were therefore adopted, adapted, and remade by the colonized in their own name. So "hybridity" can become a term *not* for the mixing of once separate and self-contained cultural traditions, but rather for the recognition of the fact that all culture is an arena of struggle, where self is played off against the purportedly "other," and in which the attempts of the dominant culture to close and patrol its hegemonic account are threatened by the return of minority stories and histories, and by strategies of appropriation and revaluation. As R. Radhakrishnan puts it in a recent essay, "hybridity is heady stuff: transgressive in more than one direction, de-territorializing . . . With hybridity, anything is possible for the simple reason that hybridity is about making meaning without the repression of a pre-existing normativity or teleology: in the exhilarating a-nomie between 'having been deterritorialized' and 'awaiting to be reterritorialized' there is all manner of unprecedented 'becoming'" (Radhakrishnan 2000; see also J. N. Pieterse 1995). Hybridity, in this usage, names the fact that the cultural mechanisms for producing affiliation are always open-ended and incomplete, and that they stall and misfire in the face of what is typically referred to as "cultural difference."

Because it has been used, after Bhabha, as the name for a transgression or a crisis that undermines closed ways of understanding the world, it can seem as if the disclosure of cultural hybridity is, in itself, somehow automatically radicalizing. "[I]deas of cross-fertilization, of the potential richness of traffic between and across boundaries," as Dennis Walder points out, "can return postcolonial theorising to a more celebratory, even . . . liberatory mode" (1998: 81). As theory embraces and celebrates this apparent liberation, it is worth remembering that hybridity is a quality of narratives or discourses in specific circumstances, rather than a quality that is radical in its own right. One only has to think of the Third Reich's use of Aryan motifs to remember that symbolic syncretism can be put to the service of the most regressive politics.

This poststructurally orientated sense of the term "hybridity" foregrounds the "constructedness" of culture. There are important reasons for this, and the insistence on recognizing the discursive creation of meaning and value is a powerful refutation of the claims of culture as a "given" category on a par with genes or blood type. As Iain Chambers says, "the idea that knowledge is constructed, produced through the activity of language . . . subverts all appeals to the idea of a 'natural' truth and its obvious factuality" (1994: 33). The danger in this refutation, however, lies in the implication that culture – especially in the most limited sense of high literary culture – is the definitive arena of social struggle. So, Bronwyn T. Williams, discussing Hanif Kureishi's generation of black British writers, describes their work as

> an attempt to disrupt the narrative forged to define the dominant culture, to hybridize the discourse, to reconfigure the concept of all cultural identities as fluid and heterogeneous. Instead of seeking recognition from the dominant culture or overcoming specific instances of political injustice, the work of these writers endeavours to reconfigure these relations of dominance and resistance, to reposition both the dominant and the marginalized on the stage of cultural discourse, and to challenge static borders of national and cultural identity.
>
> (1999: 2)

We are, I think, entitled to ask whether or not this means anything in terms of substantive political activity. What is absent is some sense of the *inertia* of cultural practices, shaped as they are by institutions and traditions that are the product of historical struggles, and of the entanglement of the cultural with the material, the concrete stuff of human consumption and survival. Culture does not exist outside history *either* in the sense of being pre-given and essential *or* in the sense of being wholly protean and amenable to acts of reformulation by individuals. When Okri writes that "the only hope is to redream one's place in the world – a beautiful act of imagination, and a sustained self-becoming" (1997: 55), it does seem as if the celebration of a radical hybridity in culture also means a celebration of *disconnection* from the strictures of daily practices and communal networks of meaning. In common with the discussion of migration, it can appear to celebrate a very privileged form of mobility and ignore the typical, everyday experience of localized forms of control and resistance.

It is, finally, important to recall that if hybridity is, in one sense, a radicalizing effect of cultural difference, it is also the operating condition of a commodity-producing capitalist system that is always reliant on the disclosure of a kind of superficial newness. Hybrid forms of popular cultural production are repeatedly recuperated under the signs of fashion and the exotic, as with henna tattoos and world music. In saying this I am following García Canclini again, specifically his argument that hybridity should be treated as ambivalent, especially given the market's hunger for seeming novelty. Culture's irreducible hybridity can be *both* a means of resistance to the attempts to "fix" and control meaning by ruling élites *and* the very tag under which cultural works become detached from a local context and are made objects for sale, among all other objects for sale, denuded of all meaning which is reliant on context and reduced to their value as items of exchange (García Canclini 1995).

Diaspora

The term "diaspora" derives from the Greek, and combines the words *speiro* (meaning "to sow") and *dia* ("over"). For the ancient Greeks, as Robin Cohen points out, "diaspora" was conceived "as migration and colonization." In its historical actualization, however – above all with reference to the Jewish people – the term "acquired a more sinister and brutal meaning. Diaspora signified a collective trauma, a banishment, where one dreamed of home but lived in exile" (Cohen 1997: ix). The convention is to use the term to refer to the dispersion of the Jewish peoples in the period following the destruction of Jerusalem in 586BC and their forced removal to Babylon; and to the existence thereafter of Jewish populations outside Palestine (Boyarin and Boyarin 1993).

The word "diaspora" suggests, therefore, a linkage asserted in the context of exile from a homeland, and a unity maintained in the varying circumstances confronting a scattered population. Such a concept refers by extension to other dispersed peoples, such as those exiled Armenians who resettled across much of Europe and Asia from the eleventh century and throughout the period of the Ottoman Empire. While we cannot think of diaspora without regard to Jewish history, we must beware of making this history *normative* for our understanding of the concept. Cohen speaks of the need both to construe and to "supersede the Jewish concept of diaspora" (1997: 3; see also Tölölyan 1991, 1996; Clifford 1994; Kirschenblatt-Gimblett 1994; Gikandi 1996; Gilroy 1994; Patterson and Kelley, 2000).

One result of capitalism's global expansion was the voluntary and (more often) forcible dispersion of increasing numbers of people and it is in relation to these impelled dislocations of modern history that the concept of diaspora becomes more widely germane as displaced populations attempted to trace a story of unity in the face of dislocation and alienation. At the same time, the rise of nationalism as the single most prominent form of modern communal organization gave the idea of the "homeland" a new state-orientated connotation, associating it with political and popular self-determination. In the wake of the French revolution, for example, it was the diaspora of Greek intellectuals across Europe that was instrumental in campaigning for an independent Greek homeland which meant also an autonomous Greek state.

From the point of view of imperial history, however, the most obvious and most brutally achieved example of forced dislocation is that from which Equiano writes: the dispersion of Africans within the Americas and elsewhere as a result of the slave trade. Particularly in this context, where the exiled population was denied control or cultural representation in the new world, it became a political act to affirm the oneness of the dispossessed. The notions of black unity proposed by African American intellectuals, such as the nineteenth-century abolitionist and preacher Alexander Crummell, specifically asserted the ties of race and tradition in the African diaspora. Later cultural movements such as *négritude* celebrated in a literary form the idea of a unitary African being, bringing together those of African origin in the Caribbean, in Europe, in America, and in the home continent itself. In these and other examples we can see the same historical pattern we found in relation to hybridity: reading *as positive* the negative difference or *otherness* which racial dogma imposed and upheld as a form of ideological control (Appiah 1992).

In the context of global migration the ideas of diaspora and of diasporan culture have become more, not less, significant, and continue to be grounded in the assertion of a unity based on something conceived of as sufficiently fundamental to override geographical separation. The "fundamental something," of course, might be precisely the promise of a future, restored geographical unity as in dreams of a Kurdish or Kashmiri homeland. Unity between scattered peoples can also be asserted on the basis of shared religious projects, shared blood ties, shared melanin levels, or shared histories of dispossession. Many of these discourses of unity are developed in the face of on-going racism or prejudice; many are also manipulated by ruling groups within diaspora populations for their own purposes of control. A diaspora is also, it should be remembered, a network whose connections can be financial. Skilled migrant workers in the UK, for example, send home on average 11 percent of their annual income (Department of Trade and Industry 2002: 64), and the world-wide economy of immigrant remittances to developing and former communist countries was estimated to be worth $100 billion in 1999 (Stalker 2003).

In postcolonial studies, however, the concept of diaspora often carries the same anti-essentialist freight as the concept of hybridity. For a writer like Stuart Hall, the notion of culture as diasporic registers the fact that ideas of essential unity based in blood or land are, at best, fictions which people put to work to think of themselves as a single congregation: "Cultural identities are the points of identification, the unstable points of identification or suture, which are made, within the discourses of history and culture. Not an essence, but a *positioning*" (Hall 1993: 395). In this theoretical context, "diaspora" becomes a term of critical intervention *against* the essentializing categories used to control and delimit peoples, including such notions as are employed by élites within diasporas themselves: "What was initially felt to be a curse" as Paul Gilroy has written "– the curse of homelessness or the curse of enforced exile – gets repossessed as a privileged standpoint from which certain useful and critical perceptions about the modern world become more likely" (1993: 111). The paradox of diaspora is that it is a concept intimately linked to a sense of territory, to the lost homeland or the once-and-future nation. Yet at the same time, because diaspora formations cross national borders, they reveal precisely the fact that cultural practices are *not tied to place*. They show culture, in other words, as *deterritorialized*. It is worth remembering again that the historical context here is that of disillusionment with the political reality of so many postcolonial states and with other "grounded" projects such as pan-Africanism. For many postcolonialists, it is precisely the mobility and fluidity of diasporan culture that becomes significant. To Hall, diasporan culture demonstrates that identity is not a thing that is given, but something always in the *process* of being asserted. Specific practices, ways of constructing meaning, allocating value, determining status, and so forth – in short all of the buttresses of identity – seem perfectly capable of being reformed and reproduced in conditions of exile and movement. In some postcolonial writing certainly, that emotional investment in a specific space, which lies at the nostalgic heart of the concept of diaspora, is seen as outdated. In Arjun Appadurai's influential account of globalization, it is culture as "a volatile form of difference," rather than an "inert, local substance" that is the distinctive modern fact (1996: 60). Likewise, Salman Rushdie's famous essay on "imaginary homelands" (1991) is interested primarily in the creative, re-creative power of the "imagination," rather the contingencies of an actual "homeland." In short, diaspora is taken to have the same kind of critical charge as hybridity, a conjuncture that exposes the formulation of identity as a positioning, or as a project, repudiating the idea of a definite and stable home (see, for instance, Brah 1996; Chow 1993; Israel 2000; Jules-Rosete 2000).

Yet the idea of diaspora returns us to those paradoxes that run like stress fractures through so many of the major discussions in postcolonial studies. What García Canclini argues in relation to hybridity holds true here: diaspora too is both a radical assertion *and* a form in which radicalism is recuperated by the market. After all, as Marx recognized, bourgeois ruling culture was and is modernity's first genuinely global, transnational class. Brand-dominated commodity capitalism has given rise to symbols that link, superficially, swathes of the world's population more numerous than any diaspora. Its price tag, however, includes the atrophying of spaces of democratic speech, increasing global disparity, and the rise of production methods that treat human and environmental resources as expendable units in the equation of profit. This ought to lead us to question whether hybridity, diaspora, migrancy, and the position of the "in-between" are, in any *necessary sense*, radical formations or qualities. Where diaspora becomes merely a synonym for the traffic of cultural capitalism it is surely stripped of its transformative possibilities. In this case, its fêted mobility becomes a form of detachment from the very circumstances in which political resistance is possible.

Criticisms

We began by saying that the relationship between storytelling and movement, between migrancy and narrative, is an old one. In the world according to postcolonial theory, however, a strange expansion seems to have occurred. On the one hand, *everyone* seems to be in some sense migrant. "Migrancy" is now ubiquitous as a theoretical term. It specifically refers to migration *not* as an act, but as a *condition* of human life. On the other hand, *everything* seems to be a story. The histories of countries whose independence was often fought for, in the most literal sense, are analyzed only in terms of national "narratives." Edward Said's intention, we might recall, was to make us remember how tangled together cultural representations are with material repression and violence. However, there is a sense in some later postcolonial theory that this concern with representations – with story or text – has swallowed up any interest in the world that is being represented.

Let us return to Equiano one more time. After a period spent slowly accumulating wealth and knowledge, treading the tightrope of a fragile, always impugnable freedom, Equiano finally gains a note of commendation from his one-time owner and heads to London: "With a light heart I bade Monserrat farewell, and never had my feet on it since; and with it I bade adieu to the sound of the cruel whip, and all other dreadful instruments of torture; adieu to the offensive sight of the violated chastity of the sable females, which has too often accosted my eyes; adieu to oppressions" (Edwards 1988: 121). Postcolonial literary studies treats migration generally in terms of its epiphanies: new sight, new knowledge, a new understanding of the relativity of things. All of which, of course, must be true in many respects. Equiano, however, forces us back to the awkward fact we touched on earlier. Migration can *also* entail a deliberate, even self-deluding blindness. Does the oppression in Montserrat end while Equiano takes up a position as a hairdresser in London? Of course not; he determinedly states the abolitionist case, sprinkling it with Pope and Milton, precisely *because* he knows the brutality continues. However, as his statement makes clear, life for the manumitted slave in London is not just easier, economically and physically, it is also easier to *live with*. In the colonies, as Marx pointed out in a slightly different context, capitalism stood exposed, stripped of the "beautiful illusions" that made it seem acceptable and rational in Europe (1976: 935). In the same way the capitalism of today is stripped, in the subcontracted clothes factories of Ras Jebel and Tae Kwang Vina, of the "beautiful illusions" held up by globalization's neoliberal proponents.

In a novel by the Nigerian author, Cyprian Ekwensi, the main character Iska says at one point: "What I want is to go away from Nigeria – to England, France, America, anywhere at all. As long as it's away! . . . From there I can read all about Nigeria from a distance. It will all be like fiction and won't hurt much" (1966: 199–200). So much work in postcolonial literary studies takes up Iska's position, treating the politics of the wider world as a narrative form, agreeing with Iain Chambers that "if what passes for knowledge emerges in language, then critical knowledge involves an exploration of language itself" (1994: 32). However, if we replace the lens of culture with that of class we have to focus on the fact that this theoretical discourse is, as Arif Dirlik (1994) and Aijaz Ahmad (1992, 1995a, 1995b) have argued in well-known critiques, the product of middle-class First-World intellectuals of Third-World origin whose geographical migrations have often *also* entailed upward class movement. We need at least to question the automatically radical associations given to migrancy in postcolonial literary theory and notice how it can also involve increased disguise. As Spivak has pointed out, there is a danger here that the postcolonial fascination with migrancy becomes a kind of *alibi*, erected in place of a genuine confrontation with the lives of those at the receiving end of global capitalism's polarizing action (1999: 361). Here is Dirlik's uncompromising charge: "postcoloniality is designed to *avoid* making sense of the current crisis and, in the process, to cover up the origins of postcolonial intellectuals in a global capitalism of which they are not so much victims as beneficiaries" (1994: 353). Seen from one angle, postcolonial theory's inside–outside stance, its "immanent" criticism of Western modes of thought *is* its most radical point. It results from its historical relationship to migrancy and explains its continuing fascination with cultural hybridity. Seen from another angle, however, this same inside–outside position can also seem like its weakest and most complicit aspect. Equiano's book is not only his life-story. It is also his attempt to "damn the vessel on which my life depended." A great deal of his time is spent arguing against the very trade in which he had been forced to work to buy his freedom. He ends his book marshaling these arguments, appealing to his reader on humanitarian and moral grounds, interlacing these with bitter ironic asides about "Christian" behavior. Primarily, though, because he knows his audience, Equiano argues that the slave trade is not in British *economic* interests. His closing gambit is a rhetorical appeal to the financially minded reader to imagine how Africa "lays open an endless field of commerce to the British manufacturers and merchant adventurer[s]" (Edwards 1988: 169). With the benefit of historical hindsight it is clear that Equiano ends up arguing for the continuation of the very system which gave rise to slavery and which later shifted its exploitation into colonial and other forms. His position in Britain, the audience he was addressing, the dynamics of publishing his book: in short, all the consequences of his migration lead into the argument he chooses. Against all its own intentions, postcolonial theory may be making similarly compromised arguments, for similar positional reasons. Timothy Brennan asks the question thus: "How is it possible to divorce the near unanimity in humanistic theory of the tropes of traversing, being between, migrating, and so forth from the climate created by the 'global vision of a capitalist or technocratic monoculture'?" (1997: 18; see also Dirlik 1995).

A return to romanticism

Postcolonial theory does reflect real changes in the order of the world, and emerges from a specific period of historical disappointment. It deals with new forms of social life and experience, and with new questions raised by unprecedented levels of human movement and interaction. Yet, scratch the surface of this newness and disconcertingly familiar archetypes of Western culture become discernible. Nowhere is this more apparent than with respect to the emblematic figure of the migrant. The producers of "high" forms of art and literature have always tended to see the outsider as an appropriate self-image. At least one brand of romanticism, for example, threatened by the fact that the marketplace was reducing artistic labor to commodity production pure and simple, responded by trying to step beyond modern life. Thomas Love Peacock, a friend of Percy Shelley, half-jokingly satirized the romantic argument as being: "all that is artificial is anti-poetical. Society is artificial, therefore we will live out of society" (Brett-Smith 1972: 14). Later in the romantic tradition Matthew Arnold would individualize this argument in the figure of the scholar–gypsy, the natural artist who deliberately withdraws from the shabbiness of modern life. Arnold urges him on his way: "fly our paths, our feverish contact fly! / For strong the infection of our mental strife / Which though it gives no bliss, yet spoils for rest." In other words, there was in romanticism, as there would be for the exiles and expatriates who led the modernist movement, a strong attachment to the idea of the "poet's painful but necessary isolation, in his creativity" (Abrams 1953: 281). Even more so to the "stereotype of the poète maudit, endowed with an ambiguous gift of sensibility which makes him at the same time more blessed and more cursed than the other members of a society from which he is . . . an outcast" (103).

My point here is that traces of this figure and this position continually re-emerge in postcolonial literary theory's trope of migrancy. This is not the result of some unremarked recycling of ideas about art and its producers. Rather it is because the position of those who produce the most valued, most acceptable art and literature under capitalism involves the same contradictions for a Rushdie or an Okri as it did for a Wordsworth or a Coleridge. Writers, academics, and artists hold a position in society that is reliant on ownership of high levels of *cultural* capital – that is, the knowledge and understanding of consecrated cultural forms. They therefore instinctively adopt a position of "distance," of detachment, of separation from the messy, muddied world of economic transactions. This is why, according to Pierre Bourdieu, there is a tendency for artistic schools, in various but repeating ways, to "transform the privation linked to exclusion . . . into a cognitive privilege" (2000: 224). Just as the romantics took up the image of the rustic traveler and just as modernism adopted the figure of the urban exile, so postcolonial literary theory takes the modern global migrant as its own self-portrait. To say this is neither to denigrate the experiences of those migrant writers and thinkers who have been so influential, nor to deflate the importance of the criticisms they have leveled at Eurocentric historical and cultural methods. It should, however, put us on our guard against the possibility of making severance from daily political struggle seem a virtue in itself. Here is Raymond Williams discussing the modernist movement in words that might equally apply to postcolonial literary theory: "Their self-referentiality, their propinquity and mutual isolation all served to represent the artist as necessarily estranged, and to ratify as canonical the works of radical estrangement. So, to *want* to leave your settlement and settle nowhere . . . becomes presented, in another ideological move, as a normal condition" (1989: 35). Another way of understanding this is to think about what migration into the West looks like from the point of view of those who have refused, or cannot make, that journey. Let me, in closing, quote the Nigerian writer Femi Osofisan, whose words hold up a mirror to the celebrations of hybridity and migrancy so prevalent in postcolonial theory:

[A]lmost all authors of the new movement are living in exile, either outside the continent, or in some other country than that of their birth; . . . all of them are published abroad, on the list of publishing houses in the capitalist centres of Europe and America. That first point, about their enforced exile, immediately positions them as disillusioned fugitives; and the second, their place of publication, dictates that their audience will be largely foreign. These two factors therefore determine their chosen style – a disjointed, postmodern prose, dissonant and delirious, in conformity with the current respectable literary fashion in the west (confirmed by their ability to win these glittering prizes); and an ahistorical, unideological vocation, in celebration of their escape from, and abandonment of, the African predicament. (1997)

REFERENCES

Abdel-Malek, Anouar 1981. *Nation and Revolution*. Trans. Mike Gonzalez. Albany: State University of New York Press.

Abrams, M. H. 1953. *The Mirror and the Lamp: Romantic Theory and the Critical Tradition*. Oxford and New York: Oxford University Press.

Abu-Lughod, Janet 1989. "On the Remaking of History: How to Reinvent the Past." *Remaking History*. Ed. Barbara Kruger and Phil Mariani. Seattle: Bay Press, 111–29.

Achebe, Chinua 1974. *Arrow of God* [1964]. 2nd edn. London: Heinemann.

1975. "The African Writer and the English Language." *Morning Yet on Creation Day*. New York: Anchor, 74–84.

1976. *Things Fall Apart* [1958]. London, Ibadan, Nairobi: Heinemann.

1984. *The Trouble with Nigeria*. London: Heinemann.

1988. "An Image of Africa." *Hopes and Impediments: Selected Essays*. New York: Doubleday, 1–20.

Achúgar, Hugo 1998. "Leones, cazadores e historiadores. A propósito de las políticas de la memoria y del conocimiento." *Teorías sin disciplina. Postcolonialidad y globalización en debate*. Ed. Santiago Castro-Gómez and Eduardo Mendieta. Mexico: Miguel Angel Porrúa, 271–85.

Adorno, Rolena 1993. "Reconsidering Colonial Discourse for Sixteenth- and Seventeenth-Century Spanish America." *Latin American Research Review* 28.3: 135–52.

Adorno, Theodor W. 1987. *Negative Dialectics* [1966]. Trans. E. B. Ashton. New York: Continuum.

Afzal-Khan, Fawzia and Kalpana Seshadri-Crooks, eds. 2000. *The Pre-Occupation of Postcolonial Studies*. Durham and London: Duke University Press.

Agamben, Giorgio 1993. *The Coming Community*. Trans. Michael Hardt. Minneapolis and London: University of Minnesota Press.

Ageron, Charles-Robert 1991. *Modern Algeria: A History from 1830 to the Present* [1964]. Trans. Michael Brett. Trenton, NJ: Africa World Press.

Ahmad, Aijaz 1992. *In Theory: Classes, Nations, Literatures*. London and New York: Verso.

1995a. "The Politics of Literary Postcoloniality." *Race & Class* 36.3: 1–20.

1995b. "Postcolonialism: What's in a Name?" *Late Imperial Culture*. Ed. Román de la Campa, E. Ann Kaplan, and Michael Sprinker. London: Verso, 11–32.

Alam, Javeed 1999. *India: Living with Modernity*. Delhi: Oxford University Press.

Alavi, Hamza 1972. "The State in Post-Colonial Societies." *New Left Review* 74: 59–81.

Alavi, Hamza, P. Burns, G. Knight, P. Mayer, and D. McEachern 1982. *Capitalism and Colonial Production*. London: Croom Helm.

Alexander, M. Jacqui 2000. "Not Just (Any) *Body* Can Be a Citizen: The Politics of Law, Sexuality and Postcoloniality in Trinidad and Tobago and the Bahamas." *Cultures of Empire: A Reader*. Ed. Catherine Hall. Manchester: Manchester University Press, 359–76.

Alexander, M. Jacqui, and Chandra Talpade Mohanty, eds. 1997. *Feminist Genealogies, Colonial Legacies, Democratic Futures*. New York and London: Routledge.

Aloysius, G. 1997. *Nationalism without a Nation in India*. Delhi: Oxford University Press.

Amin, Samir 1970. *The Maghreb in the Modern World: Algeria, Tunisia, Morocco*. Trans. Michael Perl. Harmondsworth: Penguin.

1974. *Accumulation on a World Scale: A Critique of the Theory of Underdevelopment* [1970]. 2 vols. Trans. Brian Pearce. New York: Monthly Review Press.

1976. *Unequal Development: An Essay on the Social Formations of Peripheral Capitalism*. New York: Monthly Review Press.

1989. *Eurocentrism*. Trans. Russell Moore. New York: Monthly Review Press.

1992. *Empire of Chaos*. Trans. W. H. Locke Anderson. New York: Monthly Review Press.

1994. *Re-Reading the Postwar Period: An Intellectual Itinerary*. Trans. Michael Wolfers. New York: Monthly Review Press.

1997. *Capitalism in the Age of Globalization: The Management of Contemporary Society*. London and New Jersey: Zed.

1998. *Spectres of Capitalism: A Critique of Current Intellectual Fashions*. Trans. Henry Mage. New York: Monthly Review Press.

Amin, Samir, Giovanni Arrighi, Andre Gunder Frank, and Immanuel Wallerstein 1990. *Transforming the Revolution: Social Movements and the World-System*. New York: Monthly Review Press.

Amin, Shahid 1988. "Gandhi as Mahatma: Gorakhpur District, Eastern UP, 1921–2" [1983]. *Selected Subaltern Studies*. Ed. Ranajit Guha and Gayatri Chakravorty Spivak. New York and London: Oxford University Press, 288–350.

1995. *Event, Metaphor, Memory: Chauri Chaura, 1922–1992*. Berkeley, Los Angeles, London: University of California Press.

Amireh, Amal, and Lis Suhair Majaj, eds. 2000. *Going Global: The Transnational Reception of Third World Women Writers*. New York and London: Garland Publishing, Inc.

Anderson, Benedict 1991. *Imagined Communities: Reflections on the Origins and Spread of Nationalism* [1983]. Rev. edn. London and New York: Verso.

Anderson, Perry 2002. "Internationalism: A Breviary." *New Left Review* 14 (2nd series): 5–25.

Anozie, Sunday O. 1984. "Negritude, Structuralism, Deconstruction." *Black Literature and Literary Theory*. Ed. Henry Louis Gates, Jr. New York and London: Methuen, 105–26.

Ansell-Pearson, Keith, Benita Parry, and Judith Squires, eds. 1997. *Cultural Readings of Imperialism: Edward Said and the Gravity of History*. New York: St. Martin's Press; London: Lawrence and Wishart.

Appadurai, Arjun 1996. *Modernity at Large: Cultural Dimensions of Globalization.* Minneapolis and London: University of Minnesota Press.

Appiah, Kwame Anthony 1991. "Is the Post- in Postmodernism the Post- in Postcolonial?" *Critical Inquiry* 17: 336–51.

　1992. *In My Father's House: Africa in the Philosophy of Culture.* Oxford and New York: Oxford University Press.

　2001. "Cosmopolitan Reading." *Cosmopolitan Geographies.* Ed. Vinay Dharwadker. London and New York: Routledge, 197–227.

Arac, Jonathan, and Harriet Ritvo, eds. 1991. *Macropolitics of Nineteenth-Century Literature: Nationalism, Exoticism, Imperialism.* Philadelphia: University of Pennsylvania Press.

Aravamudan, Srinivas 1998. "Postcolonial Affiliations: Ulysses and All About H. Hatterr." *Transcultural Joyce.* Ed. Karen Lawrence. Cambridge: Cambridge University Press, 97–128.

Armah, Ayi Kwei 1981. *The Beautyful Ones Are Not Yet Born* [1968]. London: Heinemann.

Arnold, A. James 1981. *Modernism and Negritude.* Cambridge, MA: Harvard University Press.

Arnold, David 1984. "Adivasi Assertion in South Gujarat: The Devi Movement of 1922–23." *Subaltern Studies* III: *Writings on South Asian History and Society.* Ed. Ranajit Guha. New Delhi: Oxford University Press, 196–230.

　1993. *Colonizing the Body: State Medicine and Epidemic Disease in Nineteenth-Century India.* Berkeley, Los Angeles, and London: University of California Press.

　2000. "Gramsci and Peasant Subalternity in India" [1984]. *Mapping Subaltern Studies and the Postcolonial.* Ed. Vinayak Chaturvedi. London and New York: Verso, 24–49.

Arrighi, Giovanni 1994. *The Long Twentieth Century: Money, Power, and the Origins of Our Times.* London: Verso.

Asante, Molefi Kete 1990. "The African Essence in African American Language." *African Culture: The Rhythms of Unity.* Ed. M. K. Asante and K. W. Asante. Trenton, NJ: Africa World Press, 233–52.

Ashcroft, Bill 1999. "Modernity's First Born: Latin America and Post-Colonial Transformation." *El debate de la postcolonialidad en Latinoamérica.* Ed. Alfonso de Toro and Fernando de Toro. Madrid: Iberoamericana, 13–30.

　2001. *On Post-Colonial Futures: Transformations of Colonial Culture.* London and New York: Continuum.

Ashcroft, Bill, and Pal Ahluwalia 1999. *Edward Said: The Paradox of Identity.* London and New York: Routledge.

Ashcroft, Bill, Gareth Griffiths, and Helen Tiffin 1989. *The Empire Writes Back: Theory and Practice in Post-Colonial Literatures.* London and New York: Routledge.

　eds. 1995. *The Post-colonial Studies Reader.* London and New York: Routledge.

Ashfar, Haleh, ed. 1996. *Women and Politics in the Third World.* London: Routledge.

Balandier, George 1951. "La situation coloniale: Approche théorique." *Cahiers internationaux de sociologie* 11.51: 44–79.

Barker, Francis, Peter Hulme, and Margaret Iversen, eds. 1994. *Colonial Discourse / Postcolonial Theory.* Manchester and New York: Manchester University Press.

Bartolovich, Crystal, and Neil Lazarus, eds. 2002. *Marxism, Modernity and Post-colonial Studies*. Cambridge: Cambridge University Press.

Basu, Amrita, ed. 1995. *The Challenge of Local Feminisms: Women's Movements in Global Perspectives*. Boulder: Westview Press.

Bauman, Zygmunt 1998. *Globalization: The Human Consequences*. New York: Columbia University Press.

Bayly, C. A. 1998. *Origins of Nationality in South Asia: Patriotism and Ethical Government in the Making of Modern India*. New Delhi: Oxford University Press.

Bell, Daniel 1960. *The End of Ideology. On the Exhaustion of Political Ideas in the Fifties*. Glencoe, IL: Free Press of Glencoe.

Bello, Walden, with Shea Cunningham and Bill Rau 1999. *Dark Victory: The United States and Global Poverty*. London: Pluto Press, in association with Food First, Oakland, and the Transnational Institute, Amsterdam.

Benjamin, Walter 1969a. "The Storyteller: Reflections on the Works of Nikolai Leskov [1936]." *Illuminations*. Trans. Harry Zohn. New York: Schocken Books, 83–109.

1969b. "Theses on the Philosophy of History [1950]." *Illuminations*. Trans. Harry Zohn. New York: Schocken Books, 253–64.

1996. "The Life Of Students" [1915]. Trans. Rodney Livingstone. *Selected Writings*. Vol I: *1913–1926*. Ed. Marcus Bullock and Michael W. Jennings. Cambridge, MA, and London: Harvard University Press, 37–47.

Bentham, Jeremy 1995. *Colonies, Commerce, and Constitutional law. "Rid your-selves of Ultramaria" and other Writings on Spain and Spanish America* [1822]. Ed. Philip Schofield. Oxford: Clarendon Press.

Berman, Bruce, and John Londsdale 1992. *Unhappy Valley. Conflict in Kenya and Africa*. London: James Currey.

Bernabé, Jean, Patrick Chamoiseau, and Raphaël Confiant 1990. *Éloge de la Créolité: In Praise of Creoleness* [1989]. Bilingual text, English trans. Mohamed B. Taleb-Khyar. Baltimore: Johns Hopkins University Press.

Bernasconi, Robert. 1996. "Casting the Slough: Fanon's New Humanism for a New Humanity." *Fanon: A Critical Reader*. Ed. Lewis R. Gordon, T. Denean Sharpley-Whiting, and Renée T. White. Oxford: Blackwell, 113–21.

Betts, Raymond F. 1998. *Decolonization*. London and New York: Routledge.

Beverley, John 1993. *Against Literature*. Minneapolis: University of Minnesota Press.

1999. *Subalternity and Representation: Arguments in Cultural Theory*. Durham and London: Duke University Press.

2000. "The Dilemma of Subaltern Studies at Duke." *Nepantla: Views from the South* 1.1: 33–44.

Bhabha, Homi K. 1984. "Representation and the Colonial Text: A Critical Explo-ration of Some Forms of Mimeticism." *The Theory of Reading*. Ed. Frank Gloversmith. Brighton: The Harvester Press; New York: Barnes and Noble, 93–122.

ed. 1990a. *Nation and Narration*. London and New York: Routledge.

1990b. "DissemiNation: Time, Narrative, and the Margins of the Modern Nation." *Nation and Narration*. Ed. Homi K. Bhabha. London and New York: Routledge, 291–322.

1994. *The Location of Culture*. London and New York: Routledge.

Bhagwati, Jagdish 2001. "Why Globalization Is Good." *Items & Issues* 2.3–4: 7–8.

Biddle, Arthur, ed. 1995. *Global Voices: Contemporary Literature from the Non-Western World*. Englewood Cliffs: Prentice Hall.

Bivona, Daniel 1990. *Desire and Contradiction: Imperial Visions and Domestic Debates in Victorian Literature*. Manchester: Manchester University Press.

Blaut, J. M. 1993. *The Colonizer's Model of the World: Geographical Diffusionism and Eurocentric History*. New York and London: Guilford.

Bloch, Ernst 1977. "Non-synchronism and the Obligation to Its Dialectics" [1932]. Trans. Mark Ritter. *New German Critique* 11: 22–38.

Blum, William 2003. *Killing Hope: US Military and CIA Interventions Since World War II*. London: Zed.

Boehmer, Elleke 1992. "Motherlands, Mothers and Nationalist Sons: Representations of Nationalism and Women in African Literature." *From Commonwealth to Post-Colonial*. Ed. Anna Rutherford. Sydney: Dangaroo Press, 229–47.

  1995. *Colonial and Postcolonial Literature*. Oxford: Oxford University Press.

Bose, Sugata, and Ayesha Jalal 2002. *Modern South Asia: History, Culture, Political Economy*. London and New York: Routledge.

Bourdieu, Pierre 1998. *Acts of Resistance: Against the New Myths of Our Time*. Trans. Richard Nice. Oxford: Polity.

  2000. *Pascalian Meditations*. Trans. Richard Nice. Oxford: Polity.

  2001. "Uniting to Better Dominate." *Items & Issues* 2.3–4: 1–6.

Boyarin, Daniel, and Jonathan Boyarin 1993. "Diaspora: Generation and the Ground of Jewish Identity." *Critical Inquiry* 19.4: 693–725.

Brah, Avtar 1996. *Cartographies of Diaspora: Contesting Identities*. New York and London: Routledge.

Brah, Avtar, and Annie E. Coombes, eds. 2000. *Hybridity and Its Discontents: Politics, Science, Culture*. London and New York: Routledge.

Brantlinger, Patrick 1988. *Rule of Darkness: British Literature and Imperialism 1830–1914*. Ithaca: Cornell University Press.

Brathwaite, Kamau 1993. "History of the Voice" [1979–81]. *Roots*. Ann Arbor: University of Michigan Press, 259–304.

Braudel, Fernand 1992. "Economies in Space: The World Economies" and "By Way of a Conclusion: Past and Present." *Civilization and Capitalism: 15th–18th Century*. Vol. III of *The Perspective of the World*. [1979]. Trans. Siân Reynolds. Berkeley and Los Angeles: University of California Press, 21–45, 617–32.

Brecher, Jeremy, and Tim Costello 1994. *Global Village or Global Pillage: Economic Reconstruction from the Bottom Up*. Boston: South End Press.

Brennan, Timothy 1989. *Salman Rushdie and the Third World: Myths of the Nation*. New York: St. Martin's Press.

  1990. "The National Longing for Form." *Nation and Narration*. Ed. Homi K. Bhabha. London and New York: Routledge, 44–70.

  1992. "Places of Mind, Occupied Lands: Edward Said and Philology." *Edward Said: A Critical Reader*. Ed. Michael Sprinker. Oxford: Blackwell, 74–95.

  1997. *At Home in the World: Cosmopolitanism Now*. Cambridge: Harvard University Press.

  2000. "The Illusion of a Future: Orientalism as Traveling Theory." *Critical Inquiry* 26: 558–83.

2001. "Antonio Gramsci and Post-Colonial Theory: 'Southernism.'" *Diaspora* 10.2: 143–87.

2002a. "Cosmo-Theory." *South Atlantic Quarterly* 100.3: 657–89.

2002b. "Postcolonial Studies between the European Wars: An Intellectual History." *Marxism, Modernity and Postcolonial Studies*. Ed. Crystal Bartolovich and Neil Lazarus. Cambridge: Cambridge University Press, 185–203.

Brett, E. A. 1985. *The World Economy Since the War: The Politics of Uneven Development*. Basingstoke: Macmillan.

Brett-Smith, H. F. B., ed. 1972. *Peacock's Four Ages of Poetry; Shelley's Defence of Poetry; Browning's Essay on Shelley* [1921]. Oxford: Basil Blackwell.

Brewer, Anthony 1980. *Marxist Theories of Imperialism*. London: Routledge and Kegan Paul.

Buck-Morss, Susan 2000. "Hegel and Haiti." *Critical Inquiry* 26.4: 821–65.

Burbach, Roger, and William Robinson 1999. "The Fin de Siècle Debate: Globalization as Epochal Shift." *Science and Society* 63: 10–39.

Busia, Abena 1989. "Silencing Sycorax: On African Colonial Discourse and the Unvoiced Female." *Cultural Critique* 14: 81–104.

Bustos, Guillermo 2002. "Enfoque subalterno e historia latinoamericana: nación y escritura de la historia en el debate Mallon–Beverley." Unpublished manuscript.

Cabral, Amilcar 1969. "The Weapon of Theory." *Revolution in Guinea: Selected Texts*. Trans. and ed. Richard Handyside. New York and London: Monthly Review Press, 90–111.

1973. *Return to the Source: Selected Speeches of Amilcar Cabral*. Ed. Africa Information Service. New York and London: Monthly Review Press.

Cain, P. J., and A. G. Hopkins 1993. *British Imperialism: Crisis and Deconstruction 1914–1990*. London and New York: Longman.

Cairns, David, and Shaun Richards 1988. *Writing Ireland: Colonialism, Nationalism and Culture*. Manchester: Manchester University Press.

Cardoso, Fernando Henrique 1977. "The Consumption of Dependency Theory in the United States." *Latin American Research Review* 12.3: 7–24.

Castells, Manuel 1998. *The Information Age: Economy Society and Culture*. Vol. I: *The Rise of the Network Society*; Vol. II: *The Power of Identity*; Vol. III: *End of Millennium*. Oxford: Blackwell.

Castle, Gregory, ed. 2001. *Postcolonial Discourses: An Anthology*. Oxford: Blackwell.

Castles, Stephen 1998. *The Age of Migration: International Population Movements in the Modern World*. 2nd edn. Basingstoke: Macmillan.

Castro-Gómez, Santiago, and Eduardo Mendieta, eds. 1998. *Teorías sin disciplina. Latinoamericanismo, postcolonialidad y globalización en debate*. Mexico: Miguel Angel Porrúa.

Castro-Klarén, Sara 1999. "Mimicry Revisited: Latin America, Post-colonial Theory and the Location of Knowledge." *El debate de la postcolonialidad en Latinoamérica*. Ed. Alfonso de Toro and Fernando de Toro. Madrid: Iberoamericana, 137–64.

2001. "Historiography on the Ground: The Toledo Circle and Guamán Poma". *The Latin American Subaltern Studies Reader*. Ed. Ileana Rodríguez. Durham and London: Duke University Press.

Caute, David 1970. *Fanon*. New York: Viking.

Caygill, Howard 1998. *Walter Benjamin: The Colour of Experience*. London and New York: Routledge.

Césaire, Aimé 1970. "The Responsibility of the Artist" [1959]. *The Africa Reader: Independent Africa*. Ed. Wilfred Cartey and Martin Kilson. New York: Vintage, 153–61.

  1972. *Discourse on Colonialism* [1955]. Trans. Joan Pinkham. New York and London: Monthly Review Press.

  1983. "Notebook of a Return to the Native Land" [1956]. *The Collected Poetry*. Trans. and ed. Clayton Eshleman and Annette Smith. Berkeley, Los Angeles, London: University of California Press, 32–85.

Chakrabarty, Dipesh 2000a. *Provincializing Europe: Postcolonial Thought and Historical Difference*. Princeton: Princeton University Press.

  2000b. "Radical Histories and the Question of Enlightenment Rationalism: Some Recent Critiques of Subaltern Studies" [1995]. *Mapping Subaltern Studies and the Postcolonial*. Ed. Vinayak Chaturvedi. New York and London: Verso, 256–80.

Chambers, Iain 1994. *Migrancy, Identity, Culture*. London and New York: Routledge.

Chandavarkar, Rajnarayan 1998. *Imperial Power and Popular Politics: Class, Resistance and the State in India, c. 1850–1950*. Cambridge: Cambridge University Press.

Chandra, Bipan 1979. *Nationalism and Colonialism in Modern India*. New Delhi: Orient Longman.

  1981. "Karl Marx, His Theories of Asian Societies, and Colonial Rule." *Review* 5.1: 13–91.

Chandra, Bipan, M. Mukherjee, A. Mukherjee, S. Mahajan, and K. M. Panikkar, eds. 1989. *India's Struggle for Independence, 1857–1947*. New Delhi: Penguin.

Chatterjee, Partha 1986. *Nationalist Thought and the Colonial World: A Derivative Discourse*. Minneapolis: University of Minnesota Press.

  1993. *The Nation and its Fragments: Colonial and Postcolonial Histories*. Princeton: Princeton University Press.

  1997a. *A Possible India: Essays in Political Criticism*. Delhi: Oxford University Press.

  1997b. "Introduction: A Political History of Independent India." *State and Politics in India*. Ed. Partha Chatterjee. Delhi: Oxford University Press, 1–39.

Chaturvedi, Vinayak ed. 2000. *Mapping Subaltern Studies and the Postcolonial*. London and New York: Verso.

Chaudhuri, Amit 2002. "Poles of Recovery." *Interventions* 4.1: 89–105.

Cheyfitz, Eric 1991. *The Poetics of Imperialism: Translation and Colonization from "The Tempest" to "Tarzan."* New York and Oxford: Oxford University Press.

Chiaramonte, Juan Carlos 1997. *Ciudades, provincias, estado. Orígenes de la nación argentina*. Buenos Aires: Ariel.

Chilcote, Ronald H. ed. 2000. *Imperialism: Theoretical Directions*. Amherst, NY: Humanity Books.

Childs, Peter, ed. 1999. *Post-Colonial Theory and English Literature: A Reader*. Edinburgh: Edinburgh University Press.

Childs, Peter, and Patrick Williams 1997. *An Introduction to Post-Colonial Theory*. London: Prentice Hall.

Chinweizu, Onwuchekwa Jemie, and Ihechukwu Madubuike 1983. *Towards the Decolonization of African Literature*. Washington, DC: Howard University Press.

Chomsky, Noam 1987. *The Chomsky Reader*. Ed. James Peck. New York: Pantheon.
1992. *Deterring Democracy*. New York: Hill and Wang.

Chow, Rey 1991. *Woman and Chinese Modernity: The Politics of Reading Between West and East*. Minneapolis: University of Minnesota Press.

1993. *Writing Diaspora: Tactics of Intervention in Contemporary Cultural Studies*. Bloomington: Indiana University Press.

1995. "The Fascist Longings in our Midst." *Ariel: A Review of International Literature* 26.1: 23–50.

1999. "The Politics of Admittance: Female Sexual Agency, Miscegenation, and the Formation of Community in Frantz Fanon." *Frantz Fanon: Critical Perspectives*. Ed. Anthony C. Alessandri. London and New York: Routledge, 34–56.

Chrisman, Laura 1995. "Inventing Post-colonial Theory: Polemical Observations." *Pretexts* 5.1–2: 205–12.

2000. *Rereading the Imperial Romance: British Imperialism and South African Resistance in Haggard, Schreiner and Plaatje*. Oxford: Clarendon Press.

Clarke, Simon 1981. *The Foundations of Structuralism: A Critique of Lévi-Strauss and the Structuralist Movement*. Brighton: The Harvester Press.

1990. "The Crisis of Fordism or the Crisis of Social Democracy?" *Telos* 83: 71–98.

Clayton, Anthony 1994. *The Wars of French Decolonization*. London: Longman.

Clegg, Ian 1979. "Workers and Managers in Algeria." *Peasants and Proletarians: The Struggles of Third World Workers*. Ed. Robin Cohen, Peter C. W. Gutkind, and Phyllis Brazier. New York: Monthly Review Press, 223–47.

Clifford, James 1992. "Travelling Cultures." *Cultural Studies*. Ed. Lawrence Grossberg, Cary Nelson, and Paula Treichler. London and New York: Routledge, 96–116.

1994. "Diasporas." *Current Anthropology* 9.3: 302–38.

Cockburn, Alexander 1997. *The Golden Age Is in Us: Journeys and Encounters 1987–1994*. London and New York: Verso.

Cohen, Robin 1987. *The New Helots: Migrants in the International Division of Labour*. Aldershot: Avebury.

1997. *Global Diasporas: An Introduction*. Seattle: University of Washington Press.

Cohn, Bernard 1985. "The Command of Language and the Language of Command." *Subaltern Studies* IV: *Writings on South Asian History and Society*. Ed. Ranajit Guha. New Delhi: Oxford University Press, 276–329.

Colás, Santiago 1995. "Of Creole Symptoms, Cuban Fantasies, and Other Latin American Postcolonial Ideologies." *Publications of the Modern Language Association of America* 110.3: 382–96.

Collingwood, R. G. 1961. *The Idea of History* [1946]. London: Oxford University Press.

Connolly, James 1997a. "What is a Free Nation?" [1916]. *James Connolly: Selected Writings*. Ed. Peter Berresford Ellis. London: Pluto Press, 138–42.

1997b. "Woman" [1915]. *James Connolly: Selected Writings*. Ed. Peter Berresford Ellis. London: Pluto Press: 189–95.

Conrad, Joseph 1982. *Heart of Darkness* [1898]. Harmondsworth: Penguin.

Coombes, Annie E. 1994. *Reinventing Africa: Museums, Material Culture and Popular Imagination in Late Victorian and Edwardian England*. New Haven and London: Yale University Press.

Cooper, Frederick, and Ann Laura Stoler, eds. 1997. *Tensions of Empire: Colonial Cultures in a Bourgeois World*. Berkeley, Los Angeles, and London: University of California Press.

Coronil, Fernando 1992. "Can Postcoloniality be Decolonized? Imperial Banality and Postcolonial Power." *Public Culture* 5.1: 89–108.

1995. "Introduction: Transculturation and the Politics of Theory– Countering the Center, Cuban Counterpoint." *Cuban Counterpoint: Tobacco and Sugar*. Fernando Ortiz. Durham and London: Duke University Press, ix–lvi.

1996. "Beyond Occidentalism: Towards Nonimperial Geohistorical Categories." *Cultural Anthropology* 11.1: 52–87.

1997. *The Magical State: Nature, Money, and Modernity in Venezuela*. Chicago: University of Chicago Press.

2000. "Towards a Critique of Globalcentrism: Speculations on Capitalism's Nature." *Public Culture* 12.2: 351–74.

2004. "Globalización liberal o Imperialismo Global: cinco piezas para armar el rompecabezas del presente." *Temas*: forthcoming.

Costello, Nicholas, Jonathan Michie, and Seumas Milne 1989. *Beyond the Casino Economy: Planning for the 1990s*. London: Verso.

Cox, Oliver C. 1959. *The Foundations of Capitalism*. New York: Philosophical Library.

1962. *Capitalism and American Leadership*. New York: Philosophical Library.

1964. *Capitalism as a System*. New York: Monthly Review Press.

Craig, Gordon 1981. *Germany 1866–1945*. Oxford: Oxford University Press.

Crane, Ralph 1992. *Inventing India: A History of India in English-Language Fiction*. Basingstoke: Macmillan.

Dangarembga, Tsitsi 1988. *Nervous Conditions*. Seattle: Seal.

Datta Gupta, Sobhanlal 1980. *Comintern, India and the Colonial Question, 1920–1937*. Calcutta: K. P. Bagchi.

David, Deirdre 1995. *Rule Britannia: Women, Empire and Victorian Writing*. Ithaca and London: Cornell University Press.

Davidson, Basil 1978. *Let Freedom Come: Africa in Modern History*. Boston and Toronto: Little, Brown and Company.

1983. *Modern Africa*. London: Longman.

1986. "On Revolutionary Nationalism: The Legacy of Amilcar Cabral." *Race & Class* 27.3: 21–47.

1989. *The Fortunate Isles: A Study in African Transformation*. London, Sydney, Auckland, Johannesburg: Hutchinson.

1992. *The Black Man's Burden: Africa and the Curse of the Nation-State*. New York: Times Books.

Department of Trade and Industry (UK) 2002. *Knowledge Migrants: The Motivations and Experiences of Professionals in the UK on Work Permits – Final Report*. London: Department of Trade and Industry.

Derrida, Jacques 1976. *Of Grammatology* [1967]. Trans. Gayatri Chakravorty Spivak. Baltimore: Johns Hopkins University Press.

　1982. "Structure, Sign, and Play in the Discourse of the Human Sciences" [1967]. *Writing and Difference*. Trans. Alan Bass. Chicago: University of Chicago Press, 278–93.

Desai, Ashwin 2002. *We Are the Poors: Community Struggles in Post-Apartheid South Africa*. New York: Monthly Review Press, 2002.

Dews, Peter 1987. *Logic of Disintegration: Post-structuralist Thought and the Claims of Critical Theory*. London: Verso.

Dirlik, Arif 1994. "The Postcolonial Aura: Third World Criticism in the Age of Global Capitalism." *Critical Inquiry* 20.2: 328–56.

　1995. "Bringing History Back In: Of Diasporas, Hybridities, Places, and Histories." *Review of Education / Pedagogy / Cultural Studies* 21.2: 95–131.

　1997. *The Postcolonial Aura: Third World Criticism in the Age of Global Capitalism*. Boulder: Westview Press.

Djebar, Assia 1993. *Fantasia: An Algerian Cavalcade* [1985]. Trans. Dorothy S. Blair. London and Portsmouth, NH: Heinemann.

Dubey, Madhu 1998. "The 'True Lie' of the Nation: Fanon and Feminism." *differences: A Journal of Feminist Cultural Studies* 10.1: 1–29.

　2002. "Postmodernism as Postnationalism? Racial Representation in US Black Cultural Studies." *New Formations* 45: 150–68.

Du Bois, W. E. B. 1977. *Black Reconstruction in America* [1938]. New York: Atheneum.

During, Simon 1998. "Postcolonialism and Globalisation: A Dialectical Relation After All?" *Postcolonial Studies* 1.1: 31–47.

Dussel, Enrique 1995. *The Invention of the Americas*. Trans. Michael D. Barber. New York: Continuum.

　1998. "Beyond Eurocentrism: The World-System and the Limits of Modernity." *The Cultures of Globalization*. Ed. Fredric Jameson and Masao Miyoshi. Durham and London: Duke University Press, 3–31.

Eagleton, Terry, Fredric Jameson, and Edward W. Said 1990. *Nationalism, Colonialism, and Literature*. Minneapolis: University of Minnesota Press.

Edwards, Paul, ed. 1988. *The Life of Olaudah Equiano*. Harlow: Longman.

Ekwensi, Cyprian 1966. *Iska*. London: Hutchinson and Co.

Enloe, Cynthia 1989. *Bananas, Beaches and Bases: Making Feminist Sense of International Politics*. Los Angeles: University of California Press.

Fabian, Johannes 1983. *Time and the Other: How Anthropology Makes Its Object*. New York: Columbia University Press.

Falk, Richard, and Andrew Strauss 2000. "On the Creation of a Global People's Assembly: Legitimacy and Power of Popular Sovereignty." *Stanford Journal of International Law* 36.2: 191–219.

　2001. "Toward a Global Parliament." *Foreign Affairs* 80.1: 212–20.

Fanon, Frantz 1965. *A Dying Colonialism* [1959]. Trans. Haakon Chevalier. New York: Grove Press.

　1967. *Black Skin, White Masks* [1952]. Trans. Charles Lam Markmann. New York: Grove Press.

　1968. *The Wretched of the Earth* [1961]. Trans. Constance Farrington. New York: Grove Press.

Ferguson, Moira 1991. "Mansfield Park: Slavery, Colonialism and Gender." *Oxford Literary Review* 13.1–2: 118–39.

Fernández Retamar, Roberto 1974. "Nuestra América y el Occidente." *Casa de las Américas* XVI.98: 36–57.

1996. "Pensamiento de Nuestra América: autoreflexiones y propuestas." *Casa de las Américas* XXXVII.204: 41–56.

Foster, John Bellamy 2002. "The Rediscovery of Imperialism." *Monthly Review* 54.6: 1–16.

Foucault, Michel, ed. 1987. *I, Pierre Riviere, Having Slaughtered My Mother, My Sister, and My Brother: A Case of Parricide in the Nineteenth Century* [1975]. Lincoln: University of Nebraska Press.

Frank, Andre Gunder 1967. *Capitalism and Underdevelopment in Latin America.* New York: Monthly Review Press.

1972. *Lumpenbourgeoisie: Lumpendevelopment – Dependency, Class, and Politics in Latin America.* New York and London: Monthly Review Press.

Frank, Andre Gunder, and Barry K. Gills, eds. 1996. "The 5,000-Year Old World System: An Interdisciplinary Introduction." *The World System: Five Hundred or Five Thousand?* London and New York: Routledge, 3–55.

Freeman, Carla 2001. "Is Local: Global as Feminine: Masculine? – Rethinking the Gender of Globalization." *Signs: Journal of Women in Culture and Society* 26.4: 1007–37.

Friedman, Thomas 1999. *The Lexus and the Olive Tree.* New York: Farrar, Strauss and Giroux.

Fukuyama, Francis 1992. *The End of History and the Last Man.* Harmondsworth: Penguin.

Fuss, Diana 1990. *Essentially Speaking: Feminism, Nature and Difference.* London and New York: Routledge.

1994. "Interior Colonies: Frantz Fanon and the Politics of Identification." *Diacritics* 24.2–3: 20–42.

Galeano, Eduardo 1973. *Open Veins of Latin America: Five Centuries of the Pillage of a Continent.* Trans. Cedric Belfrage. New York: Monthly Review Press.

Gandhi, Leela 1998. *Postcolonial Theory: A Critical Introduction.* New York: Columbia University Press.

Ganguly, Keya 2002. "Adorno, Authenticity, Critique." *Marxism, Modernity and Postcolonial Studies.* Ed. Crystal Bartolovich and Neil Lazarus. Cambridge: Cambridge University Press, 240–56.

Gaonkar, Dilip Parameshwar, ed. 2001. *Alternative Modernities.* Durham: Duke University Press.

García Canclini, Néstor 1995. *Hybrid Cultures: Strategies for Entering and Leaving Modernity.* Trans. Christopher L. Chiappari and Silvia L. López. Minneapolis and London: University of Minnesota Press.

Gates, Henry Louis, Jr. 1991. "Critical Fanonism." *Critical Inquiry* 17.3: 457–70.

Gellner, Ernest 1983. *Nations and Nationalism.* Ithaca: Cornell University Press.

George, Rosemary Marangoly 1996. *The Politics of Home: Postcolonial Relocations and Twentieth-Century Fiction.* Cambridge: Cambridge University Press.

Ghosh, Amitav 1992a. "The Slave of MS. H.6." *Subaltern Studies* VII: *Writings on South Asian History and Society.* Ed. Partha Chatterjee and Gyanendra Pandey. New Delhi: Oxford University Press, 159–220.

1992b. *In an Antique Land*. New York: Vintage Books.

2001. "Correspondence." www.amitavghosh.com/correspondence.html.

Ghosh, Bishnupriya, and Brinda Bose, eds. 1997. *Interventions: Feminist Dialogues on Third World Women's Literature and Film*. New York: Garland.

Giddens, Anthony 1991. "The Contours of High Modernity." *Modernity and Self-Identity: Self and Society in the Late Modern Age*. Cambridge: Polity, 10–34.

Giddings, Robert, ed. 1991. *Literature and Imperialism*. New York: St. Martin's Press.

Gikandi, Simon 1996. "Introduction: Africa, Diaspora, and the Discourse of Modernity." *Research in African Literatures* 27.4: 1–6.

2001. "Chinua Achebe and the Invention of African Culture." *Research in African Literatures* 32.3: 3–8.

Gills, Barry 1997. "Whither Democracy?: Globalization and the 'New Hellenism.'" *Globalization and the South*. Ed. Caroline Thomas and Peter Wilkin. London: Macmillan; New York: St. Martin's Press, 60–75.

Gilroy, Paul 1993. *The Black Atlantic: Modernity and Double Consciousness*. Cambridge, MA: Harvard University Press.

1994. "Diaspora." *Paragraph* 17.3: 207–12.

2000. *Between Camps: Nations, Cultures and the Allure of Race*. London: Penguin.

Goldberg, Theo, and Ato Quayson, eds. 2002. *Relocating Postcolonialism*. Oxford: Blackwell.

González Casanova, Pablo 1965. "Internal Colonialism and National Development." *Studies in Comparative International Development* 1.4: 27–37.

Graham, R. B. Cunninghame 1896. *The Imperial Kailyard: Being a Biting Satire on English Colonisation*. London: The Twentieth Century Press.

Gramsci, Antonio 1971. *Selections from the Prison Notebooks*. Trans. and ed. Quentin Hoare and Geoffrey Nowell Smith. New York: International Publishers.

Gray, John 1998. *False Dawn: The Delusions of Global Capitalism*. London: Granta.

Greenberger, Allen J. 1969. *The British Image of India: A Study in the Literature of Imperialism 1880–1960*. London: Oxford University Press.

Greene, Graham 1980. "Introduction" [1937]. *The Bachelor of Arts*. R. K. Narayan. Chicago: University of Chicago Press, v–x.

Grewal, Inderpal, and Caren Kaplan, eds. 1994. *Scattered Hegemonies: Postmodernity and Transnational Feminist Practices*. Minneapolis: University of Minnesota Press.

2000. "Postcolonial Studies and Transnational Feminist Practices." *Jouvert: A Journal of Postcolonial Studies* 5.1. Online journal.

Grosfoguel, Ramón 2000. "Developmentalism, Modernity and Dependency in Latin America." *Nepantla* 1.2: 347–74.

Guattari, Félix, and Toni Negri 1990. *Communists Like Us: New Spaces of Liberty, New Lines of Alliance* [1985]. Trans. Michael Ryan. New York: Semiotext(e).

Guevara, Ernesto "Che" 1969. *Guerrilla Warfare* [1961]. Trans. J. P. Morray. New York: Vintage Books.

Guha, Ranajit 1982a. "Preface." *Subaltern Studies* I: *Writings on South Asian History and Society*. Ed. Ranajit Guha. New Delhi: Oxford University Press, vii–viii.

1982b. "On Some Aspects of the Historiography of Colonial India." *Subaltern Studies* I: *Writings on South Asian History and Society*. Ed. Ranajit Guha. New Delhi: Oxford University Press, 1–8.

1987. "Chandra's Death." *Subaltern Studies* v: *Writings on South Asian History and Society*. Ed. Ranajit Guha. New Delhi: Oxford University Press, 135–65.

1988. "The Prose of Counter-Insurgency" [1983]. *Selected Subaltern Studies*. Ed. Ranajit Guha and Gayatri Chakravorty Spivak. New York and London: Oxford University Press, 45–86.

1996. *A Rule of Property for Bengal: An Essay on the Idea of Permanent Settlement* [1963]. Durham and London: Duke University Press.

1997. *Dominance without Hegemony: History and Power in Colonial India*. Cambridge, MA, and London: Harvard University Press.

Guha, Ranajit, and Gayatri Chakravorty Spivak, eds. 1988. *Selected Subaltern Studies*. New York and London: Oxford University Press.

Gunew, Sneja 1990. "Denaturalizing Cultural Nationalisms: Multicultural Readings of 'Australia.'" *Nation and Narration*. Ed. Homi K. Bhabha. London and New York: Routledge, 99–120.

Gwynne, Robert N. and Cristóbal Kay 1999. "Latin America Transformed: Changing Paradigms, Debates and Alternatives." *Latin America Transformed: Globalization and Modernity*. Ed. Robert N. Gwynne and Cristóbal Kay. London, Sydney, Auckland: Arnold, 2–30.

Habermas, Jürgen 1983. "Walter Benjamin: Consciousness-Raising or Rescuing Critique" [1972]. *Philosophical-Political Profiles*. Trans. Frederick G. Lawrence. Cambridge, MA, and London: MIT Press, 129–63. Reprinted in *On Walter Benjamin: Critical Essays and Recollections*. Ed. Gary Smith. Cambridge, MA: MIT Press, 90–128.

1987. *The Philosophical Discourse of Modernity: Twelve Lectures*. Trans. Frederick Lawrence. Cambridge, MA: The MIT Press.

2001. "Learning from Catastrophe? A Look Back at the Short Twentieth Century." *The Postnational Constellation: Political Essays*. Trans. and ed. Max Pensky. Oxford: Polity, 38–57.

Hall, Stuart 1993. "Cultural Identity and Diaspora." *Colonial Discourse and Post-Colonial Theory: A Reader*. Ed. Patrick Williams and Laura Chrisman. Hemel Hempstead: Harvester Wheatsheaf; New York: Columbia University Press, 392–403.

1996. "When Was 'the Post-Colonial?' Thinking at the Limit." *The Post-Colonial Question: Common Skies, Divided Horizons*. Ed. Iain Chambers and Lidia Curti. London and New York: Routledge, 242–60.

Hallward, Peter 2001. *Absolutely Postcolonial: Writing Between the Singular and the Specific*. Manchester: Manchester University Press.

Hannerz, Ulf 1990. "Cosmopolitans and Locals in World Culture." *Global Culture: Nationalism, Globalization and Modernity*. Ed. Mike Featherstone. London: Sage, 237–51.

1996. *Transnational Connections: Culture, People, Places*. London and New York: Routledge.

Hansen, Thomas Blom 1999. *The Saffron Wave: Democracy and Hindu Nationalism in Modern India*. Princeton: Princeton University Press.

Hardiman, David 1984. "Adivasi Assertion in South Gujarat: The Devi Movement of 1922–3." *Subaltern Studies* III: *Writings on South Asian History and Society*. Ed. Ranajit Guha. New Delhi: Oxford University Press, 196–230.

ed. 1992. *Peasant Resistance in India 1858–1914*. Oxford: Oxford University Press.

Harlow, Barbara 1987. *Resistance Literature*. London: Methuen.

Harootunian, Harry 2000. *History's Disquiet: Modernity, Cultural Practice, and the Question of Everyday Life*. New York: Columbia University Press.

Harris, Jerry 1999. "Globalisation and the Technological Transformation of Capitalism." *Race & Class* 40.2–3: 21–35.

Harris, Wilson 1983. *The Womb of Space: The Cross-cultural Imagination*. London: Greenwood Press.

1985. *Palace of the Peacock* [1960]. *The Guyana Quartet*. London: Faber and Faber.

1990. "The Frontier On Which Heart of Darkness Stands." *Joseph Conrad: Third World Perspectives*. Ed. Robert D. Hamner. Washington, DC: Three Continents, 161–67.

Harrison, Nicholas 2003. *Postcolonial Criticism: History, Theory and the Work of Fiction*. Oxford: Polity.

Harrow, Kenneth 2001. "Introduction." *Research in African Literatures* 32.3: 33–44.

Harvey, David 1989. *The Condition of Postmodernity: An Enquiry into the Origins of Cultural Change*. Oxford and Cambridge, MA: Blackwell.

1995. "Globalization in Question." *Rethinking Marxism* 8.4: 1–17.

Hegel, Georg Wilhelm Friedrich 1956. *The Philosophy of History* [1822–25]. Trans. J. Sibree. New York: Dover Publications.

1967. *Hegel's Philosophy of Right* [1821]. Trans. T. M. Knox. London, Oxford, New York: Oxford University Press.

Heller, Tamara 1992. *Dead Secrets: Wilkie Collins and the Female Gothic*. New Haven and London: Yale University Press.

Heywood, Christopher 1987. "Yorkshire Slavery in Emily Bronte's *Wuthering Heights*." *Review of English Studies* 38.150: 184–98.

Hill, Christopher 1972. *The World Turned Upside Down*. London: Temple Smith.

Hirst, Paul, and Grahame Thompson 1996. *Globalization in Question: The International Economy and the Possibilities of Governance*. Oxford: Polity.

Hobsbawm, Eric 1987. *The Age of Empire: 1875–1914*. London: Cardinal; New York: Pantheon.

1993. *Nations and Nationalism Since 1870*. Cambridge: Cambridge University Press.

1994. *The Age of Extremes: A History of the World, 1914–1991*. New York: Pantheon Books.

Hobsbawm, Eric, and Terence Ranger 1983. *The Invention of Tradition*. Cambridge: Cambridge University Press.

Hobson, J. A. 1902. *Imperialism: A Study*. London: Allen & Unwin.

Ho Chi Minh 1967. *On Revolution: Selected Writings, 1920–66*. Ed. Bernard B. Fall. London: Pall Mall Press.

Hodgson, Marshall 1974. *The Venture of Islam: Conscience and History in a World Civilization*. Chicago: University of Chicago Press.

Hogan, Patrick Colm 2001. "What's Wrong with Postcolonial Theory?" *Journal of Commonwealth and Postcolonial Studies* 8.1–2: 193–221.

Hoogvelt, Ankie 1997. *Globalisation and the Postcolonial World: The New Political Economy of Development*. London: Macmillan.

hooks, bell 1984. *Feminist Theory: From Margin to Center*. Boston: South End Press.
1994. *Outlaw Culture*. New York and London: Routledge.

Howells, J., and M. Wood 1993. *The Globalisation of Production and Technology*. London and New York: Belhaven Press.

Hrbek, Ivan 1999. "North Africa and the Horn." *General History of Africa*. VIII: *Africa since 1935*. Ed. Ali A. Mazrui. London: James Currey; Berkeley: University of California Press; Paris: UNESCO, 127–60.

Hroch, Miroslav 1985. *Social Preconditions of National Revival in Europe*. Cambridge: Cambridge University Press.

Huggan, Graham 2001. *The Postcolonial Exotic: Marketing the Margins*. London and New York: Routledge.

Hulme, Peter 1989. "Subversive Archipelagos: Colonial Discourse and the Break-Up of Continental Theory." *Dispositio* 14: 1–23.

1992. *Colonial Encounters: Europe and the Native Caribbean 1492–1797* [1986]. London and New York: Routledge.

1994. "The Locked Heart: Wide Sargasso Sea." *Colonial Discourse / Postcolonial Theory*. Ed. Francis Barker, Peter Hulme, and Margaret Iversen. Manchester: Manchester University Press, 72–88.

1996. "La teoría postcolonial y la representación de la cultura en las Américas." *Casa de las Américas* 36.202: 3–8.

2000. "Reading from Elsewhere: George Lamming and the Paradox of Exile." *"The Tempest" and Its Travels*. Ed. Peter Hulme and William H. Sherman. Philadelphia: University of Pennsylvania Press, 220–35.

Huntington, Samuel 1998. *The Clash of Civilizations and the Remaking of World Order*. London: Touchstone Books.

Hussein, Abdirahman A. 2002. *Edward Said: Criticism and Society*. London and New York: Verso.

Hutcheon, Linda 1994. "The Post Always Rings Twice: The Postmodern and the Postcolonial." *Textual Practice* 8.2: 205–38.

Inden, Ronald 1990. *Imagining India*. Oxford: Blackwell.

Irele, Abiola 1981. *The African Experience in Literature and Ideology*. London and Exeter, NH: Heinemann.

1990. "The African Imagination." *Research in African Literatures* 21.1: 49–67.

Israel, Nico 2000. *Outlandish: Writing Between Exile and Diaspora*. Stanford: Stanford University Press.

James, C. L. R. 1963. *The Black Jacobins* [1938]. New York: Vintage.

Jameson, Fredric 1986. "Third-World Literature in the Era of Multinational Capitalism." *Social Text* 15: 65–88.

2002. *A Singular Modernity: Essay on the Ontology of the Present*. London and New York: Verso.

JanMohamed, Abdul R., and David Lloyd, eds. 1990. *The Nature and Context of Minority Discourse*. Oxford and New York: Oxford University Press.

Jayawardena, Kumari 1986. *Feminism and Nationalism in the Third World*. London: Zed.

1995. *The White Woman's Other Burden: Western Women and South Asia during British Rule*. London: Routledge.

John, Mary E. 1996. *Discrepant Dislocations: Feminism, Theory, and Postcolonial Histories*. Berkeley, Los Angeles, London: University of California Press.

Johnson-Odim, Cheryl 1991. "Common Themes, Different Contexts: Third World Women and Feminism." *Third World Women and the Politics of Feminism.* Ed. Chandra Talpade Mohanty, Ann Russo, and Lourdes Torres. Bloomington: Indiana University Press, 314–27.

Joseph, Gil 1990. "On the Trail of Latin American Bandits: A Reexamination of Peasant Resistance." *Latin American Research Review* 25: 7–53.

Joseph, Gil, Catherine LeGrand, and Ricardo D. Salvatore 1999. *Close Encounters of Empire. Writing the Cultural History of US–Latin American Relations.* Durham and London: Duke University Press.

Joshi, Svati 1991. "Rethinking English: An Introduction." *Rethinking English: Essays in Literature, Language, History.* Ed. Svati Joshi. New Delhi: Trianka, 1–31.

Judy, Ronald A. T. 1996. "Fanon's Body of Black Experience." *Fanon: A Critical Reader.* Ed. Lewis R. Gordon, T. Denean Sharpley-Whiting, and Renée T. White. Oxford: Blackwell, 53–73.

Jules-Rosete, Bennetta 2000. "Identity Discourses and Diasporic Aesthetics in Black Paris: Community Formation and the Translation of Culture." *Diaspora* 9.1: 39–58.

Jusdanis, Gregory 2001. *The Necessary Nation.* Princeton: Princeton University Press.

Kabbani, Rana 1994. *Imperial Fictions: Europe's Myths of Orient.* Rev. edn. London: Pandora.

Kabeer, Naila 1991. "The Quest For National Identity: Women, Islam and the State in Bangladesh." *Feminist Review* 37: 38–58.

Kagarlitsky, Boris 2000. *The Twilight of Globalization: Property, State and Capitalism.* Trans. Renfrey Clarke. London and Sterling, VA: Pluto Press.

Kang, Liu 1998. "Is There an Alternative to (Capitalist) Globalization? The Debate about Modernity in China." *The Cultures of Globalization.* Ed. Fredric Jameson and Masao Miyoshi. Durham and London: Duke University Press, 164–88.

Kant, Immanuel 1963. "Perpetual Peace" [1795]. *On History.* Trans. and ed. Lewis White Beck. New York: Bobbs-Merrill, 85–135.

    1991. "Idea for a Universal History with a Cosmopolitan Standpoint" [1784]. *Political Writings.* Trans. H. B. Nisbet. Ed. Hans Reiss. Cambridge: Cambridge University Press, 41–53.

Kaplan, Caren 1994. "The Politics of Location as Transnational Feminist Practice." *Scattered Hegemonies: Postmodernity and Transnational Feminist Practices.* Ed. Inderpal Grewal and Caren Kaplan. Minneapolis: University of Minnesota Press, 137–52.

Katrak, Ketu H. 1989. "Decolonizing Culture: Toward a Theory for Postcolonial Women's Texts." *Modern Fiction Studies* 35.1: 157–79.

Kautsky, Karl 1970. "Ultra-imperialism" [1914]. *New Left Review* 59: 41–46.

Kaviraj, Sudipta 1992. "The Imaginary Institution of India." *Subaltern Studies* VII: *Writings on South Asian History and Society.* Ed. Partha Chatterjee and Gyanendra Pandey. New Delhi: Oxford University Press, 1–39.

Kennedy, Valerie 2000. *Edward Said: A Critical Introduction.* Oxford: Polity.

Kiberd, Declan 1995. *Inventing Ireland: The Literature of the Modern Nation.* London: Jonathan Cape.

Kiernan, V. G. 1969. *The Lords of Human Kind: European Attitudes to the Outside World in the Imperial Age*. London: Weidenfield and Nicolson.

King, Anthony D. 1995. "Writing Colonial Space." *Comparative Study of Society and History*: 541–54.

Kirschenblatt-Gimblett, Barbara 1994. "Spaces of Dispersal." *Cultural Anthropology* 9.3: 339–44.

Kissinger, Henry 1994. *Diplomacy*. New York: Simon & Schuster.

Klor de Alva, Jorge 1992. "Colonialism and Postcolonialism as (Latin) American Mirages." *Colonial Latin American Review* 1.1–2: 3–23.

　　1995. "The Postcolonization of the (Latin) American Experience: A Reconsideration of 'Colonialism,' 'Postcolonialism,' and 'Mestizaje.'" *After Colonialism: Imperial Histories and Postcolonial Predicaments*. Ed. Gyan Prakash. Princeton: Princeton University Press, 240–75.

Kolko, Gabriel 1986. *Vietnam: Anatomy of a War 1940–1975*. London and Sydney: Allen and Unwin.

　　1997. *Vietnam: Anatomy of a Peace*. London and New York: Routledge.

Kolko, J. 1988. *Restructuring the World Economy*. New York: Pantheon Books.

Krebs, Paula M. 1999. *Gender, Race, and the Writing of Empire: Public Discourse and the Boer War*. Cambridge: Cambridge University Press.

Krishnaswamy, Revathi 1995. "Mythologies of Migrancy: Postcolonialism, Postmodernism and the Politics of (Dis)location." *Ariel: A Review of International English Literature* 26.1: 125–46.

Kristeva, Julia 1993. *Nations Without Nationalism*. Trans. Leon S. Roudiez. New York: Columbia University Press.

Krugman, Paul R. 1997. *The Age of Diminished Expectations: US Economic Policy in the 1990s*. Cambridge, MA: MIT Press.

Kruks, Sonia 1996. "Fanon, Sartre, and Identity Politics." *Fanon: A Critical Reader*. Ed. Lewis R. Gordon, T. Denean Sharpley-Whiting, and Renée T. White. Oxford: Blackwell, 122–33.

Lamming, George 1984. *The Pleasures of Exile*. London and New York: Allison and Busby.

Landes, David 1998. *The Wealth and Poverty of Nations: Why Some Are so Rich and Some so Poor*. New York: W. W. Norton.

Lapham, Lewis H. 1998. *The Agony of Mammon: The Imperial World Economy Explains Itself to the Membership in Davos, Switerzland*. London and New York: Verso.

Larrain, Jorge 2000. *Identity and Modernity in Latin America*. Oxford: Polity.

Larsen, Neil 2002. "Marxism, Postcolonialism and The Eighteenth Brumaire." *Marxism, Modernity and Postcolonial Studies*. Ed. Crystal Bartolovich and Neil Lazarus. Cambridge: Cambridge University Press, 204–20.

Las Casas, Bartolomé de 1992. *A Short Account of the Destruction of the Indies* [1542]. Trans. and ed. Nigel Griffin. London: Penguin.

Lash, Scott, and John Urry 1987. *The End of Organized Capitalism*. Cambridge: Polity.

Lazarus, Neil 1990. *Resistance in Postcolonial African Fiction*. New Haven: Yale University Press.

　　1991. "Doubting the New World Order: Marxism and Postmodernist Social Theory." *differences* 3.3: 94–138.

1994. "National Consciousness and the Specificity of (Post)Colonial Intellectualism." *Colonial Discourse / Postcolonial Theory.* Ed. Francis Barker, Peter Hulme, and Margaret Iversen. Manchester and New York: Manchester University Press, 197–220.

1999a. *Nationalism and Cultural Practice in the Postcolonial World.* Cambridge: Cambridge University Press.

1999b. "Disavowing Decolonization: Fanon, Nationalism, and the Question of Representation in Postcolonial Theory." *Frantz Fanon: Critical Perspectives.* Ed. Anthony C. Alessandri. London and New York: Routledge, 161–95.

2002. "The Fetish of 'the West' in Postcolonial Theory." *Marxism, Modernity and Postcolonial Studies.* Ed. Crystal Bartolovich and Neil Lazarus. Cambridge: Cambridge University Press, 43–64.

Forthcoming. "The Politics of Postcolonial Modernism." *Postcolonial Studies and Beyond.* Ed. Ania Loomba, Suvir Kaul, Matti Bunzl, Antoinette Burton, and Jed Esty. Durham and London: Duke University Press.

Legum, Colin 1999. *Africa Since Independence.* Bloomington and Indianapolis: Indiana University Press.

Lenin, Vladimir 1975. *Imperialism: The Highest Stage of Capitalism* [1917]. London: New Left Books.

Lévi-Strauss, Claude 1966. *The Savage Mind* [1962]. Chicago: University of Chicago Press.

1969. *The Elementary Structures of Kinship.* Trans. James Bell, John von Sturmer, and Rodney Needham. Boston: Beacon Press.

1992. *Tristes Tropiques* [1955]. Trans. John Weightman and Doreen Weightman. New York: Penguin Books.

Leys, Colin 1996. *The Rise and Fall of Development Theory.* Nairobi: East African Publishing House; Bloomington and Indianapolis: Indiana University Press; London: James Currey.

Lipietz, Alain 1987. *Miracles and Mirages: The Crises of Global Fordism.* Trans. David Macey. London: Verso.

Lloyd, David 1991. "Race under Representation." *Oxford Literary Review* 13.1: 62–94.

Loomba, Ania 1998a. *Colonialism/Postcolonialism.* London and New York: Routledge.

1998b. "Teaching the Bard in India." *Subject to Change: Teaching Literature in the Nineties.* Ed. Susie Tharu. New Delhi: Orient Longman, 33–51.

Loomba, Ania, and Suvir Kaul 1994. "Location, Culture, Post-Coloniality." *Oxford Literary Review* 16: 3–30.

Love, Joseph 1980. "Raúl Prebish and the Origins of the Doctrine of Unequal Exchange." *Latin American Research Review* 15.3: 45–72.

Lowe, Lisa 1991. *Critical Terrains: French and British Orientalisms.* Ithaca and London: Cornell University Press.

1993. "Des Chinoises: Orientalism, Psychoanalysis, and Feminine Writing." *Ethics, Politics, and Difference in Julia Kristeva's Writing.* Ed. Kelly Oliver. New York: Routledge, 150–63.

Lowe, Lisa, and David Lloyd. 1997. "Introduction." *The Politics of Culture in the Shadow of Capital.* Ed. Lowe and Lloyd. Durham and London: Duke University Press, 1–32.

Ludden, David ed. 2001. *Reading Subaltern Studies: Critical History, Contested Meaning, and the Globalisation of South Asia*. New Delhi: Permanent Black; London: Anthem Press (2002).

Lumumba, Patrice 1972. *Lumumba Speaks: The Speeches and Writings of Patrice Lumumba*. Trans. Helen R. Lane. Ed. Jean van Lierde. Boston: Little, Brown.

Macey, David 2000. *Frantz Fanon: A Life*. London: Granta Books.

Mahasweta Devi 1993. "Shishu (Children)" [1978]. Trans. Pinaki Bhattacharya. *Women Writing in India*. Vol. II: *The Twentieth Century*. Ed. Susie Tharu and K. Lalita. New York: Feminist Press, 234–51.

Mahood, Molly 1977. *The Colonial Encounter: A Reading of Six Novels*. London: Rex Collings.

Mailer, Norman 1993. *The Naked and the Dead* [1949]. London: Flamingo.

Mallon, Florencia 1994. "The Promise and Dilemma of Subaltern Studies: Perspectives from Latin American History." *American Historical Review* 99.5: 1491–515.

  1995. *Peasant and Nation. The Making of Postcolonial Mexico and Peru*. Berkeley: University of California Press.

Mamdani, Mahmood 1996. *Citizen and Subject: Contemporary Africa and the Legacy of Late Colonialism*. Princeton: Princeton University Press.

Mandel, Ernest 1993. *Late Capitalism* [1972]. Trans. Joris De Bres. London and New York: Verso.

Mani, Lata 1990. "Multiple Mediations: Feminist Scholarship in the Age of Multinational Reception." *Feminist Review* 35: 24–41.

Mao Zedong 1953. *On Contradiction*. New York: International Publishers.

Maraire, J. Nozipo 1996. *Zenzele: A Letter for my Daughter*. New York: Crown.

Marais, Hein 1998. *South Africa: Limits to Change. The Political Economy of Transition*. London: Zed.

Martin, Hans-Peter, and Harald Schumann 1997. *The Global Trap: Globalization and the Assault on Prosperity and Democracy*. Trans. Patrick Camiller. Pretoria: HRSC /RGN; Leichhardt, NSW: Pluto Press; Bangkok: White Lotus; London and New York: Zed.

Marx, Karl 1976. *Capital: A Critique of Political Economy* [1867]. Vol. I. Trans. Ben Fowkes. London: Penguin.

  1981. "Theses on Feuerbach" [1846; first published 1888]. *The German Ideology. Part One*. Ed. and intro. C. J. Arthur. New York: International Publishers, 121–23.

  1991. *Capital: A Critique of Political Economy* [1894]. Vol. III. Trans. David Fernbach. London: Penguin.

Marx, Karl, and Frederick Engels 1988. *Manifesto of the Communist Party* [1848]. Beijing: Foreign Languages Press.

McClintock, Anne 1995. *Imperial Leather: Race, Gender and Sexuality in the Colonial Contest*. London and New York: Routledge.

McClintock, Anne, Aamir Mufti, and Ella Shohat, eds. 1997. *Dangerous Liaisons: Gender, Nation and Postcolonial Perspectives*. Minneapolis: University of Minnesota Press.

McGrew, Anthony 1996. "A Global Society?" *Modernity: An Introduction to Modern Societies*. Ed. Stuart Hall, David Held, Don Hubert, and Kenneth Thompson. Oxford: Blackwell, 466–503.

McLeod, John 2000. *Beginning Postcolonialism*. Manchester: Manchester University Press.

McNeill, William 1963. *The Rise of the West: A History of the Human Community*. Chicago and London: University of Chicago Press.

Melville, Herman 1988. *Moby-Dick* [1851]. Oxford and New York: Oxford University Press.

Menchú, Rigoberta 1984. *I, Rigoberta Menchú: An Indian Woman in Guatemala*. Trans. Ann Wright. Ed. and intro. Elizabeth Burgos-Debray. London: Verso.

Meyer, Susan 1996. *Imperialism at Home: Race and Victorian Women's Fiction*. Ithaca and London: Cornell University Press.

Meyers, Jeffrey 1973. *Fiction and the Colonial Experience*. Ipswich: The Boydell Press.

Mignolo, Walter D. 1993. "Colonial and Postcolonial Discourse: Cultural Critique or Academic Colonialism?" *Latin American Research Review* 28.3: 120–34.

2000. *Local Histories / Global Designs: Coloniality, Subaltern Knowledges, and Border Thinking*. Princeton: Princeton University Press.

Miller, Christopher L. 1985. *Blank Darkness: Africanist Discourse in French*. Chicago and London: University of Chicago Press.

1990. *Theories of Africans: Francophone Literature and Anthropology in Africa*. Chicago and London: University of Chicago Press.

1993. "Literary Studies and African Literature: The Challenge of Intercultural Literacy." *Africa and the Disciplines*. Ed. Robert H. Bates, V. Y. Mudimbe, and Jean O'Barr. Chicago: University of Chicago Press, 213–31.

Mitchell, Timothy 1991. *Colonising Egypt* [1988]. Berkeley, Los Angeles, and Oxford: University of California Press.

Mitter, Swasti, and Sheila Rowbotham, eds. 1995. *Women Encounter Technology: Changing Patterns of Employment in the Third World*. London: Routledge, 1995.

Miyoshi, Masao 1993. "A Borderless World? From Colonialism to Transnationalism and the Decline of the Nation State." *Critical Inquiry* 19.4: 726–51.

Moghadam, Valentine, ed. 1994. *Gender and National Identity: Women and Politics in Muslim Societies*. London: Zed.

Mohanty, Chandra Talpade 1991. "Under Western Eyes: Feminist Scholarship and Colonial Discourses" [1982]. *Third World Women and the Politics of Feminism*. Ed. Chandra Talpade Mohanty, Ann Russo, and Lourdes Torres. Bloomington: Indiana University Press, 51–81.

1995. "Feminist Encounters: Locating the Politics of Experience." *Social Postmodernism: Beyond Identity Politics*. Ed. Linda Nicholson and Steven Seidman. Cambridge and New York: Cambridge University Press, 68–87.

1997. "Women Workers and Capitalist Scripts: Ideologies of Domination, Common Interests and the Politics of Solidarity." *Feminist Genealogies. Colonial Legacies. Democratic Futures*. Ed. M. Jacqui Alexander and Chandra Talpade Mohanty. New York and London: Routledge, 3–29.

Mongia, Padmini, ed. 1996. *Contemporary Postcolonial Theory: A Reader*. London: Arnold.

Montaigne, Michel de 1991. "On the Cannibals" [1578–80]. *The Complete Essays*. Trans. and ed. M. A. Screech. London: Penguin, 228–41.

Moody, Kim 1997. *Workers in a Lean World: Unions in the International Economy.* London and New York: Verso.

Moore-Gilbert, Bart 1997. *Postcolonial Theory: Contexts, Practices, Politics.* London and New York: Verso.

Moraña, Mabel 1997. "El boom del subalterno." *Revista de crítica cultural* 15: 48–53.

Morris, William 1901. *News from Nowhere: Or, An Epoch of Rest, Being some Chapters from a Utopian Romance.* New York: Longmans, Green.

Mudimbe, V. Y. 1988. *The Invention of Africa: Gnosis, Philosophy, and the Order of Knowledge.* Bloomington and Indianapolis: Indiana University Press; London: James Currey.

Naipaul, V. S. 1979. *A Bend in the River.* New York: Vintage.

  1987. *The Enigma of Arrival.* New York: Vintage.

Nairn, Tom 1977. *The Break-up of Britain: Crisis and Neo-Nationalism.* London: New Left Books.

Nandy, Ashis 2003. *Time Warps: Silent and Evasive Pasts in Indian Politics and Religion.* London: Zed.

Narayan, Uma 1997. *Dislocating Cultures: Identities, Tradition and Third World Feminism.* New York and London: Routledge.

Nehru, Jawaharlal 1946. *The Discovery of India.* New York: The John Day Company.

  1997. "Tryst with Destiny" [1947]. *The Vintage Book of Indian Writing.* Ed. Salman Rushdie and Elizabeth West. London: Vintage, 1–2.

Ngugi wa Thiong'o 1986. *Decolonising the Mind: The Politics of Language in African Literature.* London: James Currey; Nairobi: Heinemann Kenya; Portsmouth, NH: Heinemann; Harare: Zimbabwe Publishing House.

  1988. *Weep Not, Child* [1964]. London: Heinemann.

Ngugi wa Thiong'o, Henry Owuor-Anyumba, and Taban Lo Liyong 1978. "On the Abolition of the English Department." *Homecoming: Essays on African and Caribbean Literature, Culture and Politics.* Ngugi wa Thiong'o. London: Heinemann, 145–50.

Nkrumah, Kwame 1965. *Neo-Colonialism: The Last Stage of Imperialism.* London: Thomas Nelson.

  1971. *Ghana: The Autobiography of Kwame Nkrumah* [1957]. New York: International Publishers.

  1973. *I Speak of Freedom.* London: PANAF.

Norris, Christopher 1993. *The Truth About Postmodernism.* Oxford: Blackwell.

  1994. *Truth and the Ethics of Criticism.* Manchester: Manchester University Press.

Nussbaum, Martha C., with respondents 1996. *For Love of Country: Debating the Limits of Patriotism.* Ed. Joshua Cohen. Boston: Beacon.

Nyerere, Julius K. 1979. "The Process of Liberation" [1976]. *Politics and State in the Third World.* Ed. Harry Goulbourne. London and Basingstoke: Macmillan, 248–58.

Okri, Ben 1997. *A Way of Being Free.* London: Phoenix House.

Oliver, Kelly 1993. *Reading Kristeva: Unraveling the Double-Bind.* Bloomington: Indiana University Press.

Osofisan, Femi 1997. "Warriors of a Failed Utopia: West African Writers Since the '70s." www.PostExpressWired.com.

2001. "The Challenge of Translation or Some Notes on the Language Factor in African Literature." *The Nostalgic Drum: Essays on Literature, Drama and Culture*. Trenton, NJ; Asmara, Eritrea: Africa World Press, 219–28.

Pandey, Gyanendra 1989. "The Colonial Construction of 'Communalism': British Writings on Banaras in the Nineteenth Century." *Subaltern Studies* VI: *Writings on South Asian History and Society*. Ed. Ranajit Guha. New Delhi: Oxford University Press, 132–68.

1992. *The Construction of Communalism in Colonial North India*. New Delhi: Oxford University Press.

Papastergiadis, Nikos 2000. *The Turbulence of Migration: Globalization, Deterritorialization and Hybridity*. Cambridge: Polity.

Parker, Andrew, Mary Russo, Doris Sommer, and Patricia Yeager 1992. "Introduction." *Nationalisms and Sexualities*. Ed. Parker, Russo, Sommer, and Yeager. New York and London: Routledge: 1–18.

Parry, Benita 1983. *Conrad and Imperialism: Ideological Boundaries and Visionary Frontiers*. London: Macmillan.

1987. "Problems in Current Theories of Colonial Discourse." *Oxford Literary Review* 9.1–2: 27–58.

1992. "Overlapping Territories and Intertwined Histories: Edward Said's Postcolonial Cosmopolitanism." *Edward Said: A Critical Reader*. Ed. Michael Sprinker. Oxford: Blackwell, 19–47.

1994. "Resistance Theory / Theorising Resistance, or Two Cheers for Nativism." *Colonial Discourse / Postcolonial Theory*. Ed. Francis Barker, Peter Hulme, and Margaret Iversen. Manchester and New York: Manchester University Press, 172–96.

1997a. "The Postcolonial: Conceptual Category or Chimera?" *Yearbook of English Studies* 27: 3–21.

1997b. "Narrating Imperialism." *Cultural Readings of Imperialism: Edward Said and the Gravity of History*. Ed. Keith Ansell-Pearson, Benita Parry, and Judith Squires. New York: St. Martin's Press; London: Lawrence and Wishart, 227–46.

1998a. "*Tono-Bungay*, or the Failed Electrification of the Empire of Light." *New Formations* 34: 91–108.

1998b. "Materiality and Mystification in *A Passage to India*." *Novel: A Forum on Fiction* 31.2: 174–94.

1998c. *Delusions and Discoveries: Studies on India in the British Imagination, 1880–1930* [1972]. London and New York: Verso.

2002. "Liberation Theory: Variations on Themes of Marxism and Modernity." *Marxism, Modernity and Postcolonial Studies*. Ed. Crystal Bartolovich and Neil Lazarus. Cambridge: Cambridge University Press, 125–49.

Patterson, Tiffany Ruby, and Robin D. G. Kelley 2000. "Unfinished Migrations: Reflections on the African Diaspora and the Making of the Modern World." *African Studies Review* 43.1: 11–45.

Pavel, Thomas G. 1989. *The Spell of Language: Poststructuralism and Speculation*. Chicago and London: University of Chicago Press.

Perera, Suvendrina 1991. *Reaches of Empire*. New York: Columbia University Press.

Pérez, Alberto Julián 1999. "El postcolonialismo y la inmadurez de los pensadores hispanoamericanos." *El debate de la postcolonialidad en Latinoamérica.*

Ed. Alfonso de Toro and Fernando de Toro. Madrid: Iberoamericana, 199–213.

Peterson, Kirsten Holst 1984. "First Things First: Problems of a Feminist Approach to African Literature." *Kunapipi* 6.3: 35–47.

Phillips, Tom 1996. Curator. *Africa: The Art of a Continent*. New York: Guggenheim.

Pieterse, Cosmo, and Dennis Duerden, eds. 1972. *African Writers Talking*. New York: Africana.

Pieterse, Jan Nederveen 1995. "Globalization as Hybridization." *Global Modernities*. Ed. Mike Featherstone, Scott Lash, and Roland Robertson. London; Thousand Oaks, CA; New Delhi: Sage, 45–68.

2001. *Development Theory: Deconstructions/Reconstructions*. London: Sage.

Plasa, Carl 1994. "'Silent Revolt': Slavery and the Politics of Metaphor in Jane Eyre." *The Discourse of Slavery: Aphra Behn to Toni Morrison*. Ed. Carl Plasa and Betty Ring. London: Routledge, 64–93.

Polanyi, Karl 1957. *The Great Transformation: The Political and Economic Origins of Our Time* [1944]. Boston: Beacon Press.

Poster, Mark 1975. *Existential Marxism in Postwar France: From Sartre to Althusser*. Princeton: Princeton University Press.

Prakash, Gyan 1993. "Postcolonial Criticism and Indian Historiography." *Social Text* 31.2: 8–19.

1996. "Who's Afraid of Postcoloniality?" *Social Text* 49: 187–203.

2000. "Writing Post-Orientalist Histories of the Third World: Perspectives from Indian Historiography" [1990]. *Mapping Subaltern Studies and the Postcolonial*. Ed. Vinayak Chaturvedi. London and New York: Verso, 163–90.

Pratt, Mary Louise 1992. *Imperial Eyes: Travel Writing and Transculturation*. London: Routledge.

Premnath, Gautam 2000. "Remembering Fanon, Decolonizing Diaspora." *Postcolonial Theory and Criticism*. Ed. Laura Chrisman and Benita Parry. Cambridge: D. S. Brewer, 57–73.

Quayson, Ato 1997. *Strategic Transformations in Nigerian Writing: Orality and History in the Work of Rev. Samuel Johnson, Amos Tutuola, Wole Soyinka and Ben Okri*. Oxford: James Currey; Bloomington and Indianapolis: Indiana University Press.

2000. *Postcolonialism: Theory, Practice or Process?* Cambridge and Oxford: Polity Press.

Quijano, Anibal 2000. "Colonialidad del poder, eurocentrismo y América Latina." *La colonialidad del saber: eurocentrismo y ciencias sociales. Perspectivas Latinoamericanas*. Ed. Edgardo Lander. Buenos Aires: CLASCO, 201–46.

Radhakrishnan, R. 2000. "Adjudicating Hybridity, Co-ordinating Betweenness." *Jouvert: A Journal of Postcolonial Studies* 5.1. Online journal.

Raleigh, Walter, Sir 1997. *The Discoverie of the Large, Rich, and Bewtiful Empyre of Guiana* [1596]. Ed. Neil L. Whitehead. Manchester: Manchester University Press.

Ramazani, Jahan 2001. *The Hybrid Muse: Postcolonial Poetry in English*. Chicago and London: University of Chicago Press.

Randall, Margaret 1981. *Sandino's Daughters: Testimonies of Nicaraguan Women in Struggle*. Ed. Lynda Yanz. Vancouver and Toronto: New Star Books.

Ranger, Terence 1983. "The Invention of Tradition in Colonial Africa." *The Invention of Tradition*. Ed. Eric Hobsbawm and Terence Ranger. Cambridge: Cambridge University Press, 211–62.

Rao, Raja 1963. *Kanthapura* [1938]. New York: New Directions.

Raskin, Jonah 1971. *The Mythology of Imperialism: A Revolutionary Critique of British Literature and Society in the Modern Age.* New York: Random House.

Raynal, Abbé (Guillaume-Thomas-François) 1991. *Histoire philosophique et politique des établissements et du commerce des européens dans les deux Indes* [1667]. Oxford: Voltaire Foundation at the Taylor Institution.

Read, Alan, ed. 1996. *The Fact of Blackness: Frantz Fanon and Visual Representation.* London: Institute of Contemporary Arts.

Richards, Thomas 1993. *The Imperial Archive: Knowledge and the Fantasy of Empire.* London and New York: Verso.

Rivera Cusicanqui, Silvia, and Rossana Barragán, eds. 1999. *Debates Post Coloniales. Una Introducción a los Estudios de la Subalternidad.* La Paz: Sephis/Aruwiyri.

Robinson, William 1996a. *Promoting Polyarchy.* Cambridge: Cambridge University Press.

1996b. "Globalisation: Nine Theses of Our Epoch." *Race & Class* 38: 13–31.

Rodney, Walter 1972. *How Europe Underdeveloped Africa.* London: Bogle L'Ouverture Publications; Dar-es-Salaam: Tanzania Publishing House.

Rodriguez, Ileana, ed. 2001. *The Latin American Subaltern Studies Reader.* Durham and London: Duke University Press.

Rosenberg, Justin 2000. *The Follies of Globalisation Theory.* London and New York: Verso.

Ross, Robert L., ed. 1999. *Colonial and Postcolonial Fiction in English: An Anthology.* New York: Garland.

Rostow, Walt W. 1960. *The Stages of Economic Growth. A Non-Communist Manifesto.* Cambridge: Cambridge University Press.

Roth, Michael S. 1988. *Knowing and History: Appropriations of Hegel in Twentieth-Century France.* Ithaca and London: Cornell University Press.

Roy, Arundhati 1997. *The God of Small Things.* New York: Random House.

2002. "Fascism's Firm Footprint in India." *Nation* 275.10: 18.

Ruedy, John 1992. *Modern Algeria: The Origins and Development of a Nation.* Bloomington and Indianapolis: Indiana University Press.

Rushdie, Salman 1991. *Imaginary Homelands: Essays and Criticism 1981–1991.* London: Granta.

1995. *Midnight's Children* [1981]. London: Vintage Books.

Rustin, Michael 1989. "The Politics of Post-Fordism: Or, the Trouble with 'New Times.'" *New Left Review* 175: 54–77.

Saadawi, Nawal El 1980. "Preface." *The Hidden Face of Eve: Women in the Arab World.* Trans. Sherif Hetata. London: Zed, i–xvi.

Said, Edward W. 1978. *Orientalism.* New York: Random House.

1984. *The World, the Text and the Critic.* London: Faber.

1990. "Third World Intellectuals and Metropolitan Culture." *Raritan* 9.3: 27–51.

1993. *Culture and Imperialism.* New York: Alfred A. Knopf.

1994. *Representations of the Intellectual.* London: Vintage.

2000. "The Clash of Definitions: On Samuel Huntington." *Reflections on Exile and Other Literary and Cultural Essays.* London: Granta Books, 569–90.

2002. "A Conversation with Neeldari Bhattacharya, Suvir Kaul and Ania Loomba." *Relocating Postcolonialism.* Ed. Theo Goldberg and Ato Quayson. Oxford: Blackwell, 1–14.

Salih, Tayeb 1969. *Season of Migration to the North.* Trans. Denys Johnson-Davies. London: Heinemann.

Sangari, Kumkum 1990. "The Politics of the Possible." *The Nature and Context of Minority Discourse.* Ed. Abdul JanMohamed and David Lloyd. New York: Oxford University Press, 216–45.

San Juan, Epifanio, Jr. 1988. "The Responsibility to Beauty: Toward an Aesthetic of National Liberation." *Rupturing Schisms, Interventions: Cultural Revolution in the Third World.* Manila: De La Salle University Press, 89–103.

1998. *Beyond Postcolonial Theory.* New York: St. Martins.

2002. "Postcolonialism and the Problematic of Uneven Development." *Marxism, Modernity and Postcolonial Studies.* Ed. Crystal Bartolovich and Neil Lazarus. Cambridge: Cambridge University Press, 221–39.

Santos, Theotonio dos 1978. *Imperialismo y dependencia.* Mexico City: Ediciones Era.

Sarkar, Sumit 1989a. *Modern India 1885–1947.* London: Macmillan.

1989b. "The Kalki-Avatar of Bikrampur: A Village Scandal in Early Twentieth Century Bengal." *Subaltern Studies* VI: *Writings on South Asian History and Society.* Ed. Ranajit Guha. New Delhi: Oxford University Press, 1–53.

1997. *Writing Social History.* New Delhi: Oxford University Press.

2000. "The Decline of the Subaltern in Subaltern Studies" [1996]. *Mapping Subaltern Studies and the Postcolonial.* Ed. Vinayak Chaturvedi. London and New York: Verso, 300–23.

Sartre, Jean-Paul 1968. "Preface" [1961]. *The Wretched of the Earth.* Frantz Fanon. Trans. Constance Farrington. New York: Grove Press, 7–31.

1976. *Critique of Dialectical Reason.* Vol. I: *Theory of Practical Ensembles* [1960]. Trans. Alan Sheridan-Smith. London: New Left Books.

2001a. *Colonialism and Neocolonialism.* Trans. Azzedine Haddour, Steve Brewer, and Terry McWilliams. London and New York: Routledge.

2001b. "Black Orpheus." *Race.* Ed. Robert Bernasconi. Oxford: Blackwell, 115–42.

Sassen, Saskia 1998. *Globalization and Its Discontents.* New York: New Press.

Saul, John S. 1974. "The State in Post-Colonial Societies: Tanzania." *The Socialist Register.* Ed. Ralph Miliband and John Saville. New York: Monthly Review Press; London: The Merlin Press, 349–72. Reprinted in John S. Saul, *The State and Revolution in Eastern Africa.* New York and London: Monthly Review Press, 1979, 167–99.

2001. *Millennial Africa: Capitalism, Socialism, Democracy.* Trenton and Asmara: Africa World Press.

Saussure, Ferdinand de 1966. *Course in General Linguistics* [1915]. Trans. Wade Baskin. New York, Toronto, London: McGraw-Hill Book Company.

Schell, Jonathan 2003. "Letter from Ground Zero: The Removed State." *Nation* (5 May): 8.

Schwarz, Henry 2000. "Mission Impossible: Introducing Postcolonial Studies in the US Academy." *A Companion to Postcolonial Studies.* Ed. Henry Schwarz and Sangeeta Ray. Oxford: Blackwell, 1–20.

Schwarz, Henry, and Sangeeta Ray, eds. 2000. *A Companion to Postcolonial Studies*. Oxford: Blackwell.

Scott, Alan 1997. "Introduction – Globalization: Social Process or Political Rhetoric." *The Limits of Globalization: Cases and Arguments*. Ed. Alan Scott. London and New York: Routledge, 1–22.

Scott, James C. 1985. *Weapons of the Weak: Everyday Forms of Peasant Resistance*. New Haven and London: Yale University Press.

Seed, Patricia 1991. "Colonial and Postcolonial Discourse." *Latin American Research Review* 26.3: 181–200.

Sekyi-Otu, Ato 1996. *Fanon's Dialectic of Experience*. Cambridge, MA, and London: Harvard University Press.

Senghor, Léopold 1993. "Negritude: A Humanism of the Twentieth Century." *Colonial Discourse and Post-Colonial Theory: A Reader*. Ed. Patrick Williams and Laura Chrisman. Hemel Hempstead: Harvester Wheatsheaf, 27–35.

Serequeberhan, Tsenay 1994. *The Hermeneutics of African Philosophy*. London: Routledge.

1997. "The Critique of Eurocentrism and the Practice of African Philosophy." *Postcolonial African Philosophy: A Critical Reader*. Ed. Emmanuel Chukwudi Eze. Oxford: Blackwell, 141–61.

Seth, Sanjay, Leela Gandhi, and Michael Dutton 1998. "Postcolonial Studies: A Beginning." *Postcolonial Studies* 1.1: 7–11.

Seyhan, Azade 2001. *Writing Outside the Nation*. Princeton: Princeton University Press.

Shakespeare, William 1997. *The Tempest* [1623]. *The Riverside Shakespeare*. Ed. G. Blakemore *et al*. Boston: Houghton, 1656–88.

Sharpe, Jenny 1993. *Allegories of Empire: The Figure of Woman in the Colonial Text*. Minneapolis: University of Minnesota Press.

Shohat, Ella 1995. "The Struggle over Representation: Casting, Coalitions, and the Politics of Identification." *Late Imperial Culture*. Ed. Roman de la Campa, E. Ann Kaplan, and Michael Sprinker. London and New York: Verso, 166–78.

Shohat, Ella, and Robert Stam 1994. *Unthinking Eurocentrism: Multiculturalism and the Media*. London and New York: Routledge.

Sinha, Mrinalini 1995. *Colonial Masculinity: The "Manly Englishman" and the "Effeminate Bengali" in the Late Nineteenth Century*. Manchester: Manchester University Press.

Sklair, Leslie 1991. *Sociology of the Global System*. Brighton: Harvester Wheatsheaf.

2001. *The Transnational Capitalist Class*. Oxford: Blackwell.

Smith, Adam 1910. *The Wealth of Nations* [1776]. 2 vols. Ed. E. R. A. Seligman. London: Dent.

Smith, Zadie 2000. *White Teeth*. New York: Random House; London: Penguin.

Sommer, Doris 1991. *Foundational Fictions*. Berkeley, Los Angeles, London: University of California Press.

Soros, George 1998. *The Crisis of Global Capitalism: Open Society Endangered*. New York: Public Affairs.

Soueif, Ahdaf 1999. *The Map of Love*. New York: Anchor.

Sparks, Colin 1996. "Stuart Hall, Cultural Studies and Marxism." *Stuart Hall: Critical Dialogues in Cultural Studies*. Ed. David Morley and Kuan-Hsing. London: Routledge, 71–101.

Spivak, Gayatri Chakravorty 1976. Translator's Preface to Jacques Derrida, *Of Grammatology*. Baltimore: Johns Hopkins University Press, ix–xc.

1985a. "Three Women's Texts and a Critique of Imperialism." *Critical Inquiry* 12.1: 243–61.

1985b. "Can the Subaltern Speak? Speculations on Widow Sacrifice." *Wedge* 7.8: 120–30.

1988a. "Subaltern Studies: Deconstructing Historiography." *Selected Subaltern Studies*. Ed. Ranajit Guha and Gayatri Chakravorty Spivak. New York and London: Oxford University Press, 3–34.

1988b. "Can the Subaltern Speak?" *Marxism and the Interpretation of Culture*. Ed. Cary Nelson and Lawrence Grossberg. Urbana: University of Illinois Press, 271–313.

1988c. "A Literary Representation of the Subaltern." *In Other Worlds: Essays in Cultural Politics*. New York and London: Routledge, 241–68.

1988d. "French Feminism in an International Frame." *In Other Worlds: Essays in Cultural Politics*. New York and London: Routledge, 134–53.

1988e. "Feminism and Critical Theory." *In Other Worlds: Essays in Cultural Politics*. New York and London: Routledge, 77–92.

1990. *The Post-Colonial Critic: Interviews, Strategies, Dialogues*. Ed. Sarah Harasym. London and New York: Routledge.

1993. *Outside in the Teaching Machine*. London and New York: Routledge.

1994. "How to Read a 'Culturally Different' Book." *Colonial Discourse / Postcolonial Theory*. Ed. Francis Barker, Peter Hulme, and Margaret Iversen. Manchester and New York: Manchester University Press, 126–50.

1995a. "Love, Cruelty, and Cultural Talks in the Hot Peace." *Parallax: A Journal of Metadiscursive Theory and Cultural Practices* 1: 1–31.

1995b. "Academic Freedom." *Pretexts* 5.1–2: 117–56.

1996. *The Spivak Reader*. Ed. Donna Landry and Gerald MacLean. London and New York: Routledge.

1999. *A Critique of Postcolonial Reason: Toward a History of the Vanishing Present*. Cambridge, MA: Harvard University Press.

Sprinker, Michael ed. 1992. *Edward Said: A Critical Reader*. Oxford: Blackwell.

1993. "The National Question: Said, Ahmad, Jameson." *Public Culture* 6.1: 3–29.

Spurr, David 1993. *The Rhetoric of Empire: Colonial Discourse in Journalism, Travel Writing, and Imperial Administration*. Durham and London: Duke University Press.

Stalker, Peter 2003. "Stalker's Guide to International Migration." www.pstalker.com/migration.

Stavenhagen, Rodolfo 1965. "Classes, Colonialism and Acculturation. Essay on a System of Inter-Ethnic Relations in Mesoamerica." *Studies in Comparative International Development* 1.6: 53–77.

Stavrianos, Leften Stavros 1981. *Global Rift: The Third World Comes of Age*. New York: Morrow.

Stern, Fritz 1974. *The Politics of Cultural Despair: A Study in the Rise of the Germanic Ideology*. Berkeley: University of California Press.

Stokes, Gale 2001. "Why the West?" *Lingua Franca* 11.8: 30–39.

Stratton, Florence 1994. *Contemporary African Literature and the Politics of Gender*. London: Routledge.

Strongman, Luke 2002. *The Booker Prize and the Legacy of Empire*. Amsterdam and Atlanta: Rodopi.

Suleri, Sara 1989. *Meatless Days*. Chicago: University of Chicago Press.

1992a. *The Rhetoric of English India*. Chicago: University of Chicago Press.

1992b. "Woman Skin Deep: Feminism and the Postcolonial Condition." *Critical Inquiry* 18: 756–69.

Sunder Rajan, Rajeswari 1992. "Fixing English: Nation, Language, Subject." *The Lie of the Land: English Literary Study in India*. Ed. Rajeswari Sunder Rajan. New Delhi: Oxford University Press, 7–28.

1997. "The Third World Academic in Other Places; or, the Postcolonial Intellectual Revisited." *Critical Inquiry* 23.1: 596–616.

Sunder Rajan, Rajeswari, and You-me Park 2000. "Postcolonial Feminism / Feminism and Postcolonialism." *A Companion to Postcolonial Studies*. Ed. Henry Schwarz and Sangeeta Ray. Oxford and Malden, MA: Blackwell Publishers, 53–71.

Szentes, Tamás 1988. *The Transformation of the World Economy: New Directions and New Interests*. London and Atlantic Highlands: Zed.

Tabb, William K. 1997. "Globalization Is *An* Issue, the Power of Capital Is *The* Issue." *Monthly Review* 49.2: 20–30.

2000. "Capitalism and Globalization." *Imperialism: Theoretical Directions*. Ed. Ronald H. Chilcote. Amherst, NY: Humanity Books, 315–21.

2001. *The Amoral Elephant: Globalization and the Struggle for Social Justice in the Twenty-First Century*. New York: Monthly Review Press.

Talbott, John 1981. *The War Without a Name: France in Algeria 1954–1962*. London: Faber and Faber.

Talib, Ismail S. 2002. *The Language of Postcolonial Literatures: An Introduction*. London and New York: Routledge.

Taylor, Patrick 1989. *The Narrative of Liberation*. Ithaca and London: Cornell University Press.

Tharu, Susie 1998. "Government, Binding and Unbinding: Alienation and the Subject of Literature." *Subject to Change: Teaching Literature in the Nineties*. Ed. Susie Tharu. New Delhi: Orient Longman, 1–32.

Therborn, Göran 1996. *European Modernity and Beyond: The Trajectory of European Societies 1945–2000*. London: Sage.

Thieme, John, ed. 1996. *The Arnold Anthology of Postcolonial Literatures in English*. London: Arnold.

Thomas, Alan, and Ben Crow, with Paul Frenz, Tom Hewitt, Sabrina Kassam, and Steven Treagust 1997. *Third World Atlas*. 2nd edn. Buckingham: Open University Press.

Thomas, Nicholas 1991. *Entangled Objects*. Cambridge, MA: Harvard University Press.

1994. *Colonialism's Culture: Anthropology, Travel and Government*. Cambridge: Polity.

Thompson, E. P. 1968. *The Making of the English Working Class* [1963]. Harmondsworth: Penguin.

Thurner, Mark 1997. *From Two Republics to One Divided*. Durham and London: Duke University Press.

Tilly, Charles, ed. 1975. *The Formation of National States in Western Europe*. Princeton: Princeton University Press.

Tlemcani, Rachid 1986. *State and Revolution in Algeria*. Boulder, CO: Westview Press; London: Zed.

Tölölyan, Khachig 1991. "The Nation-State and Its Others: In Lieu of a Preface." *Diaspora* 1.1: 3–7.

1996. "Rethinking Diaspora." *Diaspora* 5: 3–36.

Toulmin, Stephen Edelston 1990. *Cosmopolis: The Hidden Agenda of Modernity*. New York: Free Press.

Trinh T. Minh-ha 1987. "Difference: A Special Third World Women Issue." *Discourse* 8: 10–37.

1989. *Woman, Native, Other: Writing Postcoloniality and Feminism*. Bloomington and Indianapolis: Indiana University Press.

Urdang, Stephanie 1989. *And Still They Dance: Women, War, and the Struggle for Change in Mozambique*. New York: Monthly Review Press.

Valladao, Alfredo 1998. *The Twenty-First Century Will be American*. Trans. John Howe. London and New York: Verso.

Vanaik, Achin 1990. *The Painful Transition: Bourgeois Democracy in India*. London and New York: Verso.

1997. *The Furies of Indian Communalism: Religion, Modernity and Secularization*. London and New York: Verso.

Vaughan, Megan 1991. *Curing Their Ills: Colonial Power and African Illness*. Cambridge: Polity.

Vertovec, Steven, and Robin Cohen, eds. 1999. *Migration, Diasporas and Transnationalism*. Cheltenham, UK, and Northampton, US: Edward Elgar Publishing.

Vidal, Hernán 1993. "The Concept of Colonial and Postcolonial Discourse: A Perspective from Literary Criticism." *Latin American Research Review* 28.3: 113–19.

Viswanathan, Gauri 1989. *Masks of Conquest: Literary Study and British Rule in India*. New York: Columbia University Press; London: Faber and Faber.

Voltaire 2001. *Candide: ou l'optimisme* [1759]. Paris: Maisonneuve et Larose.

Walby, Sylvia 1996. "Woman and Nation." *Mapping the Nation*. Ed. Gopal Balakrishnan. London and New York: Verso, 235–54.

Walder, Dennis 1998. *Post-Colonial Literatures in English: History, Language, Theory*. Oxford: Blackwell.

Walker, Cheryl 1991. *Women and Resistance in South Africa*. 2nd edn. New York: Monthly Review Press.

Wallerstein, Immanuel 1974. *The Modern World-System: Capitalist Agriculture and the Origins of the European World Economy in the Sixteenth Century*. New York: Academic Press.

1984. *The Politics of the World Economy: The States, the Movements, and the Civilizations*. Cambridge and New York: Cambridge University Press.

1991. *Geopolitics and Geoculture: Essays on the Changing World System*. Cambridge and New York: Cambridge University Press.

1996. *Historical Capitalism with Capitalist Civilization*. London and New York: Verso.

Weber, Eugen 1976. *Peasants into Frenchmen: The Modernization of Rural France, 1870–1914*. Stanford: Stanford University Press.

Werbner, Pnina 1997. "Essentializing Essentialism, Essentializing Silence: Ambivalence and Multiplicity in the Constructions of Racism and Ethnicity." *Debating*

Cultural Hybridity, Multi-Cultural Identities and the Politics of Anti-Racism. Ed. Pnina Werbner and Tariq Modood. London: Zed, 226–54.

West, Lois A., ed. 1997. *Feminist Nationalism.* New York and London: Routledge.

Wilford, Rick, and Robert E. Miller, eds. 1998. *Women, Ethnicity and Nationalism: The Politics of Transition.* New York and London: Routledge.

Wilkin, Peter 1997. "New Myths for the South: Globalization and the Conflict between Private Power and Freedom." *Globalization and the South.* Ed. Caroline Thomas and Peter Wilkin. London: Macmillan; New York: St. Martin's Press, 18–35.

Williams, Bronwyn T. 1999. "'A State of Perpetual Wandering': Diaspora and Black British Writers." *Jouvert: A Journal of Postcolonial Studies* 3.3. Online journal.

Williams, Eric 1966. *Capitalism and Slavery* [1944]. New York: G. P. Putnam's Sons.

Williams, Patrick, and Laura Chrisman, eds. 1993. *Colonial Discourse and Post-Colonial Theory: A Reader.* Hemel Hempstead: Harvester Wheatsheaf.

Williams, Raymond 1977. *Marxism and Literature.* Oxford: Oxford University Press.
   1980. *Problems in Materialism and Culture.* London: New Left Books.
   1989. *The Politics of Modernism: Against the New Conformists.* London and New York: Verso.

Wolf, Eric R. 1982. *Europe and the People Without History.* Berkeley: University of California Press.

Wolpe, Harold, ed. 1980. *The Articulation of Modes of Production.* London: Routledge and Kegan Paul.

Wolpert, Stanley 1982. *A New History of India.* 2nd edn. London: Oxford University Press.

Wood, Ellen Meiksins 1997. "Capitalism, Globalization, and Epochal Shifts: An Exchange." *Monthly Review Press* 48.9: 21–32.
   1998. "Class Compacts, the Welfare State, and Epochal Shifts (A Reply to Frances Fox Piven and Richard A. Cloward)." *Monthly Review* 49.8: 24–43.
   2002. "Global Capital, National States." *Historical Materialism and Globalization.* Ed. Mark Rupert and Hazel Smith. London and New York: Routledge, 17–39.

Wood, Marcus 2002. *Slavery Empathy, Pornography.* Oxford: Oxford University Press.

Worsley, Peter 1984. *The Three Worlds: Culture and World Development.* Chicago: University of Chicago Press.

Young, Robert 1990. *White Mythologies: Writing History and the West.* London and New York: Routledge.
   1995. *Colonial Desire: Hybridity in Theory, Culture and Race.* London and New York: Routledge.
   2001. *Postcolonialism: An Historical Introduction.* Oxford: Blackwell.

Yúdice, George 1996. "Puede hablarse de la postmodernidad en América Latina." *Revista Crítica Literaria Latinoamericana* 15.29: 105–28.

Yuval-Davis, Nira, and Floya Anthias, eds. 1989. *Woman-Nation-State.* London: Macmillan.

INDEX

CAMBRIDGE COMPANIONS TO LITERATURE

The Cambridge Companion to Thomas
Hardy edited by Dale Kramer

The Cambridge Companion to Oscar Wilde
edited by Peter Raby

The Cambridge Companion to George
Bernard Shaw edited by Christopher Innes

The Cambridge Companion to Joseph
Conrad edited by J. H. Stape

The Cambridge Companion to D. H.
Lawrence edited by Anne Fernihough

The Cambridge Companion to Virginia
Woolf edited by Sue Roe
and Susan Sellers

The Cambridge Companion to James
Joyce, second edition edited
by Derek Attridge

The Cambridge Companion to T. S. Eliot
edited by A. David Moody

The Cambridge Companion to Ezra Pound
edited by Ira B. Nadel

The Cambridge Companion to Beckett
edited by John Pilling

The Cambridge Companion to
Harold Pinter
edited by Peter Raby

The Cambridge Companion
to Tom Stoppard
edited by Katherine E. Kelly

The Cambridge Companion to
David Mamet
edited by Christopher Bigsby

The Cambridge Companion to Herman
Melville edited by Robert S. Levine

The Cambridge Companion to
Nathaniel Hawthorne edited by
Richard Millington

The Cambridge Companion to Harriet
Beecher Stowe edited by Cindy Weinstein

The Cambridge Companion to Theodore
Dreiser edited by Leonard Cassuto
and Claire Virginia Eby

The Cambridge Companion to Edith
Wharton edited by Millicent Bell

The Cambridge Companion to Henry James
edited by Jonathan Freedman

The Cambridge Companion to Walt
Whitman edited by Ezra Greenspan

The Cambridge Companion to Ralph
Waldo Emerson edited by Joel Porte
and Saundra Morris

The Cambridge Companion to Henry
David Thoreau edited by Joel
Myerson

The Cambridge Companion to Mark Twain
edited by Forrest G. Robinson

The Cambridge Companion to Edgar Allan
Poe edited by Kevin J. Hayes

The Cambridge Companion to Emily
Dickinson edited by Wendy Martin

The Cambridge Companion to William
Faulkner edited by Philip M. Weinstein

The Cambridge Companion to Ernest
Hemingway edited by Scott Donaldson

The Cambridge Companion to F. Scott
Fitzgerald edited by Ruth Prigozy

The Cambridge Companion to Robert Frost
edited by Robert Faggen

The Cambridge Companion to Eugene
O'Neill edited by Michael Manheim

The Cambridge Companion to Tennessee
Williams edited by Matthew C. Roudané

The Cambridge Companion to Arthur Miller
edited by Christopher Bigsby

The Cambridge Companion to Sam Shepard
edited by Matthew C. Roudané

CAMBRIDGE COMPANIONS TO CULTURE

The Cambridge Companion to Modern
German Culture edited by Eva Kolinsky and
Wilfried van der Will

The Cambridge Companion to Modern
Russian Culture edited by Nicholas Rzhevsky

The Cambridge Companion to Modern
Spanish Culture edited by David T. Gies

The Cambridge Companion to Modern
Italian Culture edited by Zygmunt G.
Barański and Rebeeca J. West

The Cambridge Companion to Modern
French Culture edited by Nicholas Hewitt

The Cambridge Companion to Modern Latin
American Literature edited by John King